THE IMPLOSION
CONSPIRACY

Books by Louis Nizer

The Implosion Conspiracy
The Jury Returns
An Analysis and Commentary on the Official
Warren Commission Report
My Life in Court
What to Do with Germany
Thinking on Your Feet
Between You and Me
New Courts of Industry

THE

IMPLOSION

CONSPIRACY

BY

Louis Nizer

DOUBLEDAY & COMPANY, INC., GARDEN CITY

NEW YORK 1973

345.73
N 137n

The author gratefully acknowledges The Society of Authors, on behalf of the
Bernard Shaw Estate, for the use of the excerpt from Saint Joan.

PHOTO CREDITS:
United Press International—1, 11, 13, 14, 15, 16, 21
Wide World Photos—2, 3, 4, 5, 6, 7, 8, 9, 10, 12, 17, 18, 19, 20

ISBN: 0-385-03925-5
Library of Congress Catalog Card Number 72-77001
Copyright © 1973 by Louis Nizer
All Rights Reserved
PRINTED IN THE UNITED STATES OF AMERICA

FIRST EDITION

029359

To TRIAL LAWYERS,
the Civilized Warriors for Justice

ACKNOWLEDGMENT

I am indebted to Mrs. Gloria Agrin Josephson, Bob Considine and Rabbi Irving Koslowe who were generous in the interviews they gave me. I also wish to acknowledge in addition to the Court Record, the following books, which were helpful in special details, *The Rosenberg Story* by Virginia Gardner (Masses & Mainstream), *It's All News to Me* by Bob Considine (Meredith), *The Book of Daniel* by E. L. Doctorow (Random House), *The Judgement of Ethel and Julius Rosenberg* by John Wexley (Cameron & Kahn), *The Rosenberg Letters* (Dennis Dobson, London), *The Betrayers* by Jonathan Root (Coward-McCann) and *Was Justice Done?* by Malcolm P. Sharp (Monthly Review Press). I am indebted as always for the New York *Times* file on the Rosenberg case.

LOUIS NIZER

THE IMPLOSION
CONSPIRACY

INTRODUCTION

The Rosenberg trial is not only the most extraordinary spy story of the century, it is a love story. The love between Julius and Ethel Rosenberg was brought to unbearable intensity, by waiting for and sharing death. When they were permitted to converse through a mesh screen forty minutes before execution, and pushed their fingers through the screen until they touched, though bleeding, in a farewell kiss, the horror of execution was juxtaposed against sentiment, like Wagnerian thunder counterpointed by idyllic music.

The trial also produced an unexpected hero in my eyes. He was Emanuel Bloch, who, together with his father, Alexander Bloch, were the lawyers for the Rosenbergs.

While not wanting to be uncharitable, particularly since their appeal briefs were brilliant—apparently, the Blochs were better brief writers than trial lawyers, and often the twain do not meet in the same person.

Then why did I find Bloch the hero of the book? Because his dedication and emotional involvement in the cause are a shining example of the lawyer in his noblest role. He became an advocate in the classic sense, whose "hands were charged with electricity and his face ablaze with concern for his quivering client."

Bloch took care of the Rosenberg children, brought them monthly to the death house for visits and conversations which were so excruciatingly painful that hardened guards broke down and cried; he sacrificed his law practice, devoting his every energy and resource to saving his clients' lives; he pleaded at the White House gate in the last hours for an oral hearing with President Eisenhower, who twice refused clemency; he suffered to the point of tears as motions to delay the executions failed; he literally danced with joy when a last minute stay by a justice of the Supreme Court gave surcease from death over the summer; and then collapsed when the very next day the Supreme Court reconvened in an unprecedented special session to vacate the stay; he telephoned his last message to the Rosenbergs through the warden, and his sobs prevented him from finishing after he said, "Tell them I love them . . ." His exertions and emotional exhaustion were so great that he died several months later.

When I was invited by Otto Preminger to write a motion picture script of the Rosenberg spy trial, I declined without hesitation. His continued importunities resulted only in repeated demurrers. The reason was not merely that professional burdens already made my shoulders stoop lower than was right for physical or mental posture. Nor even that I had never written a play which is so different from the prose form of a book, since it is limited to dialogue and visual action and does not permit the luxury of exposition.

There was something else. I had always written about cases which I had tried myself. This assured me of intimate knowledge of every word of the record and of the personalities of the participants. Thus, immersed in fact and the emotions of the contest, I felt equipped to recreate the human drama, for that is what every trial is. Also, as a writer, I knew that complete mastery of the facts, which includes not only the external ones uttered by the witnesses, but the internal ones such as the psychological motivations, is essential to an authentic presentation. Out of such thorough preparation and participation emerge the suspense and momentum of the original events. Otherwise, there is only an account of the court stenographer's record, exciting too, but only history, not pulsating life.

Since there are dozens of cases I have tried and not written about, nor do I intend to, after *My Life in Court* and *The Jury Returns,* I saw no reason to write about a case which was remote and which I knew only as a controversial abstraction. I had no opinion about the guilt or innocence of the Rosenbergs, which might impel me, as it did many other authors, to propagandize for or against their conviction.

Furthermore, I was only halfway through with an autobiography (of a hybrid nature since it dealt with extraordinary people I had met and events I had experienced, rather than a strict recital of my life). So why interrupt that work, for which I had carved out the only writing time available—vacations and weekends?

But when Preminger's insistence and allurements had overcome me, and I shall not describe how, for fear that they will reveal my weakness and also depict his skills of persuasion, which will detract from my own, I set myself a special task.

I was going to know as much about the Rosenbergs and the trial as was humanly possible to know, without having defended or prosecuted them.

I was not going to write a word until research had put me under their skins, the prosecutors', the defense counsels', the judge's, the appellate judges', the witnesses'.

I was not going to write a word until I could achieve what the psychologists call "abreaction," the re-creation of the contemporary emotions of that day, not the coolness with which events can be viewed in retrospect.

Perspective aids the intellectual process, but it may distort the events because it superimposes upon them wisdom not available at the time. The Rosenberg case is a typical illustration. In 1943, Russia, our involuntary ally, was praised for its heroic military resistance. Eisenhower, MacArthur, Churchill, Roosevelt, all recognized its contribution in chewing up the Nazi panzer divisions. But in 1951, when the Rosenbergs were tried for stealing the atomic bomb and giving it to Russia, the atmosphere was different. Stalin had broken the Yalta agreements and the warmth of a joint war effort had turned into a freeze—the cold war. This had resulted in extreme reaction under the demagogic leadership of Senator Joseph McCarthy. The trial, which dealt with prior events, lacked the benign atmosphere of that day.

Writing about a trial involves the process of reincarnation in reverse. It is not the present life, with its supposed dim echoes of the past, which is important. It is the old life, vividly felt with all of its torments and triumphs, which must be relived. There is no place for fiction or even imaginative reconstruction. That is the path to a counterfeit presentation. Authenticity is the key. It unlocks the meaningfulness and the inevitable excitement of a trial. It gives a true picture of the American/Anglo-Saxon process of justice, which, although beset by the frailties of those who seek it and those who administer it, nevertheless approximates its objective better than any other system now or before.

The reason that truth is stranger than fiction in the courtroom is that "fiction is obliged to stick to possibilities; truth isn't." A trial is a war, in which the desire to annihilate the adversary is curbed by civilized rules. But these very restraints, which turn it into intellectual combat, cannot contain the passions which break through in the most unexpected manner. I am constantly amazed by the unexpected conduct of those caught in conflicting pressures.

The famous motion-picture director William Wyler once told me that the most effective scene in a courtroom he had ever seen was a true incident in a trial I had conducted. The witness, who was Canadian and, therefore, requested the privilege of standing in the box during his testimony, when destroyed on cross-examination, did not shriek hysterically, or run from the witness stand, or confess his error with sobs, as fiction writers would have it. He did what no imaginative writer would have concocted. He slowly sat down. That's all. He just sat down like a balloon that is gently pierced and collapses in slow motion. It was far more effective in registering his distress, than any of the stereotyped means used in stage and television trials.

In another trial, a woman artist, who had repeatedly refused to marry her lover, whom she bore a child, claiming marriage was a barbaric enslavement, nevertheless sued him as his common-law wife when he

(3)

abandoned her for another woman. A mutual friend, who wore a Croix de guerre ribbon in his lapel, testified about her views on free love, and when pressed on cross-examination, conceded that she had lived with him too. Before he could move, the outraged plaintiff ran forward, faced the witness, saluted him smartly, clicking her heels, and said, "Well done, Legion of Honor!" and fell in a faint across his path.

When Westbrook Pegler was confronted on cross-examination with the revelation that the writings I had read to him, and which he condemned as brazen Communist propaganda (believing they were Quentin Reynolds'), were his own columns, he lifted his arm in a threatening gesture as I approached him, and yelled, "Get away from me!"

The Rosenberg trial and subsequent events, which dangled death in front of their eyes hypnotically, involve a succession of unexpected climaxes of which only the truth could be the author.

So, determined to be fully equipped before I ventured forth to subdue the facts in writing, I spent my first writing vacation solely on research. I made several hundred pages of handwritten notes of every fact or argument in the trial, the appellate briefs and the many judicial opinions.

My objective was to know every inch of the thousands of pages of the record, as if I were going to write the briefs; and every word and authority in the briefs, as if I were going to argue the appeals; and every word of the many judicial opinions, as if I were going to write a critique for a law review; and every book I could find for or against the verdict, as if I were going to review each one for the Sunday *Times;* and every newspaper reference I could find, as if I were an editor preparing an editorial; and every person I could find who touched their lives or deaths, as if I were a reporter on a Pulitzer-Prize mission.

Only when I had absorbed all this, did I put pen to paper. Only then for the first time did an opinion about the Rosenberg trial begin to shape itself. I stress this delayed reaction because I am constantly astonished by the definite opinions people have about cases based on newspaper reports of a trial still in progress. At dinner tables, intelligent men and women, who would stoutly defend the presumption of innocence of any accused person, will condemn the defendant as guilty, substituting vehemence for their lack of knowledge, and holding forth authoritatively on testimony they have never heard, and of which newspaper accounts give the most fragmentary version. Barest inferences and suspicions are elevated to incontestable truth. After the debate has raged for a while, someone, out of consideration for my supposed expertise, will turn to me and ask my opinion. I reply that I do not understand how they could have judgments when the defense has not even been heard yet, and when the evidence which has been adduced might fill five hundred pages of the record and of which they have read a diluted, selected version of ten or twelve paragraphs in a newspaper. Even the jurors, who have heard all the testimony thus far presented, are warned by the judge not to form any opinion, until all the evidence has been concluded. They are even forbidden to discuss the case among themselves until the very end of the trial, lest they form a premature and, therefore, unfair judgment. The word prejudice stems from prae-judicare, to judge before one knows the facts.

To soften the blow of my strictures, I tell the jest about the judge who rendered a record number of decisions in one year. He was besieged by newspapermen to explain his achievement.

"Well," he said, "I listen to the plaintiff and decide the case immediately."

"Don't you listen to the defendant too?" they ask.

"I used to," he replied, "but I found it confused me."

Most of the writings on the Rosenberg case proceed from the author's strong conviction of innocence or guilt and a demonstration justifying his view. That is not unusual. Judge Cardozo, in his judicial process, contended that the lengthy opinions rendered by the courts are not the means to the conclusion, but rather a rationalization of a conclusion based on conscience. The law is found to justify the judgment rather than the verdict flowing from the law. The quality and sincerity of these writings preclude any theory of deliberate distortion. Bias can be innocent, and passion for "truth," as one interprets it, is a fierce light that can be blinding.

The Rosenberg case lent itself to strong feelings. There was the ideological conflict of communism joined by non-Communists, who are always eager to test civil rights on the most hostile territory.

There was the issue of capital punishment opposed by many on general principles and by others specifically in this case because other confessed spies who were in the conspiracy suffered only prison sentences.

There was the revulsion of feeling against the chief government witnesses, David and Ruth Greenglass, who testified against their kith and kin. No matter how the prosecutor and the judge praised them for their contrition and full confession, it was not delectable to see Ethel Rosenberg's younger brother, "Davey," who she said she still "loved very much," sending her and her husband to the electric chair by his damning testimony. There is an ancient unwritten law of family loyalty which resists statutory law. We may accept truth no matter how bitter its consequence but we do not necessarily honor the truth sayer.

There was the world-wide unrest protesting chiefly the death penalty, but also the verdict. Originally organized by Communists, the movement gained distinguished non-Communist support for clemency from Pope Pius XII, President Auriol of France, Professor Harold Urey, Professor Albert Einstein, and many others. United States embassies in Europe and South America were attacked by furious mobs, resulting in some deaths. The organized effort not to execute the Rosenbergs was financed by one million dollars raised from sympathizers, the published love letters written by Ethel from Sing Sing, and even the distribution of an inexpensive edition of the trial record.

The outcry against the death sentence spread like the whirling mushroom of an atomic explosion, which was the subject of Rosenbergs' claimed martyrdom.

Momentum came from disparate sources. There were religious and moral groups who did not quarrel with the verdict, but asked for mercy for the mother and father of two young children. There were those who despised legalized murder by the state even for hardened criminals. There were the Communists, who could achieve four objectives at one time: ridicule their proven spy activities, defend two loyal adherents, denounce the American judicial process and charge capitalist system with venality.

All these tributaries flowed into a river of articles, books and plays on the Rosenberg case, which have persisted for a quarter of a century.

An accompanying phenomenon is what I shall call the analytical syndrome. It is possible to take the record of any trial and by minute dissection and post-facto reasoning demonstrate that witnesses for either side made egregious errors or lied. Then by ascribing critical weight to the exposed facts, the conclusion is reached that the verdict was fraudulently obtained. This was the process by which the Warren Commission Report was challenged in a spate of books. To cite just one illustration, a constable deputy sheriff described the rifle which had been found on the sixth floor of the Book Depository Building as a Mauser, instead of a Mannlicher-Carcano, which it was. Out of this innocent error, due to ignorance or excitement, sprouted the theory that the real assassin's rifle had been spirited away and Oswald's rifle planted on the scene to involve him. Multiply this incident by many others such as someone's testimony that shots were heard coming from the mall, and the "hiding" of the death X rays of the President (since revealed), and you have a gigantic conspiracy by foreign agents, or government officials, or New Orleans homosexuals, or lord knows what to fix the blame on an innocent man, Oswald. Of course, all this was nonsense and subsequent events have confirmed the accuracy of the Report.

The analytical syndrome can be used to discredit any verdict from the commonest automobile negligence case to the most involved anti-trust or proxy contest.

The fallacy in this approach is that it assumes that all the evidence for the winning side must be believed by the jury, or it would not decide as it did. It ignores the jury's right to be selective of a witness' story and also the reality of conflict of testimony, which the jury must resolve by applying its common sense and keen observation of the witnesses. That is why the law is that not the larger number of witnesses for one of the parties determines the issue. The jury may choose to believe one

(6)

witness, and often does, against five witnesses who testified to the contrary.

The scales of justice are not laden on one side and empty on the other. If they were, we would not need trials and the complicated rules for measuring veracity. There are weights on both sides and they are not subject to precise evaluation. They must be measured by the values assigned to them in the jury's mind. Jurors often have seven senses, adding horse and common to the usual five.

Nor does it follow that because there is alloy in some of the pieces of gold on one side of the scales that the jury's recognition of its meretricious nature requires it to ignore the decisive tipping of the scales from other weights on the same scale. The opposite scale might be lighter, too, if it were not for some artificial weight.

This is the reason for the age-old rule of law which requires the judge to instruct juries that if they believe a witness has testified falsely deliberately on a material matter, they may, if they choose, disregard all his testimony. Even then, when a jury has detected conscious perjury, it may believe part of his testimony, if surrounding circumstances warrant it. My own experience has been that a jury will forgive errors. The frailty of memory, even if induced subsconsciously by self-interest, is tolerated. But a jury will rarely forgive a deliberate lie. When such a witness falls, it is seldom that he can pick himself up, brush off his dishonesty and proceed to re-establish his credibility. His fall is usually fatal.

The point is that it is the composite effect which is determinative, not a dissection of each fact as if it were the whole.

The analytical syndrome approach is particularly misleading when it challenges the *logic* of a conclusion based on conflicting testimony. Such an argument usurps the jury's role and decides whom it should have believed. The jury has very likely heard the opposing contentions from counsel. Furthermore, the jurors have an advantage no critic has. They saw and heard the witnesses! He hasn't.

No one can overestimate the importance of observation in judging credibility. Time and again, I have seen a witness discredited by the manner of his testifying rather than by what he said. A witness, on cross-examination, who glances at his counsel as if pleading for help, turns red, pauses and then hesitantly replies, "I don't remember," may well give the jury the impression that his answer is an evasion. But in cold type, he may appear to be forthright.

Jurors usually watch every mannerism of the witness, every inflection of voice, every reaction under stress. They are not unlike the cross-examiner, whose antennae are alert to every signal which the witness sends out. Witnesses who scissor their legs at certain questions; or look up at the ceiling for help at some inconsequential question although they have been untroubled by difficult ones; or become unduly em-

(7)

phatic, abandoning previous equanimity; or are assertive though their eyes register doubt; or substitute nastiness for indignation; or pretend they didn't hear the question to stall for time; or are affectedly obsequious; or pass their hands over their mouths before answering, in a gesture which might mean "I wish I didn't have to say what I am about to say" (particularly, if repeated whenever the same sensitive subject matter is posed); or claim to have been tricked by the questioner, instead of candidly admitting error; or go out of their way to express their spleen, thus exposing the hypocrisy of benignity; or, in a moment of anger, reveal a crude streak of language or attitude which contradicts a proffered cultured manner; or accept signals from others in the courtroom; or seek to elicit sympathy for being badgered; or engage in sarcastic sallies with the tormenting cross-examiner; or repeatedly introduce irrelevancies to sidetrack the persistent questioner; or dress elegantly or poorly but in apparent unaccustomed style; or are so determined to balk the examiner that they won't admit the most obvious fact; or seek to gain favor with the jury by fawning on them; or, well, who are not themselves in a thousand ways—may forfeit the jury's confidence. Yet none of this can be recorded in the printed record.

Indeed, a jury's scrutiny of a witness does not cease when counsel are conferring at the judge's bench or during a short recess. If he believes he is "at ease" and winks to a friend, or makes a disparaging gesture about his adversary, or otherwise acts out of character, his self-revelation does not go unnoticed in the jury's evaluation of his credibility.

Is all this surprising? Then how, reader, do you judge people whom you have met only at a dinner party? How do you come to the conclusion that the man or woman seated next to you is "very nice" or "not to be trusted any further than I could throw a piano"? Surely, if the stenographic record of the conversation were taken down and read, it would not support your conclusion. It was not the words uttered that gave you the impression. It was the "shiftiness of his eyes," or the fact that he was looking at others while you were talking, or his unbecoming flirtatiousness, or vanity, or pretense of intellectualism, or insipid humor, or arrogance, or, to the contrary, his sincerity, or his pleasing voice, or a thousand undefined stimuli which led you to your conclusion. But it was observation as well as the uttered word which shaped your opinion.

So important is the opportunity to see and hear the witness that it has resulted in a rule of law hundreds of years old: that an Appellate Court will not reverse a jury verdict on a question of fact. The upper court sees only the printed record. It does not see or hear the witnesses. Therefore, as appears in many appellate decisions, the judges may even differ with the jury verdict but they won't tamper with it, because they realize the importance of seeing and hearing the witnesses in judging credibility. The Appellate Court, therefore, confines itself to errors of law, not of fact.

If contentiousness between opposing views was sufficient to cast doubt on the jury's verdict, then what verdict could stand? Frequently, even Supreme Court decisions are based on a six to three or five to four vote. Often the minority vigorously takes the majority to task, and sometimes in acerbic language. If the analytic syndrome approach to discredit jury verdicts were applied to Appellate Courts, would it be right to discredit every majority opinion by quoting the minority? This would result in the paradox that where there is no unanimity, the minority view should prevail.

The law is not a science, subject to mathematical certainty. (Even *quod erat demonstrandum* is now challenged by the advanced mathematicians who contend that $2+2$ does not necessarily equal 4.) The law is the end result of logic, prior learning, experience, moral standards, ethical concepts, intuitive judgment, psychological insights, prevalent mores, religious precepts, need for certainty—all of which are in themselves subject to differing views. Therefore, our judicial system is at best an approximation of justice, not an absolute edict handed down from on high and beyond cavil. As Chief Justice Charles Evans Hughes said, "The law is the most complex of all social sciences and cannot be expected to reach the icy stratosphere of certainty."

All this applies to the plethora of works challenging the jury's verdict in the Rosenberg trial—and also quarreling with the many judicial reviews of the case.

This is not to say that criticism should be hushed. I shall take the privilege of engaging in it myself. But it must be offered with full acknowledgment that all critics are handicapped by not having heard and seen the witnesses, and also with humility, for no criminal case in American history enjoyed so many applications to the courts, twenty-three; was reviewed by so many judges, 112; only sixteen of whom dissented, and then not on the merits, but rather on stays or the opportunity for further review.

Therefore, the ubiquitous question asked, "Do you think the Rosenbergs were guilty?" is a wrong question and can only result in a wrong answer. The question should be "Do you think there was sufficient evidence warranting the jury, which sized up the witnesses, to decide that the Rosenbergs were guilty?"

It is by such guidelines that I have presented all the evidence and nuances on both sides fairly and fully. I had no difficulty being objective. I had nothing to overcome. I started with a clean slate; no prior convictions, no desire to demonstrate guilt or innocence. I let my thorough research carry me where it would. There is no stuffed ballot box. The reader will have an opportunity to judge for himself, in accordance with the guidelines I have indicated.

But make no mistake. This will not be a journey over a dusty road of dried evidence. No case I have ever tried or read has had so many extraordinary detours, booby trap surprises, climax piled on climax after one is certain the peak has been reached and there is no more.

In summing up to the jury, Rosenberg's counsel said:

> This is a very celebrated case. You have seen unfolded before you one of the most moving dramas that any human being could concoct.
>
> You have seen a brother testify against his sister in a case where her life might be at stake.
>
> You have been dealing with the atomic bomb, the most terrible and destructive weapon yet invented by man.
>
> This case is packed with drama. Playwrights and movie script writers could do a lot with a case like this. You have been fortunate. You had a front seat.
>
> But you are unfortunate because now you have the heavy responsibility of deciding whether these human beings are to be convicted with a possible death penalty.

What he could not anticipate was that the events over a period of more than two years after the trial would exceed what he described at the end of the trial as "the most moving drama any human being could concoct." For, as it turned out, the trial and its revelations were only the foundation of the story. Built upon it was a huge structure of continued struggles, the like of which have never occurred in judicial history. Time and again, events challenged precedents and broke them. Time and again, the tides of fortune lifted the hopes of the Rosenbergs and then dashed them. They, their attorneys, the children, the prosecutors, the Department of Justice, the President and our foreign embassies were pulled in the tow.

As a chronicler of all this, I could not avoid being inundated by the emotional events, but I came up determined to present the facts and law precisely as they were, not as an advocate might see them. For when we lean to one side or the other, our vision may be slanted too. Sometimes we see what we want to see or fail to see that which is unpleasant. A trial lawyer, who became a judge, once told me of his greatest difficulty —he didn't know what side he was on. I wanted to suffer the confusion of neutrality.

I had first written a motion picture script. The resolution to permit it to speak for itself, without my personal opinions, faded when this book was written. For it is an independent work, not a mere enlargement of the script. Grafting is as inimical to a literary creation as to the human body, and likely to be rejected by critic as it is by corpus.

The American judicial system has been under scrutiny and criticism. This is healthy. What institution doesn't need prodding, modernizing and improvement? Only death is perfect.

There has been such a fierce light on the Rosenberg case for so long that it has become a prototype for analysis. But it is interesting that critics derive opposite conclusions from it. Some insist that our judicial process is self-defeating because it is endless. The defendant is afforded so many appeals and applications that years intervene between a verdict and its enforcement. The interval provides escape, often on technical grounds. This is deemed an encouragement to criminals, who thrive on the uncertainties of the law.

Others complain that the courts fail to give sufficient consideration to issues raised, thus denying full justice. Several judges of the Supreme Court considered the Court's action precipitous, even after years had elapsed. They argued that more time should have been permitted to study a novel legal point.

Of course, there is the wide divergence of views as to whether the death penalty is a violation of the Constitution, which forbids cruel and unusual punishment; or, in any event, of civilized standards which abhor the extinction of life. In addition, there are sharp differences as to whether the Rosenbergs should have been punished to die, since other conspirators, who confessed sharing the crime with them, only received prison sentences. This discrimination in punishment is a separate ground for criticism, and quite understandably.

So, the Rosenberg case is not only significant in its own right, but is a symbol in the ubiquitous capital punishment debate and the general conflict between stricter law enforcement to diminish the crime wave and concern for the civil rights of those apprehended.

It also presents a sharp contrast with some modern trials concerning the behavior of counsel and defendants in the courtroom. In the Rosenberg case, the defendants were models of decorum. Their counsel were not only respectful, but went to the extreme of being obsequious to the prosecutor and to the judge. In recent years, some defendants and their counsel have cannonaded the courtroom with disrupting outbursts; defiantly attacking the court and witnesses, even to the point of abusive and obscene language; and generally interfered with the conduct of the trial so as to make completion virtually impossible. All this has been done on the theory that the trial was "political" and, therefore, should be conducted in a revolutionary setting.

For a while, the courts were unable to control the pandemonium, because counteraction might prejudice the defendants in the eyes of the jury. To remove the screaming defendant from the courtroom to his prison cell might violate his constitutional rights to be present at his trial. To remove his obstructing counsel might violate the defendant's right to choose his own lawyer. It was not until recently that the Supreme Court, in the Allen case, held that removal of an uncontrollable, insolent defendant from the courtroom, until he agreed to behave, was not a violation of his rights. Other suggestions have aided in restoring serenity to the courtroom.

(11)

Certainly, the Rosenberg case was a "political" trial in the demagogic sense in which the accusation is used. But any statute passed by Congress and signed by the President (whether it be the Espionage Act of 1917, involved in the Rosenberg case, or the Smith Act, involved in the Communist trial of 1949, or Statute Against Crossing State Lines to incite a riot, involved in the Chicago Seven trial of 1969–70) is not to be defied by defendants, because they deem it to be "political." If it is unconstitutional, it is for the Supreme Court to say, not for defendants to anticipate and proceed to make the trial a nullity.

The Rosenberg case is an example of obedience to legal processes, followed by subsequent violent protestations. Perhaps it induced the false notion that disruptive tactics should precede and prevent the verdict. Thus, the Rosenbergs and their counsel might have contributed by their very docility to the anarchy in subsequent cases, which it took much effort to curb.

All of which indicates that when we study the Rosenberg case, we are in a sense reviewing the judicial system in many aspects.

The Rosenberg case involved explosion and implosion. The triggering device of the bomb resulted from an implosion, the pinpointing inward of concentrated power, to smash the atom and release its illimitable energy. Then followed the devastating explosion.

The trial, too, involved complementary and yet contrasting forces. There was the explosive testimony of confessing conspirators, who revealed how they had managed to steal the most powerful weapon in history despite the most careful security precautions which our nation could devise. But there was also the mysterious implosive force of idealistic revolutionary doctrine, which the jury found had propelled two decent, loving people, into desperate espionage activity, without any material reward.

Inner conviction, even if mistakenly acquired and nourished, constitutes an implosive, motivating force. It is the stuff of which martyrdom is made and eagerly suffered.

Perhaps there may be less perplexity about what follows if we comprehend the concept of a psychological as well as scientific implosion.

LOUIS NIZER

September 1972

CHAPTER 1

On March 6, 1951, at 10:30 A.M., in the high, gray marbled, austere, federal courtroom in the Southern District of New York, the court clerk called out:

> The United States against Julius Rosenberg, Ethel Rosenberg, Anatoli A. Yakovlev, David Greenglass and Morton Sobell.

It was a heart-pounding moment for the defendants, their families, their lawyers, the prosecutors and even some eager spectators who filled the wooden benches to capacity in the large room. Years of preparation suddenly culminated. Neither side knew the strength of the other. Hopes and fears mingled in the torment of uncertainty. Judgment day had come, and the fact that it was for the living assured certain and immediate determination.

The United States attorney, Irving H. Saypol, announced:

> The Government is ready.

A. BLOCH   The defendants are ready to proceed.

SAYPOL   May the record show the presence of the defendants and their counsel?

COURT   Yes.

These formal announcements that the battle was joined were heard not only in the courtroom. They raced on wires throughout the world. People everywhere had been alerted that the greatest theft in history had taken place. The secret of the atom bomb had been stolen. It had been delivered to the Soviet Union. The international balance of power might have shifted. These revelations came in a series of shocks, like succeeding earth tremors, which increased their impact.

First was the startling announcement from England that Klaus Fuchs, the physicist who worked on the atomic bomb project in Los Alamos, New Mexico, had confessed to being a Communist spy. This was succeeded by the announcement that an American, Harry Gold, had confessed to being a courier who passed on atomic secrets to a top Russian agent, Yakovlev. The chain reaction of exposure then involved David Greenglass, of the United States Army, foreman of the machine shop in Los Alamos, entrusted with producing vital parts of the bomb, who confessed that he had turned over critical drawings of the bomb to an espionage ring.

The final revelation in the melodramatic events was Greenglass' confession that Julius and Ethel Rosenberg in conspiracy with others had induced him to exploit his unique vantage point in the Los Alamos project, to sneak out what was surely the most guarded secret in history.

Thus, world-wide attention focused on the trial. Communists railed against "the frame-up" intended to embarrass them. Anti-Communists seized upon these events as proof of the incorrigible, insidious nature of the Communist conspiracy to undermine and destroy the United States. These emotional forces flowed like opposing streams into the courtroom. All the participants in the trial felt the pressure of these opinion waves beating against them.

When a patient is worried about his blood pressure, the very procedure in taking it increases the count. He struggles to maintain calm, but the effort defeats him. So the attempt to conduct an impartial trial, which is watched closely by peoples in many nations, suffers from the very attention lavished on it. It is as if the normal light in the room was blotted out by a tremendous searchlight, but none of those present are supposed to blink their eyes or notice it. The result was bound to be that those who favored the procedure saw its purity in the intensified light. Those who opposed it saw flaws which might have been lost from sight under ordinary conditions. This may explain the passionate pros and cons of the past quarter of a century about what happened.

—→←—

Who were Julius and Ethel Rosenberg?

Even before the trial began, their names had become known throughout the world. They were accused of being master spies who had pierced the protective devices of our powerful nation. They were charged with achieving an unprecedented triumph of espionage for Russia.

How did Julius and Ethel Rosenberg come to occupy seats at the counsel table as alleged nefarious and successful masterminds?

If we trace their footsteps backward, as if they had always walked on snow, we might better understand how they reached their unhappy destination.

There is no logical line between origin and fame or notoriety. Genes can be responsible for genius, but there is no pattern or order by which we can predict it. Nature appears to glory in haphazard choices, skipping generations to bestow its bounties on the most unlikely recipients. Or, as is more likely, its rules are so mysterious that we cannot comprehend or trace them.

But there is one area which does not completely elude us. It is the change which takes place inside people from outward pressures. It is possible, as has been contended, that Hitler's rejection by a Jewish girl, when he was a self-conscious youth, fired his mad thrust for power and, thereafter, revenge on six million Jews.

The great jurist and legal philosopher Benjamin Cardozo was humiliated by a scandal which clouded his father's career as a judge. He was propelled thereby to live a monastic life, devoting every waking moment to study, so that his enormous natural gifts prospered abnormally and magnificently.

Franklin Roosevelt might have been only a political dilettante, were it not for the disaster of polio which gave him a compassionate view about millions who were crippled by circumstances, rather than disease. Paradoxically, his immobility propelled him to rise above his handicap.

The psychologists tell us that few of us use more than 10 per cent of our capacity. The difference in achievement is that some dig a little deeper within themselves to bring up the ore. But what is it that drives us to do so?

Poverty and injustice are the parents of revolutionary idealism. If we are to find any explanation for the Rosenbergs' presence as defendants in the courtroom, this may be the clue.

Julius' father, Harry, arrived in 1902 in steerage from Czarist Russia. He worked in a sweatshop, married and had five children. Julius was the youngest. His family lived on the top floor of a five-story tenement on Broome Street on the lower East Side of New York.

The roof leaked. The windows were cracked and stuffed with rags and papers. In winter, icicles hung from the ceiling and windows, and Julius as an infant was always cold and hungry too. He was afraid of the dark and, though he was three years old, his mother accompanied him to the bathroom to hold a lighted candle. Did that fear ever leave him? Much later, fascism substituted for the dark. When Mussolini invaded Ethiopia, he broke into a sweat. When he read of Hitler's deadly campaign against Jews, he suffered as if his own annihilation was imminent.

He was a sickly child. His mother, Sophie, would prepare a hard-boiled egg and slice it so that it could be shared by the children. She would stand on a long line to receive bread and milk from the union which was out on strike.

Julius went to Public School 88, and at the same time received religious education at the Downtown Talmud Torah. He studied Hebrew and biblical philosophy and was graduated with highest honors. He took the Scriptures literally.

Later, when he attended Seward Park High School, he was elected vice-president of the Young Men's Synagogue Organization. He had to work to help his parents. He sold penny candy and earned as much as eighty cents a day.

His father, as shop chairman, was active in a garment strike against sweatshop conditions. He lost and was blacklisted. The cruel retaliation to discourage future audacity did not go unnoticed by Julius.

Came 1933, the great Depression, with its breadlines, and Julius' bent for religion grew stronger. He derived solace from it, until one day, as he later wrote:

> . . . I stopped to listen to a speaker at a street corner meeting . . . His topic was to win freedom for Tom Mooney, labor leader who was imprisoned on a frame-up.
>
> That night I was reading a pamphlet I bought from the speaker giving the facts of this case and the next day I went and contributed 50 cents. Then I began to distribute the pamphlets and collect signatures on a Mooney petition from school friends and neighbors . . .

It is curious how a purely accidental incident can change the course of a person's life. If Julius Rosenberg had not stopped to listen to the Mooney orator, he may not have been seated in a defendant's chair in the courtroom eighteen years later.

For that pamphlet turned him to radicalism. As he read of Tom Mooney's sixteenth year in jail for murders he did not commit, he found himself burning with a new mission in life. Religion was not only vertical. It was horizontal. How could one ignore such an injustice? It would be unholy not to join in the earthly crusade. Even though he was only fifteen years old, he had felt uneasy for some time because religious devotion was directed to a force beyond us to undo evil. Human problems were immediate, and it was cowardice to avert one's gaze by looking up to heaven. There were farm foreclosures, breadlines and soup kitchens. The Depression was at home and incarnate villainy was abroad. Hitler had just burned down the Reichstag and mendaciously blamed it on the Communists. Suddenly, Julius felt that to bend one's knee to God, and do nothing more, was bending one's knee to oppressors too.

It was a short step from these thoughts to Marxist dialectic. Religion was the opiate of the people; and so were all other distractions, even baseball. His religious fervor seeped out through the sieve of his new-found idolatry.

His reading matter changed. The biblical and literary works in his room were crowded out by revolutionary tracts. He involved himself in the struggle to free the nine Negro Scottsboro boys sentenced to death for rape, on the testimony of a prostitute.

He propagandized against National Biscuit Company cookies, products of Standard Oil Company, General Motors and DuPont because they were the result of labor exploitation. He adopted the whole lexicon of Communist grievances, which offered the simplistic view that every injustice resulted from capitalism and nothing else. A Marxist considers responsibility fixed and undebatable. The only question is whether there is injustice in the world, and who could gainsay that?

He preached that newspapers were all controlled and corrupt. In his eyes, Andrew Carnegie, Jay Gould, John D. Rockefeller and Henry Ford were the great villains who "sucked the blood of the downtrodden workers." On Sundays, he went from door to door to sell subscriptions to the *Daily Worker*.

By this time, his appearance as well as his beliefs had changed too. He grew tall, very thin and nervous. His hair was jet black. He wore "intellectual looking" glasses and later a thin mustache and he spoke with nasal sing-song cadences, left over from his religious days. He had sensuous wet lips and in his intense discourse sprayed his hearers. He became a faithful recruit to the "struggle of the working class."

In 1934, he entered City College in New York. He became a leader of the radical group. His father was bewildered by his transformation from a reflective rabbinical student to a bitter revolutionist. Once Julius preened himself at home by telling how he stopped a Trotskyite from speaking against a resolution and had him thrown out.

"It's a free country," said his father softly. "Maybe he had something to say."

Julius told him he didn't understand. A Trotskyite was an "obstructionist" and a "deviationist." He had already turned the full cycle in which it was right to suppress speech in the name of the revolutionary gospel. This went for the left or right. In his freshman year, he later wrote, the college was visited by a delegation of students from Fascist Italy, whose mission it was to praise Mussolini and his works.

Rosenberg joined in the plan to prevent the visitors from speaking by booing them off the platform. The protesters yelled *"abbasso il fascismo!"* in rhythmic chant more suitable to those they denounced. A fight ensued. The police were called. Rosenberg and his friends learned a lesson in "nightstick civics." Such blows do not drive out radical convictions. They hammer them in. Pain suffered for a cause glorifies it and provides gratification, like the pain of birth which makes the child all the dearer to the mother. Twenty-one students were expelled. Rosenberg was not among them. But he was enlisted for life, and as it turned out, for death in a fanatical movement. The trial was to deal with his later activities.

Let us trace Ethel Rosenberg's steps in the snow. She was reared in the same neighborhood and in similar circumstances as Julius. Her parents lived in a cold-water tenement at 64 Sheriff Street on the lower East Side. Her father, Barnet Greenglass, worked in the basement repairing sewing machines. In winter, he could not hold the tools which were as cold as his fingers, and he would quit at noon, to huddle with his family around the coal stove in the kitchen.

Ethel's dream of escape was not religion, but art. She was going to obtain a college education and become a famous singer or actress. At the age of twelve, she pleaded for music lessons, but her mother refused on the conclusive ground that if God had wanted her to have music lessons, He would have made it possible.

Ethel graduated from Public School 22 at the age of eleven. She was slight but hippy. To her mother's displeasure, she wore her hair straight back. Ethel's first escape from squalor came when she appeared in school plays. Her fantasies of entering a better world came to life when she heard applause from the audience. Every handclap sounded like an ovation. As she bowed graciously toward her few admirers, she projected the moment to one of triumph on the Broadway stage.

Her father, who loved the Jewish theater, came to see her perform. So did her younger brother, David, whom she affectionately called "Doovey." But her mother, Tessie, refused. She condemned the nonsense they were all nourishing. Her daughter ought to stop being foolish. Her destiny was to marry, cook and rear children.

By the time Ethel entered Seward Park High School, she disliked her mother intensely. It was she who wanted to chain her to the old world. "You'll never get ahead," her mother said, "there's no room in life for arty people." Ethel was determined to disprove this prophecy, and Tessie became the symbolic enemy.

From the age of thirteen, Ethel suffered spasmodic back pains due to a ricketic curvature of the spine. This led to low blood pressure, dizziness and severe headaches, which never abandoned her. But as she grew to maturity, she looked the picture of robust health.

She was only five feet tall and weighed a hundred pounds. Her body was ill proportioned; her hands small and ungraceful. She looked better seated behind a table where her thick short legs were not visible. She always wore oversized clothes, because she could not overcome the frugal habit of the poor, to allow for future growth. It assured dowdiness, not economy.

The over-all impression of her face was pleasant and just missed being beautiful. She had a condescending look. At times it seemed beatific. The most distinctive feature was her lips, oval shaped, pursed and pinched, as if she was continually hiding disapproval. She spoke deliberately. The words were delayed by reflective selectivity. It all added up to an impression of a tight personality.

One thing was clear. There was enormous determination. Her life and death confirmed an extraordinary will—a will to rise above her environment, a will to become an artist, a will to be a revolutionist and a superhuman will to live against a death current powerful enough to have destroyed two other lives. How was this will diverted from her original ambition to be an artist, to activities which brought her into a federal courtroom charged with espionage?

In her case, it was a series of isolated incidents, each insufficient to push her off the path she was doggedly traveling, but cumulatively strong enough to drive her finally in another direction. Then she pursued her new mission with the same fierce will. Like most converts, she was more zealous than original believers.

After graduating from a six-month stenographic course in a neighborhood settlement house, she got a job at $7.00 a week in the National New York Shipping and Packing Company, at 327 West 36th Street.

She was sixteen years old. Her real interest was in the theater. She joined the Clark House Players, an amateur theatrical group sponsored by the settlement house on Rivington Street, and became its star. She lived the Cinderella story every day; desultory work until evening, then the magic and splendor of the stage. At midnight, she went home to squalor and the dreary disapproval of her mother.

She ventured into an amateur night contest at Loew's Delancey Theater. Her song was "Ciribiribin," a Chassidic ode of joy to God, which is an irresistible combination of rhythm, melody and finger snapping. She won second prize. This led to performances at all sorts of gatherings on the East Side, earning a dollar here and there. A Major Bowes talent scout put her on the circuit for amateur competition. She made "Ciribiribin" so familiar, audiences called for it when she appeared.

On one occasion she had the feminine lead in a Clark House Players' production of *The Valiant,* in which she played the teen-age sister of a man awaiting execution.

Of the $7.00 a week she earned at her prosaic job, her mother gave her $2.00 for carfare and lunches. She saved enough from this pittance and her performances to take singing lessons at a Carnegie Hall studio, paying $2.00 a lesson. Later she obtained a decrepit piano for mere cartage. Her mother grew more bitter at Ethel's "disgraceful running around theaters." The final blow to her was the piano, a space-consuming monster, which added noise to her frustration. She drowned out the piano with her outraged tirades. By this time Ethel's dislike for her mother had turned into hatred. She did not scream back at her. Her lips grew tighter and more pinched.

Her determination to pursue her "art" needed no prodding, but now there was added gratification, the chagrin of her mother. She aspired to join the famous Schola Cantorum, a professional choir under the direction of Hugh Ross. She reported to the Metropolitan Opera House rehearsal rooms for a tryout. To her dismay, sight reading of music was a requirement. She fled, but immediately set about taking lessons. Several months later she had mastered the alphabet of notes and applied again. She was accepted, the youngest singer ever to join the group. Her voice was small and resonant in the lower register, but when she ascended the scale, it became strident, a kind of musical acrophobia. When she practiced at home, her mother could not "stand the noise."

After a year, the Schola Cantorum went on tour. Ethel could not accompany the troupe. She could not leave her job. This was only the first wrench from her career.

There were other incidents which caused her to abandon the magical world of illusion in favor of an illusory solution for a better world.

It was 1932, a time of crisis. She applied for a clerk's job at a paper box factory on Bleecker Street. There were more than one thousand applicants ahead of her who had answered the advertisement. They were so desperate that they battered down the doors of the factory. Ethel was about to leave when a fire truck, which had been summoned by the police, turned its hoses on the mob. Ethel was knocked down and soaked to the skin. She was not hurt and the cold shower did not dampen her spirit. It lighted a flame of indignation.

She began to notice and resent conditions which she had previously accepted as familiar inconveniences: the squeezed subway traffic, the selfish arrogance of employers who considered their workers disposable machines on hire, the hunger of people who expended their ebbing energy looking for a job which wasn't there, the rewards for the hardy rather than the sensitive, and the general political paralysis when confronted with economic crisis.

If, occasionally, she yearned to return to the more beautiful world of unreality, she was drawn back by the clamor around her. Protesters were declaiming on every street corner. The Depression had increased oratory in the same proportion as it decreased work. Innocent people and their children were suffering. The injustice of it all stirred anger. There being no recognizable solution, any theory, no matter how wild, seemed cogent. Something is better than nothing. You can't hold on to nothing. A defiant "Then what do you suggest?" was an unanswerable challenge, even though it didn't justify the demagogic platform from which it was hurled. Radicalism was rampant. It took all forms, from blueprints for a new society, which rejected violence as anti-intellectual, to violence supported intellectually as an unavoidable ingredient of revolution. Even the arts were invaded. *Pins and Needles,* a musical produced by a union, featured "Sing Me a Song of Social Significance."

Ethel joined in union activities hesitantly. But participation revealed a new stage to her. Here, too, she stood before an audience. Here, too, she was applauded. Furthermore, her words were her own and she did not have to share credit with an author. This gave an added dimension of

(20)

power. Imperceptibly, belief and make-believe merged. It was not until she became a star in her new role that the union became complete.

This occurred in August 1935. Ethel was now nineteen years old. She led a strike of 150 woman workers which shut down New York National Shipping Company. Andrew W. Loebel, president of the company, recruited workers from the welfare rolls of New Jersey and opened the plant the very next day. Ethel and the girls she led caused such a disturbance at the office doors that newspapermen and policemen appeared on the scene to record and quell the disorder.

Though it was hot, Ethel and her army donned raincoats and, linked arm in arm, paraded up and down 36th Street barring and frightening away most of the substitute workers.

When a delivery truck arrived, the driver was dragged from his perch by the girls, who acted like a swarm of bees overcoming a bull. They tore his clothes off and holding him face downward wrote "I am a scab" on his back with lipstick. He was then permitted to drive off, accompanied by a chorus of humiliating laughter by the girls.

The battle was not over. The next day, many trucks arrived with drivers forewarned against surprise assault. But the girls changed tactics. Unable to cope with many drivers, they just lay down across 36th Street and defied the trucks to run over them. The opposing generals countered by calling the workers out of the plant, to carry the packages by hand from the stalled trucks. Ethel spared one of her battalions to cut the twine with open razor blades. Bundles of clothing spilled into the street.

The police found their power curbed because they could not apply all-out force against girls who looked more like children than law breakers. Half measures in war are half surrender, and this was industrial war. Courage is a multiplication table. Astonished by the staying power of a small group of women, fifteen thousand suitmakers and dressmakers joined the strike in sympathy. Still the battle continued for two more weeks.

Then the employer ostensibly surrendered. He cut hours and raised wages. But after a week, Ethel and ten of her lieutenants were fired. She filed a complaint with the National Labor Relations Board, which had just begun its activities. Five months later, the Board ruled that she had been punished for leading a strike and ordered that her job be restored. But by this time, she was working as a stenographer at Bell Textile Company.

One day, she was invited by the International Seaman's Union to sing "Ciribiribin" at a fund-raising party on New Year's Eve. She was out of practice and voice, and refused. But "the show must go on" also applied to the new social drama in which she had become a star. She finally agreed.

In the audience was Julius Rosenberg.

They met because both were nervous. She was sitting in a corner of the rented hall on Delancey Street. The six-piece band was blaring for the dancers gyrating under the balloons which failed to disguise the musty surroundings. Amateur talent was to follow. She had not sung for a long time and was more apprehensive than usual. Julius observed her fright, which equaled his own discomfiture at being there. He was a revolutionist, not a bourgeois seeker of petty pleasures. The cause, not the setting, had brought him there and he didn't know how to adjust.

He imagined he had seen Ethel in the neighborhood. She, too, was remote from the whirling scene. Awkwardly, he approached and asked, "Why are you so nervous?" She explained that she was supposed to sing, but was concerned because she had not performed for a long time. It led to his suggestion that she practice out loud in one of the side rooms. She would not be heard above the band, and she might regain her confidence.

His innocence and concern moved her immediately. It was an hour before the show. They went to one of the rooms off the ballroom. She rehearsed in his presence, but she felt she was performing for him alone. In order not to be heard outside, she sang pianissimo, and this made her voice mellow and sweet. He was surprised and entranced. The Chassidic melody evoked deep feelings in him, which he had subdued for a long time. He had abandoned his religious beliefs but emotions are no respecter of rational processes. She looked like a *moloch* (angel). The sudden surge of intermingled feelings brought tears to his eyes. Her heart pounded. She had never before been admired by a man. She had never before felt such tenderness.

At the end of the evening, they eagerly sought each other and walked home. The conversation, like the music, bound them together. Each was excited at the other's activities and the identical dedication to a better world. He told of his work to undo Tom Mooney's martyrdom, she of her triumph in the strike. Only one difference arose. He told her of abandoning his rabbinical career, and now he was going to give up his studies for an engineering degree. There was too much revolutionary work to be done to pursue technical education.

She stopped and seized his arm. It was their first touch. They had not experienced such excitement before. He must not give up his college career. "I'll help you," she said. This was the beginning of his dependence on her. He was thrilled in more ways than one to have a confidante; she to find love, which even her mother had denied her.

They became inseparable. She bought an old portable typewriter and typed his papers on engineering. They read the *New Masses* and the *Daily Worker* together, and turned avidly to Communist activities. He quoted Karl Marx, "Philosophers have explained the world; it is necessary to change the world."

With Ethel's help and insistence, Julius graduated from City College in February 1939, receiving a bachelor of science degree in electrical engineering. He was seventy-ninth in a class of eighty-five.

Three months later, they were married. For the sake of their relatives, the ceremony was in a synagogue on the corner of Sheriff Street. Ethel's brother Bernard was best man, but her favorite younger brother, David, was at her side. He had never overcome his jealousy of Ethel, and she had not understood his anxious inquiring look when she returned upstairs after long good-night partings with Julius in the dark hallway. But now he was resigned to her independence. He had come to admire Julius, who had inducted him into the Young Communist League.

Julius obtained a job as civilian junior engineer at the Brooklyn supply office of the United States Army Signal Corps at a salary of $2,000 a year.

The newly married couple intensified their efforts for the Communist Party. They attended lengthy meetings in cells. They passed out leaflets. They sold the *Daily Worker*. They collected funds in door-to-door canvass for Communist activities. They abandoned any discriminating judgment in their fanatical devotion to communism. So they urged peace during the period of the Hitler-Stalin pact and war afterward.

In 1943, a son, Michael, was born to them. Four years later, Robert was born. The children were extremely difficult. Ethel and Julius studied texts on child psychology to develop a relationship with them. Michael would throw a tantrum on the street and could not be controlled by either of his parents. They were mystified by this. It didn't occur to them that their political fanaticism had deprived their children of the warmth and intimacy which they insisted would come to the world if their theories prevailed. Blueprints for Utopia never take into account human frailties. That is why they are so alluring in print and so ineffectual in practice. The Rosenbergs had a microscopic illustration of this right in their own home and with their own flesh and blood. But they failed to perceive it.

Whatever failure of love there was with the children didn't affect theirs. When Ethel and Julius went away for a rare weekend, friends would see them lying in a hammock together, she singing softly to him while he caressed her.

In late 1943, they stopped their open Communist activities. They did not buy the *Daily Worker*. A few months later, Army Intelligence investigators appeared to make inquiries among the neighbors. In March 1945, Julius was fired from his job on charges that he was a Communist. He filed an appeal. Ethel became so ill she spent four months in bed. They began to see less of their friends and their lives became shrouded in mysterious privacy if not secrecy. Julius looked for a new job. He obtained one at Emerson Radio Corporation in Manhattan.

Julius' father, Harry, could not square his patriotism and gratitude to America with his son's activities. Abandoning his rabbinical career was regrettable, his religion, despicable, and his country, outrageous. When Harry learned that his son had been deemed unfit to serve the Signal Corps, he felt disgraced. He refused to see Julius, and barred him for the rest of his life. But when he lay dying of a kidney infection in Mount Sinai Hospital, the Greenglasses arranged for Julius to visit him. He shaved his father at bedside and made light conversation to disguise the approaching tragedy.

Three hours later, Harry was dead. It was merciful timing, for had he lived to read that his son had been arrested by the FBI for conspiring against the United States, his shame would have been worse than his death.

Now Ethel and Julius, still holding hands in the courtroom, were to hear hostile voices give a detailed description of their later activities.

CHAPTER 2

The Rosenberg trial followed procedures which were evolved over centuries.

Guilt or innocence used to be determined by trial by ordeal. The accused would plunge his arm into boiling water to pick up a stone. Then bandages would be applied by a Catholic priest, who attended for three days. When unwrapped in his presence, if there was no scalding, he was innocent. Another ordeal was walking over nine rods of hot plowshares. Freedom depended on whether the accused's soles were not burnt. The theory that God would intervene in each case to do justice was finally abandoned by the Catholic Church and outlawed by Henry III in England in 1219.

There followed trial by combat. For centuries, duels with various weapons determined that the victor was righteous. To overcome the possibility that God might not always choose to play his part against the iniquitous, disputants were permitted to select representatives for combat.

The present jury trial, developed under Anglo-Saxon law, nurtured by Judeo-Christian ethics, was the result of a slow and painful evolutionary process.

Why twelve jurors? That number has a mystical tradition. There were twelve gods in mythical history, twelve tribes of Israel and twelve disciples. Whatever the number, the multiplicity of lay judgments is intended to establish an approximate cross-section of opinion, which tends to cancel out prejudices or undue sympathies.

Fear of tyrants, or even of the power of benevolent governments, is responsible for the extraordinary obstacles we place in the path of the prosecutor. The law has constructed a protective fence around the accused citizen.

(25)

The Rosenbergs and Sobell were the beneficiaries of these rules. The judge instructed the jury that there was a presumption of innocence, until the very moment that the jury might decide them guilty.

Even if the jury believed they were guilty, it could not find them so, unless they believed them guilty "beyond a reasonable doubt!" Thus, preponderance of evidence, which is all that is required in a civil case, is not enough. The scales must not just tip, they must tip decisively.

Even if that severe test is met, the jury must be unanimous. If one juror is unconvinced, there can be no verdict of guilty.

The fact that they were indicted must not be considered by the jury as any indication of guilt, and the judge so instructed the jury.

The defendants need not take the stand to defend themselves. If they did not, the jury might not draw any inference against them for failing to do so. The burden to establish their guilt rested entirely on the government and was not shared. The Rosenbergs chose to testify, but Sobell did not, and he was protected by this instruction.

The fact that the United States of America brought the action, or that the FBI testified, was not to impress the jurors. All litigants, including the government, stood equally before the law—so the jury was instructed.

There are many more protective devices for a defendant. A jury of his peers, which means fellow citizens, who will apply their common experiences in life, decide his fate. The judge is excluded from fact-finding. He tells the jury so. His function is to rule only on questions of law. The jurors are the sole judges of the facts.

Then there are rules of evidence, designed to weed out irrelevancies; hearsay (what someone else told the witness, when that someone is not available for cross-examination to test his veracity, and for the jury to observe him); conclusions rather than a statement of facts on which they are based, which prevent the jury from drawing its own conclusions; and hundreds of other precautionary rules which fill volumes marked EVIDENCE.

In addition, there are court rules, designed to prevent surprise. For example, both sides must list the names of their witnesses in advance. The government must provide the defendant with a bill of particulars of its claims. Sometimes, the grand jury minutes must be shown to the defendant before trial. Under certain circumstances, which we will see occurred in the Rosenberg trial, the written reports of FBI agents may be examined to see whether their testimony on the stand is different from what they previously wrote.

Joseph Conrad once described a storm at sea with such detail and imagery that one heard every groan of the masts, every howl of the wind, every lash and crash of the giant waves and even experienced malaise from the violent seesawing of the boat as it was tossed out of the ocean only to fall into cavernous troughs. After forty-seven pages of such description, Conrad wrote, "And this was only the beginning."

Everything I have described about our judicial system is only the beginning of an effort to achieve an exquisite balance of fairness.

In the long process of adopting procedures for justice, difficult choices had to be made. Should we sacrifice thoroughness to save time? For example, should we limit questions in selecting a jury, or the length of opening statements, or summations or even cross-examination? We opted for unlimited opportunity for presentation, despite crowded calendars.

Should the losing party be required to pay the victor the real costs it suffered, as in England, or only nominal costs? We have adopted the latter, because we do not wish to discourage poor people from asserting their possible rights, fearing the disastrous consequences of losing.

Should appeals be limited? To prevent error or prejudice, we permit multiple appeals.

These are only a few illustrations of the perfectionism we have struggled to achieve.

No other judicial system in the world has set so high a goal. This is evident from their more pragmatic procedures, accepting affidavits in lieu of oral testimony, thus eliminating the opportunity to test truth through cross-examination; barring jury trials in most disputes, so as to place more power in the hands of a single judge; substituting "masters" for judges to conserve judicial time; and severely curtailing the opportunity to appeal.

We are solicitous about the precious rights of the individual. We are loath to diminish them for the sake of over-all efficiency. Ultimately, this poses the question whether the individual, too, may not suffer because he is part of the general public, which is threatened by delay and even the breakdown of a hand-tailored system, unable to cope with a mass problem.

Does our finely sculptured judicial system function with intended purity? Of course not. Like any ideal, there is a gap between concept and performance. The holy grail is sullied by human handling. Particularly in an area uncharted by the certainties of science, it is difficult to eliminate the frailties of men. While science has progressed phenomenally in the last fifty years (if all the scientists who ever lived were listed, 90 per cent would be alive today; that is how few there were in past centuries), human nature has improved, if at all, almost imperceptibly. Consequently, corrupting influences, whether sordid or subtle, whether intentional or the psychological consequence of prejudice and ignorance (are they synonymous?), and the many mysterious bedevilments of true objectivity mar the judicial system.

Indeed, just as we tolerate a limited amount of adulteration in food, before we forbid its consumption, so the law tolerates some error in the judicial process. This stems from the realization that in a long

(27)

trial, it is virtually impossible to avoid some mistakes, whether they be admission of evidence which should have been excluded, or exclusion of evidence which should have been admitted, or the judge's intrusion into the factual area of the trial beyond the permissible limits of clarification or inflammatory statements by the prosecutor. The more delicate and intricate the construction of the judicial scales to avoid imbalance, the more likelihood there is that its sensitive parts will be violated by use.

The rule is that only errors which are so substantial that they resulted in a verdict which would not otherwise have been given require reversal. But if, for example, the evidence which was wrongly excluded was only corroborative of a fact which has been established, or a prejudicial comment by the prosecutor, has been overcome by a vigorous instruction by the judge to disregard it, or if the evidence is so overwhelming that the result would and should have been the same, irrespective of the errors, then the Appellate Court will point out the legal defect, condemn it, caution judges and counsel in future proceedings not to repeat it, but nevertheless, affirm the verdict.

The Rosenberg trial should be evaluated by these standards. Were there errors? If so, how prejudicial were they?

Also, were there tactical mistakes, missed opportunities in cross-examination, or inadequate preparation, which might have altered the result?

We embark on the tour of the trial on two levels. One is the drama in the courtroom. The other is a critical eye on the events.

CHAPTER 3

Ceremonial tradition is as much part of the judiciary as of royalty. In England, judges wear white curly wigs, which frame the most nondescript faces with wisdom. In France, lawyers wear black robes, with red or purple stripes to distinguish them from austere judicial robes. In the United States, formality has been gradually crowded out by the notion that democracy is equalization rather than equal opportunity for unequals. The requirement that lawyers should wear frock coats and striped pants when appearing before the Supreme Court of the United States or Appellate Courts has yielded to plain black or blue suits. Even judges sometimes leave their black gowns in the robing room.

So judges have denuded themselves of adornments, which some might well use to look impressive, and warrant the appellation "Your Honor" or "Your Lordship."

Nevertheless, no matter who the judge is, there is that moment of quickened anticipation when a brightly badged attendant emerges from the judge's chambers, facing the seventy-five-foot crowded courtroom, pounds his knuckled fist on the door three times and calls out, "Everyone, please rise." Before the noise of scraping feet has died down, a robed figure sweeps out of the room and up the three steps to the huge bench. There he stands while the court clerk announces that the court is now in session. "All ye having business before this Court, come forward and ye shall be heard. God bless the United States of America. God bless this Honorable Court."

In the Rosenberg case, the judge was Irving R. Kaufman. He nodded an impersonal greeting and settled his five-foot six-inch frame into the large leather chair, built as if it was intended for a man twice his size. His head was barely seen above the bench. The audience and counsel were seated again, leaving shuffling echoes.

Judge Kaufman was only forty years old. He was the youngest judge on the federal bench. This was natural for him. In his short life, his accomplishments had always outdistanced his age. He received his law degree from Fordham University at the age of twenty, one year too early for admission to the bar. In 1935, he became special assistant to the United States Attorney for the Southern District of New York. Only a year later, he advanced to Assistant United States Attorney, and because he was still in his twenties, he became known as "the boy prosecutor." After an interval of successful private practice, he became special assistant to the Attorney General of the United States, Tom Clark, who later ascended to the Supreme Court. Then he received President Truman's appointment for life as a federal judge.

When the Senate and the public examine the qualifications of a judge, they concentrate upon his legal antecedents, giving insufficient attention to his family and environmental antecedents. No judge can divest himself of these influences upon his judicial conduct. It is no coincidence that Judge Pierce Butler of the United States Supreme Court, who had been counsel for the railroads, wrote brilliant opinions on Interstate Commerce from the vantage point of his former predilections, or that Judge Louis Brandeis, whose career as a lawyer was defending the public interest against "predatory corporations," evolved the technique of judicial decision by economic studies often based on his own research.

The law is rarely prescribed in terms which permit precise application. Interpretation equivalent to translation is required. What is "due process" when we face the problem of women jurors or Negroes disproportionally represented on jury rolls; or when a tax law places a heavier burden on certain businesses than others; or when laws forbid employment of children or women under certain circumstances; or limit welfare payments in various ways; or forbid non-fireproof clothes or plastic toys, which small entrepreneurs protest put them out of business; and the thousands, yes, many thousands of questions arising from a flood of new laws, which could not be anticipated by Congress whose eyes were on one target, without realizing the enveloping nature of language? Or to cite just one more illustration, what does the definition of "negligence" mean when it is defined as conduct contrary to how a reasonable man would act under the circumstances? How would a reasonable man act when his automobile confronts a problem at an intersection, at a certain hour, in certain light, and with variable counterforces in flow?

Contrary to some misconceptions, the judge cannot find the law by looking it up in a book. He must look it up in himself. What he finds there has been implanted in his daily experiences from childhood on. His interpretive judgment is based on stimuli resulting from his religious, economic and social background. His relationship with his parents, his sisters and brothers and his friends; his illnesses; his sexual experiences and growth; his love relationships; the toughness he acquires from collisions in the competitive world, and the shield he builds to prevent it from encroaching on the soft core essential to his ideals; everything he reads; every person he meets and every conversation he has; every admiration and hate he develops; every defeat and every triumph, often in trivial matters, which affect his psyche, not his worldly stance; these and infinitely more leave their marks inside him. Every man is a conglomerate enterprise, and his values and judgments derive from a mysterious jumble of life's acquisitions.

To evaluate Judge Kaufman, therefore, requires some knowledge of his background.

Irving Kaufman is a native New Yorker. He is one of five children. His father was a manufacturer of tobacco humidifiers. Although he attended a Catholic university and even excelled in a course on Christian Doctrine, he is a devout Jew, attending synagogue.

He began his legal career by working in the law office of an outstanding lawyer, Louis Rosenberg. He fell in love with his daughter, married her and reared a family of three children. So now, the judge, who was married to a Rosenberg, presided over a trial of two other Rosenbergs. Did this subconsciously produce sympathy or resentment that a name he revered should be besmirched? Was he inclined to lean backward to demonstrate there was no subtle unintended influence on him?

There once was a judge in New York State's highest criminal court by the name of Otto Rosalsky. He was a proud Jew and made no attempt to hide his contempt for any convicted Jew because he had sullied the reputation of Jews as good citizens. He became a terror to Jewish criminals. He would impose long sentences upon them, openly announcing that they were receiving harsh treatment because they were Jews and should have known better. It was reverse chauvinism and every sentence ended with an exclamation point.

As we already see, all the leading figures in the trial were Jews—the prosecutor and the judge. The jury had no Jews upon it, and this has been the subject of comment by the critics of the verdict, but it should be observed that Jews were on the panel and in the jury box, but were excused by both the defense as well as by the prosecution. There was considerable resentment in Jewish circles against the Rosenbergs and defense counsel might have feared the "Rosalsky reaction" from Jewish jurors.

A judge who must depend upon his gavel, rather than his presence, to maintain order seldom succeeds. Kaufman quickly exerted his authority effortlessly. His black, flattened-down hair, brown eyes framed by glasses, wide mouth and heavy clamping jaws created a stern-visaged face. Yet it was scholarly and sensitive.

When Julius Rosenberg first saw him on the bench, he whispered to his lawyer, "He looks like a cross between a rabbinical student and an Army sergeant."

❊❊❊❊❊

CHAPTER 4

We come to the selection of the jury in the Rosenberg case. It is a vital step in a trial, because it affords the litigants a unique opportunity to pick their own judges. The art in doing so involves psychological insights. Is the juror sympathetic or severe? There is little opportunity to analyze his personality. The readings must be instantaneous and gathered from such stimuli as there are, no matter how minor. Is his smile bright or tight? What newspaper or magazine is tucked in his pocket? Are his eyes hostile while his words are friendly? What kind of glances does he throw at the defendants when he thinks he is unobserved? The defense seeks to eliminate individualists. Such jurors tend to be leaders who win over unconvinced jurors to their side, thus achieving unanimity. This is usually to the advantage of the prosecution. It cannot afford to have a single dissident. That creates a hung jury—and no verdict.

If the defense is strong enough, it can win an acquittal by the required unanimous vote. If it is not, it has everything to gain from conflict in the jury room. Disagreement is more likely to occur if the twelve jurors are equally matched in their persuasive powers. Defense wants no "strong" juror who may overwhelm the others. That is why a defense lawyer should scrutinize the juror for individualistic traits. Do his clothes reveal any? Does he wear strange cut lapels, a leather watch fob, daring colored shirt, a bow tie, a boutonniere or unusual eyeglasses? Has he a beard or mustache? Counsel should listen carefully to the juror's voice and diction. Is he fluent and forceful? What is his background and work? Is he in business for himself? Does he hold a job which requires authority?

As with all rules, there are exceptions to mock the maker. Jurors deemed weak sometimes turn out to be mulishly obstinate, though in-

(33)

articulate. A keen mind is not the only bulwark against a false argument. Refusal to listen or understand achieves the same immunity.

One of the professional jokes which point up the unpredictability of jury conduct is about the guilty defendant who manages to corrupt a juror in a murder case. No matter how conclusive the evidence, he is to hold out for manslaughter. The jury disagrees. He reports his triumph. "All the other jurors voted for acquittal, but I wouldn't budge."

The most significant test of an acceptable juror is an imponderable one.

Is there a bond of affinity between the juror and the counsel which will redound to the client's benefit? This may be felt as well as discerned. Does he follow counsel as he walks to the other end of the jury box, or does he look straight ahead, relieved that the questions are ended? Does he join in the smile of the questioner or rebuke him by deadpan or even a frown? Does he react as if he admired opposing counsel and might subconsciously identify with him?

Will he be likely to accept the word of certain witnesses who counsel know will appear? Yes, racial, religious and social factors may play a part in credibility. The lawyer tries to obtain a jury which is disposed toward his client. Since both lawyers have this objective, they cancel out each other's partisanship and an impartial jury is the most likely result. The philosophy of the law is that each side in the contest shows its best profile and justice sees truth full face.

However, all this assumes that it is the lawyer who questions the prospective juror.

In federal courts, some judges do all the questioning of the jurors themselves, permitting the lawyers to challenge on the basis of what they hear. They invite counsel to submit written questions which, if proper, the judge puts to the jurors. Here is an illustration of reducing a litigant's rights in the interest of saving time. Purists, who believe an individual's precious rights should not be compromised for efficiency reasons, therefore criticize this practice, which excludes the lawyer from direct questioning of each juror.

There are two kinds of challenges of a juror. Those for cause, such as a juror's admission of prejudice or his acquaintance with a party, witness or lawyer in the case. Such challenges are unlimited in number. Then there are peremptory challenges, which either side exercises in its discretion. These are limited.

In the Rosenberg case, the judge announced that he would question the jurors. He ruled that the government would have twenty challenges and the defendants collectively thirty challenges.

To be fair, these challenges would be alternated. Otherwise, one side would have the advantage of sitting by while the adversary excused a juror he might have decided to challenge, thus obtaining an extra challenge for himself. The judge ruled that there should be eight rounds, three by the defendants, two by the government. Then there would be a ninth round, three by the defendants, one by the government, and thereafter three rounds, one apiece to each side.

This was an opening illustration of the extreme care the law takes to see that the scales of justice are truly balanced, before the weights of testimony are placed in them.

On the clerk's desk in the courtroom was a revolving closed wooden cage, not unlike those used in picking numbers in a bingo game or in a draft. In it were the names of a panel of jurors, picked at random from the rolls. The clerk whirled the cage and called out the name of a juror until twelve were seated. Judge Irving Kaufman addressed them and the prospective jurors waiting in the rear who might be called to the box as it emptied from challenges:

COURT   To the gentlemen in the jury box and to the ladies and gentlemen in the courtroom, I shall attempt to speak loud enough so that all of you can hear my questions.

Now, I will address certain questions to the jurors, and the purpose of these questions is to elicit such information from the jurors that would bring out any bias or any sympathy or any prejudice against either side, if such exists; and if in my questioning you feel that there is something that you ought to reply to, don't hesitate to make the answer.

To those who are not in the jury box, I ask you to merely make a note to the particular question, that will require an answer if you are ultimately put into the jury box . . . you can volunteer your reply to that particular question. . . .   .

It is our purpose and object to secure a jury that has no feeling, no bias, no prejudice as to either side of this controversy. To put it another way, the minds of the jurors should be the same as a white sheet of paper with nothing on it, with respect to this case, and you should only take the testimony as it comes from the witnesses and from no other source.

It is the object of this Court to select jurors who will keep their minds open during the entire trial and at no time during the proceedings to say, "Now, I know what I am going to do." If a juror takes that position, he might just as well go home and come back when the matter is submitted. Now, that is important. A piece of evidence might come in later that will change your opinion one way or the other, and that is why it is important that your minds remain open until all the evidence is in, until you have heard the summations of counsel and until you have heard the charge of the Court. If you don't do that, you might have such pride of opinion that it may cause you to adhere to a position which you took in the early part of the trial and your minds would hence be closed.

(35)

He gave them the classic instruction that the indictment is not proof of guilt and should be completely disregarded; that the defendants are presumed to be innocent "until it is established beyond a reasonable doubt that they have offended against the law."

He asked whether any juror had had dealings "directly or indirectly" with the Attorney General of the United States or the prosecuting attorneys, each of whom he introduced and asked to stand. He followed the same procedure with each of the defense lawyers and then the defendants.

When the judge asked whether "you or any member of your immediate families or friends are connected with the FBI, police department or investigating agency public or private," several jurors raised their hands. One had a brother who was a policeman in Elmsford, New York. Another had a neighbor who was with the FBI. Both, however, assured the judge, "It wouldn't have any effect on me." This, of course, barred a challenge for cause, but not a discretionary or peremptory challenge by defense counsel.

The judge asked whether any of the jurors was employed by a company which had contracts with the government. One juror, Mr. Fritz, said he worked for the National Carbon Division of Union Carbide, which did work for the government. Another, Mr. Miclo, reported that he worked for the New York Telephone Company. He didn't know whether it had contracts with the government. Still another, Mr. King, worked for the General Drafting Company, which produced maps for the federal government. But all were certain that they would not be embarrassed to sit in a case brought by the government and that their minds would be open.

The judge obtained satisfactory negative answers when he asked whether any juror had any interest in a case pending in the federal court; or any dispute with the government.

Then the clerk read a list of witnesses submitted by both sides and the judge asked whether any juror knew any of them. None did.

COURT Do you have any hesitancy in accepting the proposition that each of the defendants is presumed to be innocent? And that a defendant can only be found guilty when you are convinced beyond a reasonable doubt of the defendants' guilt?

PROSPECTIVE JUROR NO. 12 Your Honor, I never served in a criminal court before, but under the present circumstances, and even though I had not read the indictment, I don't feel that I could give the defendants a fair and equitable opinion.

COURT Very well. You are excused.

There followed a judicial lecture on the jury's obligation to practice godly impartiality:

When you are asked to serve on a jury, you are asked to leave all your prejudices behind. No matter how distasteful your service may be, no matter how distasteful your verdict might be, if it is based upon the evidence, that is what is expected of you. It is just like adding a column of figures and you get a result. You may not like the result you have gotten but that is the result. And that is the same situation here. So you can see that we are searching to see whether or not we can get jurors who can receive this evidence with an open mind, without any prejudice or bias for or against either the defense or the Government.

Now, I repeat, would any of you be so prejudiced that you could not leave your mind open to decide this case on all the evidence by the fact that the defendants are alleged to have engaged in a conspiracy to violate the espionage laws of the United States, or that it is asserted that the spying was done on behalf of the Soviet Union.

Juror No. 6, George N. Melinette, replied that he served in the Navy in the Pacific and that he would be prejudiced. The court excused him.

When the judge asked whether any juror had a prejudice against capital punishment, Juror No. 1, Richard H. King, said he had and was excused.

None of the jurors opposed the government's research and development of atomic weapons or believed they should be revealed to Russia.

Many hands were raised when the judge inquired whether any members of the jurors' families had served in the Armed Forces. Jurors Troy and Cuff each had had four brothers in the Army. Two jurors had served in the Navy in the First World War. Several others had had brothers and nephews in the Second World War.

Each juror assured the court that he could be fair and unprejudiced, and that he could "serve with propriety." The defense counsel took full notes of these answers.

In reply to the judge's question, almost all jurors stated that they had read in the newspapers or heard on radio or television about the "arrest and conviction of one Harry Gold and one David Greenglass for espionage."

Now I want you to listen to this question: Have you formed any opinions or impressions as to the merits of the charge unfavorable either to the Government or to the defendants or any of them, which would prevent or hinder you from holding your mind fully open until all of the evidence and the instructions of the Court are complete?

Juror Cornelius Troy spoke up:

Your Honor, I am afraid on that question about Harry Gold, I would be a little prejudiced there. In fact, the way I feel about it, after reading it.

COURT Very well, you are excused.

The judge then read a list of newspapers and publications, the names of which had been submitted by opposing counsel, and asked whether any juror had been a subscriber or reader or connected in some way with any of them. The list was so comprehensive that it took ten minutes to read. It included daily newspapers, *Red Channels,* Chicago American Committee for Yugoslav Relief, German-American Bund, Ku Klux Klan, Hollywood Writers Mobilization for Defense and many, many others.

One juror advised that he supplied ink to the *Daily News,* but he assured the court that he would render a verdict based solely on the evidence and that he would not be embarrassed by his business association to do so.

Another juror announced that he was once in the advertising department of Hearst's *Journal-American,* and was presently on *Time* magazine. He asserted that this would not affect him in any way.

The judge read a special list of newspapers (undoubtedly submitted by the government).

COURT I want you to listen to these other papers and I will address a question based on them.

Daily Worker, The Worker, The Communist, Political Affairs, morning *Freiheit, New Masses, In Fact, People's World, The German-American, Soviet Russia Today, Masses & Main Stream, People's Voice, The Protestant, Contact, The National Guardian, New Foundations, New Times.*

Have any of you read or been associated with any of these publications?

A juror, Mr. Layman, told the court that as a journalist he had read *In Fact* but he did "not come to the jury box with any prejudice for or against either side." Later, however, he talked to the judge who excused him.

The judge asked whether any juror had made a contribution or had been associated with any organization "contained on a list published by the Attorney General pursuant to a Presidential Executive order?"

The clerk read a lengthy list beginning with the Abraham Lincoln Brigade and concluding with China Aid Council. There was a negative response.

The court elicited the information that the jurors had read or had heard of Westbrook Pegler, Walter Winchell, John O'Donnell, Frederick Woltman, Melton Frank, Howard Rushmore, Louis F. Budenz, Fulton Lewis, Jr., Elizabeth Bentley. But all answered that they would not be prejudiced thereby.

A juror, Samuel G. French, who had taken the place of Layman, revealed that he had worked on a sedition case "directly under O. John

Rogge," who was now the attorney for the defendant Greenglass. He believed that there was a possibility of prejudice and the court excused him.

COURT Has any juror or member of the juror's family attended the College of the City of New York known as C.C.N.Y.? If so, would the fact that some of the defendants also may have graduated from that institution prejudice you one way or the other in your consideration of the evidence in this case?

A juror, Mrs. Pincus, revealed that her nephew had attended City College and "got out four years ago" and she said "that wouldn't have any bearing on her verdict at all."

The jury gave negative answers to a series of searching questions such as whether they or any member of their family had ever been the subject of investigation by any committee of Congress or grand jury; or whether they had known any congressman who had been a member of the House Un-American Activities Committee, or any investigator of the committee; or had testified before it; or had borne any bias against the committee; or had prejudice against "the loyalty oath"; or had been a member of any organization which advocated the overthrow of the government of the United States by force; or had signed a Communist petition; or had belonged to any organization which had been either friendly or opposed to communism?

JORDAN (Juror No. 4) The American Legion.
COURT (To Juror No. 4)
Q Now, would the fact, Mr. Jordan, that the American Legion has made some expressions on the subject influence you, or have you been so influenced, that in a case of this character you couldn't come in here with an open mind and decide it upon the evidence and the evidence alone?
A No, your Honor. It has been many years. I belonged to it for twenty years, but in the last thirteen years I haven't belonged.
Q And you feel you can conscientiously perform your duty as a citizen and decide this case based on the evidence and the evidence alone?
A I do, your Honor.
COURT Is that the general feeling of each and every member of the jury? If it is not, will you please speak up?
(Prospective jurors nodded in the affirmative.)

The judge then put a critical question to the jurors. If the defendants "assert their constitutional privilege against testifying to matters which may tend to incriminate them," in other words, if they took the Fifth Amendment, would that influence the jurors against them, even though the court instructed them that the government must "prove its charges beyond a reasonable doubt?"
The jurors indicated that they would not be prejudiced thereby.

(39)

Would the fact that witnesses for the government, like Harry Gold and David Greenglass, had confessed to espionage for Russia so prejudice the jurors that they would be unable to accept as truthful anything these witnesses said? Conversely (another illustration of the effort to keep a gyroscopic balance in the prejudicial winds), would the jurors scrutinize such testimony "by the same standards" as those for defense witnesses in accordance with the legal instructions by the judge?

The jurors answered these questions satisfactorily to both sides.

But when the next question was put, whether the jury would give the same weight to the testimony of either an FBI agent or a member of the Communist Party, as he would to other witnesses, William H. Fritz, Juror No. 8, said: "I am afraid I wouldn't be able to do that," and was excused.

The judge phrased two civil rights questions:

COURT Do you subscribe to the principle that every one, regardless of race, color, creed or position in society, and regardless also of his political or religious beliefs, is entitled to a fair trial, according to our laws?

(Prospective jurors nodded in the affirmative.)

COURT Has any juror any prejudice, bias or sympathy, based solely upon a person's educational background or personal appearance?

(Prospective jurors indicated in the negative.)

To impress the jury with its duty to disregard public pressure, the judge asked:

Is there anything that has happened in connection with this case which would give you any fear or hesitancy in declaring the defendants not guilty, if the evidence in law warranted such a verdict?

(Prospective jurors indicated in the negative.)

This concluded the general questions appropriate to all jurors. The court then announced, "I shall call on each one of the jurors to tell me something about their occupation." He urged them to speak up, because he was not prying into their personal business, "but everybody in the litigation is entitled to know something about your background." Were they married; children; occupation; was wife employed and other questions which filled in the colors on a bland portrait.

The judge invited counsel on both sides to submit questions which, if he deemed proper, he would ask, or permit the attorney to ask.

E. H. Bloch, attorney for the Rosenbergs, asked whether any juror had been the victim of a crime:

A PROSPECTIVE JUROR I have been the victim of a crime. I was in a holdup about three weeks ago.

(40)

Q Would the fact that you were the victim of a holdup in any way prejudice you in serving in this type of case?

A No, your Honor.

The defense exercised three peremptory challenges, and jurors Baring-Gould (who was questioned by the FBI concerning an applicant for a government position), Cuff (whose brother was a policeman and who had four brothers in the war) and Jordan (who had worked on the Hearst newspaper and then on *Time*) left the jury box.

Three others took their places, and the questions began over again.

One of them, Raymond Mitchell, admitted that his reading of the *National Guardian* had prejudiced him and he was excused for cause.

The challenges accelerated. The government had its rounds of exclusion. New faces appeared. Marvin G. Barrett and Julian M. Walldorf didn't believe in capital punishment. They were out. Another, Albert E. Molsaka, had served in the war and believed he could not be impartial. New questions occurred to defense counsel:

E. H. BLOCH If your Honor pleases, I am going to ask your Honor to ask a question of those jurors who have stated that they were in the armed services in the last World War, and ask them whether or not they have any bias or prejudice against any men of the age group that were eligible for Selective Service but who were not in the active armed forces of the United States?

COURT You may consider that question asked of you, and I want the entire panel to consider that question put to them also.

(Prospective jurors and panel indicated in the negative.)

The turnover of jurors gave rise to new problems. Here was one whose relative "is attached to the Atomic Energy Commission" and he didn't feel "able to serve." Another had a cousin who had been killed in the war, and would rather not sit. Still another, Howard B. McGowan, worked with the investment banking firm of F. S. Mosely and Company and he feared that "while I am considering the evidence, I probably unconsciously would be thinking of my contacts." He was excused.

Possible bias was not the only reason for release from service. One juror asked permission to approach the bench and talk to the judge privately.

Your Honor, my daughter is a spastic. She is in the Bancroft School in New Jersey. Because of her brain condition, anything is liable to happen at any time, and I want you to know that, because if anything did happen, I naturally would have to ask the Court to release . . . In a long case like this, why I—

(41)

COURT Is she at a stage now where something acute is about to arise?

JUROR As you know, spasticism is an infection of the vasomotor section of the brain and it is a hard thing to—I mean, in point of time—

COURT You think you would rather be excused?

JUROR I think I would, your Honor, for that reason.

COURT All right.

As each card was picked from the revolving wheel, it was placed in a slotted flat board, with room for twelve names. This board was handed back and forth between defense counsel and government counsel. When each side had exercised its peremptory challenges, the card was removed, and the replacement slip inserted.

Psychologically, it was best for the jury not to know who was exercising the challenge. The reason was that the remaining jurors might deem the challenged juror fair and draw unpleasant inferences from the fact that he was thrown off. So a subtle way of not exposing the challenge was to indicate to the clerk, as unostentatiously as possible, the numbers of the jurors to be excused. It was he who called out their names.

Government counsel followed this practice, which made his challenges least noticeable. But defense counsel openly announced their challenges to the judge. The clerk then took the cards from them and repeated the names.

Sometimes defendants' counsel openly consulted with Julius Rosenberg, thus drawing him into the possible prejudicial area. For example, the record reveals:

(Board containing names of jurors handed to defense counsel.)

E. H. BLOCH Will you bear with us for a moment, your Honor. (Consults with defendants Rosenberg.)

The defendants ask that 9, 11 and 12 be excused.

(Mr. Sexton, Mr. Meisner and Mr. Crawford excused by the defense.)

The peremptory challenges began to run out. The government had only two left. The prosecutor announced, "I pass." This phrase used in poker is not inappropriate. It means that I waive my challenges of new jurors, who have just been seated, so that I may hoard my challenge in the event the defense excuses them, and someone less acceptable comes into the box. The skillful use of challenges is important. Counsel often looks to the rear of the courtroom to see the kind of jurors still available. Perhaps the replacement will be worse than the juror in the box about whom he has doubt. Indeed, it is wise to have at least one or two peremptory challenges left. Otherwise, one cannot displace a juror who is especially displeasing, but who cannot be removed for cause.

The jury selection had consumed several days. After a few more skirmishes, both sides felt that they had a fair jury.

SAYPOL Challenges waived and the jury is satisfactory to the Government.

COURT Very well.

KUNTZ Satisfactory to the defendant.

COURT Jury satisfactory all around.

E. H. BLOCH Satisfactory all around.

(Jurors sworn in by clerk.)

Thus after extensive elimination and selection, and after all the jockeying for jurors who would not be favorable to the opposing side, the following jurors appealed to both sides as acceptable:

NO. 1 (Foreman) Vincent J. Lebonitte, manager for R. H. Macy branch in White Plains.

NO. 2 Richard Booth, a caterer for a tennis club in Forest Hills, called the Seminole Club.

NO. 3 Howard G. Becker, an auditor for the Irving Trust Company for twenty-four years.

NO. 4 James A. Gibbons, an accountant for the New York City Omnibus Company for twenty-eight years.

NO. 5 Charles W. Christie, an auditor for the Tidewater Associated Oil Company.

NO. 6 Harold H. Axley, a restaurant owner.

NO. 7 Emanuel Clarence Dean, a black, who worked for the Consolidated Edison Company.

NO. 8 Chauncey E. Miller, secretary of the Board of Commissioners of Pilots, an agency of the state of New York for twenty years.

NO. 9 Mrs. Lisetts D. Dammas, a housewife.

NO. 10 Charles J. Duda, a bookkeeper for Davis and Lawrence Company.

NO. 11 James Mitchell, an accountant for Harris, Kerr, Forster & Company.

NO. 12 James F. Tessitore, an estimator for the Alco Gravure Division of Publications Corporation.

Four additional jurors were chosen to be available if any jurors became ill or unable to serve because of some emergency. This would prevent a mistrial for lack of a full jury. They were:

ALTERNATE NO. 1 John F. Moore, a business representative for the Consolidated Edison Company.

ALTERNATE NO. 2 Emerson C. Nein, an officer and auditor for the Empire State Bank.

ALTERNATE NO. 3 Richard Lombardi, a government employee (Post Office).

ALTERNATE NO. 4 Mrs. Edna Allen, housewife.

(43)

For the first time, the judge addressed the jurors as official partners in the judicial process. They would share the burdens with him for weeks to come.

COURT   Madam and gentlemen, you have been selected as jurors in this case. My bailiff will escort you when we take our recess for lunch, to the jury room, which is behind the courtroom, here, where you will leave your hats and coats. You will in the mornings, go to that jury room, leave your hat and coat there and wait until you are sent for; the same thing during your luncheon recess. . . . I admonish you now and I ask you to carry it with you at all times throughout this trial, not to discuss it with your fellow jurors, not to discuss it with anybody at home, not to permit anybody to discuss the case with you, and, of course, not to read a newspaper, read anything in a newspaper concerning this case, not to listen to the radio, not to watch television, at no time to read any magazine that deals with this particular case.

The jurors had been transformed from citizens to citizen judges. As surely as if they had been clothed with black robes, they were the exclusive judges of the facts. The fate of the Rosenbergs and Sobell were in their hands.

CHAPTER 5

What is the real purpose of opening statements by respective counsel? Why not permit the witnesses to tell it from the stand, without speeches by lawyers?

In an involved case, there are many witnesses and dozens of exhibits. The jury may not understand the significance of each bit of testimony and its relationship to the whole case. To avoid the confusion of fragmented presentation, the law permits each counsel to tell the jury in advance his theory of the case and what he intends to prove.

The prosecutor usually outlines his case quite fully. He must present his case first. The burden is heavy upon him to overcome the presumption of innocence beyond a reasonable doubt. He, therefore, has no reason to hold back. He wishes to educate the jury to the nature of the crime and the evidence to support it.

The defendant is in a different position. He is not certain how much evidence the government has or how impressive it will be. He does not want to commit himself too early. If the case against him does not meet the severe test of proof "beyond a reasonable doubt," he may decide not to testify. The law protects him against any adverse inference from his silence. Why should he risk cross-examination if it is unnecessary? So he must bide his time to watch the developments. He is not certain what claims he may have to defend or which will not require an answer. This limits his opening statement to discreet generalities such as pleas for an open mind until all the evidence has been presented.

Julius and Ethel Rosenberg chose to take the stand and subject themselves to harrowing cross-examination. Morton Sobell did not, with extraordinary consequences.

The opening statements followed this pattern of vigorous accusation by prosecutor and cautious statement by the defense.

The opening statement for the government was made by the United States Attorney for the Southern District of New York, Irving H. Saypol.

He was then forty-five years old, but his fading brown hair had already surrendered to a little white at the temples. He was a solidly built man above medium height. His light horn-rimmed glasses underneath heavy eyebrows lent a scholarly look to his firm, square face. Like so many persuaders, who lack the voice and eloquence to set the atmosphere around them ablaze until the flames jump over the jury rail and set fire to the conviction of the jurors, he adopted the opposite technique. He spoke in flat tones, unemotionally, but fluently and directly. The effort was to create a no-nonsense, factual approach. The louder the opposition, the quieter he was. The more flamboyant the adversary, the more homey was his approach. He could seldom be heard in the back of the courtroom.

Saypol was thoroughly experienced. He had already won the second case against Alger Hiss. He had been Chief Prosecutor of the eleven Communist leaders, of William Remington, and of Abraham Brothman, and in all instances successfully. He had received national recognition as "the nation's number one legal hunter of top Communists."

His record revealed an almost vertical rise to the point of now being the chief actor in one of the most important government prosecutions in American history. After graduation from Brooklyn Law School, at the age of twenty-two, Saypol had become an assistant in the Law Department of the city of New York. Thereafter, he became Assistant United States Attorney and after five years earned the prestigious post of United States Attorney. His interests were not professionally limited. He led the United Jewish Appeal and the Salvation Army drives.

Saypol was effective because of an inner conviction that he was fighting a wicked enemy. It armed him with sincerity. There is no more effective weapon to pierce a juror's doubts. Also, it made him determined to convict, thus offsetting fanatical Communist convictions. Throughout the trial, he did not give an inch. Defense counsel treated him deferentially and sometimes fawned upon him, conceding he was right about some minor controversy, or accepting his word, "if you say so," and thanked him for his "courtesies." But there was no reciprocal gesture by him. He was intense. Every word he uttered was calculated to further the impression that the defendants were tampering with or dodging the truth, and that even their counsel were confused or embarrassed by their duty. His was a one-track mind, and the track led to the death house.

The government had created a team to conduct the case. Saypol's chief assistant was Myles J. Lane, who had presented the evidence to the grand jury, which indicted the Rosenbergs and Sobell. Lane was a former hockey player, and even without the protective paraphornolia of his sport, he loomed huge and overpowering. He had ably assisted Saypol in other prosecutions. They had worked together with the same anticipatory smoothness which team athletes develop. Saypol and Lane later became judges of the State Supreme Court of New York, where they now sit, gazing down on the arena they once occupied.

There were other assistants. One was Roy M. Cohn, slender, short and dark visaged. His sleepy eyelids with heavy shadows underneath gave his face a brooding old look, despite his twenty-four years. His hair was slicked down. His lips were loose and his tongue constantly darted out to wet them even while he was talking. His tantivy movements added to the impression of nervous energy.

His father, Albert Cohn, was an able and universally liked judge of the appellate division of the New York State Supreme Court. Upon graduation from law school, Roy went directly to an important post in the United States Attorney's office. Here he had rendered valuable service to Saypol in the trial of the eleven Communists before Judge Harold Medina and a jury.

After the Rosenberg trial, he became counsel for Senator Joseph McCarthy's committee, which set him on a stormy path he has followed ever since. While Saypol and Lane became judges, Cohn has been a defendant in several criminal cases, and acquitted in each.

The two other assistants were James B. Kilsheimer III and James E. Branigan, Jr.

Saypol rose from the midst of his assistants and corps of FBI investigators to make an opening statement on behalf of the government.

He struck a high and appropriate note in his opening. He disavowed the role of partisanship. He spoke of his obligation "on one hand to protect the rights of each individual, and, on the other hand, to protect the rights and the security of all the people."

> My colleagues and I at the counsel table for the Government will so conduct ourselves to the end that a fair trial is had in this courtroom by both parties in interest, the defendants and the Government of the United States.

He attempted to reduce the accusation to simplicity—always the objective of a prosecutor, because the more complicated the issue the more difficult it is to obtain unanimous agreement. The charge, he said, was that the Rosenbergs and Sobell conspired among themselves and with Harry Gold, David Greenglass, his wife, Ruth, and Anatoli Yakovlev, an agent and official of the Soviet Union, to deliver "information, sketches and material vital to the national defense of our country" to Russia.

While conceding that only the judge could instruct them on the law, he believed that "for purposes of clarity" that he should explain

(47)

what a conspiracy is. It is an agreement between two or more people to violate the law—in this case "espionage on behalf of a foreign power."

He tried at the outset to reduce the principle that one conspirator was responsible for the acts of his fellow conspirator to simple logic.

> . . . common sense tells us that when a number of people enter into a widespread agreement and conspiracy, such as we have here, each one cannot do all of the dirty work himself; one can only perform one's particular task. The law wisely holds, however, that the particular acts that any one of the conspirators may have performed or did perform to help along this conspiracy binds not only the doer of the act, but also his partners in crime, for that is exactly what co-conspirators are, partners, but in crime. That is so because he is not acting for himself alone, but with all of them and for all of them, as well as for himself.

Whenever a criminal confesses, thus involving his former associates, the jury listens to him with understandable skepticism. Is he worthy of belief? Prosecutors are aware of this resistance and Saypol addressed himself to it. The defendants, he warned, would attempt to attack government witnesses who were formerly their partners in crime, "but you will hear and see that these witnesses are telling the truth" and the difference between them and the Rosenbergs and Sobell, was that "they have not added to their past sins by refusing to tell you the truth." He assured the jury that the testimony and documentary evidence which the government would present could not be contradicted, "because of the truth."

His next comment touched a sensitive nerve and caused defense counsel to jump. It was the first skirmish on this point which was to reoccur continuously through the trial.

> The evidence will show that the loyalty and the allegiance of the Rosenbergs and Sobell were not to our country, but that it was to communism, communism in this country and communism throughout the world.
>
> E. H. BLOCH   If the Court pleases, I object to these remarks as irrelevant to the charge before this Court and jury and I ask the Court to instruct the District Attorney to desist from making any remarks about communism, because communism is not on trial here. These defendants are charged with espionage.
>
> SAYPOL   I object to this interruption.
>
> E. H. BLOCH   I beg your pardon, Mr. Saypol, but I am forced to do it.
>
> COURT   Will somebody permit me to make a ruling here?
>
> The charge here is conspiracy to commit espionage. It is not that the defendants are members of the Communist Party or that they

(48)

had any interest in communism. However, if the Government intends to establish that they did have an interest in communism, for the purpose of establishing a motive for what they were doing, I will, in due course, when that question arises, rule on that point.

SAYPOL That is the purpose of my remarks.

A. BLOCH Defendants except to your Honor's statement.

COURT Very well.

The prosecutor did not relent. He insisted that the Julius Rosenbergs' "love of communism and the Soviet Union led them into a Soviet espionage ring." He was admitted "into its inner sanctum and he devoted himself to the service of 'Russia' at the expense of betraying his own country."

The government, he said, would prove that the Rosenbergs and Sobell reached into wartime projects including the Army and Navy to obtain secret information and turn it over to agents of the Soviet Union "to speed it on its way to Russia."

The government would prove that the defendants recruited promising members for their Soviet espionage ring:

> The evidence will reveal to you how the Rosenbergs persuaded David Greenglass, Mrs. Rosenberg's own brother, to play the treacherous role of a modern Benedict Arnold, while wearing the uniform of the United States Army.

Saypol promised to prove how Greenglass "at the behest of the Rosenbergs" turned over to Harry Gold, a co-conspirator, "at secret rendezvous, sketches and descriptions of the very bomb itself."

By this time, Saypol had dropped his cool manner and appeared to be carried away by the enormity of the crime:

> There came a day, however, that a vigilant Federal Bureau of Investigation broke through the darkness of this insidious business and collected the evidence that would bring these culprits before the bar of justice, before an American jury like you. These defendants and their Soviet partners in crime, had at their command various amounts of money, with which to finance the escape from American justice into safe havens behind the Iron Curtain the members of this espionage ring. When one spy after another was caught and confessed, Klaus Fuchs, Harry Gold, David Greenglass, these defendants and their Soviet superiors quickly put into operation an elaborate prearranged scheme to flee the country of their birth, to seek refuge behind the Iron Curtain. These efforts to flee the borders of our country and avoid facing you followed a carefully planned pattern. Fortunately, in most instances these attempts to escape were nipped in the bud, were thwarted.

You will hear how the defendant Sobell actually succeeded in getting out of the country, in a desperate and fortunately unsuccessful attempt to flee the country.

He concluded that the evidence would prove not only beyond a reasonable doubt, "but beyond any doubt, that all three defendants have committed the most serious crime which can be committed against the people of this country."

The attorney for Ethel Rosenberg, Alexander Bloch, moved for a mistrial on the ground that "the opening statement of the learned United States Attorney was inflammatory" and introduced an irrelevant issue, communism. The court denied the motion.

One of the attorneys for Sobell, Harold M. Phillips, objected to Saypol's comments about his client's flight to Mexico, because it occurred after the claimed conspiracy and was irrelevant.

COURT I suggest that if you will examine the law books, Mr. Phillips, you will find that it is quite relevant in a criminal case to introduce evidence of flight on the question of guilt.

PHILLIPS After the proof of the act itself has been advanced, but not in advance.

COURT Well, the United States Attorney hasn't introduced any proof yet. He is telling the jury what he intends to prove.

PHILLIPS My point is, he had no business to state what he intends to prove before proving the act itself.

COURT The motion for a mistrial is denied.

The attorney for Julius Rosenberg, Emanuel H. Bloch, son of Ethel's attorney, renewed his objection to the mention of communism.

This stimulated the judge to explain the rule of law which requires the jury to steer a narrow path, avoiding prejudice against the defendants merely because they may be Communists, but considering dedication to communism as a motive, if proof of espionage was presented.

COURT You are not to determine the guilt or innocence of a defendant on whether he or she was a Communist. The charge is not Communism.

Now defendants' counsel had the opportunity to make opening statements.

CHAPTER 6

Alexander Bloch was seventy-four years old. He was a tiny, thin man with a fringe of gray hair, bridged by strands which looked thicker because his scalp was white too. His glasses had a light frame and emphasized the pallor of an old man.

After fifty, everyone has a face he deserves. His had the furrowed, wizened look of a curmudgeon, and he spoke and acted like one, avoiding circuitous formalism, for the direct route.

He had been a business lawyer all his life, specializing in the sale of bakeries. Criminal law was foreign to him. In a sense, so was all other book law. He was no scholar and didn't aspire to be one. He relied on his judgment based on experience. He practiced law by the seat of his pants, not by the books in the library. He did not fail to see the forest of practical solution, because of the trees of technical involvements.

So his view was wide and objective. He served as a realist and adviser to his son Emanuel, who became enmeshed in the emotional tides of the case.

He loved Emanuel and was proud of him, but it was not his style to tell him so or fawn upon him with fatherly pride. On the contrary, he hid his feelings with severity, but "Manny" understood.

The same kind of critical, direct advice to Ethel Rosenberg by "the old man" was not received with equal grace. She was under too much strain to take the bitter medicine he handed out, because it was good for her. She needed sympathy, not abrasive questioning. So they screamed at each other. Ultimately she recognized that his "hostility" was concern for her. There was even some relief in knowing that at least from him, she would get the unsugared truth. His skepticism at times about her story did not insult her, though she responded furiously.

Was he not warning her about how the jury might feel? Why stick her head in the sand of loyal confidence, and not see the effect of the testimony upon the jury?

So from a stormy beginning, Alexander Bloch's relationship with Ethel and Julius became affectionate, in the sense that children appreciate a stern father's attitude. Ethel later wrote that she grew to love Alexander as if he were her father.

Emanuel Bloch was the opposite of his father in appearance and personality. He was taller and stockier, and looked older than his fifty-one years because his shoulders were stooped. He was scholarly and accustomed to poring over books. Whether this had bent him, or only contributed to his collapsing posture, he seemed to be carrying an invisible load on his back. His hair was thick and inconsistently brown and gray. His eyes were light, turning into the surrounding color, but could hardly be seen, because of very heavy dark pouches. His head looked top heavy, so that his finely shaped nose and fine lips were hardly noticed.

He wore conservative, dark suits with striped ties. He also wore his heart on his legal sleeve. He had made a local reputation on the East Side, in several civil rights cases. It was natural that he should be called into the Rosenberg case. He was not only versed in constitutional law, but he had been drawn to such representation because of sympathy for the downtrodden and helpless. He knew the enemy to be mob psychology, and the Rosenbergs appeared to be its victims.

So although he had little experience in criminal cases, he was temperamentally suitable to the challenge, and a fine lawyer who would adjust to the new exigencies.

One thing was certain. He could not be, like his father, an objective observer. From the first moment, he identified with the plight of his clients, as if it was his own. He suffered with them. With adversity, he was not ashamed to cry. When good news came, he was more jubilant than they. Unlike his father, he had no doubts. It was impossible for him to have them, unless he was prepared to doubt himself.

All this led to intense partisanship. He and the Rosenbergs were one in fighting his father's "realism."

Emanuel Bloch became so emotionally involved with the cause that he deemed it necessary to take care of the Rosenbergs' two young children. He arranged for their stay in a custodial home and visited them regularly, as if this was part of his legal duty. He became their foster father during the three years of their parents' incarceration.

Bloch neglected his paying practice to serve the Rosenbergs. Due to the inability of the Rosenbergs to pay counsel fees, an application was made *in forma pauperis* to the federal court for assignment of counsel. It designated the Blochs, and provided a modest fee for that purpose.

The case became an international sensation, and Emanuel Bloch became a famous figure. However, even this precipitous rise from a humble, local attorney to world fame did not give him any satisfaction. He was too immersed in the difficulties of the case to enjoy his sudden prominence.

In a way, the more celebrated the cause became, the greater he felt his burden. He had spent anguished, sleepless nights, when all that was involved were the civil rights of a teacher or minor governmental employee. Now he had two lives at stake. To be entrusted with such responsibility bent his shoulders more, and deepened and darkened the rings under his eyes.

He also felt the weight of government forces, unlimited in number, while all he could muster were his father's common-sense guidance and the legal research of a bright young woman lawyer, Gloria Agrin.

Bloch himself read cases late at night to familiarize himself with intricate legal problems. He became more tired as sleeping hours shrank. Between factual preparation, legal research, holding his clients' hands, battling a determined prosecutor, appeasing a querulous judge and even contesting with counsel for Sobell, he had to function on nervous energy.

Most wearing of all were the surprise blows which came from the witness stand. "Co-conspirators" pointed fingers at Ethel and Julius, confessing joint involvement in crime. The plight of his clients was constantly growing worse. They seemed to be sinking into a quagmire of accusation, which enveloped them and sucked them downward. He feared that instead of pulling them out, he was being tugged into the abyss. So even when he had some hours to rest, he was tossed about by his vivid mind filled with terrible fears.

He accelerated his efforts, but grew weaker inside. Ultimately his morale was shattered. His exhaustion prevailed over his will. He died in the service of his clients.

———→←———

Emanuel Bloch spoke first on behalf of Julius Rosenberg. He told the jury that he did not know what the evidence would be. "We have to wait. We have to see." Julius was arrested in July 1950 and had asserted his innocence ever since.

Bloch described his role in modest and patriotic terms. When he made objections, he would be simply doing his duty.

> Pay very little attention to it because we are not the clients. This is the clients' case, not the lawyers'. Lawyers tend to dominate the

atmosphere of a courtroom. I think the Court will tell you that we are mechanics and mechanics alone. We are here to aid in the administration of justice. And that is true whether or not it is the prosecutor or whether or not it is the defense counsel, because all of us as lawyers have taken an oath to loyally support the Constitution, and inherent in that is the oath to support the administration of justice.

He reminded them of their oath to be impartial. "We ask you, we plead with you, don't be influenced by any bias or prejudice or hysteria." He conceded that the crime charged "is very grave." There was a tense international atmosphere.

I think all of us delude ourselves that we believe that we are completely free from all of those pressures and influences that every minute of the day are upon us. All we are asked to do is to take this charge against these defendants, and particularly I am speaking, of course, for the defendant, Julius Rosenberg, and see whether the Government will succeed in proving this charge and in proving all these things that Mr. Saypol said the prosecution is going to prove. We say now that the Government will not be able to prove these charges beyond a reasonable doubt.

May I repeat, and I hope you forgive me if I repeat, all we ask of you is a fair shake in the American way. All we ask of you is to keep your minds open until all the evidence is in, and until the Court has charged you. All we ask you is to follow the fundamental precept of law that the defendant is presumed to be innocent until you find him guilty, and that can only come after all the evidence is in. We ask you to keep your minds open. We ask you to judge this defendant, an American citizen, as you would want to be judged yourself if you were sitting as a defendant. In short, we ask you to keep your mind open and be fair. If the evidence satisfies you that these defendants are guilty and you bring in such a verdict, let it be on the evidence, not on any collateral issue, not on any political issue unconnected with the case.

Knowing the witnesses who might do most damage, he tried to alert the jury to look at them with a jaundiced eye. He pointed a finger at David Greenglass, a self-confessed spy, who would testify against his own sister, and Ruth Greenglass, who would testify against her brother-in-law and sister-in-law. He also mentioned Harry Gold, without specifying any reason to disbelieve him.

He concluded with the generalization that the jurors should not be swayed by emotion. "Keep your minds open."

Bloch's father followed with a brief statement on behalf of Ethel Rosenberg:

You are not to condemn her because her brother is a self-confessed traitor.

Surprisingly, he committed Ethel to take the stand and deny the charges before he knew the extent to which she would be involved.

She did not transmit or conspire to transmit any information to any government. She was a housewife, basically a housewife and nothing more. She was dragged into this case through the machinations of her own brother and her own sister-in-law, who in order to transfer and lighten their burden of responsibility, accused her of being a co-conspirator.

He asked the jurors "as my son did" to reserve its judgment to the very end of the case. He was confident that they would find that Ethel Rosenberg had committed no crime, and "should be sent back to her family to take care of her children."

Opening statements by counsel were like trumpet calls announcing that the battle of sworn words was about to begin. The government called its first witness.

CHAPTER 7

One of the ironies which ran through the Rosenberg trial, like a theme in a musical composition, was that the accused betrayers were constantly being betrayed by their relatives or friends. This is the rule when conspirators fall out.

As Max Elitcher was sworn in to testify for the government, Sobell and Rosenberg must have felt the special pain of one of their own turning against them.

Sobell and Elitcher were friends at Stuyvesant High School. They had both decided to enter the School of Engineering at the College of the City of New York. There they had become friendly with Julius Rosenberg. After graduation, Sobell and Elitcher both became junior engineers with the Navy's Bureau of Ordnance in Washington and shared an apartment together.

Yet, now he was on the stand to offer his intimate knowledge against Sobell and Rosenberg. How far would he go to condemn his friends? If the defendants expected mercy at his hands, they were in for a shock.

SAYPOL Did Sobell ever invite you to join meetings of the Communist Party?

ELITCHER Yes. At first, I declined, but he continued to ask me and I finally visited a cell of the Communist Party and joined it.

SAYPOL Did you thereafter attend meetings of this Communist cell with Sobell?

ELITCHER Yes.

In 1944, Elitcher was working on military equipment for the Navy Department. It involved anti-aircraft control and computers involving fire control.

Saypol asked him whether Julius Rosenberg visited him in Washington. Suddenly, Elitcher's reply launched the first revelation of Julius' espionage activities:

ELITCHER Yes, he called me and reminded me of our school friendship and came to my home.

After a while, he asked if my wife would leave the room, that he wanted to talk to me in private. She did. Then he began talking about the job that the Soviet Union was doing in the war effort and how at present a good deal of military information was being denied them by some interests in the United States, and because of that their effort was being impeded. He said there were many people who were implementing aid to the Soviet Union by providing classified information about military equipment, and so forth, and asked whether in my capacity at the Bureau of Ordnance working on anti-aircraft devices, and computer control of firing missiles, would I turn information over to him? He told me that any information I gave him would be taken to New York, processed photographically and would be returned overnight—so it would not be missed. The process would be safe as far as I am concerned.

The next question implicated Sobell:

SAYPOL Was Sobell mentioned in this conversation?
ELITCHER Yes, Rosenberg said Sobell was one of those who were getting military information for him.
SAYPOL For what purpose?
ELITCHER To transfer to the Soviet Union.

Rosenberg pursued him, but Elitcher evaded, saying if he had anything and wanted to give it to Rosenberg, he "would let him know."

SAYPOL Later, did Rosenberg warn you of a leak in espionage?
ELITCHER Yes. He said, we must be more careful—not to visit him any more, or see him. Also, he advised that I discontinue my Communist Party activities.

I told him I couldn't. That was my life and I could not withdraw.

When Elitcher saw Sobell, they talked about espionage and Elitcher promised to give him information if it came along.

Spies who are married run a special risk. If they fall out with their wives, who know of their activities, they are subject to exposure. Elitcher had such a problem, and when he told Sobell about it, Sobell inquired with understandable anxiety whether Mrs. Elitcher knew of his espionage activities. Elitcher thought she did, but "If she knows, she knows, and I just can't do anything about it."

Elitcher testified that when he was about to leave his job with the government, Rosenberg pleaded with him to stay.

> . . . he needed somebody to work at the Navy Department for this espionage purpose and he wanted me to change my mind.

SAYPOL Did Rosenberg tell you how he got into espionage?

ELITCHER He told me that a long time ago he decided that this is what he wanted to do, and he made it a point to get close to people in the Communist Party, until he was able to approach a Russian.

Elitcher testified that in 1948 he decided to leave Washington. He drove with his wife and child to New York to seek a permanent residence. As a temporary stopover, he arranged to go to the home of his friend Sobell.

While on the road, he noticed he was being followed. At first, he was not certain, but at Baltimore he made a detour to buy some dishes, and when he returned to the main road, the same car appeared behind him. He could not shake the shadower any more than his fears.

When he arrived at Sobell's home, he was greeted warmly. He put the child to bed. After a while, he confided to Sobell, "I think I was followed on my trip here."

SOBELL Followed? Are you sure?

ELITCHER Pretty sure.

SOBELL Then why in hell did you come here? You know you are welcome under ordinary circumstances, but do you think you should set up here and bring the FBI right to our door?

ELITCHER What could I do? I'll leave tomorrow.

SOBELL I want you to leave right now. Drive to the mountains, or any place. You have no right to endanger us, when you know you are being tailed.

Elitcher pleaded that he didn't know where to go. There was the baby. His wife too was exhausted from the trip. He had to stay. He would arrange to leave as quickly as he could the next day.

Sobell relented. He had no choice. But he fretted over the danger Sobell had dragged into the house. Suppose the FBI decided to make a search. He had incriminating evidence in the apartment. He had to get rid of it. Elitcher's description of what followed was one of the most telling pieces of evidence in the trial:

> . . . A little later, Sobell said he had some valuable information in the house, something he should have given to Julius Rosenberg some time ago. It was too valuable to be destroyed and too dangerous to keep around. He said he wanted to deliver it to Rosenberg that night. He said he was tired and he wanted me to go along. He might not be able to make the trip back. He took

a 35 millimeter film can. We drove to Catherine Slip. I parked the car facing the East River. He left with the can. I waited. He came back about a half hour later and as we drove off, I said, "Well, what does Julie think about my being followed?"

He said, "Don't be concerned about it; it is OK." Rosenberg told Sobell that he once talked to Elizabeth Bentley on the phone but he was pretty sure she didn't know who he was and, therefore, everything was all right.

After Saypol established that Elitcher had seen in Sobell's apartment "photographic equipment, a Leica camera and an enlarger and material for processing film" and that while Sobell worked at Reeves Instrument Company, he saw him "take material out in a briefcase, though he didn't know what the material was," Elitcher was turned over for cross-examination. He faced several lawyers in lengthy questioning. First, Emanuel H. Bloch tackled him on behalf of Julius Rosenberg.

Elitcher admitted he had hired a lawyer. Why? He had testified he had not given any secret data to Julius Rosenberg.

E. H. BLOCH   As a matter of fact, from your own story on direct examination, you rejected all overtures on the part of anybody to try to enlist you in stealing information from the Government; isn't that correct?

ELITCHER   Well, I didn't reject them. I went along. I never turned over material, but I was part of it, I mean, it was part of the —I was part of discussions concerning it until 1948.

E. H. BLOCH   Did you at any time tell him that you would turn over material to him?

ELITCHER   Well, I said that I might and I didn't say I would not turn over information, I said that I might.

After some fencing, Bloch struck hard at Elitcher's credibility:

E. H. BLOCH   Did you ever sign a loyalty oath for the Federal Government?

ELITCHER   I did.

E. H. BLOCH   Do you know the contents of the oath you signed and swore to?

ELITCHER   I signed a statement saying that I was not or had not been a member of an organization that was dedicated to overthrow the Government by force and violence. I don't remember whether the statement specifically mentioned the Communist Party or not.

E. H. BLOCH   At the time you verified that oath, did you believe you were lying when you concealed your membership in the Communist Party?

ELITCHER   Yes. I did.

E. H. BLOCH   So you have lied under oath?

ELITCHER Yes.

E. H. BLOCH Were you worried about it?

ELITCHER Yes. . . .

E. H. BLOCH As a matter of fact, didn't you leave the Government service to try to get a job in private industry because you were afraid you might be prosecuted for perjury?

ELITCHER That is not the entire reason for my leaving.

E. H. BLOCH But that was one of the substantial reasons?

ELITCHER I would say, yes.

Elitcher had been interviewed at length by the FBI men.

E. H. BLOCH Now when you were interrogated by the FBI for the first time, did that fear of prosecution persist in your mind?

ELITCHER Yes, I realized what the implications might be.

E. H. BLOCH You felt that the Government had something over you, didn't you?

ELITCHER I couldn't tell; I thought, yes, perhaps.

One of the most difficult decisions which a cross-examiner must make is when to take his profit from the questions and quit the market of inquiry. If he stays too long, he may be hurt. Bloch, having scored, persisted, and the witness had a chance to rehabilitate himself. Had he confessed because he feared government prosecution? Elitcher replied:

Well, partly, yes. I didn't know what information the FBI had; I had no idea. However, I felt that I didn't want to fight the case. When they came to me, I freely told them the story, and as they might know about it anyway, I felt the only course was to tell the complete story, which I did.

E. H. BLOCH It wasn't out of any sense of patriotism that you told the FBI the story?

ELITCHER Well, in a sense, yes.

E. H. BLOCH It was to save your own skin, wasn't it?

ELITCHER No, because I didn't know what would happen to my skin even when I told the story—and I knew of nothing I was doing that would save my skin.

Bloch then approached his most difficult task. How was he going to tear down the testimony of the auto trip at night to deliver a can of film to Julius Rosenberg because it was too incriminating to keep in his apartment? It resulted in the first skirmish with the judge.

E. H. BLOCH You voluntarily came up to New York, you say, for the purpose of discussing espionage with Julius Rosenberg; is that right?

ELITCHER Yes.

COURT Was it pursuant to your talk with Sobell?

ELITCHER Yes.

PHILLIPS We object to your Honor's question. The word "pursuant" is objectionable. It calls for a conclusion.

COURT Denied . . . Where the Court is of the opinion the jury may not follow the sequence of events, the Court will not hesitate to call that to the jury's attention.

It was evident that the judge's question was intended to tie Sobell into the testimony. His question elicited the fact that it was Sobell who induced Elitcher to discuss espionage with Rosenberg.

This was one of the few times that defense counsel, and it was Sobell's, challenged the judge because he was intervening "to aid the prosecution."

However, the judge's retort was justified. The federal rules follow the English procedure which permits the judge to take an active part in questioning witnesses and even commenting on their credibility. The only limitation is that he must instruct the jury that its recollection and impression are conclusive and not his. Later, Judge Kaufman gave such direction to the jury emphatically in his charge to the jury.

It is interesting that in state courts, the judge's interference in the development of testimony is far more limited, and Judge Kaufman's conduct might have created reversible error. Bloch continued his attack and again the judge attempted to blunt his sword.

E. H. BLOCH When you were questioned by the FBI, did you tell them about the automobile trip you took with Sobell to Catherine Slip?

ELITCHER I did not.

E. H. BLOCH Tell me, Mr. Elitcher, have you ever been treated by a psychiatrist?

ELITCHER Yes, for about a year in Washington and for a similar period in New York.

E. H. BLOCH How continuous were those visits?

ELITCHER Approximately twice a week.

COURT Did the treatment consist of a discussion with the psychiatrist?

ELITCHER Yes.

COURT It didn't include any so-called shock therapy or anything of that character?

ELITCHER No shock or other therapy involved.

Bloch did not object to the court's questions. He merely continued:

Did your wife also take psychiatric treatment?

ELITCHER Yes.

E. H. BLOCH Did both of you go to the same psychiatrist?

ELITCHER No, that is not done.

It is common practice for prosecutors to recommend lenience for criminals who turn "state's evidence." Honest citizens are rarely in a position to reveal the facts of a crime. "It takes a thief to catch a thief."

(62)

Those who plotted and performed the crime can tell most. But, being criminals themselves, how reliable are they even when they confess? This is the perennial dilemma. The prosecutor urges the jury to accept such testimony, because it is authentic. The witness was there. The symbolism often used is that conspirators do not plot in broad daylight. They meet in a dark cellar at candlelight with no one else present and only one of them can reveal what really happened.

The defense, on the other hand, hammers away at the characterless witness, who it claims is ready to lie to extricate himself.

So the jury has a difficult choice to make. Will it believe the witness who concedes that he has previously lied and has a criminal past, but insists that now he is telling the truth? Or will it discount his confession because his evil character may extend to implicating others falsely in order to gain reward from an overzealous prosecutor? Once again, their sizing up of the witness is a determinative factor in their conclusion.

Elitcher was the subject of such an encounter, of which there were many in the Rosenberg trial.

E. H. BLOCH   You have come here voluntarily, without any compulsion, isn't that right?

ELITCHER   That is correct.

E. H. BLOCH   Were any promises made to you in return for your testimony before the grand jury or this Court?

ELITCHER   Absolutely none. In fact, I was told that there were no promises to be made, nothing—the Government would make no statement in regard to what would happen to me.

When Bloch pressed again, he elicited the strongest statement from Elitcher in support of his truthfulness.

E. H. BLOCH   Did you at the time you were first interrogated by the FBI entertain any hope that if you told a story in which you said that Julius Rosenberg and Morton Sobell tried to recruit you in espionage work, that the Government would go easy on you or would not prosecute you criminally for any crime you may have committed?

ELITCHER   From the first time that I was approached by the FBI, I decided I would tell the whole complete story. I had no idea at the time of what would happen to me. Frankly, I didn't know whether I would be arrested the same day, and to this day, I don't know what is going to happen, and I decided that purely on the basis that I would tell the whole truth and at least in the future I would not be subjected to any perjury, and I would hope in that way I would come out in the best way. I could see no other course but to tell the truth.

Bloch tackled Elitcher's story that Rosenberg had brazenly solicited him to spy and deliver secrets.

E. H. BLOCH Now, you had merely the most casual relationship with Julius Rosenberg during your student days, isn't that right?

ELITCHER Yes.

E. H. BLOCH And you didn't see him for six years after graduation?

ELITCHER That is right.

E. H. BLOCH Now, not having seen him for six years, he then comes to your apartment, asks your wife to step into the bedroom, and this man who hardly knows you, launches into an overture for you to be a spy?

ELITCHER Yes.

E. H. BLOCH What did you reply?

ELITCHER Well, I told him I would see about it. I didn't say I would not engage in this activity; I would think about it. I said, "I can't make trips to New York on my own without my wife's knowledge. It is just impractical . . . I will consider it, and if something comes up and I feel I should bring it, I will."

E. H. BLOCH Was there any question of money raised?

ELITCHER No.

E. H. BLOCH Did you pass any information, secret, classified or otherwise of the Government of the United States, to the defendant Julius Rosenberg at any time?

ELITCHER I did not.

E. H. BLOCH Well what particular crime did you have in mind you may have committed when you went to a lawyer?

ELITCHER I know I had discussed a transfer of such material, and I knew that was not legal.

Bloch announced that he was through with the witness "temporarily." He had submitted a request to the judge to direct Saypol to produce the FBI statements which Elitcher had signed. He wanted to see if they differed from his testimony. The judge was studying the question. If he ruled favorably, Bloch would be permitted to continue his cross-examination.

One of Sobell's attorneys, Edward Kuntz, rose to question Elitcher. He was a stocky, gray-haired man of long experience in criminal trial representation. He was gruff in manner and diction, the kind of lawyer who attacks witnesses boldly and loudly, permits his sarcasm to flow over the head of his adversary, and even crosses swords with the judge. Within a minute he was in conflict with the judge.

KUNTZ Mr. Elitcher, during all the time you knew Sobell, did he in any way offer you any documents belonging to the United States Government?

(64)

ELITCHER   No.

COURT   Did Sobell ask you to see Rosenberg?

ELITCHER   Yes.

KUNTZ   I object to the interjection by the Court.

COURT   Your objection is overruled. I will ask questions whenever I think I ought to.

KUNTZ   Well it seems to—

COURT   You proceed. Let's not argue the point.

KUNTZ   Now on each occasion that you had a conversation with Rosenberg or Sobell, where they made invitations to you, did you accept those invitations to commit espionage?

ELITCHER   I accepted the invitations. Yes.

KUNTZ   Did you get any documents from the United States Government?

ELITCHER   No.

KUNTZ   Your trip to Catherine Slip, that loomed rather important in your mind, did it not?

ELITCHER   Yes.

KUNTZ   As a matter of fact, according to your testimony, the only contact you have ever had with secret stuff was on that trip; right?

ELITCHER   Yes.

KUNTZ   But you didn't tell this to the FBI on the first visit?

ELITCHER   No, I did not.

KUNTZ   Were you trying to conceal it?

ELITCHER   At that time, perhaps.

KUNTZ   In other words, you were trying to lie to the FBI, weren't you?

ELITCHER   I omitted it, but I didn't—all right, I lied.

KUNTZ   And in other respects, you continued to lie, did you not, by not reporting fully, is that it?

ELITCHER   Yes.

The questions continued to come one on top of another, their speed generating heat.

Despite Elitcher's position that he agreed to engage in espionage but didn't perform, it developed that he did. He said that Sobell had asked him to "see Rosenberg" about certain pamphlets in the Ordnance Department where Elitcher worked. He delivered an "unimportant one," the "important one" not being finished.

Elitcher testified that Sobell had asked him to look for engineering students who were "progressive" and "whom it would be safe to ask for espionage material."

Kuntz took the witness through his testimony on the night he drove in from Washington and was followed.

Sobell was working on government projects at Reeves Instrument

Company. Might not his anger have been due to his concern that he would be involved, though innocent? This, of course, did not explain why he drove at that hour "nine or ten o'clock" at night to Rosenberg's home with a film. The judge intervened again to bring the point home.

COURT Did he tell you why he was going at that hour of the night?
ELITCHER Yes, he said it was too valuable to destroy and he didn't want to keep it around the house because of the danger.
COURT The danger of what?
ELITCHER The danger resulting from my being followed to New York, to the house.

Kuntz smarted from the clarification. He changed direction.

KUNTZ And you offered to go into the car with Sobell, to take a ten-mile trip, knowing he had dangerous stuff?
SAYPOL Just a minute now. That is not the testimony. It was Sobell who made the suggestion, not the witness.
KUNTZ May I suggest that the United States Attorney just make an objection without characterizing whether it was or was not the testimony. If he doubts that it was the testimony, let the stenographer read it, because I don't think it is fair to characterize what is or is not testimony during my questioning.
COURT Are you finished?
KUNTZ Yes, sir.
COURT I sustain the objection.
KUNTZ I didn't hear your Honor's ruling.
COURT I sustain the objection, because you are assuming something that hasn't been testified to.
KUNTZ Well, when you say that Sobell told you he had some very dangerous, some very important material to deliver to Rosenberg, did you believe him?
ELITCHER Yes.
KUNTZ Nevertheless, you got into this automobile with Sobell and made that ten-mile trip; is that right?
ELITCHER Yes.

As in all combat, neither side came out entirely unscathed. Elitcher scored by supplying impressive detail, when he was pressed. He and Sobell "checked as we went outside, and as we drove" to Rosenberg's home to be sure "no one was following." As to who brought up the name of Elizabeth Bentley, the ex-Communist who turned informer, Elitcher in reply to the court's questions explained:

The name Bentley was brought up by the FBI agents and I said I had nothing to do with Miss Bentley. At a much later period, I told them that the name Bentley had been mentioned to me by Sobell.

Kuntz again protested the judge's intervention:

COURT   Don't raise your voice to me.

KUNTZ   I am sorry, Judge; I am sorry, Judge; it means nothing. It is my customary way, your Honor.

COURT   I will accept your answer.

KUNTZ   I have never tried a case in any different way.

COURT   Proceed.

KUNTZ   I assure you.

COURT   All right.

KUNTZ   All the judges have occasion at times to say the same thing, but after a while they get to know me.

COURT   Very well.

KUNTZ   I am sorry.

Later the prosecution put Elizabeth Bentley on the stand, and the defense had full opportunity to inquire into her double life, politically and morally.

The cross-examination of Elitcher had ended, and the prosecutor took over for redirect examination. This was the final opportunity to repair damage which the cross-examiner had caused.

The impression had been created that Elitcher might be unreliable because he had taken psychiatric treatment. Saypol addressed himself to this point. He asked whether it was a matrimonial problem which drove him to psychiatry. Bloch objected on the ground that Elitcher "was not an expert."

COURT   But you got into the field and I think you have left a certain implication, which all laymen have, when somebody goes to see a psychiatrist. I think this witness should be permitted to tell what motivated him in going to the psychiatrist.

SAYPOL   What was it that made you go or caused you to go to a psychiatrist, to a doctor?

ELITCHER   Well, after our marriage we found that we had domestic difficulties and we found it difficult to live with each other. We found that I had personality problems and she had personality problems which prevented a happy existence together. I found it difficult to meet with people to have a good time, to talk in front of an audience. I think, to jump a step, without the aid that I went to, it would be difficult for me to present myself in front of this audience in this matter, and because of that my wife decided that she would attempt to correct her problems which were of a similar nature to mine, but perhaps not exactly the same. She

(67)

went to a psychiatrist and felt that she was being benefited by it, but because I wasn't going, so that it would be a two-way arrangement, that both of us would be improved by it, she insisted that I go. It was upon her insistence that I finally did go to a psychiatrist. It was only after I had gone and had been able to recognize some of my problems, that our married life did adjust itself, and I will say right now that it couldn't be much happier as married life goes.

SAYPOL In taking these treatments from the doctor did it require that you remain away from your work?

ELITCHER No.

Since the defense had requested the right to inspect the statements Elitcher had signed for the FBI, Saypol developed the circumstances under which he was questioned.

SAYPOL Was there any coercion?

ELITCHER No.

SAYPOL Was there any loud shouting?

ELITCHER No.

Once more the court intervened and this time Kuntz made a concession:

COURT Would you say the agents at all times behaved themselves like gentlemen?

ELITCHER I would say so.

KUNTZ Oh, I am sure they did.

COURT Are you willing to concede that?

Saypol established that the FBI had advised Elitcher of his constitutional right not to answer, and his right to counsel:

SAYPOL At any time in your relation with the agencies of the Government, and I couple them all, has anybody tried to color your story or suggest to you anything other than the truth as you know it?

ELITCHER No.

Then Saypol painstakingly traced the events to explain why Elitcher had not told the full story to the FBI, which he had recited from the witness stand. A series of statements had been taken by the FBI in long interviews. They were typed and submitted for signature at different times. On each occasion the FBI dug deeper into certain subjects and Elitcher filled in detail or recalled more incidents. Therefore when he was asked by Bloch whether he had told the FBI agents a certain fact when he first talked to them, he was not sure he had, although if all statements were considered collectively, his information to the FBI was the same as his testimony:

ELITCHER   When I said I had lied I meant that I had not told them that story at that particular time. Otherwise I didn't lie to them.

This is a typical illustration of attempted rehabilitation of the witness. The defense was not content to leave the matter there. On recross Bloch established the many hours he had spent with the FBI and that he had "deliberately omitted mentioning the automobile ride with Sobell" to Rosenberg's home.

At last all were through with Elitcher, but the judge asked him to return "Monday morning" to be cross-examined further if the court should rule that his statements to the FBI must be shown to the defendants.

Sobell never took the stand to deny Elitcher's testimony. The judge instructed the jury that no inference was to be drawn against Sobell because of his failure to testify. But, of course, his silence left undenied, as far as he was concerned, the story of his trip with a "hot" can of film to Rosenberg on the very night that an alarmed Elitcher arrived at his home. Sobell's decision to exercise his constitutional right not to testify was later regretted by his own lawyers.

But Julius Rosenberg did take the stand. He denied Elitcher's testimony that he had been approached by Julius in Washington to enlist him in espionage.

There is a continuous dilemma in trial tactics. Which is worse, silence which forfeits a denial of the accusation or testifying and risking cross-examination? Statistics favor the latter. Of those convicted, a large percentage did not testify. Of those acquitted, a large percentage did. Yet no rule gives guidance in a particular situation. The decision must be made by evaluating the circumstances of each individual case. The personality of the defendant, his vulnerability due to his past record or for other reasons, the strength of the prosecution evidence, the rebuttal available from others than the defendant are only some of the factors to be considered. It is a decision often made after agonizing discussion among counsel, the defendant and his family into the early hours of the morning.

However, a negative decision should never be reached because the defendant is unprepared to take the stand. True, the decision to have him testify or not must be made at the last moment because it depends largely on the proof actually offered against him. But the defendant must not be in the panicky position of not knowing the facts thoroughly and feeling as if he were being tossed into a stormy sea before he has learned to swim. The events he must know stride across many years. Dates are important. Letters must be reread and related to incidents which may have escaped him. All this requires careful and repeated review so that the truth can be reconstructed. To leave him to the mercy of a cross-examiner without such knowledge is to risk admissions and distortions due to confusion. Only by thorough preparation can the truth be approximated. He should be drilled to cope with a skilled cross-examiner. He must be encouraged to tell the truth at all times, even if it is harmful to him at times. This is the best way to the jury's belief in him.

Rosenberg did not take the stand until the prosecution case was completed. This took weeks. But this recital permits us to move up his testimony, so that it can be compared with Elitcher's, without a lapse of reading time to dim the accusation.

—————→←—————

Rosenberg admitted that he had visited Elitcher in Washington, D.C., but denied that it was Sobell who suggested that he do so. He had not seen Elitcher for four years, but being in Washington he telephoned him:

ROSENBERG   I was there alone and I was lonesome and I looked up in the telephone book for Mr. Elitcher's number, and I called him one evening.
E. H. BLOCH   Did he invite you over to the house?
ROSENBERG   Yes, he did.

Emanuel Bloch developed the innocent character of the visit. Rosenberg had some pie and coffee. They talked about their respective jobs:

E. H. BLOCH   Did you during the course of that evening ever say to Mr. Elitcher in specific words or by implication, that you wanted him to engage in espionage work, or let me put it this way, or that you wanted him to get certain information from the Government by reason of this access to certain secret information?
ROSENBERG   I never said anything of the sort.

They discussed politics, the war, and "that the Russians had been carrying a very heavy burden in the war."

Rosenberg testified he had never met Sobell and Elitcher together, except once at a swimming pool in Washington, D.C. He also denied that Sobell ever brought "any microfilm can or microfilm" to him.

Rosenberg's explanation that it was "loneliness" and not espionage which induced his visit to Elitcher was a temptation to cross-examine:

SAYPOL   Now, how well did you know Elitcher in college?
ROSENBERG   Very casually.
SAYPOL   Did you go out with him socially?
ROSENBERG   I did not.
SAYPOL   Did you have girls, girl friends together?
ROSENBERG   We did not.
SAYPOL   And you graduated in 1939, I think, didn't you?
ROSENBERG   That is correct.

(70)

SAYPOL   Then the next time that you saw him was at a swimming pool for a minute in Washington, in 1940; is that right?

ROSENBERG   That is correct.

SAYPOL   How long did you see him, for just a minute?

ROSENBERG   That's right.

SAYPOL   What did you talk about in that minute, very much?

ROSENBERG   Just, "Hello. I am working in Washington." That is what he said to me.

SAYPOL   Then you didn't hear from him or see him again until when?

ROSENBERG   Until sometime in '44.

A cross-examiner picks up acorns as he heads for the meadow. Saypol asked him whether Elitcher was right in saying it was "D Day" and they drank a toast to the second front. No, he only remembered having coffee:

SAYPOL   Were you happy when the second front was opened?

ROSENBERG   Yes, I was happy when the second front was opened.

But the main thrust was an attack on Rosenberg's denial that he solicited Elitcher, who was working in a naval department, to join him in espionage:

SAYPOL   And then four years later, when you were in Washington, you decided that you wanted to call him and pay him a visit?

ROSENBERG   That's right.

SAYPOL   Well, what was it that you wanted to see him about?

ROSENBERG   I was lonesome and I just wanted to see somebody to talk to.

SAYPOL   And out of the clear sky you looked in the telephone book under "E" for the name Elitcher and you called him up?

ROSENBERG   Mr. Saypol, I was looking in the phone book for any names that I could recognize as former classmates or people I knew at one time.

COURT   What names were you looking for?

ROSENBERG   For some names I might recognize.

COURT   You mean, you started with "A" and started going—

ROSENBERG   No, I didn't just start with "A"; I thought of a couple of people's names who might be in Washington; I remembered the incident at the swimming pool at that time, that Elitcher was in Washington, and perhaps he had a telephone.

The court intervened to ask what other names he looked up. There was a long pause. Bloch urged Rosenberg to answer. "The judge asked you a question," he said. Rosenberg replied, "Sobell." It may have appeared to the jury that he was reluctant to combine Sobell with Elitcher. The cross-examiner continued to add to his discomfort. Why had he not called other people with whom he had worked at the Bureau of Standards in Washington?

ROSENBERG I didn't know them socially.

SAYPOL Did you know Elitcher socially?

ROSENBERG No, but he had been a former classmate.

The questions began to drip with sarcasm. He looked up Elitcher's telephone number and called him. What was the conversation?

ROSENBERG I said something to the effect: "I am in town; can I come over to see you."

SAYPOL Well, did you tell him what your name was?

ROSENBERG Sure.

SAYPOL Did he recognize your name right away?

ROSENBERG I don't recall if he did or if he didn't, but he says, "Come over."

SAYPOL Did you tell him before that you were the fellow who used to go to school with him and saw him at the swimming pool for a minute four years ago?

ROSENBERG I told him I was a classmate of his.

SAYPOL Did you tell him about the swimming pool?

ROSENBERG I didn't tell him on the telephone.

SAYPOL Now tell us, what did you talk about? Did you tell him why you came to see him? Didn't he ask you, "Just why out of the clear sky do you pick on me to pay a visit to like this? I never really knew you."

ROSENBERG He didn't say that.

Suddenly Saypol pointed to Elitcher's activities in communism. Bloch objected but withdrew.

SAYPOL Had you known of Elitcher's activities in the Young Communist League at City College?

E. H. BLOCH Well, if the Court please, I think that presupposes a state of facts that is not proven. I do not recollect that Elitcher testified that he was a member of the Young Communist League.

COURT Yes, I am quite sure of that.

E. H. BLOCH All right, I will withdraw my objection, your Honor.

Sobell later fled to Mexico when the FBI swooped down on the accused. This could have been interpreted by the jury as indirect proof of his guilty mind. But Elitcher's story of his visit to Sobell and the delivery of the microfilm to Rosenberg constituted virtually the only direct evidence of Sobell's complicity in the conspiracy. Indeed, the judge later charged the jury that if it did not believe Elitcher, it must acquit Sobell! So although no one knew it at the time, when Elitcher, the first witness in the long trial, stepped off the stand, Sobell's fate was sealed. He

(72)

would either go free, receive the death penalty, or be caged in a cell for thirty years. It all depended on whether the jury believed Elitcher.

But Rosenberg's fate was far from determined. Elitcher's testimony that Rosenberg had solicited him to steal secrets from the Navy, was a serious cloud over his head. If this were all, it might be dissipated by Rosenberg's denial. However, as was soon evident, the cloud was the mere harbinger of a fierce storm. The thunder came from the next government witness. It was Ethel Rosenberg's younger brother, David, her beloved "Doovey."

CHAPTER 8

Greenglass immediately admitted that as one of the defendants he had pleaded guilty. He was in jail, awaiting sentence.

His father was dead, his mother Tessie, still alive. He was married and had two children, one four years old, the other only nine months old.

He had had political discussions with Ethel and Julius Rosenberg. They preferred Russian socialism to capitalism. This opening sally was to create a background against which the incredible events would appear credible. Bloch's objection on the ground that "this leads to matters which may be inflammatory," was overruled, because the Supreme Court in the Haupt case had held that a defendant's sympathy with Hitler and hostility to the United States could be shown in a treason case. It went to motive.

How had David Greenglass landed in Los Alamos in a strategic position to learn the secret of the atom bomb? He had joined the Army in 1943, and being a graduate machinist, was assigned to the Manhattan Project in Oak Ridge, Tennessee. In August 1944, he became a machinist at Los Alamos, New Mexico.

He did not know what the project was until his wife visited him and informed him that he was working on the atomic bomb. How did she know? Julius Rosenberg had told her.

This brought a vigorous objection. But the judge ruled correctly that "a conversation of a conspirator is admissible against the other conspirators."

Government counsel Roy Cohn elicited a description of the surroundings and personnel of the huge secret enterprise at Los Alamos. There were separate buildings for different studies. Greenglass worked in the "E" building. The leader of the "E" group was Professor George B. Kistiakowsky of Harvard University, an expert in thermodynamics (physical chemistry). Greenglass later "got to know" other scientists who worked there, "some of world fame, for instance, Dr. J. Robert Oppenheimer," Dr. Harold Urey and Dr. Niels Bohr, who went under the disguised name of Baker, so that nuclear physics would not be identified as the subject of the experiments. He also met Professor Walter Koski, whom he pointed out in the courtroom. This was a signal that he, too, would be a government witness.

The "E" staff was concerned with high explosives. Greenglass became assistant foreman and later was promoted to foreman of the shop.

To emphasize the importance of secrecy, a book of instructions was issued to all employees marked "Restricted." It was offered in evidence, and a few passages read to the jury:

> Everyone must maintain a constant and intelligent interest in the prevention and reporting of all incidents which may endanger security of the project . . .
> There must no conversation and no information in letters conveying information about
> 1. The purpose of the project.
> 2. The general problems worked on.
> 3. The personnel employed on the project.
> Your address is P. O. Box 1663, Sante Fe, New Mexico. Do not use Los Alamos.

Every employee had to wear a badge. The colors were different and significant.

A white badge was authorized to go to the seminars and be let in on all the information that was available on the atom bomb.

A red badge allowed the bearer to get all the information necessary to be able to do his job.

A blue badge allowed the bearer to enter the technical area to do various jobs like steam fitting or ditch digging, but not to be around any of the equipment.

Greenglass had a red badge.

Then came the real thrust. Had Julius and Ethel Rosenberg ever asked him "to divulge information about the atomic bomb?" "Yes, they sent a message to me through my wife when she visited me in Los Alamos in November 1944." The questions and answers which followed were like strings drawn from him and winding around Ethel and Julius.

———→←———

Later, Ruth Greenglass took the stand and confirmed her husband's story. One day Ruth had visited the Rosenbergs in their apartment at 10 Monroe Street in Knickerbocker Village, lower Manhattan.

RUTH GREENGLASS November 29th is our second wedding anniversary, and I am going to Albuquerque to be with David. How I am looking forward to it.

(76)

ROSENBERG He is at Los Alamos, isn't he?

RUTH GREENGLASS Yes, but I am not permitted there—so we meet at Albuquerque.

ROSENBERG I hope you have a wonderful stay. Ethel and I have wanted to talk to you about something important—something which will contribute to the peace of the world.

RUTH GREENGLASS Peace of the world?

ROSENBERG Yes. Maybe you have noticed that for some time Ethel and I have not been active in the Communist Party. We don't buy the *Daily Worker* at the usual newsstand. The reason is that we have reached a higher phase of activity to help the Russian people. For the past two years, I have developed contacts with Russians and others to do work which will lead to real peace, when this war is over. You can help, Ruth. David is in a key spot. He is working on the atomic bomb—

RUTH GREENGLASS Are you sure? How do you know this, Julius? I received notice from the War Department telling me that all mail between David and me would be censored, because David's work was a secret. So how do you know it is on the atomic bomb?

ROSENBERG My friends know. The atomic bomb is the most destructive weapon ever invented. It will have dangerous radiation effects.

The United States and Britain are working on this project jointly, but they are not sharing with our most valuable ally, Russia.

You see, Ruth, if all nations had the information, then one nation couldn't use the bomb as a threat against another.

When you are in Albuquerque explain this to David. After all, Russia has suffered more casualties in our joint effort against Hitler than any other nation. Tell him to give you information which I can pass on to the Russians.

RUTH GREENGLASS This is dangerous stuff, Julius, and I don't think it's right. The people in charge of the work are in a better position to know whether the information should be shared with Russia or not. I don't want to get David involved in this. He is in the Army. He is under strict security orders. We have two children. This is not for us. I am against it.

ETHEL ROSENBERG I don't think you have a right to decide this for David. No matter what your opinion is, he has a right to make his own decision. I am his sister. Do you think I want any harm to come to him or to you, or the children? But there are certain things in the world more important than any individual. David has a chance to prevent a third world war. He can help create a balance of power to preserve peace. I think he will want to do this. Why don't you tell him about it and let him decide?

RUTH GREENGLASS Well, I am against it, but I will think it over. Perhaps I will tell David about it. I suppose I should.

ROSENBERG That's fair enough. Now tell him what information we want. We want a physical description of the project at Los Alamos, the number of people employed, the names of some of the scientists working there—whether the place is camouflaged, what the security measures are and the distance of the project to Albuquerque and Santa Fe.

Do you think you can remember all this—I don't want you to write it down.

RUTH GREENGLASS I'll try.

ROSENBERG Tell David to be very careful. Not to indulge in any political conversations and be very careful not to take any papers or sketches or blueprints—not to be obvious in seeking information. Just have him tell me what he retains in his memory.

(Took money from his pocket.)

Here is $150 for the trip, Ruth.

(She hesitated to take it.)

Oh, go ahead and take it. It will pay for your expenses.

She had taken the money reluctantly. When she visited David in Los Alamos to celebrate their anniversary, she told him of the Rosenberg invitation to violate the secrecy of the project on the alluring theory that it would be a noble deed in aid of world balance and peace.

His reply was:

At first, I told my wife I agreed with her and I wouldn't do it. But I thought about it all night. Russia was our ally. If the two great powers had the atomic bomb, they would offset each other. Perhaps this was the best road to peace. The next morning, I told my wife I had decided to give the information.

—→←—

Greenglass returned on furlough to New York. The next morning Rosenberg came to his home at 266 Stanton Street, on the lower East Side, and Greenglass delivered to him "a sketch of the lens mold" with definitions of the explanatory markings "on separate pieces of paper."

COHN Now, Mr. Greenglass, have you at our request prepared a copy of the sketch of the lens mold which you furnished to Rosenberg on that day?

GREENGLASS Yes.

COHN Is this it?

GREENGLASS Yes.

COHN We offer it in evidence.

E. H. BLOCH Before I make any objection, may I ask the witness several questions?

COURT Yes, you may have a *voir dire*. Go ahead.

E. H. BLOCH When did you prepare this?

GREENGLASS During the trial yesterday.

E. H. BLOCH Are you saying that that paper represents a true copy of the sketch you turned over to Rosenberg?

GREENGLASS To the best of my recollection at this time, yes.

Over objection, the sketch was admitted into evidence and shown to the jury.

Greenglass then explained the various markings which indicated the

(78)

curve of the lens, its width, its four-leaf clover design with a hollow center to pour high explosives into it. It was the real secret of the implosion bomb.

Greenglass did not hesitate to draw his sister, Ethel, into the vortex of conspiratorial conduct:

> My wife, Ruth, in a passing remark said that my handwriting was bad and would need interpretation, and Julius said there was nothing to worry about as Ethel would type it up, retype the information.

Spy stories abound with ingenious devices. Those who make a science of secrecy do not trust even their own. There must be no chain in which one link leads to another. There is safety only in isolated movements among anonymous participants. How then, when they must meet, can they be sure that they are comrades? Necessity is the mother of invention, but also tension. The emotional pressure on the couriers was unbearable.

Through Greenglass' testimony we are given an insight into the ingenuity of plotters. Of all things, it involved a Jell-O box.

Rosenberg asked David and Ruth Greenglass to visit him in Knickerbocker Village. When they arrived, a woman by the name of Ann Sidorovich was also there. Greenglass described what happened:

ROSENBERG I wanted you to meet Ann Sidorovich because she is probably going to be the one who will come out to Albuquerque when you are both there, to pick up any information you may have.

GREENGLASS I think I met her before. I know her husband, Mike.

ETHEL ROSENBERG That's right. Julius, you better explain how the information is to be handed over.

ROSENBERG Well, Ruth, you and Ann Sidorovich will go to a motion picture theater in Denver. We'll specify which one. While in the theater, you will exchange your purses. So put any information Dave gives you in your purse, and keep out other personal possessions.

GREENGLASS You said Ann Sidorovich will probably be the one to visit us. Does that mean you are not sure? Suppose it has to be someone else, how will Ruth and I be able to identify him?

ROSENBERG I'll give you something which will act as an identification. Come in here.

(Julius led Ethel and Ruth into the kitchen. David stayed behind. Julius took a Jell-O box from the shelf. He tore off the thin side. He looked for a scissors. Then he cut the side irregularly. He gave Ruth Greenglass one piece and kept the other. They returned to the living room.)

Look, David, I have given one part of the Jell-O box side to Ruth. She'll keep it. I'll give the other part to whatever person we send out. You see how they match up.

(He took Ruth's cardboard a moment and fitted it with the piece he

(79)

retained. Of course, they joined perfectly. He gave Ruth back the piece he took from her. She put it in her purse.)

GREENGLASS Say, that's very clever.

ROSENBERG The simplest things are always the cleverest.

ETHEL ROSENBERG This is so good, I think we ought to discard the Denver movie idea.

RUTH GREENGLASS Well, where are we going to meet?

GREENGLASS There is a Safeway store in Albuquerque. It is the only one. Why don't Ruth and whoever comes with the Jell-O identification meet in front of the store?

ROSENBERG That's a very good idea. We'll have to set a date and exact time later, when we know Ruth has returned. And Ruth, I want you to stay there for quite a while. Take the child with you. I want you to know how happy we are that both of you have come in with us in this work. Don't worry about the money. It will be taken care of. If you can't work there, it won't matter. The money will be forthcoming and it is not a loan. It is coming to you for this work. The Russians want you to have it.

ETHEL ROSENBERG You can be sure what Julius says will be done. So take money off your mind.

RUTH GREENGLASS It's nice of you to tell me not to worry. Look how tired you look.

ETHEL ROSENBERG Between taking care of the children and staying up late at night typing over notes Julius brings me in this work, I get a little worn out at times. But it is nothing. I don't mind it so long as Julius is doing what he wants to do.

ROSENBERG Before you go back, David, I want you to meet a Russian and talk to him about the lenses you told me about. He will understand better how this device may be able to trigger the atomic bomb, because he has scientific knowledge. Will you do that?

GREENGLASS Sure. You arrange it.

Julius did so. One night, in a car borrowed from his father-in-law, David drove with Julius up First Avenue in New York City. When they reached 50th Street, Julius saw a man walking slowly in the dark near the curb. Julius instructed David to stop at the corner. He got out of the car and silently ushered "the Russian" into his seat. The visitor, looking straight ahead, plied David with questions. He learned that the lens was made of metal and a mold taken from it.

GREENGLASS The whole purpose is to so shape the lens that the high explosive goes inward toward the uranium, and so increases its impact.

RUSSIAN It is designed to be a detonator.

GREENGLASS That's right.

RUSSIAN Were there many different models built?

GREENGLASS Oh, yes. Our machine shop was busy day and night building lenses of different sizes and curvature.

RUSSIAN Do you know which model was considered the most effective?

GREENGLASS I am not sure about that.

RUSSIAN Do you know the formula of curve on the lens?

(80)

GREENGLASS No I built according to specification, but I don't know what the formula was.
RUSSIAN What kind of H.E. is used?
GREENGLASS I don't know. I was never present at the explosions.
RUSSIAN Tell me the names of all scientists and workers besides those you already gave Julius.

After twenty minutes of questioning in the crawling car, it returned to the original scene where the Russian was taken aboard. David was instructed to stop. The Russian got out. A figure emerged from the dark. It was Julius, who walked off with the Russian. David drove home alone.

When he arrived home, he told his wife, Ruth, about the incident. Later, when she was on the stand, she confirmed it.

When Greenglass had finished this recital, the prosecutor handed him a Jell-O box and a scissors and asked him "to cut the correct side in two parts, resembling the two pieces" he had seen that night in Rosenberg's apartment. The jury watched the surgery of the Jell-O box, and then the two pieces were offered in evidence and handed to the jury for inspection.

When Greenglass returned to Los Alamos, he took an apartment in Albuquerque. His wife came there to live with him. He was permitted to leave Los Alamos on Sunday and return Monday morning.

Ann Sidorovich was not the courier sent to receive the information he was spiriting out of Los Alamos. Instead, Harry Gold arrived. A photograph of Gold was placed in evidence. Later, Gold was to appear in person as a witness.

Greenglass and his wife, Ruth, were in their apartment when there was a knock on the door.

COHN Would you tell us exactly what happened from the first minute you saw Gold?
GREENGLASS There was a knock on the door and I opened it. We had just completed eating breakfast, and there was a man standing in the hallway who asked if I was Mr. Greenglass and I said, yes. He stepped through the door and said, "Julius sent me," and I said, "Oh" and walked to my wife's purse, took out the wallet and took out the matched part of the Jell-O box.

He produced his piece and we checked them and they fitted, and the identification was made.

I offered him something to eat and he said he had already eaten. He just wanted to know if I had any information, and I said, "I have some but I will have to write it up. If you come back in the afternoon, I will give it to you."

I started to tell him about one of the people who would be good material for recruiting into espionage work. He cut me short and he left and I got to work on the report.

COHN Where did you work on the report?

GREENGLASS In my combination living room and bedroom.

COHN Tell us exactly what you did.

GREENGLASS I got out some 8 by 10 ruled white paper, and I drew some sketches of a lens mold and how they are set up in the experiment, and I gave a description of the experiment.

COHN Was this another step in the same experiment on atomic energy concerning which you had given a sketch to Rosenberg?

GREENGLASS That is right, and I also gave him a list of possible recruits for espionage.

COHN Did Harry Gold come back in the afternoon?

GREENGLASS Yes at 2:30. I gave him my report in an envelope and he gave me an envelope, which I felt and realized there was money in it and I put it in my pocket.

COHN Did you examine the money at that point?

GREENGLASS No, I didn't. Gold said, "Will it be enough?" and I said, "Well, it will be plenty for the present." And he said, "You need it" and we went into a side discussion about the fact that my wife had a miscarriage earlier in the spring, and he said, "Well, I will see what I can do about getting some more money for you."

COHN How much was in the envelope?

GREENGLASS My wife and I counted it later. There was $500. I gave it to her.

COHN Have you prepared a sketch of the drawing which you gave Gold in June 1945?

GREENGLASS Yes.

COHN I offer it in evidence as Exhibit 6.

E. H. BLOCH May I ask one question on the *voir dire,* before your Honor rules?

COURT Go ahead.

E. H. BLOCH When you made this sketch in 1950, did you rely solely on your memory as to what you had given Gold five years earlier?

GREENGLASS I did.

E. H. BLOCH I object to its admission.

COURT I am admitting it. The weight to be given it will be . . . entirely up to the jury. It is being done for the purpose of permitting the jury to visualize what was turned over, and only insofar as that. It is not being introduced as the document which was given to Gold, because for apparent reasons the Government couldn't introduce that at this time.

Greenglass explained the sketch. It showed a high explosive lens mold and how it worked with the detonator on, and the steel tube in the middle which was exploded by the lens mold. He had also prepared "a schematic view of the lens mold setup," which he delivered to Gold. It, too, was admitted in evidence after he conceded having drawn it from memory for the trial.

This sketch was also accompanied by descriptive material on a separate sheet, identified with letters "A" to "F." Greenglass gave a brief explanatory lecture. "A" was the light source which projected a light "through this tube E." There was a camera set up to photograph the light source. The tube was surrounded by the high explosive lens "C," shown in a cross-section. There was a detonator marked "B." The way the experiment was conducted was to detonate the tube which imploded it. The camera through the lens "F" photographed the effect of the implosion, and "D" was the resulting picture. In this way, the scientists could measure the effectiveness of different-shaped lenses and different explosives.

All this was, of course, highly "secret" information. It was unlikely that the jury could understand this technical testimony. However, it did establish that Greenglass not only had access to the bomb's secret, but that he had sufficient understanding to translate it into sketches.

The prosecution engaged in a well-conceived plan to pin down this impression scientifically. It asked the court to permit Greenglass to suspend his testimony temporarily, so that Professor Walter Koski could take the stand "concerning these matters." Such procedure was in the discretion of the judge. There was no objection by defense counsel. The judge granted the request. He "temporarily excused" Greenglass. He was replaced on the stand by a distinguished scientist, the purpose being to give depth to Greenglass' revelations with the effect on the jury of hearing stereo-echoed testimony. Furthermore, this resulted in Professor Koski being cross-examined before Greenglass, with the possibility of blunting some of the attack on a lay witness.

$$\longrightarrow \longleftarrow$$

Professor Walter S. Koski was sworn in. The jury was about to be treated to an explanation of experiments by which the power locked in an atom from the beginning of time was finally released. It was to learn the meaning of implosion.

Under questioning by Saypol, Koski recited his credentials which were of the highest. He was associate professor of physical chemistry at Johns Hopkins University and consultant at Brookhaven National Laboratories. There he worked in a program "to measure certain properties of radioactive nuclei." This was called nuclear chemistry. He had been a research chemist at the Hercules Powder Company. In 1944, the United States Government engaged him as an engineer at the Los Alamos Scientific Laboratory, where he worked for three years. At Los Alamos all work was "secret and of a highly classified nature." At first, even he did not know what the project was. Later, he learned it was "to construct a nuclear weapon or atomic bomb."

SAYPOL   What did your work involve?

KOSKI   My work was associated with implosion research connected with the atomic bomb.

SAYPOL   So that we, as laymen, may understand when you say implosion research, does that have something to do with explosives?

KOSKI   The distinction between explosion and implosion is in an explosion the shock waves, the detonation wave, the high pressure region is continually going out and dissipating itself. In an implosion the waves are converging and the energy is concentrating itself.

SAYPOL   I take it, concentrating itself toward a common center?

KOSKI   Toward a common center.

SAYPOL   In other words, in explosion it blows out; in implosion it blows in?

KOSKI   Yes.

SAYPOL   Is implosion one of the physical reactions incident to the overall action in the atomic bomb?

KOSKI   It is.

SAYPOL   So, as I understand you, your precise job was to make experimental studies relating to this phenomenon of implosion?

KOSKI   It was.

SAYPOL   Mr. Koski, in the performance of that work, did you have occasion to use what has been called here a lens, a device called a lens?

KOSKI   I did.

SAYPOL   What is the lens as you knew it in connection with your experiments?

KOSKI   A high explosive lens is a combination of explosives having different velocities and having the appropriate shape so when detonated at a particular point, it will produce a converging detonation wave.

SAYPOL   Well, once again, so that we as laymen might understand, I take it our common conception of a lens is a piece of glass used to focus light, is that right?

KOSKI   Yes, that is right.

SAYPOL   What is the distinction between a glass lens and the type of lens you were working on?

KOSKI   Well, a glass lens essentially focuses light. An explosive lens focuses a detonation wave or a high pressure force coming in.

He described the procedure by which he experimented with different lenses in order to achieve the desired implosion. It brought him into direct contact with Greenglass.

(84)

He would design a lens and take it to the Theta shop where Green-glass was foreman. There the mold would be prepared under Koski's supervision. He would talk to Sergeants Fitzpatrick and Marshman and at times to Greenglass. When the machine shop had completed the mold, he would take it to a laboratory "at a remote site" because the explosions created "heavy shocks." There he would shape high explosive into the lens. The power of the implosion effect was photographed and measured. New lenses were then designed from what had been learned.

In the middle of 1945, "a flat type lens" was the subject of experiment.

Then came the clinching testimony confirming the knowledge and accuracy of Greenglass' testimony of his reproduced sketches. It established a link in the implosion chain. The prosecutor showed him the sketch Greenglass had drawn.

SAYPOL   Would you recognize it as a reasonably accurate replica of the one you submitted to the Theta machine shop?
KOSKI   Yes.

There was a skirmish about a date.

E. H. BLOCH   Now, if the Court please, I have no objection to the substance of this question, but I ask that the time be more definitely fixed.
COURT   You do remember that they were some time during the years 1944 and 1945?
KOSKI   They were.

Koski went on to testify that the last sketch prepared by Greenglass accurately described the experiments being conducted in 1945 at Los Alamos in "the development of the atomic bomb."

Had any other nation been conducting similar experiments at that time?

KOSKI   To the best of my knowledge and all of my colleagues who were involved in this field, there was no information in textbooks or technical journals on this particular subject.
SAYPOL   In other words, you were engaged in a new and original field?
KOSKI   Correct.
SAYPOL   And up to that point and continuing right up until this trial, has the information relating to the lens mold and the lens and the experimentation to which you have testified continued to be secret information?
KOSKI   It still is.
SAYPOL   Except as divulged at this trial?
KOSKI   Correct.
COURT   As far as you know, only for the purpose of this trial?

KOSKI Correct.

SAYPOL Will your Honor allow a statement for the record in that respect? The Atomic Energy Committee has declassified this information under the Atomic Energy Act and has made the ruling as authorized by Congress that subsequent to the trial it is to be reclassified.

COURT Counsel doesn't take issue with the statement?

E. H. BLOCH No, not at all. I read about it in the newspapers before Mr. Saypol stated it.

So it was brought out without defense objection that the Atomic Energy Committee had permitted the revelation of how the bomb was created and its secret solely for the trial.

The arrangement to classify the information again after the trial was as ineffectual as letting the genie out of the lamp and then trying to stuff him back again. As matters developed, the Committee to Free Rosenberg later published the record of the trial in a ten-dollar edition and sold thousands of them. The great secret was peddled across the globe. We shall see the court's struggle to prevent the testimony of more secrets by inducing defendants to stipulate to certain conclusory facts. Bloch not only agreed but volunteered the suggestion. But Sobell's counsel balked. It was an interesting drama within a drama.

It has been argued in ensuing years that Greenglass delivered no secrets, because Russia and other countries had known of the atomic formula long before. Professor Koski's testimony contradicted this. The defense never offered testimony to the contrary.

The prosecution turned over Professor Koski for cross-examination. The court matched the opening question with its own:

E. H. BLOCH Dr. Koski, did you turn over any of the sketches requested in Government's Exhibits 2, 6 and 7 to the defendant Greenglass?

KOSKI I did not.

COURT Was the defendant Greenglass in a position where by reason of his employment in the Theta shop he could see the sketches which you turned over?

KOSKI He was.

The judge permitted Bloch, over objection, to establish that "Greenglass was a plain, ordinary machinist," and that Koski rarely conversed with machinists.

Bloch then referred to the two exhibits which were sketches of the mold, and Exhibit 7 which was a description of an experiment, and sought to demonstrate that none of them were precise enough to be of scientific value:

KOSKI   This is a rough sketch and, of course, is not quantitative but it does illustrate the important principle involved.

E. H. BLOCH   It does omit, however, the dimensions?

KOSKI   It does omit dimensions.

E. H. BLOCH   It omits, for instance, the diameter, does it not?

KOSKI   Correct.

COURT   You say it does, however, set forth the important principle involved, is that correct?

KOSKI   Correct.

COURT   Can you tell us what that principle is?

KOSKI   The principle is the use of a combination of high explosives of appropriate shape to produce a symmetrical converging detonation wave.

E. H. BLOCH   Now, weren't the dimensions of these lens molds very vital or at least very important with respect to their utility in terms of success in your experiments?

KOSKI   The physical over-all dimensions that you mention are not important. It is the relative dimensions that are.

E. H. BLOCH   Now the relative dimensions are not disclosed, are they, by these exhibits?

KOSKI   They are not.

E. H. BLOCH   That is all.

The prosecution resorted to redirect examination to salvage its contention.

SAYPOL   The important factor from the experimental point of view is the design, is it not?

KOSKI   Correct.

SAYPOL   That was original, novel at the time, was it not?

KOSKI   It was.

SAYPOL   Can you tell us, Doctor, whether a scientific expert in the field you were engaged in could glean enough information from the exhibits in evidence so as to learn the nature of the object of the experiment that was involved in the sketches in evidence?

KOSKI   From these sketches and from Mr. Greenglass' descriptions, this gives one sufficient information, one who is familiar with the field, to indicate what the principle and the idea is here.

Saypol pressed for one more point and provoked recross-examination. He asked Koski whether the design in the sketch was "the primary fact of importance" rather than "the relative dimensions." Koski replied, "It was." Block then had him admit that the lens "had to be a precision job." The judge summed up by asking, "The substance of your testimony, as I understand it, was that there was sufficient in

(87)

these sketches to reveal to an expert what was going on at Los Alamos?" Koski replied, "Yes, your Honor." All counsel then released the witness.

—————→←—————

So the record stood when Greenglass resumed his testimony. He had previously testified that it was Julius Rosenberg who told him that the project in Los Alamos was to develop an atomic bomb. How had Rosenberg described it?

GREENGLASS He said there was fissionable material at one end of a cube and at the other end of the cube there was a sliding member that was also of fissionable material and when they brought these two together under great pressure, a nuclear reaction would take place. That is the type of bomb that he described.

This, Greenglass later learned, was the type of bomb dropped on Hiroshima. It was never used again. A more powerful bomb was developed through implosion.

Greenglass described his efforts to get information about the new experiments without creating suspicion. He listened in on conversations among his friends in the Theta shop. Sometimes he would express his interest and ask questions, as if they were prompted solely by curiosity. And, of course, there were his own assignments in making high explosive lenses—"These were molds used on the atom bomb."

Nine months later, in September 1945, Greenglass returned to New York on another furlough. Rosenberg visited him the morning after he arrived.

GREENGLASS He came up to the apartment and he got me out of bed and we went into another room so my wife could dress.
COHN What did he say to you?
GREENGLASS He said to me that he wanted to know what I had for him.
I told him "I think I have a pretty good description of the atom bomb."
COHN The atom bomb itself?
GREENGLASS That's right.

Rosenberg wanted a written description immediately of the new experiments. Greenglass told him to return and he would have it ready. Rosenberg left $200 with him.

Greenglass suffered momentary jitters as the role he was playing became more significant and dangerous. He discussed the matter with his wife. She didn't want him "to give the rest of the information to Julius." He overruled her. "I have gone this far and I will do the rest of it, too." The suction of his prior perfidy drew him in all the way.

COHN Did you draw up a sketch of the atom bomb itself?

GREENGLASS I did.

COHN Did you prepare descriptive material to explain the sketch of the atom bomb?

GREENGLASS I did.

COHN Was there any other material that you wrote up on that occasion?

GREENGLASS I gave some scientists' names, and I also gave some possible recruits for espionage.

COHN Now, about how many pages would you say it took to write down all these matters?

GREENGLASS I would say about twelve pages or so.

Then he and his wife drove in his father-in-law's car to Julius' home and "handed the written material including this sketch over to Rosenberg" in the presence of Ethel Rosenberg. Thus, Greenglass' confession directly enveloped Ethel and Julius.

Greenglass had prepared a replica of that sketch for the trial. When it was offered in evidence, Bloch astonished the court by suggesting that it be impounded so that it would remain secret from the public.

SAYPOL That is a rather strange request coming from the defendants.

E. H. BLOCH Not a strange request coming from me at the present.

SAYPOL And I am happy to say that we join him.

COURT It will be sealed after it is shown to the jury.

However, when the first question was asked, Bloch asked for a conference at the bench out of the hearing of the jury.

BLOCH Even at this late day this information may be of advantage to a foreign power. So I am satisfied that this be kept secret.

SAYPOL The Department of Justice took up the matter of revelation with the Atomic Energy Commission and with the Joint Congressional Committee on Atomic Energy, and it was left to my discretion how much of this material should be disclosed, on the premise that the primary obligation in the administration of justice was that the defendants were entitled to be apprised of the nature of the case against them.

COURT Perhaps we can avoid this matter of clearing the courtroom if counsel can stipulate right now that the matters he is about to describe were of secret and confidential nature to national defense.

SAYPOL Mr. William Denson, chief of the litigation section of the Atomic Energy Commission is here, and I will obtain his consent to such procedure.

COURT How do counsel for the defense feel about this?

E. H. BLOCH May I consult with co-counsel?

(They huddle for a discussion, and return.)

(89)

E. H. BLOCH   Your Honor, we cannot agree. I would like to stipulate it as an American citizen and as a person who owes his allegiance to this country.

COURT   May I ask counsel for Sobell why aren't you stipulating this?

PHILLIPS   I do not feel that an attorney for a defendant in a criminal case should make concessions which will save the prosecution from the necessity of proving things which we may be able to refute.

SAYPOL   If counsel are not unanimous, I am inclined to go forward with my proof.

COURT   (Addressing jury) Ladies and gentlemen, when a defendant is put on trial, under our form of government, I am happy to say, he is entitled to confrontation of all the evidence which the Government contends proves his guilt. That is his constitutional right. In view of the nature of the testimony we are about to hear, I am going to ask all spectators to leave the courtroom on the balance of this particular testimony. I am going to permit the press to be present, but we are going to trust to your good taste and good judgment on the matters of publishing portions of this testimony.

SAYPOL   There is also present in the court a representative of the Department of Justice, and a representative of the Joint Congressional Committee on Atomic Energy. I take it that is agreeable?

COURT   That is agreeable.

So the public was barred, but the press which reports to it, was permitted to stay with the plea that it restrain itself. The defense counsel agreed with this procedure.

The jury was apprised by the initiative of the defense itself that the sketch delivered by Greenglass to the Rosenbergs revealed the most important secret of the atomic age.

Continuing his testimony, Greenglass said that when Rosenberg received the sketch and papers, he went into another room to study them. He came out enthused, and suggested that the explanatory material be typed immediately. A bridge table was brought into the living room. A portable typewriter was placed on it. Ethel Rosenberg did the typing while Julius and Ruth Greenglass helped to make the script clearer and more grammatical.

As if jealous of Greenglass' supreme accomplishment, Julius commented that he had once stolen a proximity fuse while he was working at Emerson Radio. When Bloch objected that this was a charge of a separate crime and ought not be injected into the trial, the court asked:

Did he tell you what he did with that proximity fuse?

GREENGLASS   He told me he took it out in his brief case. That is

the same brief case he brought his lunch in with, and gave it to
Russia.

The court overruled the objection on the ground that the indictment
was not limited to the atomic bomb. It encompassed any information
pertaining to national defense.

Bloch's motion for a mistrial because of the "prejudicial" ruling was
denied.

When the material had been typed by Ethel Rosenberg, Julius put
the original notes in a frying pan, burned them and flushed them down
the drain.

Greenglass hoped to get out of the Army. Rosenberg urged him to
live in Los Alamos as a civilian so that he could continue to obtain
information from his friends. But Greenglass wanted to come home.
In February 1946, he was honorably discharged and came back to New
York City.

He went into business with Julius Rosenberg and his brother, Bernard,
for the next three years operating a machine shop.

Julius felt that Greenglass' services were far more valuable in
espionage. He attempted at various times to induce him to go to
certain colleges which specialized in nuclear physics, so that he could
cultivate friends there and pass on new military developments. He said
the Russians would pay for his schooling. Rosenberg urged Greenglass
to enter Chicago University because some of his Los Alamos friends
had returned there. He also suggested M.I.T. and later N.Y.U. because it had "a nuclear engineering course he wanted me to take."

Greenglass said he would consider these proposals, but he never acted
on them. Either his disinclination to study or his dislike of the spying
role kept him from continuing a career in espionage. Perhaps also he
was relieved that he had come away unscathed after symbolically toying
with explosives. Here he was, the man who had scored the greatest
coup in the history of espionage, living unobserved at 265 Rivington
Street, on the lower East Side, just another resident among nondescript
people. He must have dreamed of the reception he could have received at the Kremlin if all could be revealed. Whatever excitement
he and Ruth shared had to be suppressed. Only Gold and the
Rosenbergs knew their secret, and they, according to David and Ruth
Greenglass, were even more exhilarated by the feat of delivering the
bomb to Russia, for they were fired by revolutionary zeal. They had
a mission, and fate, through Greenglass' presence in Los Alamos, had
enabled them to serve their ideals beyond their wildest dreams. Had
they remained religious, they would have believed that the almighty
made it possible for them to save the world by balancing its terrors.

While Greenglass had silently retired, the Rosenbergs were fanatically
active. Greenglass testified that Rosenberg was spreading his espionage

web across the country. He was paying people to go to various schools. In return he was receiving information from upstate New York and Ohio. He had a source at General Electric at Schenectady, and at the Hugh Warner-Swasey turret lathe plant in Cleveland. He was in touch with Communists like Joel Barr who left the country in 1947.

On one occasion in 1947, Rosenberg told David Greenglass in the presence of his brother, Bernard, that he had learned from one of his informants about a sky platform:

COHN How did he describe it?
GREENGLASS He said that it was some large vessel which would be suspended at a point of no gravity between the moon and the earth and as a satellite it would spin around the earth.

Since the trial itself took place almost twenty years before our space men went to the moon, even the jury could not appreciate the pre-science of this testimony. When Rosenberg later testified and completely denied all that Greenglass had testified to, he claimed that the sky platform idea came from a harmless science fiction magazine. This was the explanation also for Greenglass' testimony that Rosenberg's informants had given him the mathematical solution for an atomic-energy-driven airplane.

Rosenberg revealed to Greenglass the communication devices used to contact Russia:

GREENGLASS He told me that if he wanted to get in touch with the Russians, he had a means of communicating with them in a motion picture theater, an alcove where he would put microfilm or messages and the Russians would pick it up.
   If he wanted to see them in person, he would put a message in there and by prearrangement they would meet in some lonely spot in Long Island.
COHN Did you in the report you wrote for Rosenberg tell him about atomic explosion which would take place at Alamogordo, New Mexico?
GREENGLASS Yes, in June 1945.
COURT How long before the explosion did you tell him?
GREENGLASS About a month before.

Idealists can best be rewarded by recognition, not money. Rosenberg proudly told Greenglass that Russia had presented him and Ethel with watches and "a citation which had certain privileges with it if we ever went to Russia."

Up to this point Greenglass' testimony was of crime triumphant. Nothing had gone wrong. Success had been complete. The security forces of the United States had been outwitted. What was supposed to be locked in an inaccessible isolated compound in the far West, behind electrical barbed fences and gates, a veritable army of guards, and security precautions designed and enforced by the FBI, had been sneaked out with ridiculous ease. Sketches and cross-sections of the bomb with full explanations of the experiments lay spread out on a table in Rosenberg's home in New York City, and were typed up as if a child's history lesson was being transcribed. Soon after, they were delivered directly to Russian agents to be sped to Moscow where, ostensibly, scientists gathered to read them with the same fascination that they later examined moon rocks.

———→←———

Not only had all this been carried off without a hitch, the danger was now past. For, as long as Greenglass was in Los Alamos, meeting with couriers, it was possible he would be followed and detected. Even his excursions in subtle questioning of his co-workers might arouse suspicions. Perhaps someone might become curious about his curiosity. Also, Ruth Greenglass might be under observation as she carried data back to New York.

But now, he had been honorably discharged from the Army (had dishonor ever been more misjudged?). He was a thousand miles out of the orbit of secrecy, where scrutinizing light pervaded everything. He was no longer hemmed in by security regulations, which made him suspect if there was the slightest violation. He had disappeared into the crowd.

Ruth breathed more freely too. She had returned to the normal annoyances of being housewife, nursemaid, cook and complainer. Her heart need not beat wildly at the mere thought of detection.

So a daring deed had come off well. There were great crimes which have never been detected. This one seemed destined to join that list.

However, there was "talk" that David had stolen "a specimen of uranium," and also had engaged in black market sale of precision tools in Albuquerque. Although such evidence was not presented by the government at the trial, Rosenberg later made references to it in explanation of the Greenglasses' fears, rather than his own.

Whatever revelations David made to Ruth in the intimacy of their bedroom may have revived the trembling anxiety which had become part of her existence. Perhaps it was responsible for an accident which almost killed her. While standing at the gas stove, she absent-mindedly moved too close in her flowing nightgown. It caught fire. In a second she was enveloped by devouring flames. Her screams brought David, who finally beat the fire into cinders. His hands were severely burned. She lay unconscious and was rushed to Gouverneur Hospital for emergency transfusions.

She was six months' pregnant at the time. Two lives were at stake.

(93)

For several days, she kept sinking, but transfusions poured continuing life into her.

The flames had not only charred her body, but as if they wanted to perpetuate themselves, left fevers which sent her into delirium. Then, she would call out for David, her boyhood sweetheart, whom she had married when she was eighteen and he twenty. Four months later, he had been drafted into the Army and she had followed him to various Army posts, finally landing at Albuquerque. Now, even while irrational, she needed him. He was summoned repeatedly to soothe her. She finally graduated from the "critical" listing, and after two months, induced the doctors and David to take her home. Then her younger sister, Dorothy Abel, was relieved of the chore of caring for David and the three-year-old child.

By this time, Ruth, her wounds still festering, was ready to give birth. She was taken to Beth Israel Hospital where a daughter, Barbara, was born. Upon return, her fevers again took over. Once more, she was rushed to the hospital. David had to take a leave of absence from work to care for the children, and when Ruth finally came home again, still not healed, he was not relieved of his burdens. He had one more person in his charge.

They had settled down in a fretting mood to the even misery of their lives, when all that had preceded seemed trivial and highly acceptable.

An incident occurred in a distant corner of conquered Germany which reverberated throughout the world. A file was discovered listing the names of Communist spies. The name of Klaus Fuchs appeared on it. The news sped to London and caused an explosion at Scotland Yard and in government circles. Soon there were revelations which created a similar explosion in the United States, at FBI headquarters and the White House. The chain reaction traveled to Philadelphia and New York and directly into the homes of the Greenglasses and the Rosenbergs.

The significance of Klaus Fuchs's name was that he was the nuclear physicist who had been designated by England to go to Los Alamos and co-operate with the United States in the construction of an atomic bomb. Now it was discovered that a Communist spy had been inserted into secret chambers at Los Alamos.

England was shocked. Prime Minister Clement Atlee made a public statement in the House of Commons to explain that it was not negligence on the government's part to have placed its faith in Fuchs.

Klaus Fuchs had come to England seventeen years earlier as a refugee from the Nazis. He was then only twenty-three years old. He enrolled in Bristol University to continue his studies in mathematical physics. His reputation was spotless and his talents unique. There had been no way of checking his past. The British Government had trusted him.

When Klaus Fuchs was arrested, he confessed to being a Russian spy. Attorney General Sir Hartley Shaw cross-presented the case at Bow Street Court in London. Resigned to his fate, Fuchs told all. Soon there came a joint announcement from Attorney General McGrath and J. Edgar Hoover that Harry Gold had been arrested in Philadelphia as a Communist spy. It was Gold who had received secret data from Fuchs and Greenglass.

Would Gold, too, talk? Then Greenglass was next. And, if so, would Greenglass be prevented by brotherly devotion from pointing a finger at Julius and Ethel Rosenberg?

The implosion chain from Fuchs's confession had reached Rosenberg. It drove him in panic to Greenglass' home.

CHAPTER 9

Ruth and David Greenglass were asleep in bed. It was very early in the morning. They were awakened by urgent, repeated knocking on the door. David finally shuffled to the door.

"Who is it?"

"It's Julius."

Greenglass was startled not only by the early visit, but the hushed, hoarse voice which signaled distress.

He unbolted the door. Rosenberg entered quickly without even a greeting. He was distraught. He tried to give the impression of complete control. This made him even more intense. He was on the edge of panic.

By this time, Ruth had pulled on a bathrobe and had joined them. The alarming news burst out of Rosenberg as if the valve of his restraint could not hold any longer:

"Something very serious has happened. Klaus Fuchs, the English physicist, who was working with us, has been arrested in England. Gold, the man who came to see you in Albuquerque, was also his contact. He has just been arrested too. Look at this."

He showed Greenglass a copy of the *Herald Tribune* with Harry Gold's picture on the front page, and the heading "ARRESTED FOR ESPIONAGE."

"Apparently Fuchs has confessed and mentioned Gold. It is possible Gold will mention you. You must leave the country at once!"

"That's impossible. You know Ruth has just returned from the hospital with the baby. She is still weak from her burns. We have no money. As a matter of fact, we are in debt."

"Don't worry about that. I'll see that you have whatever money you need. The Russians will take care of us. I have $1,000 here for you now."

He handed him an envelope. "I will bring you $6,000 more."

"How are we going to get passports to leave? You don't think it's wise for me to go to the consulate under these circumstances, do you?"

"They let other people out more important than you. Joel Barr got out, and he was in our group. I'll tell you just how everything can be managed, if you listen to me. Get dressed. We'll go for a walk and talk."

Greenglass stood frozen. The blow had come so suddenly and hard that it had not caused pain. Rather he felt numb. Obedience was the easiest response. After a moment's hesitation, he walked to the bedroom to dress, leaving Ruth staring at Julius. She looked at him with anger, as the bearer of fateful news she had always feared. They said nothing. Slowly, her eyes filled with tears.

Greenglass returned, dressed sloppily, and followed Rosenberg out silently. They walked down Sheriff Street and into Hamilton Fish Park where the open spaces provided privacy.

"We'll get you into Mexico first," Julius began, taking it for granted that Greenglass would be acquiescent to orders.

"We'll get a tourist card near the Mexican border. You won't have to do anything in New York. You have to be inoculated for smallpox. We'll do this near Mexico and get a letter from a doctor down there that you had it done. Now I am going to give you instructions which you'll have to memorize. I'll go over it with you until you've got it down perfectly. But concentrate on what I tell you. You'll have to learn every word by heart. Listen carefully."

Greenglass still floated in fear. "I don't know. All right. I'll try."

"When you get to Mexico City, write a letter to the Secretary of the Russian Ambassador to Mexico, praising the arguments of Russia at the United Nations. Sign it 'I. Jackson.'"

"Jackson?"

"'I. Jackson.' Then three days after you have sent the letter, go to Plaza de Colón at five o'clock in the afternoon, where there is a statue of Columbus. Carry a travel guidebook, with your middle finger in the pages of the book. Have you got it so far?"

"Go ahead. Did you say Plaza de Colón?"

"Yes. Stand there and a man will come up close to you. Then say, 'That is a magnificent statue. I come from Oklahoma and I haven't seen a statue like this before.' He will say, 'Oh, there are much more beautiful statues in Paris!' That will be your identification and contact. This man will give you passports and money to get to Vera Cruz from where you will sail to Sweden."

"Where will we stay in Mexico City?"

"Anyplace away from the center of town. You'll only be there a few days.

"Now when you get to Sweden, go to Stockholm. Then send the same kind of letter to the Secretary of the Russian Ambassador to Sweden.

You know, praising Russia's position at the United Nations and sign that letter 'I. Jackson.'

"Three days later go to the statue of Lineus in Stockholm. Carry a travel guide again, with your middle finger in its pages. Go there at five o'clock in the evening. Wait until a man steps close to you and say the same thing you did at Plaza de Colón in Mexico City. Can you repeat it?"

"I say I have never seen such a beautiful statue."

"That you come from Oklahoma, and you have never seen such a beautiful statue. And he will reply?"

"That there are more beautiful statues in Paris."

"Right. There are much more beautiful statues in Paris. He will then give you passports and money to get to Czechoslovakia. When you get there just write the Russian Ambassador that you are there and sign 'I. Jackson.' He will make plans with you, whether to stay there or go to Russia, and he'll supply you with funds. Have you got all that?"

"I think so."

"Well, I'll go over it with you until you have it letter-perfect.

"Now one more thing. You will have to get passport photos, and I'll need lots of copies. You can go to any photographer in New York. That's safe enough. Get five copies of a picture of yourself. Five of yourself and your wife, five of yourself and the children. Five of your wife and the children. And five of the whole family."

"How about yourself?"

"I'm leaving too. Jacob Golos knows me. And Bentley knows him. So that will probably lead to me. I am sure we can all manage this, but as an extra precaution, you ought to get a lawyer in the meantime, in case you are picked up before you can leave. I've done that too."

The next morning, again at an insomniac's hour, Julius was at Greenglass' door. This time his knocks were a signal rather than a mysterious alarm. Greenglass knew it was he and, still clad in pajamas, opened the door hastily.

Rosenberg was more composed. Action had drained part of his nervousness. He had a package under his arm wrapped in brown paper.

"Good morning, David. How is Ruth?"

"She's better, but worried as hell."

"I understand, but you'll all be all right. Here, I've brought you some money. It is $4,000."

He put the money in brown paper on the mantelpiece.

"Let's go for a walk. I want you to repeat the instructions I gave you. Have you memorized them perfectly?"

"I took the photos."

"Good. How many sets have you for me?"

"I took six sets. How many do you want?"

"Give me five. You'll only need one for yourself."

(99)

Greenglass got dressed and once more they walked toward the park. As they walked down Columbia Street to Delancey Street, Greenglass saw two of his friends on the opposite sidewalk. They were Hermie and Dianne Einsohn. He was about to greet them. Julius told him to ignore them. Greenglass said, "They are friends of mine and they would wonder why I walked by without saying anything."

He crossed the street to greet them. It happened that the Einsohns owed him $40. They took this occasion to pay it. Julius had walked ahead, and Greenglass hurried to catch him. Then they entered the park, circling it to avoid bench sitters. They were like an actor and a coach rehearsing over and over again to get the script letter-perfect. Preparation for flight gave them hope. Perhaps they could escape the trap before it clamped down on their necks.

Fear of doom swelled the senses. New sounds and sights must have entered the Greenglasses' lives. The ring of a telephone became an alarm bell of impending catastrophe. A knock on the door became an insistent challenge to open immediately or it would be battered down. Every passer-by on the street was an FBI man, or else why would he be so ostentatiously casual? Every cold greeting by a neighbor was significant. Had investigators tipped them off that the Greenglasses were under surveillance? Every glance was accusatory.

The nights were worse. Fears were like nails. How could one sleep on them? Their minds ran rampant with hideous possibilities. Their muscles tensed from fighting their imagination. The knots spread to their hearts and there was pain and tossing. The disintegration continued until they lost the will to resist. Surrender was the only relief. It provided the victory of peace. What would be, would be.

No planning. No fear of detection. No more struggle. It is the mechanism by which confessions are voluntarily made. "Let's get it over with" is a great sedative.

Only the completely amoral criminal can escape the torment of guilt. He glories in it, as witness Manson and others who are unrepentant, because they consider evil the rule of life. Hitler had no pangs of remorse, except for defeat. But most criminals, reared to recognize the difference between right and wrong, suffer punishment imposed silently by themselves. The pressures within seek release through confession.

Greenglass was pushed by a primitive force to imitate animals who, having been beaten and exhausted in a cruel and bleeding contest, turn over on their backs submissively and bare their throats to the enemy for final disposition.

Julius Rosenberg was not aware of the transformation which had taken place in the Greenglasses. He went on an urgent trip upstate. When he returned, he immediately went to the Greenglasses. His own experience prompted his first question:

"Are you being followed?"

"Yes, I am."

"I just came back from upstate New York to see some people, and I was going to Cleveland—but I am not going any more."

He, too, was face to face with futility. But although distressed, he was far from surrender. Rather, he was alarmed by the impending defection of David and Ruth Greenglass. He feared to ask the question, but he did:

"What are you going to do now? Are you ready to leave?"

"I feel I am being followed every second. There is no use trying to leave. I am not going to do anything. I am going to stay right here."

The answer was deadly in its hopelessness and abject surrender. Julius knew he could not quarrel with it. Death was not subject to persuasion. He took a long look at David to see his own reflection in his lifeless eyes. Then he shook his head dolefully, took his hat and walked out slowly without saying another word.

$$\longrightarrow \!\! \longleftarrow$$

David Greenglass had just put Stephen to bed and was mixing the baby's formula. There was a knock on the door. It did not evoke terror as previously. Ruth and he were resigned to their fate and, psychologically, would be relieved if the sword dropped. Greenglass knew it was Rosenberg. Must he tell him again that he was too tired to run? He asked:

"Is it you, Julius?"

"It is the FBI. Open the door."

Greenglass looked at his wife in panic. She was white with fright, and intuitively put a protective hand around the child. Greenglass, with trembling hands, opened the door. Four FBI men entered. Two of them gave their names, John Harrington and Leo Frutkin. One said politely:

"You are Mr. David Greenglass?"

"Yes, sir."

"You are Mrs. Ruth Greenglass?"

She stared at him without answering. Her silence was an affirmation.

The agent produced his credentials and turned to David. "We are from the FBI. We have a warrant. You are under arrest. We have a search warrant."

Two other agents, John Lewis and William Norton, joined Harrington in a thorough search. Frutkin remained guard over the Greenglasses.

$$\longrightarrow \!\! \longleftarrow$$

Having drawn all this out of Greenglass, the prosecutor now took him back over his testimony to fill in evidentiary gaps. His purpose was to provide detail which gave credence to the recital. Rosenberg would deny all, but the jury would have to consider whether the Greenglasses had the imagination or acuity to invent so much.

Where had Greenglass taken the passport pictures which he gave to Rosenberg? It was at a photo shop on Clinton and Delancey streets "near the Apollo Theater." He remembered that it was Memorial Day because that night he had some guests at his house when Julius came to collect the pictures. Greenglass met him in the hallway. He didn't want his guests to see him.

The sixth set of passport photos which he had kept, were in a drawer, and the FBI took them. The prosecutor produced them, and offered them in evidence. There was an acrid exchange between the judge and Bloch:

E. H. BLOCH   Objection. Not binding on the defendant Rosenberg.

COURT   Did I understand the testimony to be that they were taken pursuant to instruction?

E. H. BLOCH   You heard the testimony, your Honor, as well as I did.

COURT   I am asking you a question, counselor.

E. H. BLOCH   I think it is a fair implication that these pictures were taken in accordance with instructions.

COURT   Objection overruled.

They were given to the jury which peered at them as if the photographs had said, "I am guilty and want to escape. Julius told me this was my passport to freedom."

The FBI also found and took the brown paper in which the $4,000 was wrapped. It was produced in court. Greenglass identified it, and it was put into evidence. The money was "in tens and twenties" and Greenglass gave it to his brother-in-law, Louis Abel, to keep for him.

The prosecutor asked a concluding question. Had any promise of any kind ever been made to Greenglass for testifying?

Bloch objected. The prosecutor registered his surprise at the objection, and with a gesture, said:

I will withdraw the question, your Honor.

He turned the witness over for cross-examination.

CHAPTER 10

Why had the prosecutor drawn out of Greenglass the trivial incident of his meeting the Einsohns while he was walking with Rosenberg to rehearse his instructions? It was to place two witnesses on the scene, so that Rosenberg could not deny the walk to the park which Greenglass said was to review flight plans.

The jury might later have taken note that both Julius and Ethel denied incidents whenever there were no third parties present, and when there were, admitted at least the meeting without conceding the conversation. For example, Julius and Ethel denied the Jell-O box incident completely. It never happened, they swore. They denied the delivery of $200, later, $1,000 and $4,000. But both conceded separate confrontations with David and Ruth Greenglass when the Einsohns, or Dorothy Abel, or Elitcher's wife were present even momentarily. This distinction in denial may have been coincidental. It was not observable until the end of the trial. From the present vantage point, it may be examined by setting forth Julius Rosenberg's version of his meeting with Greenglass. It was not to give him instructions on how to get out of the country. When he later took the stand, Rosenberg was asked by his lawyer:

E. H. BLOCH   You heard Greenglass testify that you took him for a walk in Hamilton Fish Park and you gave him instructions how to get to Mexico. Did you walk with Greenglass in the park?
ROSENBERG   Yes.
E. H. BLOCH   Tell us the circumstances.

—→←—

Greenglass entered Rosenberg's office in the machine shop. He was sweaty with nervousness.

"Julie, come outside. I want to talk to you."

"I'm expecting some customers. Sit down, Dave. What's on your mind?"

"I can't talk here. This is urgent. I must talk to you. Come on out."

"I don't understand all this. All right," he said resignedly.

"Dave—Dave," he sighed, got his hat and walked out with him. They entered Hamilton Fish Park, before Greenglass opened up.

"Julie," said Greenglass mysteriously, "you've got to get me $2,000 right away. I need it at once."

"Dave, you know I haven't got it. I obligated myself to David Schein. I gave him a down payment of $1,000 and I owe him money. What's the trouble? What do you need it for?"

"I need the money. Don't ask me questions."

"Calm down. What is the matter with you?"

"I must have the money. I just must."

"If I had it, I would give it to you. But I haven't got it, Dave."

"Look, if you can't help me with money, you must do something else for me."

"What is it? If I can help, I will."

"Will you go to your doctor and ask him if he would make out a certificate for a smallpox vaccination?"

"Why don't you go to your doctor?"

"Don't ask me that. I can't do it."

Julius looked at Greenglass intently and appraised his desperation. "It is highly irregular, but I will ask my doctor if he will do that."

"Don't tell him who it is for, and also, while you are talking to him, ask him if he knows what kind of injections are required to go into Mexico."

"Dave, what trouble are you in?"

"Don't ask me anything about it. You've got to do this for me. If you can't give me the money I need, at least do this for me."

Rosenberg testified that he related this extraordinary incident to Ethel when he got home.

"I've just had a talk with David," he told her. "He asked me for money. He said he needed it desperately."

"What is the matter? Is Ruthie nagging him again for money?"

"No, it doesn't seem to be that. He must be in some trouble. I don't know what it is."

"Do you remember last February, he told us about the FBI coming around to ask him about some missing uranium. Do you think that might be it?"

"I don't know. He won't tell me, but I feel it is serious."

"Well, we must help him, whatever it is."

Rosenberg's version of his second walk with Greenglass also contradicted the rehearsal-for-flight theory. On the contrary, it was Green-glass who had sent for Julius.

Rosenberg testified to the following scene:

It was eight in the morning. Rosenberg knocked on Greenglass' door. He was admitted by a haggard-looking Greenglass.

"You said it was urgent, so I am here," said Rosenberg. "What in the world is the matter?"

"I'll be dressed in a minute. Let's go down."

Ruth entered in a bathrobe. "Have some breakfast, dear?"

David didn't answer. "Let's go," he said to Julius.

"Don't be too long," called Ruth.

David led Julius and walked toward the East River Drive, but he did so furtively, taking a diagonal route, up Columbia Street.

"You are very agitated," said Rosenberg. "Calm yourself, take it easy. What's troubling you?"

"Julie, I'm in a terrible jam."

"I realize that. You have been asking me for money, telling me to get a doctor's certificate, talking about Mexico. Tell me what's the trouble?"

"I can't tell you anything about it. All I want you to do for me, Julie, is I must have a couple of thousand dollars in cash. I must."

"David, I don't have the money. I can't raise that kind of money."

"Julie, can't you borrow it from your relatives?"

"No, Dave. I can't do that. They haven't got it."

"Can you take it from the business for me?"

"Dave, I can't do that. You know that."

"Well, Julie, I just got to have that money and if you don't get me that money, you are going to be sorry." His manner was as ugly as his words. Julius bristled.

"Look here, Dave, what are you trying to do, threaten me or black-mail me?"

Rosenberg couldn't have used a worse word than "blackmail." Clearly it meant that Greenglass was "threatening" to expose him. It was an indirect confession of involvement in a crime. It contradicted Rosenberg's stance during the trial that he was an innocent bystander, maliciously drawn into the case by a venal prosecution which "paid off" Greenglass and his wife, to involve Ethel and Julius.

Here the prosecution missed its opportunity for cross-examination. Indeed, Julius repeated the word during cross-examination and even then the prosecutor didn't pick it up. The court did, but the incident passed with comparatively little impact, much to the benefit of the defense.

SAYPOL You told us about Greenglass taking you for a walk and demanding $2,000 from you. Did you tell your wife about this?

ROSENBERG Yes, she wanted to help him even though I thought we should not after he tried to blackmail me.

COURT Blackmail you?

ROSENBERG Well, he threatened me to get money.

COURT You said he told you that you would be sorry if you didn't get the money.

ROSENBERG Yes. I consider it blackmail when someone says that.

COURT Did he say what he would do to you?

ROSENBERG No, he didn't.

COURT Did he say he would go to the authorities and tell them that you were in a conspiracy with him to steal the atomic bomb secret?

ROSENBERG No.

COURT Do you think that was what he had in mind?

ROSENBERG How could I know what he had in mind.

COURT What do you mean by blackmail then?

ROSENBERG Maybe he threatened to punch me in the nose or something like that.

The prosecutor went right on to another subject.

Julius continued his recital of how the talk with Greenglass ended. He observed that "David is puffing" and had a "wild look in his eyes." He testified that he decided "to cut the conversation short." They were walking down the Drive "near Houston or Stanton Street." Julius said:

"Look, Dave, you go home, take a cold shower. I have some work to do and I am going to the shop. Good-bye."

Rosenberg turned and headed home. He "won't have anything more to do" with David. He was "agitated" too by the distressful conversation winding up with a threat to him. When he got home, Ethel asked him:

"Did you see them? What happened?"

"I don't know. Whatever it is, it is terrible. I saw only David. He took me for a walk mysteriously. He wouldn't talk to me in the house. He didn't even want Ruth to hear his troubles.

"He is like a wild man with worry. He demanded that I get him $2,000. I mean 'demanded.' He didn't ask. He practically threatened me. I got so angry. I just told him to cool off and left him."

"Did he tell you what it was? Why he needed the money?"

"No. That's just it. He won't talk. 'Don't ask me,' he kept saying. 'Just get me the money.' "

Ethel was very upset. "Let's call Ruthie. Let's talk to her."

"I don't know. She just came home from the hospital. I understand the burns are not healing. They are festering. She has the baby. I don't even know whether Davey is home. I don't think she knows what trouble he's in. We'll only add to her worries without helping the situation. I don't think we ought to bother her. Besides, he may get sore if we tell Ruthie. You know, he's always had it in for me."

"Julie, he's my kid brother and the least I can do is help him. We can't stand on ceremonies when he is in time of need."

"I don't think our interference is going to help. But I'll see if I can do something."

"Let's get a sitter for the children," Ethel suggested. "Maybe that will take some pressure off."

"I'll drop over in the morning and take a look at them. I want to be sure he is not going to do anything rash. I won't even talk to him about his troubles."

This accounted for his next early visit to the Greenglass apartment. David and Ruth were at the kitchen table. When Rosenberg entered, they were both cold as ice to him. Embarrassed by their hostility, he sat down at the kitchen table. All he had been greeted by was "Hello." Not a word had been spoken. After a few moments:

"How is the baby?"

He got up and went to the bedroom to take a look into the crib. They sat stony-faced. Rosenberg returned and observed that Greenglass was calmer than the day before. He fumbled about for a moment in the unwelcome atmosphere.

"Well," he said, "I'm off to the shop. Good-bye."

They did not respond.

Rosenberg said this was the last time he saw David Greenglass until after the arrest.

COURT   And you can't think of any reason whatsoever, can you, why David Greenglass would, of all the people he knew, his brother, all the other members of his family, single you out, as he did apparently and as you say he did, and say that you would be sorry unless you gave him the money?

ROSENBERG   Well, he knew that I owed—he had an idea that I owed him money from the business, and I guess that is why he figured he wanted to get money from me.

It was up to the jury to determine whether Greenglass' or Rosenberg's descriptions of the early morning visits were the truth. Was it Julius who took David for walks to give him involved instructions on how to travel the spy route into Russia; or was it David who pleaded with Julius to walk with him so that he could demand $2,000 to escape from the unspecified scrape he was in?

Cross-examination of both aided in this determination. Let us first examine the attack made on Greenglass' entire testimony by the defendants' lawyers.

CHAPTER 11

Since Greenglass was a confessed spy, it was not difficult to assail his character. Bloch went right to it. When Greenglass undertook to spy, he did so of his "own free will." He was twenty-two years of age, old enough to know better.

E. H. BLOCH You knew at that time, did you not, that you were engaging in the commission of a very serious crime?
GREENGLASS I did. . . .
E. H. BLOCH Did it occur to you at the time that you finally said to your wife, "I will do this" and then transmitted to her certain information that there was a possible penalty of death for espionage?
GREENGLASS Yes.
E. H. BLOCH Are you aware that you are smiling?
GREENGLASS Not very. . . .
E. H. BLOCH And from the time in the latter part of November 1944, during your entire career in the Army, you continued to spy, did you not?
GREENGLASS I did.
E. H. BLOCH And you received money for that, did you not?
GREENGLASS I did.
E. H. BLOCH You received $500 from Harry Gold in Albuquerque, New Mexico, for that, did you not?
GREENGLASS I did.
E. H. BLOCH Did you ever offer to return that money?
GREENGLASS I did not.

He conceded that when he decided that he could not escape, he did not return the $1,000 or $4,000 given to him by Julius for that purpose.

Quite obviously an espionage agent is not morally concerned about such matters.

But the attack on Greenglass' responsibility of statement did not fare so well. Very early in his questioning, Bloch had Greenglass repeat his testimony that when his wife first reported Rosenberg's invitation to espionage, he refused. The next morning, he acquiesced. Had he consulted with anybody overnight? His answer was:

I consulted with memories and voices in my mind.

Greenglass' curious references "to memories and voices in my mind" were manna from heaven for a cross-examiner. It opened the door to a possible demonstration that he was a "kook." It should have been pursued endlessly. "What did the voices say?" "How often did he hear them?" "Whose voices were they?" "What memories did he consult?" He could have been led on in a friendly way to expatiate and expose himself.

Even if he retreated by claiming he was sarcastic, the opportunity for attack was broad. It would reveal a nasty rather than a beaten man. Also, when such untraveled roads, off the beaten path of his preparation, are taken by a witness, he may get lost in thickets of contradiction. When he attempts to find his way out by improvisation, he usually loses all sense of direction. No one knows what triumphs may lie ahead for the cross-examiner in such a situation.

Even if Greenglass had had sufficient wits about him to translate his answer as meaning that he consulted his conscience, he was in for another stormy hour or two of cross-examination. What did his conscience tell him about the dastardly deed he was performing for money? Even if he admired Russia, did he think it was right to betray his own country? How about the oath of secrecy he had taken at Los Alamos, and his oath to defend the United States when he became a soldier?

Yet Emanuel Bloch reacted as if the witness had frustrated him by a skillful evasion. His very next question sought to bring him back to the harmless path of his narrow question.

Physically, did you consult with anybody?

GREENGLASS No.

Those who argue for or against the verdict do so on the record before them. What is missing is what the record might have been. Jurors must decide on what is put before them. They cannot respond to stimuli which are not there. That is why it is possible for a good case to be lost and a bad one won.

No mystical power places all the facts into the courtroom for the jury to weigh. The theory that heaven would provide the answer permeated trial by ordeal. Where men must do so, the facts must be reconstructed by diligence and research. Cross-examination must excise the truth from a hostile witness' mind. Experts must be engaged to present the defense's side of a scientific postulate. (If there was any doubt, as critics have since argued, about the real value of Greenglass' revelations, no witnesses were presented by the defense to say so. Of course, the defense was handicapped by the reluctance of experts to testify for the Rosenbergs, lest their disrepute envelop them.)

Does this mean that justice depends partly on the skills of the advocate? Of course. We would prefer it to be an abstract procedure vested with sublime certainty. But justice is administered by human beings and the variations in their abilities affect the outcome as they do in every other enterprise. While acknowledging our regret that justice is not an infallible edict from on high, we can take solace from the fact that no better system of determining controversy has ever been devised.

Greenglass was especially vulnerable on one point, and the cross-examiner took full advantage of it. How was it that his wife, Ruth, an active co-conspirator, was not even arrested? Was this a pay-off for Greenglass' testimony against the Rosenbergs?

E. H. BLOCH You have known your wife Ruth since childhood days?
GREENGLASS Yes.
E. H. BLOCH Did you love her when you married her?
GREENGLASS I did.
E. H. BLOCH Do you love her today?
GREENGLASS I do.
E. H. BLOCH Do you love her more than you love yourself?
GREENGLASS I do.
E. H. BLOCH Do you love your children?
GREENGLASS I do. . . .
E. H. BLOCH Did you at any time think of your wife while you were down here telling your story to the FBI?
GREENGLASS Of course, I thought of her.
E. H. BLOCH Did you think of your wife with respect to the fact that she may be a defendant in a criminal proceeding?
GREENGLASS I did. . . .
E. H. BLOCH Now, Mr. Greenglass, your wife has never been arrested, has she?
GREENGLASS She has not.
E. H. BLOCH And she has never been indicted, has she?
GREENGLASS She has not. . . .
E. H. BLOCH And your wife is at the present time home, taking care of your children, isn't that right?
GREENGLASS That's right.

All this, despite the fact that Greenglass himself had told the FBI that it was his wife who came to Albuquerque and carried the invitation from Rosenberg to spy; that it was she who participated in the Jell-O box incident and co-operated in the later espionage efforts.

The defense also tried to establish pressure upon Greenglass until he confessed.

E. H. BLOCH After you were arraigned, were you taken to jail and put in solitary confinement?

GREENGLASS Yes, for three days. The reason I was confined, was because there was an erroneous story in the newspapers that I was going to commit suicide; so the keeper felt, well, he wasn't going to take it on himself, so he had me put in solitary and had my laces taken off my shoes and my belt taken away from me so I wouldn't commit suicide. That was the whole story. There was no other reason.

E. H. BLOCH Now when for the first time did you have a visitor?

COURT May I ask what the relevance of this is?

E. H. BLOCH The relevancy of this entire line of testimony is to show that this witness is lying, in order to save his wife.

In the light of the treatment accorded to him by the prison authorities, and the subsequent change of treatment, inferences can be drawn.

E. H. BLOCH After three days in solitary you were treated just the way all other prisoners were treated?

GREENGLASS That's right.

As Greenglass was badgered, he lost his composure and volunteered a strange statement.

E. H. BLOCH Did you tell the FBI about your wife's participation in the Jell-O box incident?

GREENGLASS I did, but let me point out, I wasn't a lawyer. I didn't know it was an overt act or anything else. How was I to know that? I just told them the story as it happened. That was all. I was interested in getting out.

E. H. BLOCH You were interested in getting out?

GREENGLASS I said, all I was interested in was getting out the story. Don't misconstrue my words.

Greenglass' reference out of the blue to an "overt act" was an invitation to deep examination. Where did he learn that legal phrase? Had the prosecutor discussed and explained it to him? Did the government tell him that Ruth's conduct constituted "an overt act" and, therefore, she, as a conspirator, was as deeply involved as he was?

Although the cross-examiner could not demonstrate past favorable treatment, he succeeded in raising the question as to whether Greenglass was now beholden to the prosecution.

E. H. BLOCH How long ago have you pleaded guilty?

GREENGLASS A year ago.

E. H. BLOCH Have you been sentenced?

GREENGLASS No.

E. H. BLOCH Do you believe the Court will be easier on you because you are testifying here?

GREENGLASS I don't believe that in testifying I will help myself to that great extent.

E. H. BLOCH Will you clarify that?

GREENGLASS To any great extent.

E. H. BLOCH Would you say to any extent?

GREENGLASS To any extent.

E. H. BLOCH All right. Do you believe that by testifying here that you will help your wife?

GREENGLASS I don't know what the Government has in mind with my wife and I can't answer for them.

To throw a cloud over Greenglass' ability to reproduce the sketches of the bomb, the defense, having looked up his school record, put an embarrassing question to him, and drew a self-conscious answer:

E. H. BLOCH When you went to high school and Brooklyn Polytech, did you fail in your subjects?

GREENGLASS I was quite young at the time, about eighteen, and I liked to play around more than I liked to go to school, so I cut classes almost the whole term. Simple.

E. H. BLOCH How many of the eight courses that you took did you fail?

GREENGLASS I failed them all.

E. H. BLOCH Did you go to Pratt Institute?

GREENGLASS Yes, for a semester and a half. I had to work at night. I got good marks there.

E. H. BLOCH Congratulations.

COURT Strike that from the record.

But when the cross-examiner gambled beyond this, he lost.

E. H. BLOCH You never got a science degree?

GREENGLASS No.

E. H. BLOCH Did you ever study calculus, or thermodynamics, nuclear physics, or atomic physics?

GREENGLASS I did not.

E. H. BLOCH Do you know what an isotope is?

GREENGLASS I do.

E. H. BLOCH What is it?

GREENGLASS An isotope is an element having the same atomic structure, but having a different atomic weight.

E. H. BLOCH Did you learn that in Los Alamos?

GREENGLASS I picked it up here and there.

Bloch also fared badly when he challenged the witness to explain how he picked up information. Greenglass filled in detail which lent authenticity to his story.

E. H. BLOCH You told us you snooped around to get information, is that right?

GREENGLASS Yes.

E. H. BLOCH Can you give me an instance?

GREENGLASS A man came to me with a sketch—with a piece of material and said, "Machine it up so that I would have square corners, so I could lay out a lens; come over and pick it up." I would go over to his place. He was a scientist. I would say, "What is the idea?" He would tell me the idea.

E. H. BLOCH Tricky like, eh.

GREENGLASS Nothing tricky about it.

COURT Strike that out.

Greenglass was raked fore and aft on his confessed role as despicable betrayer and his disloyalty to his family, which exceeded that to his country. Still contemptuous and criminal as was his conduct, was he now telling the truth? The jury must have watched him closely as the following skirmishes occurred.

E. H. BLOCH Now when you were inducted into the Army, you took an oath, didn't you? You know you have violated that oath?

GREENGLASS I did.

E. H. BLOCH Did you consider you were doing an honorable or dishonorable thing?

GREENGLASS On the basis of the philosophy I believed in, I felt it was the right thing to do at that time.

E. H. BLOCH Did you continue to think it was the right thing?

GREENGLASS I was having my doubts.

E. H. BLOCH When did you begin to have doubts?

GREENGLASS Almost as soon as I started to do it.

COURT Did you tell Mr. Rosenberg that you had doubts about the propriety of it?

GREENGLASS I had a kind of hero worship there and I did not want my hero to fail, and that I was doing the wrong thing by him. That is exactly why I did not stop the thing after I had the doubts.

E. H. BLOCH You say you had hero worship? Who was your hero?

GREENGLASS Julius Rosenberg.

E. H. BLOCH I see. Did you have doubts when you took the money?

GREENGLASS I had plenty of headaches and I felt the thousand dollars was not coming out of Julius Rosenberg's pocket. It was coming out of the Russians' pocket and it didn't bother me one bit to take it, or the $4,000 either.

E. H. BLOCH   Do you consider that the services you rendered to the United States during your army career warranted an honorable discharge?

GREENGLASS   I did my work as a soldier and produced what I had to produce, and there was no argument about my work, and since the information went to a supposed ally at the time, I had no qualms or doubts that I deserved the honorable discharge.

COURT   Do you feel that way today?

GREENGLASS   No, I don't.

E. H. BLOCH   When did you change your mind as to whether or not you were entitled to an honorable discharge?

GREENGLASS   I never thought about it until this moment.

E. H. BLOCH   Now that you have thought about it, do you believe that you were entitled to an honorable discharge?

GREENGLASS   In the light of today's events, I was not entitled to an honorable discharge.

E. H. BLOCH   Do you feel any remorse now for what you did down at Los Alamos?

GREENGLASS   I do.

What were Greenglass' feelings toward his sister, Ethel, who sat gazing at him from a defendant's chair twenty feet away? Every word he uttered was shattering her life. He did not flinch:

E. H. BLOCH   Do you bear any affection for your sister, Ethel?

GREENGLASS   I do.

E. H. BLOCH   You realize the possible death penalty in the event Ethel is convicted by this jury?

GREENGLASS   I do.

COURT   Do you realize also that the matter of penalty is entirely in my jurisdiction, not within the jurisdiction of the jury?

GREENGLASS   I understand that, too.

E. H. BLOCH   And you bear affection for Ethel?

GREENGLASS   I do.

E. H. BLOCH   This moment?

GREENGLASS   At this moment.

E. H. BLOCH   Do you bear affection for your brother-in-law, Julius?

GREENGLASS   I do.

E. H. BLOCH   You and Ethel were brought up in your parents' home together?

GREENGLASS   Certainly.

E. H. BLOCH   You both lived in that house until Ethel was married to Julius?

GREENGLASS   That is correct.

(115)

E. H. BLOCH How old was Ethel when she married Julius?

GREENGLASS It was 1939. I guess she was about twenty-two.

E. H. BLOCH How old were you at the time?

GREENGLASS I was about seventeen.

So he loved her, but he continued to testify against her.

Despite his admiration for Julius, it appeared that their business relationship had caused great friction between them—even physical violence.

E. H. BLOCH Did you have any quarrels with your brother-in-law, Julius?

GREENGLASS Only business quarrels. It didn't amount to anything.

E. H. BLOCH Did you ever come to blows with Julius?

GREENGLASS No, I didn't.

E. H. BLOCH Do you remember an incident in the corner candy story at Houston and Avenue D when your brother, Bernie, had to separate both of you?

GREENGLASS It slipped my mind.

E. H. BLOCH Did you hit Julius?

GREENGLASS I don't recall if I actually hit him.

COURT Do you remember what occasioned that?

GREENGLASS It was some violent quarrel over something in the business. I don't recall exactly what it was. As a matter of fact, I didn't even recall the fight until just this moment.

COURT Subsequent to that, did you patch things up?

GREENGLASS Certainly. We were very friendly after that.

E. H. BLOCH After you were arrested, did you not instruct your attorney to sue Julius Rosenberg for money you claimed he owed you?

GREENGLASS I did.

When Greenglass was cross-examined about the watches he said Russia gave to Julius and Ethel, he described the one to Julius as "A sweep, second-hand, round-face watch with a leather strap." He never saw Ethel's watch.

Immediately, thereafter, the cross-examiner was staggered by a revelation he had not expected:

E. H. BLOCH You told us that Rosenberg told you about receiving a console table from the Russians. Was that console table used for eating purposes?

GREENGLASS That console table was used for photography.

E. H. BLOCH For photography?

GREENGLASS That's right. Julius told me that he did pictures on that table.

When Ruth Greenglass took the stand she developed this testimony. The console table was to become a dramatic issue in the trial and indeed long afterward, in applications to the higher courts. It had a life all its own.

It is good timing for counsel to score heavily at the end of the day, right before adjournment. It gives a victorious aura to the whole day's struggle. Bloch succeeded in this maneuver.

He showed Greenglass a Jell-O box and asked him if it was similar to the one he had cut up years before. Greenglass replied, "They made a darker-colored box at that time."

There followed the surprising question:

E. H. BLOCH   Are you color blind?
GREENGLASS   I am.
E. H. BLOCH   Do you know what color this is?
GREENGLASS   I do not.
E. H. BLOCH   May we recess until tomorrow, your Honor? I have worked hard all day.
COURT   We will recess at this point, ladies and gentlemen, until 10:30 tomorrow morning.

The next morning Bloch extended the color chart of Greenglass' infirmity. He showed him the brown paper (Exhibit 10) in which he said the $4,000 had been delivered to him by Rosenberg, and asked, "Can you tell us what color that bag is?"

GREENGLASS   From previous experience, when I see a shading of this nature, I say it is brown. I don't actually see the color brown, but I say it is brown and I know that I have heard words to the effect that "brown paper bag," "brown manila paper," I realize that it is brown; everybody accepts it as brown, so I call it "brown."
E. H. BLOCH   Even though you are not sure this is brown?
GREENGLASS   No.

There followed a lengthy examination of the description of the brown paper in an effort to question Greenglass' ability to identify it from any other brown "bag," as the particular wrapper in which the money came. Greenglass had no difficulty with these questions and actually strengthened his identification with further detail. It was not a paper bag but a torn bag with ragged edges made into a wrapper with Scotch tape on it, which it still had. He illustrated how the money was packed in it. When a dispute arose as to whether he had not originally testified that it was a paper bag, the stenographic record was read back and he was right: "It was wrapped in brown paper." He said the $4,000 was in twenty-dollar and ten-dollar bills.

Bloch then took him back to the Jell-O box and went on a fishing expedition for contradiction. There was none. Greenglass had an opportunity to fill in testimony which lent more credence to his story. So, for example, he said that when Ruth arrived in Los Alamos, she had the cut piece of the Jell-O box which Rosenberg had given her.

GREENGLASS I saw it when my wife came out to see me to stay. I said, "Do you have it, the Jell-O side, I mean? You didn't forget," and she showed it to me.

Bloch had him repeat Gold's visit and the way he and Gold matched the pieces of the Jell-O box:

E. H. BLOCH They fitted?
GREENGLASS That's right.

The damning identification signal, tracing back to Julius and Ethel Rosenberg, was thus given new emphasis. One of the cardinal rules is never to cross-examine aimlessly in the hope of finding a crevice. Repetition only hammers in the original testimony.

It is an old trial axiom that a cross-examiner should aim for the jugular. Bickering over minor matters is unproductive, even if successful, and counterproductive when unsuccessful. Example: Block wanted to know what was the denomination of $500 given to Greenglass by Rosenberg. He said they were all twenty-dollar bills. How many were there?

SAYPOL Is this a test?
E. H. BLOCH Yes, it is a test.
GREENGLASS You divide 500 by 20?
SAYPOL The jury would know the answer without testimony.
COURT He wants to see now whether he knows mathematics.
GREENGLASS Twenty-five 20-dollar bills.
SAYPOL Will counsel concede that he passed the test?
E. H. BLOCH Yes, I think—well, I better not say.

After reviewing Greenglass' losing venture into business with Rosenberg, Bloch was through. His father, Alexander Bloch, representing Ethel, had no cross-examination. Neither did Kuntz, attorney for Sobell.

The prosecutor had only two questions on redirect examination:

SAYPOL By the way, Mr. Greenglass, you told us that you are color blind, is that correct?
GREENGLASS Yes.
SAYPOL Can you nevertheless distinguish shadings and dark and light?
GREENGLASS I can do that.

David Greenglass stepped off the stand. He had done his best to bury his sister and brother-in-law.

CHAPTER 12

The Rosenbergs were not through yet with their "loving" relatives. Ruth Greenglass took the stand. She was more deadly than David. Also she was clothed in some sympathy. She was the mother of two children. She had literally been through the fires of hell, and now she was to confess that her husband had been a spy and that she had co-operated—all to give authenticity to her accusation that Ethel and Julius were the masterminds of the whole stinking mess.

Saypol's assistant James B. Kilsheimer III did the questioning.

She was not a defendant, but the indictment named her a conspirator.

It was she who had carried Rosenberg's message to her husband to engage in espionage. How had this come about? Neither David nor she knew what the secret project was in Los Alamos, but one night Julius and Ethel told her that David was working on an atomic bomb. It was "the most destructive weapon used so far, that it had dangerous radiation effects, that the United States and Britain were working on this project jointly."

The Russians ought to be helped. Ethel and Julius had graduated from mere Communist activities in the United States. They had made contact with Russians and had entered a higher echelon of service, espionage. This was why for the past two years they had taken special camouflage precaution. They no longer attended Communist meetings. They did not even buy the *Daily Worker* at the usual newsstand.

A great opportunity was now presented to render a historic service to Russia. David Greenglass was in a strategic position in the secret atomic enterprise. Russia was our ally. They urged upon Ruth the argument that

> If all nations had the information then one nation couldn't use the
> bomb as a threat against another. Julius said that he wanted me to

tell my husband, David, that he should give information to Julius to be passed on to the Russians. And at first I objected to this. I didn't think it was right. I said that the people who are in charge of the work on the bomb were in a better position to know whether the information should be shared or not.

Ethel Rosenberg said that I should at least tell it to David, that she felt that this was right for David, that he would want it, that I should give him the message and let him decide for himself.

Julius knew that the waters David was entering were deep and dangerous. His first assignment was temptingly easy. It required just wading in. What was the physical description of the project? Was it camouflaged? How far was it from Albuquerque and Santa Fe? How many people were employed? Could he learn the names of scientists who worked there? Even then Ruth was to begin her training in artfulness:

> Oh—and he told me, I am sorry—he told me also to tell David to be very circumspect, not to indulge in any political conversations and to be very careful not to take any papers or sketches or blueprints, not to be obvious in seeking information, to relate to me only what he retained in his memory.

Also, she took $150 from Julius "for expenses for the trip," a subtle commitment to treachery even before David had made a decision.

Ruth went to Albuquerque to be with David on their wedding anniversary, November 29, 1944. They stayed at the Hotel Franciscan. She was fully aware of the portentous nature of her proposal. She had already caught the fever of outdoor privacy. She took David for a walk on Route 66 on "the outskirts of Albuquerque near the Rio Grande River."

> I told my husband that I knew that he was working on the atomic bomb. He asked me how I knew and who had told me. I said that I had been to Julius Rosenberg's house and that he had told me that David's work was on the atomic bomb, and he asked me how Julius knew it and I told him of the conversation we had had, that Julius had said they spent two years getting in touch with people who would enable him to do work directly for the Russian people, that his friends, the Russians, had told him that the work was on the atomic bomb, that the bomb had dangerous radiation effects, that it was a very destructive weapon and that the scientific basis, the information on the bomb should be made available to Soviet Russia.

She told him that she thought he ought to refuse to have anything to do with this plan, but that Ethel and Julius had insisted she owed it to David to make his own decision, because he would understand how right it was not to have Russia at a disadvantage in the balance of world power.

> . . . my husband did not give me an immediate answer; at first he, too, refused, and the following day he told me that he would consent to do this.

KILSHEIMER Now, did you inform your husband as to the type of information that Julius Rosenberg had asked you to obtain?

RUTH GREENGLASS Yes, I did.

Thereafter, David made his own easy down payment on a debt which could never be paid in full. He answered the simple questions she had conveyed to him.

> He said that Los Alamos had formerly been a riding academy, that it was forty miles from Santa Fe and about 110 miles from Albuquerque, that the project itself was on the top of a hill and it was secluded; you could hardly see it until you were almost on top of it; that there was a guard at the entrance at all times, and everyone was checked going in and out. He told me the names of the scientists, Dr. Urey, Dr. Oppenheimer, Kistiakowsky, Niels Bohr. David told me that he worked in an experimental shop, that he made models from blueprints that scientists brought in to him.

She began her training in being a courier without notes, repeating the information he gave her, until she had mastered it by memory. And having been taught by Julius, she became a good teacher, too.

> I told him to be very careful in getting the information, not to take any papers, not to take any blueprints, not to be obvious in seeking information from other people, and be careful not to get involved in political discussions.

When she returned to New York and told Julius "that David had consented to give him the information," he was "very pleased." If all she said was true, this must have been a great understatement of his feelings. At one stroke, Julius had pierced the impenetrable walls of the government's citadel. He would be the biggest man in what was reputed to be the largest, most skillful and dedicated world-wide espionage network which ever existed.

She told him the information she had memorized. He asked her to write it out. She did so. The waters were getting deeper.

When David came to New York City on New Year's Day in 1945, for a furlough, Julius visited him. His first approach was to Ruth. How would she like to move to Albuquerque and live there? She was thrilled with the prospect of being near David. She had followed him to camps in his previous army service. She was lonely and lost without him. But how could she get a job to support herself and the children in a faraway city?

"You are going there," said Julius imperiously. "You don't have to worry about the money." In view of the new arrangements, she would receive gifts not loans. They would be paid "by his friends, the Russians." Julius turned to David. They had "a technical discussion about David's work," which Ruth didn't understand. Julius asked him to write it down. That night he did, and delivered it the next morning.

Then Julius arranged a meeting at his house attended by a woman, Ann Sidorovich. Plans were developed for routing secrets to a top Russian agent, Anatoli Yakovlev. Ann Sidorovich was to come to Denver to meet Ruth in a motion picture theater, and silently exchange purses. In this way, David's information would be passed on.

Ruth asked whether Mike Sidorovich knew of his wife's role. It was believed he did not, and would disapprove if he did. This set in motion other plans. Whoever the visitor to Albuquerque would be, there must be a sure way of identifying him, even though he was unknown.

A Jell-O box came off the kitchen shelf to achieve fame never before accorded a commercial product. Ethel, Julius and Ruth went into the kitchen, while David remained in the living room. The instruction side of the Jell-O box was cut in two. Julius handed one piece to Ruth. Whoever came to visit her for information would have the other matching piece. When the signal was explained to David, he commented, "That's very clever," and Julius philosophized, "The simplest things are always the cleverest."

While the wives chatted amiably, Julius and David talked "about how the bomb was detonated." Even Ruth's recital of the woman's talk pulled Ethel into the vortex of spying activities.

KILSHEIMER What did you say to Ethel Rosenberg at that time?

RUTH GREENGLASS Well, Ethel said that she was tired, and I asked her what she had been doing. She said she had been typing; and I asked her if she had found David's notes hard to distinguish. She said no, she was used to his handwriting. Then she said that Julie, too, was tired; that he was very busy; he ran around a good deal; that all his time and his energies were used in this thing; that was the most important thing to him; that he was away a good deal and spent time with his friends; that he had to make a good impression; that it sometimes cost him as much as $50 to $75 an evening to entertain his friends; and then we spoke further. I said that I expected to be very lonely in Albuquerque; and Ethel said that I would make friends; that after a while I would probably meet other people there from New York.

It was decided that Ruth would meet the courier bearing the Jell-O box signal at a Safeway store in Albuquerque.

(122)

One day in February 1945, Julius visited Ruth. Her sister, Dorothy, was there. He asked her "to take a book and go into the bathroom," because he "had something private to discuss." Dorothy was ushered out of the room. Then Julius gave Ruth instructions on how to meet a Russian agent in Albuquerque. In the last week of April and the first week in May, she was to stand in front of a Safeway store on Saturday, at 1:30 P.M. Someone would identify himself with the Jell-O box piece and she would deliver information to him.

—→←—

When Rosenberg took the stand much later, he conceded an incident involving the dismissal of Dorothy from the room, but the conversation was entirely different. He testified to the following scene:

ROSENBERG Hello, Ruthie. Hello, Dorothy. How are you?

RUTH GREENGLASS We're fine. How is Ethel?

ROSENBERG O.K.

RUTH GREENGLASS (Whispered in Rosenberg's ear) Tell the kid to go into the bathroom. I want to talk to you alone.

ROSENBERG Dorothy, get a book and leave us, will you? We have something to talk over.

(Dorothy picked up a magazine and headed for the bedroom.) Not there. Go into the bathroom and shut the door.
(She did, casting a strange look at both of them.)

RUTH GREENGLASS The reason I called you is that I am terribly worried about David, and I must talk to you.

ROSENBERG What's the trouble?

RUTH GREENGLASS Well, he has ideas about taking some things from the Army and making some money. He says others are doing it. I don't know—gasoline—or what, and cashing in.

ROSENBERG That's terrible. He'll get himself in trouble as sure as fate. Warn him to stay away. Stealing is stealing and stealing from the Army isn't any different. If anything, it's worse. He'll be caught.

RUTH GREENGLASS I told him exactly that. But he says the boys are taking automobile parts and other things and that it is a regular practice. I'm really worried. I can't sleep nights.

ROSENBERG Well, impress upon him the danger of the thing. Insist that he give up this idea. What else can I say?

So, the jury had to decide who was telling the truth: Ruth Greenglass, who said Julius ushered her sister out of the room and then gave her instructions about meeting an espionage agent in front of a Safeway store, or Julius Rosenberg, who said that on that occasion the only conversation was Ruth's plea for advice because David was in trouble for stealing from the Army. Somebody was lying.

—→←—

Ruth testified that she was unable to keep her appointment in front of a Safeway store because she took ill. On April 18, she had a miscarriage. She wrote Ethel Rosenberg about her misfortune and received a reply. Theoretically, this was a signal to Julius that the rendezvous at the Safeway store would have to be delayed.

She no longer had Ethel's reply letter. If its loss could be explained, she would be permitted to tell its contents orally. This provoked a request by Bloch to examine her for a few moments on the *voir dire*, which means preliminary questions concerning the lost or destroyed document.

He asked her whether she had looked for the letter. She said she had but couldn't find it. Yes, her husband had seen it. But Bloch wavered in his attack between accusation and courtesy.

E. H. BLOCH   Are you in the habit of destroying mail?

RUTH GREENGLASS   Sometimes.

E. H. BLOCH   Personal mail, social mail?

RUTH GREENGLASS   Sometimes. You can't keep everything you receive.

E. H. BLOCH   I am not trying to draw any implications, Mrs. Greenglass. I just wanted to know the fact.

RUTH GREENGLASS   Sometimes I did.

Ruth was permitted to give "secondary evidence," that is, her recollection of its contents:

> Ethel said that she was sympathetic about my illness and that a member of the family would come out to visit me the last weeks in May, the third and fourth Saturdays.

She took this as an instruction to keep her appointment in front of the Safeway store the third and fourth Saturday in May. David accompanied her the second time. She had her Jell-O box cardboard with her, but no one showed up.

However, on the first Sunday in June 1945, Harry Gold came to their apartment on North High Street in Albuquerque. He flashed the Jell-O box identification. She took the matching piece from her pocketbook.

KILSHEIMER   Where was the last time you had seen the portion of the Jell-O box side which Harry Gold produced?

RUTH GREENGLASS   In Julius Rosenberg's hand.

She corroborated David's testimony that Gold returned to receive the written data her husband prepared. He gave David "a white sealed envelope." They escorted him as far as the USO, where Gold went on, while the Greenglasses mixed with the soldiers they had just betrayed. Later they opened the envelope. It contained $500. There was no longer any pretense that the sole motivation for stealing secrets was in aid of world peace.

Ruth testified that the next day she deposited $400 in the Albuquerque Trust and Savings Bank, used $50 for household expenses, and $37.50 for a $50 defense bond.

In September 1945, David received another furlough. He and Ruth came to New York and stopped with David's mother at 64 Sheriff Street. Julius immediately came to see them. He and David "went into the back bedroom." When they emerged, Ruth heard Julius ask him to write out the information and bring it to his house.

When Julius left, Ruth protested David's further involvement. By this time, they both knew how perilous the venture was and its enormous import:

> . . . I did not want him to give the information to Julius. The bomb had already been dropped on Hiroshima and I realized exactly what it was and I didn't feel that the information should be passed on. However, David said that he was going to give it to him again.

The material was written down and the Greenglasses delivered it to Julius and Ethel Rosenberg. The Rosenbergs' son was present.

Julius retired to another room to read the report. He was elated when he came out and insisted that it be typed up immediately. Ethel was assigned the task. She fetched a portable Remington, put it on a bridge table, and proceeded to transfer David's notes into a coherent statement. Ruth described the remarkable scene in which two women and two men poured over data which President Roosevelt and the Security Council thought was secure from the military intelligence of our own highest officials and from those of other nations.

RUTH GREENGLASS Well, Ethel was typing the notes and David was helping her when she couldn't make out his handwriting and explained the technical terms and spelled them out for her, and Julius and I helped her with the phraseology when it got a little too lengthy, wordy.

When they were finished, "Julius burned the notes in the kitchen and then he flushed the ashes in the bowl." Later, Julius gave David $200. He turned it over to Ruth.

Suddenly, the prosecutor skipped to 1946. A console table took the center of the stage. It was in a legal spotlight from that moment on, for several years.

KILSHEIMER When David left the Army, did you for a while live in the Rosenberg apartment?

RUTH GREENGLASS Yes, Julius and Ethel were going away and they wanted us to stay in their apartment in case any important mail or telephone calls were to be received.

KILSHEIMER Did you notice any particular piece of furniture?

RUTH GREENGLASS A mahogany console table.

KILSHEIMER Did you have a conversation with the Rosenbergs concerning that table?

RUTH GREENGLASS Yes, I did.

KILSHEIMER Was your husband present?

RUTH GREENGLASS I think he was, yes.

KILSHEIMER What was the conversation?

Ruth narrated the dramatic story.

RUTH GREENGLASS (Touching the mahogany console table admiringly) This is beautiful, Ethel. When did you get it?

ETHEL ROSENBERG It is a gift. It is nice, isn't it?

ROSENBERG My friend sent us this gift. Let me show you.

(He turned the table on its side and revealed a hollowed section underneath, with room for a lamp to be put inside.)

You see you can take photographs in this compartment. I microfilm Ethel's typewritten notes this way.

(He switched on the lamp, then turned out the light in the apartment. The leaf of the table stood up as a shield.)

In this way, no one can see from the outside that photographs are being taken.

(He switched on lights in the apartment and turned the table back on its feet.)

Ruth repeated David's testimony that after he was discharged from the Army, he had an opportunity to obtain a civilian job at Los Alamos "at a very nice salary." He refused. Julius was "very displeased," because David "would have access to valuable information" there. But David was apparently ready, if not indeed eager, to shed his spy's cape. Nor would he accept Julius' similar overtures "to study nuclear fission even though finances would be taken care of—$75 or $100 a week to live on." Julius indicated this was a Russian project. "The students got their expenses first; it was the most important thing as far as the Russians were concerned."

Ruth was asked the question directly:

KILSHEIMER Did Julius Rosenberg tell you where he got the money, the $75 or $100 a week, if it were needed?

RUTH GREENGLASS From the Russians.

The fateful day of May 24, 1950, arrived. The jury was bombarded for a second time with the details of Julius' panicky visit to the Greenglass home. Ruth gave her version of the events. Julius showed them Harry Gold's picture on the front page of the *Herald Tribune*. He was jittery.

ROSENBERG This is the man who came to see you in Albuquerque. You will be the next to be picked up. You have to get out of the country.

RUTH GREENGLASS We can't go anywhere. We have a 10-day-old infant.
ROSENBERG (Impatiently) Your baby won't die. Babies are born on the ocean and on trains every day. My doctor said if you take enough canned milk, and boil the water, the baby will be all right.
(He took a small package of money out of his pocket.)
Here is $1,000. Buy everything you need. Don't be too obvious in your spending. You have a month to spend it in, and I will bring you more. Leave all your household effects. Just take your clothing and what you need for the children and leave. Ruth, do you think you can get a certificate from the doctor stating that you have all been inoculated against smallpox?
RUTH GREENGLASS I can't ask my doctor for a fake certificate.
ROSENBERG All right. I'll take care of it. My doctor will give it to me. David, come down for a walk. I have instructions to give you, which you'll have to memorize.

The court asked whether there was any discussion about how Ruth and her family were to get to Russia. Yes, David reported the plan when he returned from his walk.

The $1,000 given to her was traced by the prosecutor. Five hundred dollars was deposited in the Manufacturers Trust Company. The rest "was put in a metal closet to pay household debts and expenses."

She confirmed Julius' direction that they take six sets of passport photos and turn five sets over to him. On May 28, 1950, they took these pictures of the family. They gave Julius five sets. The FBI later seized the sixth set. It had been marked as an exhibit in the case.

Ruth testified that she was present when Julius came to her house on June 4.

KILSHEIMER Now, what took place at that time?
RUTH GREENGLASS He gave my husband a package wrapped in brown paper and he said it was $4,000, that there would be more money available in Mexico when we got there.
KILSHEIMER What did you do with the $4,000?
RUTH GREENGLASS We put it in the chimney in our fireplace and afterwards my husband gave it to my brother-in-law.
KILSHEIMER Did Rosenberg on that occasion tell you when you would have to leave the country?
RUTH GREENGLASS He told us that we would have to leave sooner than expected, that they were closing in and getting ready to make an arrest.

The judge wanted to know whether Julius revealed any plan of his own to leave the country.

RUTH GREENGLASS I asked him what he was doing. He said he was going too, that he would not leave at the same time, and he would meet us in Mexico. We would see him there, and I asked him what Ethel thought about it and he said Ethel didn't like

(127)

the idea of it herself but she realized it was necessary and they were going to go.

Several days later on June 7, Julius came to her house again. Her brief description of the conversation was as vivid as it was incriminating.

> He came and spoke in whispers. He said he thought he was being followed and that he was going to bring $2,000 more but he didn't because he was being extra careful.

After David was arrested by federal officers in the middle of June 1950, Ethel Rosenberg visited Ruth. The conversation she related was not only an admission of guilt by the Rosenbergs, but involved a separate crime of suborning perjury.

> Ethel came with pie for me and gifts for my son, and after we talked in my mother-in-law's house for a few minutes she asked me would I please go out and walk with her. We walked around the block several times and she said her counsel advised her to see me personally and get assurances from me that David would not talk. She said it would only be a matter of a couple of years, and in the long run we would be better off; that Julius had been picked up by the FBI for questioning. He said he was innocent and that he had been released; that she had no doubt that he would probably be picked up again. He would continue to say he was innocent. That if David said he was innocent and Julius said he was innocent, it would strengthen their position; everybody would stand a better chance, and she said do you think it is a dirty shame for David to take the blame and sit for two?

Before I examine the way in which defense counsel battered at Ruth, let me move up Ethel Rosenberg's reply to this last conversation, which she made much later when she took the stand. It will present the sharp contrast of the two versions and give an immediate perspective of the testimony which even the jury didn't have.

———>*<———

E. H. BLOCH Did you have any such conversation with your sister-in-law, Ruth?

ETHEL ROSENBERG Well, I had a conversation with her, but it wasn't like that at all.

E. H. BLOCH Tell us what happened?

ETHEL ROSENBERG Well, Ruth and my mother had gone to visit David in jail. I waited for them at my mother's house. When they returned, they were worn out. My mother suggested we all have a bite. Then Ruth said she would take the baby home.

She put her in a carriage and I walked with her. She said it was beautiful out, so we went around the block.

She described the conversation while Ruth was wheeling the baby carriage, and Ethel walked beside her.

"Look, Ruth, I would like to know something. Are you and Davey really mixed up in this horrible mess?"

Ruth hesitated to reply and was uncomfortably silent. Ethel made an effort to encourage her: "You know how I feel towards Davey. You know how I always felt towards him and how I have always felt towards you, although I must say that you people haven't always reciprocated, especially this last year.

"However, that is beside the point. I want you to know that even if you and Davey did do this, my attitude towards you and my feelings towards you won't change. I will stand by and help in any way that I possibly can. But I am his sister and I have a right to know."

Ruth flared up. "What are you asking such silly questions for? He is not guilty and, of course, I am not guilty, and we have hired a lawyer and we are going to fight this because we are not guilty. Did you think we were?"

"I really don't know what to think any more. There have been reports in the newspapers about confessions, and much as I always believed in Davey, I really began to wonder. I had to hear it from your own lips."

"Well, now you have heard it and it is the truth. Neither of us is guilty."

Ethel turned sympathetic. "How are you making out as to living expenses? Have you enough money?"

"I have been asking my relatives and I am trying to raise money. It is pretty hard." She looked at Ethel as if seeking help without saying so. Ethel replied to the unasked question.

"Look, Ruthie, I don't know what I would give to be able to say that I have some money that I can give you. I wish I could do that, but I really can't at the moment. You know how it is. We are living from hand to mouth and owe money. However, if I can think of anyone that might possibly lend me some money for you, you can be sure I will do whatever I can."

When they reached East Houston Street, where Ethel would take a bus home, she put her arm around Ruth and kissed her. Ruth remained rigid and didn't return the kiss. She mumbled, "Good-bye," turned on her heels and left abruptly. Ethel left rejected. She gazed after Ruth and slowly walked away.

Bloch resumed his questioning of Ethel Rosenberg.

E. H. BLOCH   That was the last talk you had with your sister-in-law?
ETHEL ROSENBERG   That is right.

COURT Did you want David to confess or deny his guilt?

ETHEL ROSENBERG I wanted him to tell the truth, whatever it was.

COURT Even if it implicated him?

ETHEL ROSENBERG That is right.

COURT Then what do you mean by standing by him?

ETHEL ROSENBERG Well, I wouldn't love him any less.

Which story would the jury believe: Ruth Greenglass' that Ethel appealed to her to keep David silent and save all of them, even if he went to jail for a year or two, or Ethel Rosenberg's that she wanted to know whether David and Ruth were really involved in espionage?

CHAPTER 13

Cross-examining Ruth Greenglass was a formidable task. Her testimony was lighted with detail which made it stand out in factual relief. Also, there was corroborating objective evidence framing her story with reality: moneys received which found their way into banks; passport photos marked as exhibits; brown wrapper with tape on it, in which the $4,000 was delivered (the money finding its way into the lawyer's hands as fees).

Above all, there was the truth, not challenged even by the Rosenbergs, that David Greenglass had stolen highly classified material from Los Alamos and delivered it to Russian agents; and the truth that Ruth Greenglass, though supposedly unhappy with her role, had assisted in effectuating her husband's espionage activities. The Rosenbergs were so close to the Greenglasses, in blood and family ties, in business relationships and in ideological activities, that the confessions which entwined the Rosenbergs with them had verisimilitude.

However, there were two areas of cross-examination which were bound to be productive. One was the conceded venality of the witness. She had outlined her participation in as foul a deed against her country as could be imagined. The second was the probability that she was serving the prosecution's cause in consideration of not being indicted or punished.

It was one thing to say that the government was willing to reward a witness for telling the truth, which otherwise might be unprovable. It was another to say that the reward was for telling lies which would enmesh others the government was eager to punish. The defense might easily establish the first, and proceeded to do so. But could it make the jury believe that David and Ruth were being "bought" to concoct a false story about two innocent people, Julius and Ethel Rosenberg?

The older Bloch, Alexander, undertook the task. He took the easiest and most effective road first.

A. BLOCH Do you think that acting as a spy against the interests of the United States is a crime?

RUTH GREENGLASS I think it is wrong.

A. BLOCH When did you first realize that it was wrong?

RUTH GREENGLASS I have always known it was wrong.

When she brought the information to Rosenberg she "didn't think it was right" to do so. She thought the FBI was after someone more important than her husband. This suggested to the cross-examiner that she might have sought escape for her husband and herself by pointing to someone else. But she parried such a question with a surprising statement.

> I told my husband in 1946 that I wanted to go to the FBI with the story. However, there had been nothing happening, everything was very peaceful, and we thought perhaps it would die down and the thing would never come to light, so we did nothing about it.

However, she never freed herself of fear and torment.

RUTH GREENGLASS It's not easy to live with something that you know is wrong.

A. BLOCH Well, when you say you know it's wrong, was it wrong in your opinion morally?

RUTH GREENGLASS I felt that we had taken something into our hands that we were not equipped to handle with, we were tampering with things that were beyond our knowledge and understanding, yes.

A. BLOCH And you realized that in 1946?

RUTH GREENGLASS I realized it in 1944.

A. BLOCH And you kept on doing what you said you did?

RUTH GREENGLASS I have told the truth about what I did.

When she painted herself in a sympathetic role by declaring that she didn't want David to spy "but my husband felt he wanted to and as his wife I went along with him," Bloch threw the first jibe at her about taking and keeping the money paid for his treachery. She fought back:

> Julius was my relative. He said to "go to Albuquerque and I am giving you this to meet your expenses," and I accepted it in the same light.

He pinned her down, and she characterized the payments in as ugly a phrase as Bloch would have wished:

A. BLOCH   And you knew that that $500 was paid to your husband by Gold?

RUTH GREENGLASS   From Julius.

A. BLOCH   And you knew that that was compensation for spy work?

RUTH GREENGLASS   No, I was under the impression at first that Julius said it was for scientific purposes we were sharing the information, but when my husband got the $500, I realized it was just C.O.D.; he gave the information and he got paid.

Then Bloch tried one of the oldest devices of cross-examination, made famous by the great trial lawyer Max D. Steuer. He was defending the owners of a factory who were charged with murder, because they had locked the doors to prevent malingering trips by employees. A fire broke out and the helpless workers were trapped. Many perished. One of the girls who had escaped the fiery furnace by jumping out of the window into a net was the chief witness for the prosecution.

She told a damning story of the defendants' greed, the warnings to them not to violate safety standards, their deliberate locking of the doors which were supposed to be free safety exits in the event of an emergency, and the terrified screams of the young girls, their clothes and hair ablaze, as they beat their fists against the closed fire doors until they became crumbling pyres. The jurors and spectators wept openly as she testified in vivid detail to the horror she had lived through.

The craven defendants were subjected to the barometric pressure of the testimony in the court and the indignation of the public and press outside the court. Steuer observed something about the witness. She was letter-perfect. There was no faltering, no search for words to describe the agonizing event. Although uneducated, her words flowed easily and in precise, logical sequence. Her descriptions had just the right color to create a feeling of outrage. Even more remarkable, her testimony adroitly filled in the gaps necessary to meet the legal tests of criminal responsibility. Every factual requirement, which Steuer's research showed was necessary, but unlikely to be supplied, was being met with what appeared to be accidental artlessness. It was all too pat.

He decided to take an enormous risk—perhaps it wasn't a risk at all, since his clients were doomed anyway. He asked the witness to repeat her testimony from the beginning. Ordinarily, this is a cardinal sin in cross-examination. The lawyer who takes the witness over the ground she has covered, in the hope of finding a crevice, usually winds up emphasizing the harmful testimony and still groping for an opening.

So Steuer's invitation to the witness to repeat her deadly testimony violated a basic rule of cross-examination. But genius determines the exception to every rule. While his assistants furiously scribbled her testimony, Steuer, an immobile figure soaking up every word, relied on his memory. When she was through, he astonished everyone by asking her whether she would mind telling the court and jury once more what had happened. Objections to "repetition and waste of time" were overruled. The court, too, had noticed the identical phrasing in identical sequence, as if a phonograph record of her first testimony was being replayed.

By this time, the witness was becoming flustered. Her memorization broke and she paused. Steuer helpfully supplied the next words. She adopted them as if a rope had been thrown to her in stormy waters and she could pull herself to the conclusion. At another juncture, she omitted a phrase. Steuer apologized for interrupting her and asked whether she had not left out certain words which he supplied. She looked up at the ceiling, her lips moving in backward recital, and then acknowledged the omission, by inserting the proffered words in her continued recital.

The tears in the jury's eyes were displaced by indignation. Steuer filled out the contours of the hoax by probing into the number of hours the witness had spent in the District Attorney's office; whether she had reviewed her testimony with him; whether he had made any suggestions to her; whether they were written out; whether she had recited "the facts" to him many times; whether she had gone over them at home; and so on. It did not matter what her answers were. Her working-girl language when on her own, as contrasted with her impeccably phrased testimony, made the transplant transparent. The defendants were acquitted.

Inspired by this example, Alexander Bloch asked Ruth to repeat her testimony of her conversation with Julius when he suggested that David steal secrets. She was surprised. He urged her on. "Go ahead, start right from the beginning." She complied. At one point, she stopped and asked, "Do you want that too?" He replied, "Give us the whole conversation."

When she finished, he asked her whether she had memorized the statement she had just made.

RUTH GREENGLASS I never memorized it. I knew it too well.

A. BLOCH Well, are you aware of the fact that the narrative you just gave us is almost identical with the verbiage used on your first giving of the testimony of that particular occurrence?

RUTH GREENGLASS No, I am not.

SAYPOL Just a moment. I appreciate so expert an opinion as to the accuracy of the witness's recollection, but I object to the form of the question.

COURT Your objection is sustained. I don't know exactly what the point is. If the witness had left out something, Mr. Bloch would say that the witness had left out something. Mr. Bloch would say that the witness didn't repeat the story accurately. And the witness repeats it accurately, and apparently that isn't any good.

A. BLOCH What I am referring to is the verbatim repetition of the verbiage.

COURT Well, we don't know that it is verbatim. We haven't had the record yet.

A. BLOCH Well, it is a matter, of course, of comparing the testimony after we get it written up.

COURT Mr. Bloch asked the question; the witness has answered.

A. BLOCH Very well.

I set forth a comparison of her testimony, given on direct examination and as repeated:

Direct Examination

KILSHEIMER Now will you state as best you can recollect, the substance of that conversation which you had with the Rosenbergs on that occasion?

RUTH GREENGLASS Yes. Julius said that I might have noticed that for some time he and Ethel had not been actively pursuing any Communist Party activities, that they didn't buy the *Daily Worker* at the usual newsstand; that for two years he had been trying to get in touch with people who would assist him to be able to help the Russian people more directly other than just his membership in the Communist Party, and he went on to tell me that he knew that David was working on the atomic bomb and I asked him how he knew, because I had received an affidavit from the War Department telling me—I said that I had received an affidavit from the War Department telling me that my mail to David would be censored and his to me, because he was working on a top secret project. And he said—I wanted to know how he knew what David was doing. He said that his friends had told him that David was working on the atomic bomb, and he went on to tell me that the atomic bomb was the most destructive weapon used so far, that it had dangerous radiation effects, that the United States and Britain were working on this project jointly and that he felt that the information should be shared with Russia, who was our ally at the time, because if all nations had the information then one nation couldn't use the bomb as a threat against another. He said that he wanted me to tell my husband, David, that he should give information to Julius to be passed on to the Russians.

KILSHEIMER And what information did he ask you to obtain from your husband if he should be willing to do it?

(135)

RUTH GREENGLASS He wanted a physical description of the project at Los Alamos, the approximate number of people employed, the names of some of the scientists who were working there—something about whether the place was camouflaged, what the security measures were and the relative distance of the project to Albuquerque and Santa Fe.

Cross-Examination

Julius said that I might have noticed that he and Ethel had not been openly participating in any Communist Party activities; that they hadn't been buying the *Daily Worker* at their usual stand. He told me that David was working on the atomic bomb; that the atomic bomb had dangerous radiation effects; that it was the most destructive weapon used to date; that Britain was working with the United States on this project; that the information had not been shared with the Soviet Union; that he felt that for scientific purposes it should be shared with the Soviet Union, so that one nation couldn't use the weapon as a threat against another; and he told me the type of information he wanted me to get from David; that David would consent to pass it on—do you want that, too?

A. BLOCH Give us the whole conversation.

RUTH GREENGLASS All right. He said that he wanted a physical description of the project at Los Alamos and the approximate number of people working there; who the prominent scientists were; how the place was camouflaged; what the security measures taken were; what David's work in particular was and the distance of the project from Santa Fe and Albuquerque.

The point was not whether she repeated the same substance, but whether her recital revealed a carefully rehearsed and memorized speech. This had to be decided by the jury.

In his charge to the jury, the judge made amends for his intrusion, by stressing the jury's sole right to decide the truthfulness of a witness.

> The facts presented by the defendants and those by the prosecution are completely irreconcilable. You are the sole and exclusive judge of the facts.

He even emphasized the negative:

> No matter how careful a judge may be to avoid it, there is always the possibility that the jury may get an impression that the judge has some opinion concerning guilt or innocence, or that some witness is more credible than another. If you have formed any such impression, you must put it out of your mind and utterly disregard it. And so I tell you again, you are the exclusive judges of the facts.

1. Julius Rosenberg with guard.

2. Julius and Ethel Rosenberg heading for prison following their conviction.

3. Emanuel Bloch, defense attorney for the Rosenbergs, with an aide after hearing of his clients' death in the electric chair.

. Alexander Bloch, father of Eman-
el Bloch, leaving Federal Court
House.

5. Federal Judge Irving R. Kaufman before setting execution date for the Rosenbergs.

6. Prosecuting attorney Irving H. Saypol.

7. David Greenglass being escorted from Federal Court after pleading guilty.

8. Ruth Greenglass in anteroom in Federal Court House.

9. Elizabeth T. Bentley, star witness in the congressional Red spy hearing, 1948.

10. David Greenglass, right, Harry Gold, left, testifying before Senate Internal Security Subcommittee, 1956.

Nevertheless, the judge's attack on Bloch for his Steuer stratagem was later cited on appeal as an instance of the judge's bias. We shall see how the upper courts dealt with it.

Bloch could have, as Steuer did, followed with a piercing examination of how many hours or days Ruth had spent with the government lawyers; how many times she had reviewed her testimony; had she ever been asked the precise questions which were put to her on the stand; when was the last time those questions were put to her; did she write out her answers. Every answer she might have made would give birth to a new series of questions.

However, Bloch, in summation, did stress the similarity in the two versions.

The elder Bloch turned to another attack. Since Ruth Greenglass testified that she and David had decided from the very beginning to tell the truth, why had they retained a lawyer to defend them? Why had they paid him a fee of $4,000 which had been delivered to them in brown paper? During the skirmish, the judge again interfered, but this time Bloch stood his ground and won.

A. BLOCH   Well, at the time you told him to go to Mr. Rogge, you say you had made up your mind and your husband had made up his mind to tell the truth; is that the idea?

RUTH GREENGLASS   I had always intended to tell the truth.

A. BLOCH   Yes, that means to confess?

COURT   It means to tell the truth.

A. BLOCH   That means to confess?

COURT   That means to tell the truth.

A. BLOCH   Yes, but I want the witness to answer, not your Honor. I know what is in your Honor's mind. I want to know what is in the witness' mind, and the jury wants to know what is in the witness' mind.

COURT   Can you answer that question?

RUTH GREENGLASS   Well, I have confessed everything I know about it.

COURT   Very well.

A. BLOCH   And you nevertheless told your brother-in-law to pay Mr. Rogge $4,000?

RUTH GREENGLASS   Yes.

Ruth denied telling newspapermen that she and David were innocent. She insisted she told her attorney, O. John Rogge, the truth as she had testified on the stand.

It wasn't much of a point. Even if Ruth and David had thought of defending themselves, and changed their minds because they recognized the futility of it all, it would not be a fatal inconsistency. Many a defendant has planned to put the prosecution to its proof, and then thought better of it. Of course, they hope to gain consideration for "coming clean" and helping the government prove its case.

This raises a moral and ethical question. In some European countries such a "deal," even if only implied, is deemed improper. In Switzerland, for example, there can be no consideration for a criminal who confesses. He must be prosecuted, and he cannot buy a lighter punishment by co-operating with the government. The Howard Hughes-Clifford Irving case was an illustration. The American prosecutors were willing to give Mrs. Irving consideration if her husband confessed the hoax and told all. But the Swiss authorities were intransigent. She had forged a signature on a check, withdrawing funds paid by the publisher McGraw-Hill for the Hughes biography and she must be prosecuted.

What is the rationale of the American practice? It is that serious crimes may go unpunished unless evidence can be obtained from some of the perpetrators. It is deemed more important to convict the higher-ups in dope traffic or in kidnapping and gang murders than it is to be sensitive to the fact that those who make possible catching and convicting such criminals will receive some reward in the form of lighter punishment.

The need for internal evidence arises partly from our solicitous rules for defendants. In order to protect the accused citizen, the law requires corroborating evidence in certain crimes. If only one witness testifies, it is not enough, and the defendant walks out free, though guilty.

We are caught in the vise of strong civil liberty provisions to protect the accused individual, and the public interest to put vicious criminals behind bars, so that they will not continue to prey on innocent people.

Other nations do not face this dilemma in such acute form. They do not have so many safeguards for the accused, and, therefore, do not find it so difficult to convict. They haven't as much need to encourage confession. Having given less moral consideration to protecting a defendant, they do not have to sacrifice moral considerations in inducing a defendant to turn "state's evidence." So, as often is the case, the matter is not one of honor against dishonor, but rather a choice between two policies, depending on which principle is more in the public interest.

Even before the case progressed further, it was evident that Ruth Greenglass had been spared indictment, because her husband confessed. Later, this was openly acknowledged by the prosecutor, and there was frank talk that if we want to induce criminals to assist the prosecution by confessing the truth, then we must give them "a pat on the back" for doing so. Otherwise, this source of effective prosecution would dry up.

All this did not deprive the Rosenbergs from claiming that this was not a case of honest confession, but of a reward for concocting a falsehood, to railroad them. It was for the jury to decide whether the government had stooped to such chicanery. There was much more testimony to come, upon which that judgment could be made. But Ruth Greenglass

(138)

kept the balance tipping in favor of the government. Time and again, she frustrated Bloch by insisting that she was telling the truth and it was not tarnished by any selfish consideration. Her most emphatic answer came when Bloch asked:

... today you entertain a hope that your husband is going to be treated by the Court with lenience?

RUTH GREENGLASS I am telling the story because it's true and I hope and pray that my husband will come home. That is what I want, but I am not telling the story for that, no.

A. BLOCH Did Julius tell you not to jot all this information down in writing?

RUTH GREENGLASS That's right.

A. BLOCH Did Greenglass tell you that you were to memorize that information?

RUTH GREENGLASS He did.

A. BLOCH And to transmit it to Rosenberg?

RUTH GREENGLASS Yes.

A. BLOCH Did you ask him why you weren't to take it down in writing?

RUTH GREENGLASS I didn't have to ask him. Julius had instructed me not to.

A. BLOCH Well, did you realize then that there was danger in your taking this thing down in writing, all these items down in writing?

RUTH GREENGLASS I think I was too young to realize the whole thing fully at the time.

A. BLOCH How old are you?

RUTH GREENGLASS Twenty-six.

A. BLOCH And at that time you were approximately twenty?

RUTH GREENGLASS That's right.

A. BLOCH So you now say, because you were young you didn't realize the danger?

RUTH GREENGLASS No, I don't say that. I say I don't think I understood the significance of what was happening.

A. BLOCH Oh, you didn't, and the first time you began to realize it was when?

RUTH GREENGLASS I think I realized it most clearly after Gold left and then again after the bomb had been dropped on Hiroshima.

Alexander Bloch asked the court's permission to approach the bench. He whispered to the judge, who then declared a recess until the next morning at 10:30 A.M.

Counsel gets exhausted toward the end of the day. He shares the strain with the witness. He wins or loses ground with each exchange. The prosecutor harasses him with objections. Sometimes, he must stand up to rebukes from the judge. His associates pull his coattails with suggestions. And all the time, he must practice severe self-discipline, lest by any gesture or word he should offend the jury.

So he is in the center of the storm and yet he must be imperturbable. The jury will notice his disappointment or distress, and enlarge its meaning. One of the gifts of a good trial lawyer is to act as if he hadn't been touched when he receives a painful blow from the witness and proceed on in the even flow of verbal exchange.

The elder Bloch must have been tired and asked for the adjournment. But there is no rest for the advocate—unless he recoups his energy at the expense of his duty. Every evening, he must plan more cross-examination; review that day's stenographic minutes, which are delivered to him late at night, and having mastered them, try to utilize them the next day to contradict the witness' testimony with what he said only the preceding day. What a triumph it is for a cross-examiner to have the witness concede that he doesn't remember what he testified to twenty-four hours earlier, when he is peddling to the jury the accuracy of events years before.

It is difficult for counsel to sleep. He is enacting in his mind what will happen, and the excitement of the imagined event grips him.

Perhaps the most wearing of all are disputes among the lawyers about strategy, and the nervous intervention of the clients.

Certainly, the Blochs, father and son, must have been shocked by the testimony given by Elitcher and the Greenglasses. No matter how fearful they were that David and Ruth would turn against their clients, the evidence pouring into the record was worse than they could have anticipated. They were faced with the delicate task of asking Ethel and Julius, "What can you tell us about these terrible details?" It became more evident as time went on that Julius would have to take the stand to overcome the impact of the Greenglass confession.

So late at night, in the prison cell underneath the courtroom, the defendants were subjected to cross-examination by their own lawyers. Based on their answers, the Blochs continued to attack David and Ruth while on the stand. Unfortunately, for the defense, the leads they gave to the Blochs did not work out too well. The Greenglasses stuck to their stories.

This increased the conflict among defense counsel about what attacks to launch and when to stop. It was all the more tense because the lawyers who differed were father and son. Deference and respect for seniority were increased by paternal authority. It was obvious that Alexander Bloch, the father, took a different tack from Emanuel Bloch, the son. Toward the end, the son's emotional involvement became so intense and even fanatical that it impinged on their relationship.

As we follow the continuing cross-examination of Ruth Greenglass and the many government witnesses who followed, we can spot the disagreements not only between the Blochs, but between them and

Kuntz and Phillips, counsel for Sobell. Indeed, there was a clash be tween Sobell's lawyers, which was later openly stated in court.

When Ruth Greenglass resumed her testimony the next morning on March 15, 1951, she was asked about the passport photographs she had taken at Julius' direction in preparation for flight. She insisted that David and she had decided not to run away.

A. BLOCH Nevertheless, on the 28th of May 1950, you took passport photographs?

RUTH GREENGLASS That is right.

A. BLOCH Six copies of them, is that right?

RUTH GREENGLASS Yes.

A. BLOCH And at the time these photographs were taken you knew that you were not leaving the country?

RUTH GREENGLASS That is right.

A. BLOCH Did you talk it over with your husband as to the reason you were taking photographs when you did not intend to leave the country?

RUTH GREENGLASS Yes.

A. BLOCH Was it to deceive Rosenberg?

RUTH GREENGLASS Yes.

A. BLOCH And make him believe that you were going away?

RUTH GREENGLASS That is right.

A. BLOCH Did you have in mind that you were going to get additional money?

RUTH GREENGLASS No, it wasn't a question of giving him the pictures for the money.

A. BLOCH Well, what was the object of deceiving him?

RUTH GREENGLASS Because we didn't want Mr. Rosenberg to think we were going to stay in the country, because we were harmful to him.

A. BLOCH Didn't you have in mind at all the $4,000, or the $5,000 that you were to receive?

RUTH GREENGLASS That was not the purpose of taking the pictures.

A. BLOCH You took the $4,000?

RUTH GREENGLASS Yes, he gave it to my husband.

A. BLOCH You were there at the time, weren't you?

RUTH GREENGLASS I was in the house.

To make the point that David and Ruth were greedy, Bloch was having her repeat the deadly story of the receipt of $4,000 from Julius Rosenberg. A cross-examiner must determine in the scales of persuasion whether the concession he gets is worth the price he pays.

An even worse imbalance resulted from Bloch's question why she had not deposited the $4,000 in the bank, instead of giving it to Abel, her brother-in-law, who turned it over as a fee to Rogge. She replied, "It would seem very odd for us to deposit $4,000 at one time."

(141)

In a lengthy examination on the business relationships among the Rosenbergs and the Greenglasses, including Bernard Greenglass, Bloch established disputes among them concerning the losses they were suffering. Ruth insisted that while she was angry, she did not bear resentment against Ethel and Julius then or now.

At this point, Alexander Bloch turned over continued cross-examination to his son, E. H. Bloch.

He showed her the cut piece of the Jell-O box in evidence and she testified that there was a thin red line around the instruction, not a green line, which represents lime flavor.

The questioning led to her assurance that the cardboard piece given to her by Julius was "in my wallet at all times, and I saw the red line."

When he asked whether she had read the "instructions" on the Jell-O box, and she said she hadn't, the court stepped in "to clear matters up" by questions which revivified the damaging testimony:

COURT   Now, let me ask you this; what was important to you?

RUTH GREENGLASS   I had the Jell-O box side to identify myself to whoever was to come out with the other matching half. It wasn't necessary for me to memorize what was written on the instruction. I memorized the instructions Mr. Rosenberg gave me and the information my husband gave in return. This had nothing to do with it.

E. H. BLOCH   Maybe you didn't understand my question.

RUTH GREENGLASS   Oh, I did.

E. H. BLOCH   All I wanted to know is whether or not you noticed what was written or printed on this side, that you said you got.

RUTH GREENGLASS   Sufficiently to know that it was the instruction side, but not the other side, with the picture of the little girl on it.

COURT   Excuse me. When the bearer of the other half of that side of the Jell-O box was to come to you, was it your primary purpose in seeing whether the two sides would fit together like a jigsaw puzzle?

RUTH GREENGLASS   Yes.

COURT   Very well.

When Bloch pressed her about the business dispute with the Greenglasses, she blurted out that Julius didn't care about salary, "because he could get $10,000 or $15,000, as a front for his activities."

So for the first time, and as a result of a cross-examination question, there was sworn testimony that the Rosenbergs were using a business as a front for spy activities.

Bloch could not hide the effect of the blow.

E. H. BLOCH   As a front?

RUTH GREENGLASS   That is right.

He partly recovered by establishing that Schein, a legitimate business man, had invested $15,000 in the business. She admitted he was not a front. But she insisted Julius had considered the business a front for espionage.

The cross-examination contest continued, Ruth getting stronger and actually taking the offensive. "Do you want me to tell you what Mr. Rosenberg said?" she challenged Bloch. "No," he replied. "You will have an opportunity to tell, but I would like an answer to that question." Finally, pushed by an impatient court ("We have already got that, let us get on."), Bloch quit. "That is all," he announced. But he changed his mind.

My dad points out just one question which he thinks I overlooked.

The question was whether Julius Rosenberg had told her he couldn't pay the claim she was asserting against him, because he had paid $1,000 to Schein.

RUTH GREENGLASS No, my husband didn't ask for payment on his stock. Julius Rosenberg said that he would bring my husband $6,000 more. That was not coming from the business, Mr. Bloch.

E. H. BLOCH What was not coming from the business?

RUTH GREENGLASS $6,000, that he promised us.

E. H. BLOCH Yes, but I didn't ask you that.

RUTH GREENGLASS Well, it wasn't being paid for the investment.

COURT Who was it coming from?

RUTH GREENGLASS From the Russians, for us to leave the country.

On this incriminatory note, the cross-examiner said he had no more questions and sat down.

Understandably, the prosecutor announced he had no redirect question. And not so understandably, Kuntz, counsel for Sobell, announced, "No cross."

Ruth Greenglass walked off the stand. In retrospect, those who have reviewed the case, and indeed the Appellate Court, agreed that her testimony was an enormous weight in the scale of guilt. Added to that of David's, the defense had its task cut out for it.

The jury had now heard Ethel Rosenberg's brother and his wife confess that they had co-operated in stealing the secret of the atomic bomb, and that they had been inspired, instructed and guided in doing so by the Rosenbergs.

And the government's case had hardly begun.

CHAPTER 14

The next witness was Ruth Greenglass' sister, Dorothy Abel. It was she who was present when Julius Rosenberg visited Ruth Greenglass. Ruth had testified that Julius came to give her espionage instructions, and, therefore, asked her sister to leave the room. Julius later testified that Ruth had invited him to come to the house to ask for advice about David's stealing from the Army. So Julius said it was Ruth who whispered in his ear to tell "the kid" to get out.

Even before the government knew whether Julius would testify and what he would say, it was presenting Dorothy Abel's version of the event. This was calculated to make it impossible for Rosenberg to deny the incident in its entirety, and to force him to give another version if he claimed Ruth was lying. It was a sort of trap play.

Kilsheimer questioned the witness. Quickly, she confirmed Ruth Greenglass' story. It was Rosenberg who said "he wanted to speak to Ruth privately." It was he who asked Dorothy, only sixteen years old at the time, to leave the room. Furthermore, it was Rosenberg who took precautions that she should not overhear the conversation.

> Well, he asked me to take a book with me, and I said all right, I would go into the bedroom; he said no, he wanted me to go into the bathroom and close the door, and I did.

While she was on the stand, the prosecutor tried to establish the Rosenbergs' Communistic beliefs.

> I remember a time when the five of us, Ruth, David and Julie and Ethel and I were going out to a show, and Julius and Ethel were comparing our form of government to the form in Russia, and they said that Russia was the ideal form of government, the Russian form of government. That is all.

"You may cross-examine," said Kilsheimer.

E. H. Bloch did not attempt to contradict the witness' testimony on the main point, that it was Rosenberg who wanted to talk privately to Ruth Greenglass and not vice versa. He limited himself to the Communist issue.

> . . . did the Rosenbergs say anything specifically about the United States form of Government?

DOROTHY ABEL   They didn't think that it compared at all with the Russian form of Government.

E. H. BLOCH   Can you tell us specifically what criticism they made of the United States form of Government?

DOROTHY ABEL   Well, they said that it was a capitalistic form of Government.

The court attempted to open the door to more testimony on this point, but when challenged, withdrew.

COURT   Was there discussion of the relative merits of the capitalistic form of Government as against Communistic form?

E. H. BLOCH   Pardon me, if the Court please, with the utmost deference and respect to the Court, I would like to register my objection to the Court's questions at this time.

COURT   I will withdraw the question. Go ahead.

Bloch also withdrew and the witness was excused.

She was followed by Louis Abel, her husband and brother-in-law of Ruth Greenglass. He merely supplied the physical link between Julius' alleged delivery of $4,000 and the final destination of the money. A week before the FBI took David Greenglass into custody, he called Abel and told him to hold the $4,000, still wrapped in the brown paper. Abel hid the money inside a hassock in his home.

After Greenglass was arrested, he sent word to Abel to retain Rogge as his lawyer. Rogge visited him in jail and returned with instruction to have Abel deliver the $4,000 to him. This was done.

In the course of this brief testimony, the prosecutor showed Abel the brown paper (which was an exhibit) with the tape on it. He too identified it as the original wrapper around the money.

There was only a feint at cross-examination.

E. H. BLOCH   Now was it your intention at the time you put this package in this hassock to put it in a place where nobody would know where it was?

LOUIS ABEL   Of course.

E. H. BLOCH   I think that is all.

Even if David and Ruth Greenglass told the truth, they were despised witnesses. First, because they confessed to being spies, and second,

(146)

because they were testifying against their own close family. The prosecutor, to the very end of the trial, tried to make a virtue of this. He insisted that they didn't add to their sins by committing perjury, as the Rosenbergs were doing. But the fact remained that the Greenglasses had obtained immunity for Ruth, and a hope for lenient punishment for David. So they had a selfish motive in "peaching" on the Rosenbergs. The prosecutor's picture of them as noble penitents was tarnished by the fact that they had already obtained some benefits from their contrition, and as their counsel later openly contended, felt they were entitled to more. The prosecutor's claim that the Greenglasses were not committing perjury had to include the fact that they still expected consideration for this negative virtue.

Also, there was something inhuman, even if legally proper, in a brother destroying his sister. Later, when Julius and Ethel Rosenberg testified, they cried out that they did not believe that one member of a family should destroy another when he is down. These answers burned with outrage, and if anything touched the jury, this must have.

The law cannot condone withholding of guilty information except in special exempted cases such as a priest, doctor or lawyer. But society certainly has no admiration for the mother who turns in her son or a David Greenglass who sends his sister to the electric chair. Human loyalties are admired even when they conflict with legal duty. This explains the public empathy with criminals in such motion pictures as Bonnie and Clyde and The Godfather. The very use of "Family" or the "Cosa Nostra" depicts the inner ties, which evoke sympathy and even a rooting interest by the general public.

So Ruth and David Greenglass, and the Abels, who thrust the sword of justice through the breasts of their own, were subject to scorn.

This was particularly so because they did not do so reluctantly. What is evident from a study of the record is the eagerness with which David and Ruth Greenglass involved the Rosenbergs. David did not spare his sister in the slightest. When asked who was present during some incriminating incident, he never had a doubtful memory. He placed his sister, Ethel, in the room. At times, he and Ruth volunteered information pillorying Ethel Rosenberg. One senses when a witness is required by his oath to make an unpleasant answer. The Greenglasses gloried in doing so.

The jury could interpret this in two ways. One, that the Greenglasses were furious with the Rosenbergs for having drawn them into an enterprise which destroyed them and their children. They were not going to be the sacrificial goats, while those who were the masterminds of the scheme escaped. Two, that the only hope for lesser punishment was to serve the government to the hilt, and thus earn its gratitude.

Neither did the Rosenbergs any good. But the second at least permitted them to claim that the Greenglasses had lied to save their skins.

In either event, one can understand the Blochs, father and son, telling the jury in sputtering indignation during summation that there were no lower animals in the world than the Greenglasses. The lawyers were beside themselves with rage at the Greenglasses. And yet, the jury may have considered their almost apoplectic anger as nothing more than a natural reaction to a betrayal, profound, but true.

If the Greenglasses were the most despised witnesses in the trial, surely the next witness, Harry Gold, was the most pitiful.

CHAPTER 15

Harry Gold was brought from jail, where he was beginning a thirty-year sentence after confessing espionage. Klaus Fuchs had revealed that he had given secrets to him. Having no way out, either physically or legally, he gave up the ghost. He told the FBI, who swooped down on him at the Philadelphia hospital, where he was working at the heart station, that he had been a Russian agent almost all his adult life. He was indicted. He could not defend himself. He admitted everything. A federal court sentenced him to a living death for the equivalent of his remaining years. Being forty years old, his chance of getting out of jail, even with probationary allowance for good behavior, was slim. At best, he was doomed to spend the vigorous years of his life in a cell.

The pity of it all was the waste of an intelligent man's life in a desultory career in pursuit of some invisible and murky ideal.

At the age of fourteen, he came to the United States with his parents from Berne, Switzerland, where he was born. Eight years later, he became a United States citizen on his father's papers. His seventy-five-year-old father, a cabinetmaker, was still living. One can imagine his anguish, similar to that of Rosenberg's father, at his son's betrayal of the adopted country they loved. What was happening to these sons of loyal parents?

Certainly, it was not lack of education. Harry Gold graduated from public school in Philadelphia and South Philadelphia High School. Then he attended Drexel Institute of Technology at night, and received a diploma in chemical engineering in June 1936.

Thereafter, he went to Xavier University in Cincinnati, Ohio, and obtained a degree of Bachelor of Science, *summa cum laude*.

He did not stop his studies. In 1936, he took a number of specialized courses relating to the chemical field. In addition, he took a course in practical psychology. All this equipment he placed in the service of another nation he had never seen and at the risk of his life. He talked freely on the stand, but nothing he said cast light on the mystery of his choice of occupation as a Russian spy courier. It would be an interesting study in itself to find out how and why this had come about. But we are limited to the revelations at and surrounding the trial.

Gold dealt directly with Anatoli Yakovlev, the chief of the spy network. As befitted Yakovlev's high rank, he was sheltered by an official position with the Russian delegation to the United Nations. Gold may have been the only American spy to see and talk to Yakovlev. As he explained on the stand, the system called for no contact among the agents, and particularly with the chief, Yakovlev. Gold had given fifteen years' service to the Russians and he was the one entrusted to receive the atom bomb secrets from Fuchs and Greenglass and report directly to Yakovlev.

When the spy ring was cracked, Yakovlev was indicted, along with the Rosenbergs and Greenglasses, but the Russian Embassy had no difficulty in speeding him out of the country. He was the absent defendant.

Gold was in a position to tell the whole story from the inside. His revelations were not based upon some discovery of documents in some archive. They were a living documentary. The jury was in for a dramatic treat.

Gold was an extremely impressive witness for the government. No one could claim that he had an interest in the outcome. Unlike the Greenglasses, he was not awaiting sentence. It could not be argued that he was concocting testimony to receive lighter punishment. Justice had finished with him. It had imposed a severe sentence in a federal penitentiary upon him. He had risen from the tomb, shackled and hopeless, to repeat his confession and fill out its contours. There was no apparent reason to disbelieve him.

He fitted the rule in some other countries which requires that a witness who participated in the crime and confessed may not testify against his collaborators while awaiting sentence. Only after he has received his punishment and his self-interest is ended, may he condemn them. Gold was such a disinterested witness.

His appearance on the stand was as ominous for the Rosenbergs as it was fascinating to the public. He could and did give an authentic description of Russian espionage activities. For the first time, there was revealed the methods and actions of what was reputed to be the most effective spy organization in history.

Having served the Russians faithfully, Gold was instructed to meet Anatoli Yakovlev for the first time in March 1944. Even then he didn't know his name. He was to meet "John." The place was in front of a bar entrance of a Childs Restaurant at 34th Street, near Eighth Avenue, in New York City. Thereafter, Gold served directly under "John" for almost three years until 1946.

The prosecutor, Myles Lane, in this instance, showed Gold a photograph of "John," and he identified him as Yakovlev. He added a verbal description. It was a perfect picture of a top Russian spy:

GOLD Yakovlev was about twenty-eight or thirty years of age at the time I knew him. He was about 5 feet 9 inches in height; had a medium build, which tended toward the slender. He had dark or dark brown hair and there was a lock of it that kept falling over his forehead, which he would brush back continually. He had a rather long nose and a fair complexion, dark eyes. He walked with somewhat of a stoop.

Could Hollywood do better?

It is rare that secret, melodramatic personages look their part. Indeed, it is one of their requirements that they should not. For years, the English looked for the leader of the Irgun, an underground revolutionary leader in Israel, equivalent to the IRA in Ireland. His exploits made those of the Scarlet Pimpernel look pale by comparison. He led his troops in invading military barracks and kidnapping officers; he broke into impenetrable prisons to rescue his men before execution; he blew up a wing of the King David Hotel in Jerusalem despite an army of defenders, and repeatedly performed other feats which would have defied the imagination of the most daring fiction writer. The English put the highest price on his head, in their long empire tradition.

After Israel's independence, he emerged. Indeed, he now heads a political party in the Knesset, and his political competence does not compare with his military exploits. His name is Menachim Beigin.

He had lived in a little house next door to an English police station. He walked about Tel Aviv and later Jerusalem totally unnoticed. I met him later in New York. One of the reasons for his spectacular anonymity then became clear. He looked like a timid clerk in a grocery store. He was short, frail, baldly blondish and had a face which looked like a composite of all of the ordinary men in the world. It was devoid of any suggestion of leadership qualities. His voice was thin and weak. He was the kind of man who would apologize for being in your way, if you pushed him aside. He told me modestly that there were others in his troops more suited than he to command, but that he had been chosen because of his harmless appearance. Nature had provided him with the best camouflage.

Yakovlev, on the other hand, was a prototype of a Russian spy. His protective covering was superb secrecy technique and the immunity of the Russian consulate.

Yakovlev's furtive demeanor, an occupational trait, would change to military barking at the slightest disobedience. He was either quietly appreciative or explosively displeased. Gold's story showed him in all these moods.

(151)

The Blochs and Kuntz were flabbergasted by his revelations. They fought bitterly to limit his testimony. The judge gave them no comfort. The result was the angriest exchanges of the trial.

When Gold told of his first conversation with Yakovlev, A. Bloch objected because it took place two months before the period mentioned in the indictment.

COURT   I suggest that you read the opinion of this Circuit Court in United States v. Dennis, et al. which deals with that subject directly.

Your objection is overruled.

The very next question brought a more vigorous outburst. Gold testified that as a result of his meeting with Yakovlev, "I continued in my espionage work for the Soviet Union," reporting directly to Yakovlev.

This time, the son, E. H. Bloch, protested:

E. H. BLOCH   I am sorry but I have got to get up to object to this. I think it is damaging evidence, and I think it is incompetent.

The jury heard Bloch's characterization of Gold's testimony as "damaging evidence." He should have taken the course in practical psychology, which Gold had attended. A lawyer should only make such an admission to a judge out of the presence of the jury (he can ask for a conference at the bench), when he is trying to impress upon him the prejudicial nature of the testimony which might make its admission reversible error. Even then it should be done rarely because the judge, too, should not learn counsel's distress, in the event he feels he must rule against him.

A lawyer's face is a mirror into which the jury looks for a reflection of the impact of the testimony. A triumphant demeanor may be discounted as acting, and when too often indulged in, mugging. But distress is genuine and heightens the jury's evaluation of the damage done. Even assistants must be warned against registering horror at some development. The jury watches them too.

Therefore, it was unwise for Bloch to exclaim that Gold's testimony "is damaging." He could have made his objection without describing it. He should only characterize the testimony when he can say the very opposite. "It is not your Honor, that the testimony is meaningful, but it certainly has no place in this record." In this particular instance, defense counsel's argument should have been that "we are hearing testimony of treachery of the Greenglasses and of Gold, all of whom have confessed. But the evidence offered does not mention our clients, Ethel and Julius Rosenberg. Even if your Honor admits this evidence as background corroboration, the jury should be told it is not pertinent to the guilt or innocence of the Rosenbergs."

This objection would have been legally sound, but in any event it would have kept a flag flying before the jury, "Are the Rosenbergs involved by this testimony?" This was the way to turn the flood of testimony aside, so that it would not touch the Rosenbergs.

The Blochs could not know what was coming, but this was a proper posture for all testimony which did not mention or relate to the Rosenbergs.

As it turned out, and with the benefit of hindsight, Gold's damning story concerned his dealings with Greenglass and Fuchs. Only four times did he mention "Julius"; once his greeting, "I come from Julius"; the second time when Greenglass gave him Rosenberg's telephone number, the third when Greenglass told him that Julius had asked him to seek recruits for espionage, and the fourth when he suggested to Yakovlev that they get in touch with Julius "to get further information."

The danger of Gold's testimony was that unless the jurors were alerted to its limited circumference, they might assume that everything testified to involved the Rosenbergs.

Since the Blochs, like all lawyers, were identified with their clients, their indignant objections combined with the statement that Gold's story was "damaging," created the impression of the Rosenbergs' total involvement, which the prosecution hoped for.

The battle continued on this unfavorable terrain. When Bloch objected to Gold's statement that he had engaged in "Soviet espionage work," because the phrase was too general, the court challenged him:

COURT   Are you saying, Mr. Bloch, that you would rather have this witness tell you how he arrives at the conclusion that he was engaged in espionage work for the Soviet Union? Would you rather have that?

E. H. BLOCH   Are you asking my personal opinion?

COURT   Yes. Is that what you are asking? Do I understand you are asking for that? You don't want the conclusion?

E. H. BLOCH   May I respond to your Honor's question?

COURT   Well, I assume that you may.

E. H. BLOCH   I want to do it.

COURT   Well, then do it.

E. H. BLOCH   I want to differentiate myself as a person, a personality from myself as acting as counsel for a defendant in a criminal case.

COURT   My question doesn't call for that type of reply. My question doesn't call for that.

E. H. BLOCH   I say yes, your Honor. I believe that this defendant is entitled to competent proof on each and every essential allegation of the indictment and that is the reason—

COURT   In the interest of your client you prefer to have this man detail all of his Soviet work, is that right?

E. H. BLOCH   No, I am not going to say—

COURT   Is that what you are asking?

E. H. BLOCH   No. I am asking for a proper foundation to be laid from which the Court and jury may infer that this witness was engaged in what he characterizes—

COURT   Before I go ahead, I want to make certain that I understand what you are asking for. You therefore say that before this witness can give what you call conclusions—that you would like to have from the witness the steps which he took which finally caused him to arrive at the conclusions which he testified to here in court today.

E. H. BLOCH   Now if the Court please, before I respond to that, I want to have an opportunity to consult with co-counsel because there are many considerations involved, one of which may be the shortening—

COURT   Do you want to withhold your objection then for the time being or do you want to have your conference right now?

E. H. BLOCH   May we have it now?

COURT   Go ahead.

After the conference, Bloch announced that he still objected. The court then invited Gold to "give the facts which led you to believe that you were engaged in espionage for the Soviet Union." This time, Kuntz, representing Sobell, objected, thus putting his client into the prejudicial arena upon which the jury was gazing. The judge pressed his point:

> I want the record to be clear that you objected to conclusions, you wanted to have each and every step which led to that conclusion, and in view of that objection and in view of your conference and in view of the statement made by Mr. Bloch on behalf of all counsel, I understand that counsel are asking for the steps which led to the conclusion.

KUNTZ   May I respectfully ask that your Honor's remarks be stricken from the record?

COURT   Oh, no.

Kuntz persisted and set forth his view of the usual procedure when an objection is made to a conclusion without the facts upon which the jury can evaluate the correctness of the conclusion. This infuriated the judge:

COURT   Mr. Kuntz, don't give me any course of instruction as to what is usually done in a courtroom. This is the way I am running this courtroom, Mr. Kuntz, and I think I understand the way a courtroom should be run. I don't care to hear anything further from you. Your objection is noted.

KUNTZ   Thank you.

COURT   Now, Mr. Bloch, I ask you, shall the witness now detail steps that led to the conclusion?

The prosecutor, having obtained the advantage of these heated exchanges, made a generous gesture.

LANE   If the Court please, I think perhaps we can simplify this a little bit by my withdrawing my question and I will come back to it a little later, with the Court's permission, and I think perhaps in that way we may be able to obviate Mr. Bloch's objection.

COURT   All right.

The fact of the matter is that you did plead guilty to an indictment charging you with espionage for the Soviet Government; is that correct?

GOLD   That is correct, your Honor.

COURT   All right.

Gold was then led by questions to describe his various meetings with Klaus Fuchs and his reports to Yakovlev. In June 1944, he was able to advise "John" that at the next meeting with Fuchs he would receive "information of the application of nuclear fission to the production of a military weapon."

In June 1944, after involved arrangements, Fuchs turned over to Gold a package of information near Borough Hall in Brooklyn. There was not a word spoken. Within minutes, Yakovlev appeared a short distance away and received the papers, just as silently.

A month later, Gold met Fuchs at 96th Street and Central Park West, in early evening. They had a long conversation lasting an hour and a half. Gold memorized it, wrote up a report and turned it over to Yakovlev. It reported "the progress on the joint American and British project which aimed at producing an atomic bomb."

Spy organizations develop procedures like military units. They, too, have rank, discipline and tactical training. The great difference, of course, is that the armed forces stress identification by uniform, epaulets, salutes, flags, bands and various insignia. The spy organization makes a science of anonymity and total secrecy.

Gold revealed the technique. Whenever he had to meet "a contact" to receive information, "an object or piece of paper was involved." Identification was thus effected by having the pieces match, or a strange object exhibited. Rosenberg's cutting up the side of a Jell-O box, as Greenglass testified, was, therefore, not an improvised idea. It accorded with espionage training.

Also, there was a code phrase "usually used in the form of a greeting." Gold said he always used a false name and never gave his true residence.

(155)

His meetings with informants were carefully arranged at a precise time and place. Some were long and some short.

> In other words, if we were just going to discuss the possibility of obtaining certain types of information, the hazards involved, just how much information should be obtained, and just what source was needed, then a rather long meeting was scheduled. If I was going to actually get information, very usually a brief meeting was scheduled, the idea being to minimize the time of detection when information would be passed from the American to me. In addition to this I made payments of sums of money to some of the people whom I regularly contacted and always I wrote reports detailing everything that happened at every meeting with these people; and these reports I turned over to Yakovlev.

COURT   And where would you get the money from, that you paid to some of these people for the information?

GOLD   The money was given to me by Yakovlev.

How did Gold get in touch with Yakovlev? He had "a set pattern":

> This is how it worked: We had an arrangement not only for regular meetings but we had an arrangement for alternate meetings, should one of the regular ones not take place, and then in addition to that we had an arrangement for an emergency meeting. This emergency meeting was a one-way affair. A system was set up whereby Yakovlev could get in touch with me if he wanted me quickly, but I couldn't get in touch with him because I didn't know where. Yakovlev told me that in this way the chain was cut in two places. The person from whom I got the information in America did not know me by my true name, nor did he know where I lived, nor could he get in touch with me and I couldn't get in touch with Yakovlev. Yakovlev said this was a good thing.

Spies go on the assumption that they are constantly observed. Any transfer of information must be so disguised that there isn't the slightest indication of an exchange. Gold revealed the technique for this sleight of hand. If a document had to be copied and returned to its file:

> I would take the information and put it between the folds of a newspaper and Yakovlev and I would exchange the newspapers. The one that I got was just a newspaper. The one that he got had the information between the folds, the information usually being in some sort of an enclosure.

Rosenberg's suggestion, according to Greenglass, that Ruth Greenglass and Ann Sidorovich should exchange purses in a dark motion picture theater in Albuquerque was another version of the same technique.

In early 1945, Gold met Klaus Fuchs in Cambridge, Massachusetts. He received another package of precious secrets, hurried to New York and delivered them to Yakovlev. He also reported that Fuchs "was now stationed at a place called Los Alamos, New Mexico," that it was a large experimental station which had formerly been a select boys' school. The startling fact was that a tremendous amount of progress had been made. In addition, he had made mention of "a lens which was being worked on as a part of the atom bomb."

In view of the developments, Yakovlev dispatched Gold to Santa Fe, New Mexico, where by arrangement on the first Saturday in June 1945, he was to meet Dr. Fuchs.

In the meantime, by utilization of circuitous devices to arrange a meeting, Gold met Yakovlev on a Saturday at a combination restaurant and bar called Volks at 42nd Street and Third Avenue in New York City. After trained glances in all direction to be sure they were not under surveillance, they slipped into a secluded booth in the rear. It was four in the afternoon. They ordered drinks. Yakovlev was agitated. Gold described the incident:

YAKOVLEV What else—what else did Fuchs tell you about the lens?

GOLD As I told you, he said it was a new device to trigger the atom bomb which would make it more powerful.

YAKOVLEV You told me that. I want more information about the lens. We must have it.

GOLD I have told you everything he said. I can't remember anything else.

YAKOVLEV (Impatiently) Every time you think hard, you remember a little more about it. I want you to dig—dig—dig into your mind. There must be more detail.

GOLD I have told you everything. There is nothing more. I will write a report and search my mind to be sure everything is in it.

YAKOVLEV (With sudden calm) You will meet with Fuchs again the first Saturday of June at the same place. Be sure you get off from your job. This meeting must be kept. When you return from Santa Fe, we will arrange two meetings; one at which you give me his written report, and a second one to give an oral report, and this time get every detail and remember it.

GOLD O.K.

YAKOVLEV I want you to perform an additional mission on this trip. After you are through with Fuchs at Santa Fe, you'll go to Albuquerque, New Mexico—

GOLD I don't want to make two visits. It's too dangerous. It doesn't make sense—

YAKOVLEV This is vital, or I wouldn't ask you to do it. A woman was supposed to go out to get this information, but she couldn't make it. You have to go.

GOLD You know how dangerous it is to make contact with Dr. Fuchs. He is a leading scientist, and is probably under surveillance every second. To add to the risk with a second contact is insane. Where is your sense of caution?

YAKOVLEV You don't have to remind me of caution. I have been guiding you idiots through every step. If I depended on your sloppiness and carelessness, you would all be in jail cells years ago. You don't realize how important the mission to Albuquerque is.

GOLD Suppose it is important. Someone else should—

YAKOVLEV *You* are going. That's an order!

GOLD (Nodded silently in frustrated acquiescence.)

YAKOVLEV (Took an onionskin paper out of his breast pocket. On it was typed: "Greenglass 259 North High Street." Underneath were the words "I come from Julius")

This is the contact and address. The recognition signal is "I come from Julius."

(Yakovlev then took a piece of cardboard out of another pocket, which was a piece of the Jell-O box oddly cut, and slipped it surreptitiously to Gold, looking around to be sure they were not observed. Gold only glanced at it and quickly put it into his pocket.)

Show this to Greenglass. He will show you the other matching piece. Then you will be sure. If Greenglass isn't there, you can talk to his wife. She will produce the matching cardboard.

GOLD Will she have information to give me, if he isn't there?

YAKOVLEV Yes. She will turn it over to you. If not, she will arrange for you to get it. One thing more. Give either Greenglass or his wife this envelope. It has $500 in it. (Gold took it and again hastily put it in his pocket.) Now I know that two missions are more dangerous than one. Don't go from Santa Fe to Albuquerque directly. First go to Phoenix, Arizona; then to El Paso; and from there to Santa Fe. This will minimize the danger of your being followed. But, of course, keep your eyes open. When you leave here, memorize the address and password and destroy that paper.

GOLD (Somewhat proudly) Of course. I have already memorized it. "Greenglass, 259 North High Street. I come from Julius."

YAKOVLEV Put the cardboard in a book as if it were a place mark.

GOLD (Teasingly) And, of course, the money I'll spend.

YAKOVLEV (Smiled for the first time and called for the waiter for some drinks.)

Like a good soldier, Gold proceeded on his double mission. First, he met Dr. Fuchs at Santa Fe on Saturday, June 2, 1945. He received more papers. Then, confident he was not observed, he went to Albuquerque, arriving there about eight-thirty in the evening on the same day. He went directly to Greenglass' apartment on High Street but they were out for the evening. So he went downtown and "managed to obtain a room in a hallway of a rooming house." Sunday morning, he registered at the Hotel Hilton in his own name. Thus, the prosecutor telegraphed his intention to prove that Gold was in Albuquerque on that day. On Sunday morning, at eight-thirty, he tried the Greenglasses again. His knock on the door was answered by "a young man about twenty-three with dark hair." He described what followed:

(158)

GOLD Mr. Greenglass?

GREENGLASS Yes.

GOLD I come from Julius.

GREENGLASS Come in.

(Gold took the Jell-O cardboard out of his pocket and showed it to Greenglass, who went to a bureau, picked up his wife's handbag and removed the matching piece of cardboard. They held the two pieces together. Then each returned the piece to the original source.)

(Ruth Greenglass entered from the bedroom.)

GREENGLASS This is my wife.

GOLD Hello. I am Dave from Pittsburgh.

RUTH GREENGLASS That's a nice coincidence. My husband's name is Dave, too.

GREENGLASS I didn't expect you this early. So I haven't the material ready. If you come back in the afternoon, I'll write it up in the meantime.

GOLD How about 4 o'clock?

GREENGLASS O.K.

RUTH GREENGLASS Have you had breakfast? Would you like a cup of coffee?

GOLD Just coffee, thanks.

GREENGLASS I have talked to a number of people who I think will be excellent recruits for our work. Some of them should have good information about the atomic work. I'll give you the names—

GOLD Wait a minute. You must be crazy. Don't you realize how dangerous it is to proposition anyone for espionage? You'll bring the whole FBI down on us. I wonder if you haven't spilled the beans already. (He was very agitated, and became dictatorial, like Yakovlev. He had learned how to talk to inferiors.)

Look. Stop talking to anyone about this. That's an order! Even when you yourself are trying to get information be very cautious. Don't ask questions so directly that you arouse suspicion.

GREENGLASS (Defensively) But Julius asked me to give names of possible recruits. I was only following directions.

GOLD Sure, if you learn from social contact, and without any initiative on your part that somebody believes in Russia and might want to give information, you can tip us off, and we'll try to develop the contact. But to make direct approaches, as apparently you have been doing, is a direct road to jail. You'll get us all into trouble with your clumsiness.

GREENGLASS Don't get excited. I haven't approached anybody directly. What do you think I am—an idiot? "Mister, do you want to spy for Russia?" I have learned that some of the men feel as we do, that Russia has done a hell of a job in this war, and I have made a mental note of the people who talk that way—that's all.

GOLD All right. No more. I'll be back at 4. Have everything ready. (Left abruptly)

Gold gave Greenglass time to write out his descriptions of the atom bomb experiments. He returned that afternoon and received a heavy envelope. In turn, Gold gave him the envelope with $500 in it. What puny prices were being paid for information which cost a billion dollars.

Greenglass told Gold that he would return to New York during his

Christmas furlough. If Gold wanted to reach him, he could do so through Julius Rosenberg, whose telephone number he gave. Gold returned to New York laden with nuclear riches. One envelope containing Fuchs's information, he marked "Doctor," and the one from Greenglass, he marked "Other." He looked at Greenglass' material sufficiently to see that "it consisted of three or four handwritten pages plus a couple of sketches" with letters on them.

By devious arrangements, he met Yakovlev "in a very lonely place at ten o'clock in the evening at Metropolitan Avenue in Brooklyn where it runs into Queens." Yakovlev wanted to know whether Gold had made contact with "the doctor and the man." Gold reported that his mission had been accomplished without incident and delivered the two envelopes.

When he met Yakovlev again, he received a rare compliment. The material he had delivered about the atomic bomb was "extremely excellent and very valuable," and had been sent immediately to the Soviet Union.

By this time, Gold had learned that the first test of an atomic explosion would "take place in July, in New Mexico." The information was correct as was proven a month later.

Fuchs had a premonition that he was in trouble. He had read that the British had gotten to Kiel, Germany, ahead of the Russians. He feared they might discover a dossier on Fuchs which would reveal to British Intelligence "his strong Communist background and ties." It was also suspicious that the British had recalled him to England.

Yet for a while there was no revelation and indeed regular contact was maintained with him. The greatest precautions were taken. Gold described them.

> Every first Saturday of the month at 8 P.M. Fuchs was to be on the street level of the British subway in London at Paddington Crescent station. He was to carry five books bound with strings and held by two fingers of one hand, and two books in the other hand. The man who would contact him would be carrying a copy of a Bennett Cerf book, *Stop Me If You Have Heard This.*

Gold knew that Greenglass would be coming home at Christmas time on a furlough. Desiring to impress his superior with his alertness, he suggested to Yakovlev that "we ought to get in touch with his brother-in-law, Julius, so that we could get further information from him." Yakovlev did not appreciate Gold's reminder. He did not want his inferiors to meddle in strategy. It was presumptuous for them to think they could advise on matters which the high command had well in hand. He told Gold unceremoniously "to mind your own business." His rebuke was accompanied with a sharp gesture which warned him to limit himself to obeying orders in the future.

But this fracas was mild compared to the eruption which occurred at Gold's next meeting with Yakovlev.

In December 1946, after a long lapse of time, Gold received two tickets to a boxing match in the mail. This was a signal that three days after the date of the tickets, he was to meet Yakovlev in the lounge of the Earl Theater.

With guarded glances, to be certain they were not observed, they met, and walked silently to a bar on Second Avenue. They took a booth. Gold described what happened.

GOLD   It's almost a year I haven't heard from you.

YAKOVLEV   Ten months. I had to stay low. A contact I was to meet was under surveillance every time we arranged a meeting. It is better to give up information than to fall into a trap. Have you been followed?

GOLD   No. I watched for an hour before I entered the theater.

YAKOVLEV   Fuchs is now in Paris. You have been picked to meet him. You'll go to London first and fly to Paris. Make plans to take off from your job in about two weeks.

GOLD   Things are easing up at Brothman. I'll arrange it.

YAKOVLEV   Who did you say? Is that Abe Brothman and Associates?

GOLD   That's right. You wanted me to have a regular job. That's where I work.

YAKOVLEV   (In a rage, as if an electric shock had struck him) You fool! You idiot! I told you in 1945 that Brothman was under suspicion by the United States Government for espionage. Don't you remember anything I tell you? You have ruined eleven years of work.

GOLD   (To calm him) I assure you—

YAKOVLEV   (Even more furious) You assure me! You've been a sitting duck all the time. We probably are being watched right now. How we pick such morons, I'll never understand.

(He threw twice as much money on the table as the drinks required, and stormed out of the door. Gold tried to catch up with him on the street.)

GOLD   (Walking behind Yakovlev and pleading with him) I am sure I have not been followed. Please listen—

YAKOVLEV   (To himself) What a disaster. We'll never repair this damage. We have been living in a fish bowl. Idiot—idiot.

GOLD   Listen to me. You are alarmed when you don't have to be. Let's sit down somewhere.

YAKOVLEV   (Stopped) I am leaving this country immediately. I'll never see you again. Just go away. Don't follow me.

(He rushed off. Gold stood there looking at the infuriated Yakovlev as he disappeared.)

Yakovlev, protected by his diplomatic post in the Russian Embassy, had no difficulty returning to Russia. He did so promptly. His anticipation of trouble was not unwarranted. When the Fuchs scandal broke, Gold was arrested by the FBI while he was in his office at Brothman Associates. Brothman was later convicted for espionage.

The prosecutor announced that he had no further questions.

At this point, the court adjourned with the following statement to the jury:

> Ladies and gentlemen, again I want to admonish you that you should not read the newspapers in connection with this case or trial, or anything related to it; or listen to the radio, watch television, read any magazines which in any way deal with this case or anything related to it, and I assume that you followed my admonition right along in this case.
>
> You are excused until 10:30 tomorrow morning.

The next morning, Harry Gold settled in his seat facing counsel. He was ready for lengthy cross-examination by the various lawyers. To everyone's amazement, he was off the stand in thirty seconds:

LANE   The Government, your Honor has no further questions.
COURT   Any cross?
E. H. BLOCH   The defendants Rosenberg have no cross-examination of this witness.
PHILLIPS   No cross.
COURT   The witness is excused.

$$\longrightarrow\!\longleftarrow$$

Failure to cross-examine may well mean that the accused accepts the testimony and cannot contradict it. To forfeit cross-examination is a dangerous tactic, which should be used only in special circumstances. Those are either that the testimony does not affect the defendant, or if it does, it is not damaging, or fear that the witness is capable of doing far greater injury, if he is badgered.

So, for example, if Gold had limited himself to his own espionage activities, without bringing Julius Rosenberg into the picture, his counsel might indicate that since it didn't involve his client, he waived cross-examination. He would thus signify that he didn't care whether Gold's story was true or false. There was nothing for him, as counsel for the Rosenbergs, to be concerned about. In such a case, Bloch's announcement of "no cross-examination" could colloquially be translated into "so what?"

But that was not the situation here. Gold had directly involved Julius Rosenberg. He claimed that the greeting signal which he used when he visited Greenglass in Albuquerque was "I come from Julius." Also, he said Greenglass gave him Rosenberg's telephone number to follow up any further revelations, and that Rosenberg had asked him to seek new recruits for espionage. Finally, he had advised Yakovlev to get in touch with Rosenberg since Greenglass would be returning on his Christmas furlough. He thereby made Rosenberg a link in the entire scheme, involving Gold's contacts with Yakovlev and Fuchs.

Furthermore, he thus confirmed Greenglass' testimony that Rosenberg was his mentor and superior in espionage, and that Gold had received this knowledge from a higher source, namely Yakovlev. Where else had he gotten the signal "I come from Julius"?

Bloch, himself, had characterized Gold's testimony as "damaging." So that failure to cross-examine could not be justified on the ground that Rosenberg had not been touched.

Bloch had to make a difficult choice. Should he gamble on cross-examination which might provoke fatal retaliatory statements, or should he take no risk at all, in view of the limited injury Gold had done the Rosenbergs?

Had he decided on the first course, several tempting possibilities presented themselves:

He could pick up Gold's statement that he never used correct names; have him expand on the fact that it was a cardinal rule of espionage technique to give false names. He, Harry, was "Dave from Pittsburgh" and Anatoli was "John." Gold might gladly have given more illustrations. The jury might infer that since real names were never used, "Julius" was not Rosenberg, but a false name for someone else.

Another possibility for cross-examination was really uncross-examination, often the most effective. In a friendly way, he could have invited Gold to characterize the report of "the atom bomb material" which he had received from Fuchs as highly important and authentic. His pride in his achievement as an espionage courier, his scientific training, his excellent memory and important role in the great spy scoop might well have induced him to yield affirmative answers concerning the great value of what he had passed on. After all, Fuchs was a leading physicist. Why would he not have been more equipped than a machinist, Greenglass, to reveal and explain the atomic secret? Since Gold had testified that he obtained data from Fuchs before he got it from Greenglass, the fact could have been established that the secret was out long before Greenglass gave it. Gold might even have admitted that through his contacts with Dr. Fuchs, the Russians had the necessary knowledge of implosion before anything Greenglass did.

Of course, this would have provoked the prosecution to demonstrate that Greenglass' delivery of the "secret" to Rosenberg directly, rather than through Gold, came first. Also, a machinist might know more about a lens than a physicist.

The court properly ruled that the crime was transmitting classified data to a foreign government, and that whether such material was highly useful or not did not matter. But it certainly affected the degree of punishment. The court conceded this when he attributed fifty thousand deaths in Korea to Russia's knowledge of the bomb and linked this fact to the Rosenbergs in deciding what sentence to impose on them. Therefore, any cross-examination which pointed up Fuchs's

(163)

authoritative data would have toned down the value of what the Rosenbergs took, even if they were guilty.

Finally, the Blochs knew that Gold had testified six months before in the espionage trial of Abe Brothman. He had been on the stand in direct and cross-examination for four days in a one-week trial. The stenographer's minutes of that testimony were available.

The greatest boon to a cross-examiner is to have prior testimony by the witness. If anything in his earlier words touches the subject matter of the trial, there is the possibility that it can be used to contradict him. Is there anything more indigestible than eating one's own words, hour after hour?

In civil cases, the parties are permitted to examine each other under oath before trial. This prevents surprise. A trial is not a game. The testimony before trial can be used to contradict the witness if he strays from it at the trial. Since these examinations may cover hundreds of pages, and sometimes thousands, it is not unusual for the witness to forget his earlier words when he testifies in direct examination. Then the confrontation with his own different version in the examination before trial disrupts his credibility and equanimity at one and the same time.

In criminal cases, such examinations before trial are not permitted, one obvious reason being that a defendant may not be compelled to testify against himself. Therefore, to have prior sworn testimony on virtually the same issue is a gift from heaven for defendant's counsel.

Gold claimed in the prior trial that he had been instructed by his superiors to lie to his employer, Brothman. So he invented a series of lies about having a wife, twin children, and a brother killed in military action, although:

> Contrary to that story . . . I actually had no wife and two twin children . . . I was a bachelor and always had been one . . . my brother was still alive.

Judge Kaufman who presided in the trial, too, at one time chided Brothman's attorney:

> The witness [Gold] said he concocted these things from beginning to end. Are you going to take each and every detail he concocted?

This would have branded him as a practiced liar in the performance of his work, and might taint his confession although the setting was different.

There was more in his prior testimony which could be used, if not to telling effect, at least to lift the veil of contrition. Indeed, his own testimony in the Brothman trial showed him to be utterly without principle, even to his own cause. Surprisingly, he testified that "I didn't like Communists . . . I thought they were a lot of wacked-up Bohemians," and his lawyer at the time of the thirty-year sentence told the court:

> Let the record in this case show . . . that Harry Gold has never been a Communist and he is not a Communist now, nor was he in those younger days.

Bloch chose to say "no cross-examination." There was one weighty reason for such a tactic. Fear. Gold might have been far more destructive than he was. If he was attacked, might he blurt out something which, true or false, would sink the Rosenbergs? Suppose he suddenly volunteered that Yakovlev had mentioned Rosenberg's valuable work, or that Rosenberg was supplying mechanical lens data, while Fuchs could only give theoretical data? The judge would very likely strike out such comments as hearsay, but eliciting them would be foolhardy. The risks were unlimited.

Also, the decision had to be made on the spur of the moment. Bloch had no opportunity to debate the problem with his confreres or his clients. He knew Gold might testify because his name was listed, but he could not anticipate what he would say. A trigger judgment had to be exercised the second after the prosecutor turned him over for cross-examination. Undoubtedly there was relief in the defense ranks that Gold had not done more damage. They played it safe. "No cross, your Honor."

—→←—

The next witness the government put on the stand was Dr. George Bernhardt, the physician for the Rosenbergs. He filled in a piece in the Greenglass mosaic of testimony by telling how Rosenberg called him one day in May 1950.

> Julie said, "Doctor, I would like to ask a favor of you. I would like to know what injections one needs to go to Mexico," and I hesitated a little, and he laughed and said, "Don't get scared, it is not for me; it's for a friend of mine." And I then proceeded to give him that information, and then as an afterthought I told him that he would need typhoid injections and a smallpox vaccination, and I then asked him if this friend of his was a veteran, telling him that if he was a veteran all he would need would be booster doses instead of going through the entire series of injections, and he said, "Yes, he is a veteran."
>
> I then asked him if this friend of his was going to stay in Mexico City or whether he was going to go into the interior because if he went into the interior he would need typhus injections, and he said, "Yes, he will probably go into the interior," and then I told him that if he decided to go, to give me a little

notice because I don't usually stock a typhus vaccine and I would have to get it, and he said he would let me know.

So, here was testimony that Rosenberg did try to get information necessary to Greenglass' flight to Mexico.

Before the doctor was permitted to tell his story, Emanuel Bloch, hearing that the conversation about to be elicited took place on the telephone, assumed that it was wiretapped by the government. Since this might be illegal, he asked for a conference at the bench, out of the hearing of the jury.

E. H. BLOCH I am not saying to the Court this as of my own knowledge but I have been informed that this witness was told either directly or indirectly that this particular telephone conversation was a wiretapped conversation. Now if that is so then under the Nardone cases and the cases following it—

COURT All right, let us find out. Is there any wiretapping?

SAYPOL A lot of arid nonsense, and I do not like this procedure. I object to it. Let us hear the testimony.

COURT It is ridiculous.

SAYPOL I do not like these interruptions. Counsel ought to know the way to proceed.

E. H. BLOCH Now Mr. Saypol—

COURT All right.

E. H. BLOCH Wait, your Honor.

COURT Yes.

E. H. BLOCH If this particular conversation, this telephone conversation was not wiretapped, of course, he can testify. If, on the other hand, it was, I would like to be able to ask a few questions.

COURT You just heard the answer, it was not wiretapped. Why go further when the United States Attorney told you that?

SAYPOL I haven't the slightest knowledge that it was ever indulged in.

E. H. BLOCH O.K. Now, look, Mr. Saypol, I said I didn't know this of my own knowledge.

SAYPOL I know, but those things don't help any.

E. H. BLOCH Now don't you think it is my duty—

COURT Yes. All right, let us not get into it any further.

Bloch scored in cross-examination. The doctor admitted that when he had previously been asked by an FBI representative whether Rosenberg had ever approached him "to sign a certificate of vaccination for his brother-in-law [Greenglass], without having vaccinated him," he said that he had not.

He attempted to recover by stating that two or three days later, he remembered Rosenberg's inquiry on the telephone and he volunteered it to the FBI.

→←

The government then turned on Morton Sobell, with a sideswipe at Julius Rosenberg. It put on the stand William Danziger, a classmate of both Rosenberg and Sobell at City College. He had tried to give Rosenberg some machine-shop work but was turned down because Rosenberg was "rather tied up." The remote inference was that Rosenberg's preoccupation was with espionage, else why would he refuse an order his machine shop needed so badly?

The real thrust was Danziger's recital that his friend Sobell wrote him from Mexico City, giving his name for return mail as "M. Sowell" and later as "Morty Levitov," and stating that when he came back he would explain the use of these aliases. Neither Rosenberg nor Sobell's counsel sought any cross-examination.

So, not only Sobell's flight, but his disguises stood uncontradicted. It was interesting that even in the course of simulation, he used names so similar to his own. Psychologists might deduce a secret desire to be detected. Certainly, his conduct and that of his counsel in not challenging evidence against him until after the trial, when it was too late, fitted the pattern of self-immolation.

The government then produced the records of the Hotel Hilton in Albuquerque to show that Harry Gold had been there on June 3, 1945, and the bank records of the Albuquerque National Bank to show that Ruth Greenglass had deposited $400, as she had testified she did, out of the $500 she received from Gold. This kind of documentation gave physical corroboration to the words spoken, and also served as a reminder of prior testimony.

Repetition has never injured the persuasive process.

CHAPTER 16

The government had the burden of establishing that the information pilfered by Greenglass would be "of advantage to a foreign government." It chose to do so in a dramatic manner. It called Colonel John Lonsdale, Jr., who was in charge of security for the project. He was a lawyer who had served in the Military Intelligence Division of War Department, General Staff, and had been assigned by Dr. Conant, president of Harvard University and chairman of National Defense Research Committee, to guard the secrecy of the undertaking. Saypol gave it the light touch when he asked the witness "to dispel the illusion" that lawyers "make the worst witnesses."

It was soon developed that our atomic project was provoked by fear.

> We believed that the Germans were working on the atomic bomb and were far in advance of our efforts. We believed also that should information as to our having undertaken in any major way work on an atomic bomb, if this were to leak out to the Germans, it would result in a redoubling of their efforts, as well as efforts on their part to ascertain what we were doing, and might well in and of itself defeat our objective.

The United States and Germany were engaged in a race to find the weapon which would give ultimate victory. Every clue was invaluable. The most important indication of what others were exploring was the expertise of those working on the project. One could know by the names of the scientists what theory was being pursued. So, if any other country knew, as was the fact, that experts on nuclear fission were gathered at Los Alamos, it would be invaluable information. It was by such deduction that the United States learned "the extent and nature of the German effort on the atomic bomb."

Colonel Lonsdale was asked to describe the extreme precautions taken to preserve secrecy. The more he testified on this subject, the more the mystery increased of how all these measures could have proven so ineffective. He told how fifty thousand acres had been chosen "on this lonely mesa, in the wastes of New Mexico, because it was isolated, and only one or two means of access to it"; how no names were used, so that Los Alamos was known only as "Site Y"; how "a specially selected military police detachment" was recruited to guard the place physically; how each area inside the compound was separated from the others by "a high wire fence," separately policed; how mail and telephones were censored; how "undercover agents were placed in all of the surrounding towns"; how "extremely careful" they were "in the selection of personnel"; how they watched the "movements of the people in their social intercourse"; how, in order to prevent sabotage, the locations of buildings were secret, and "no aircraft was permitted to fly over."

At one point, E. H. Bloch objected to this detail stating that it was merely cumulative, and that he was willing to concede the secrecy of the project. When Saypol asked whether Bloch would also admit that "any breach of secrecy was of advantage to a foreign government," he refused, saying, "I can't concede that, because I just don't know."

The court stated that this was an element of proof.

E. H. BLOCH   I think it is, and if the purpose of Mr. Saypol is to elicit that kind of testimony from the witness then I certainly want to sit down. I don't want to stop Mr. Saypol from doing it.

Lonsdale then described how each activity was "compartmented" so that "the right hand" didn't know "what the left hand was doing." The words "atomic bomb" or "nuclear fission" were ruled out of the vocabulary and communication. Only the President of the United States had "a direct contact" with all phases of the enterprises.

LONSDALE   Indeed, the President had personally directed that this project was the one with the highest order of secrecy of any project which the Government had undertaken.

In order to determine what progress any other nation, friend or foe, was making in extracting the power from an atom, our government had a list of the limited number of scientists in the world, "who had the capacity to do work of this kind," and ascertained where they were, where they traveled and where they worked. The Russians apparently had no project in progress on these studies, but "were much interested in what we were doing."

Since Niels Bohr was recognized "as a pioneer and granddaddy, you might say, of nuclear physics," his name was disguised as Nicholas Baker, so that his visits to Los Alamos would not be "a dead giveaway."

Even his coming to the United States was declared to be at the behest of the Rockefeller Foundation rather than by invitation of the President.

Colonel Lonsdale characterized the experimentation on the high explosive lens "a top secret." He then stated that the over-all purpose of the security procedures was to prevent information which was sought by foreign governments and would be of advantage to them from coming into their hands. When Bloch objected because the witness hadn't testified on the basis of knowledge obtained in the course of his official duty, Saypol revised the question. Bloch withdrew his objection. Lonsdale then had an opportunity to emphasize his former answer:

LONSDALE It was the expressed opinion of the chief of staff of the Army that this weapon, should we be able to develop it, would be decisive of this war and decisive on the question of the future security of this country.

SAYPOL And that mainly was the basis for keeping it, doing everything possible to keep it away from any foreign country, any foreign nation?

LONSDALE Yes.

SAYPOL You may examine.

Might it not have been a fair cross-examination to ask the witness what checking had been done before accepting David Greenglass as a machinist in a key spot? Didn't the records show that he had been a member of the Young Communist League? If this was not a disqualification, then why all the questions about Rosenberg's communism? At least would it not have warranted close scrutiny of Greenglass' movements even when he went on furloughs to New York?

These and many others were never asked.

———→←———

Again, the government advised the court that it was putting a witness on the stand who would reveal the secret of the atom bomb. The judge cleared the courtroom, leaving only the press. When the room was emptied of disappointed visitors, the judge instructed the stenographers not to transcribe whatever testimony would be given concerning "the operation of the atom bomb." He impounded the stenographer's minutes, stating, however, that the lawyers would have access to them.

Then John A. Derry was sworn in. He had been associated with the Atomic Energy Commission and had acted as a liaison officer for General Groves to report on technical progress of research and production of the bomb.

Saypol requested the court stenographer to read Greenglass' description of the bomb. The judge interrupted to invite the press to "exercise the same good judgment that they exercised in publishing the information as it came from the lips of Mr. Greenglass."

(171)

The witness was asked whether from the description and sketch by Greenglass a scientist could "perceive what the actual construction of the bomb was?" He answered in the affirmative.

On cross-examination, Bloch asked whether the description of the bomb could be compressed within twelve pages, as Greenglass had done. He replied, "You could give substantially the principle involved."

The Greenglass testimony, which had been brought to life from its frozen interment in the stenographic minutes, was ordered resealed.

—→←—

The government again turned its guns on Sobell.

The prosecutor called for a Spanish interpreter because his next witness spoke little English. He was Manuel Giner de los Ríos, an interior decorator in Mexico City. He testified that Morton Sobell had taken an apartment in the building in which he lived. They had become acquainted. Sobell pumped him on how to get to Vera Cruz and what papers he needed to get out of Mexico. Sobell feared returning to the United States, because he would have "to return to the U. S. Army." He had already been in a war and did not want to serve in another. He thought the military police were looking for him. Of course, all this was untrue.

Sobell left for Vera Cruz, leaving his wife, Helen, behind. From there he wrote Ríos, enclosing a letter for "Dear Helen." Six days later, he wrote Ríos from Tampico, another seaport in Mexico. Again, there was enclosed a letter for "Dear Helen."

Later, he returned to Mexico City, but when Ríos asserted that Sobell was "deported to the United States," Kuntz and Phillips objected. The question was withdrawn. There was no cross-examination.

The government had other witnesses to prove "deportation."

A young lady, Minerva Bravo Espinosa, followed on the stand. She worked in an optical store in Vera Cruz. A man by the name of M. Sand had ordered eyeglasses. She pointed out Morton Sobell as the one who had signed a card on that occasion as M. Sand. It was admitted in evidence. There was no cross-examination.

The next witness, who had been flown in from Vera Cruz, was on the stand only a minute. He was one of the "administrators of the Grand Hotel Diligencias" and identified the registration card and bill in the name of Morris Sand. Kuntz conceded it was the writing of Sobell. Again, no cross-examination.

Another witness from Tampico, Mexico, identified a registration card in Tampico Hotel in the name of Marvin Salt as being signed by Morton Sobell, whom she recognized in court.

Glenn Davis, an official of the Mexican Airlines, produced a manifest of a trip from Vera Cruz to Tampico on July 30, 1950, signed by one

N. Sand, whom he identified as Morton Sobell. Sobell must have gotten tired having so many witnesses point a finger at him.

It all added up to a proof of a series of aliases which, together with his original flight from the United States, created an impression of guilt. Or could it be merely fear of an innocent man, running from circumstantial evidence? Sobell never took the stand to explain.

There followed a wrangle which was significant because it revealed disarray among the lawyers for the different defendants and even more their psychological awe of government counsel.

The incident resulted from an effort to stipulate facts concerning documentary proof, so as not to require witnesses to be brought from far distances. Bloch and Myles Lane agreed on such a stipulation. When Lane proceeded to read it into the record, Phillips, the attorney for Sobell, protested because he had not been consulted. To appease him, Bloch said, "Will you take my word that our stipulation here will not harm you in any way?" Phillips was content, but Saypol was outraged by the comment.

> I don't care to have Mr. Bloch's observation on the record to his fellow counsel representing another defendant, giving them his word that in his judgment that testimony doesn't hurt their client.

The judge pointed out the law that a conspirator is liable for the acts of a co-conspirator, and, therefore, that Sobell might be affected by any stipulation binding the Rosenbergs.

Bloch's comment had not been for the insidious purpose of characterizing government evidence as harmless. He was attempting to live up to his stipulation which he intended in good faith to be binding on all defendants. Solely for that reason, he had assured Sobell's lawyers that his client would not be harmed thereby, and that he ought not sabotage the agreement reached. The fact is that the stipulation didn't affect Sobell. It concerned the departure from the United States of Yakovlev, which could be proven without a stipulation.

So although Bloch's evaluation of testimony in the presence of the jury was technically improper (he would have to wait until summation to exercise that privilege), it was innocently motivated and could easily be overlooked in the many exchanges during a long trial. Indeed, Saypol was guilty of equally offensive comments intended to be jests or sarcastic asides. Even his statement about a representative of the Atomic Energy Commission being in the courtroom was prejudicial, although made to seek the court's permission for his presence.

But Saypol grew more insistent and indignant as Bloch retreated:

> I don't propose to display any lack of diligence on my part when one counsel undertakes to evaluate and characterize testimony, as

it affects another defendant, because I want to be heard loudly and forcefully on that.

Finally, the jury heard the stipulation. It stated that if the witness R. B. Waklett of the United States Lines had testified, he would produce ship records which would show that Anatoli Yakovlev and his wife and two children sailed on the S.S. *America* (the irony of that name, for a boat which was taking a spy to safety, may not have been lost on the jury), and that he was listed as vice-counsul of the U.S.S.R. in New York City. This proof explained why, although named as a defendant, Yakovlev was not present in court.

The next witness, Lan Adomian, identified a photograph of Yakovlev. The jury had an opportunity to check Gold's description of "a master spy" with his picture.

——→←——

The government's case was only two weeks old, and yet it was coming to a close. The prosecutor had decided to omit most of the witnesses listed in the notification to defendants. This is not unusual. Each side plays safe in setting forth its prospective witnesses. If not listed, the witness may not be called, unless special explanation is given, and the court approves. This is to avoid surprise. However, it is always permissible not to use witnesses listed.

The prosecution had estimated that it would take at least four weeks to present its case. The defense, therefore, felt it had more time to prepare as the evidence came in. It now found itself in the predicament of having to put its witnesses on in a day or two.

Judge Kaufman had repeatedly called conferences at the bench to inquire about the time elements. This was fair to the defense. It received running notice of how much longer the prosecution estimated its case would take before resting.

As the government's presentation shrank, the elder Bloch called for a bench conference. He spread on the record that he had been misled by Saypol's estimates of time, and that he and his son did not have adequate opportunity to prepare, especially since the Rosenbergs were not available to him on weekends. Even on weekdays, they were returned to their respective House of Detention at five o'clock. He, therefore, asked for a brief adjournment after the prosecution rested, before he would be obliged to begin his defense.

The judge pointed out that Bloch had not requested him to make the prisoners available at off hours and weekends, and that he would have granted this relief. Saypol said that if such a request had been made of him, he "would have extended" himself "to see that" the lawyers had such access. The judge expressed, rather mildly, his displeasure with Bloch's tactics: "You have something in mind in putting it on the record," Of course, he had. It could be reversible error if a defendant is not given fair opportunity to prepare his defense.

The judge granted Bloch's request that the defense would not have to proceed until the following afternoon. Both Blochs said, "That will be all right." Also, the judge directed the marshal:

> Now this is a direction to the marshal. Will you see that their clients are left right here in the courthouse until the lawyers are through with them? I don't know what time it is going to be but arrangements will have to be made, and that will have to go now until the case is over.

So please tell whoever is in charge that I have so directed.

DEPUTY MARSHAL All right.

The flurry was over. From then on, the Rosenbergs were available to their counsel into the early hours of the morning, in the improvised jail in the basement of the Federal Court House. I shall examine later the tormenting questions of strategy which had to be determined. The court attendants heard loud voices of disagreement during these meetings.

CHAPTER 17

Lawyers plan the sequence of witnesses not merely on chronological consideration. It is best to begin and end with the strongest witnesses. The prosecutor had begun with Elitcher and the Greenglasses. It was certain that a powerful witness was being reserved for the end of the case. The defense anticipated such strategy and braced itself for the blow. Who was the government going to trot out last?

It was Elizabeth Bentley. She was forty-four years old and had already lived two political lifetimes. After graduating from Vassar and receiving a master's degree from Columbia University, she had gone to Italy to study at the University of Florence. She became enamored with Fascist philosophy under Mussolini, and joined the university Fascist organization. However, after she returned to the United States, she joined the Communist Party. There, as she described on the stand, she rose to the very top rank. She became a spy extraordinaire.

Then she flip-flopped again, going to the FBI and confessing her role. She was asked to continue her Communist activities, and report to the FBI. She did. So she had become a double agent.

Finally, she was permitted to come out into the open. She became a leading witness for congressional investigating committees before grand juries and in trials of Communists. She wrote a book which John Gunther would have titled *Inside the Russian Spy Organization*. She lectured throughout the United States. In short, she became a professional informer.

Before analyzing her testimony, two observations are in order. First, is the phenomenon of interchangeable roles between Fascists and Communists. Mussolini was a radical socialist, before leading the Fascist movement. Hitler professed to be a democratic socialist, and even carried over part of the name to the Nazi leadership principle.

(177)

Elizabeth Bentley didn't find the transition from fascism to communism any more difficult. The extreme points of the circle do meet. The deadly antagonism of radical and reactionary movements involves more a quest for power than ideology. Their parallelism in authoritarian control and the denial of any consent of those ruled makes all differences in "principle" sheer sophistry. The objective is the same; "A few of us will tell all of you what is good for you."

The second observation is that in accepting converts from communism, we overlook their defective character. Is the flaw which made a Whittaker Chambers, a Louis Budenz, a Harvey Matuso or an Elizabeth Bentley a Communist conspirator in the first place eliminated by confessing and informing?

Intellectual reversal may be admirable. Youngsters in college who sought a new approach to society's injustices and ultimately realized that perfectionism of a blueprint is subject to imperfection of human beings are not involved in this analysis. They were simply disillusioned idealists. Indeed, many of them withdrew the moment they recognized the despotism which paraded itself as discipline. But here we are not dealing with mere ideas. What is involved is corrupt character—people who were ready to and did betray their own government and friends (many of whom they entrapped), who adhered to a nihilist philosophy that it was right to violate ethics and law to serve "a higher cause."

Some of them believed that it was not only right to lie and spy, but even to kill for the ism which they served. Are such people to be trusted when they turn a fanatical cheek the other way? Has their character been reformed with their change in position? Having once adopted the credo that lying is virtuous if it serves the cause, this conviction may persist when the cause has changed. Matuso, an ex-Communist, who testified for the government in anti-Communist trials, was later convicted of perjury. I have always doubted their reliability, no matter to which side they gave their allegiance. The lack of scruple which made them spies in the first place is not necessarily corrected by conversion. Surely, their revelations should be examined with a suspicious eye, particularly when it absolves them from punishment and aggrandizes their fame and earnings. Budenz, a former editor of the *Daily Worker,* earned $60,000 a year from lectures after he converted to democracy. Whittaker and Bentley exploited their prior infamy in books and lectures. Since their popularity depended on new sensational exposures, the temptation existed to "tell more." Their belated, refreshed recollections of other Communists "in high government posts," whose names had not appeared in the first gush of catharsis, should have been subjected to skeptical scrutiny. But in the inflamed atmosphere of the 1950s, discriminating judgment was not the rule.

So the appearance of Elizabeth Bentley had an impact far beyond the relevance of her testimony. Its pertinence was correctly described by the judge: Was the Communist Party just another American political movement? If so, adherence to it was immune from sanctions. Or was it an arm of Russian communism and subject to direction from abroad? Then it was a foreign agency, not entitled to the protection afforded indigenous movements, no matter how much we may dislike them. Put simply, was the American Communist Party a fifth column? Bentley's testimony was relevant insofar as it supplied the answer.

Trepidation in the defendants' ranks was due to other disclosures she might make. Would she give direct testimony that the Rosenbergs were part of the Russian espionage apparatus? Would she spill out facts learned while she shared the innermost confidences, which would complete the condemnation of the Rosenbergs by their own family with that of their brothers and sisters in the Russian movement? Expecting the worst, all defense lawyers were on their feet objecting to almost every question. She could barely be heard through the barrage.

Elizabeth Bentley first described her apprenticeship in the Communist Party. She "put out" a shop paper and "infiltrated the Teachers College newspaper and various religious and cultural organizations on the campus." Later, she graduated to the underground:

> I no longer attended any unit meetings. If I met fellow Communists on the street, I was to pretend I didn't know them. If they asked me what I was doing, I was to dodge their questions; if necessary, I was to tell them that I had walked out of the Communist Party. I was to be responsible to only one man.

That man was Jacob Golos who was on a Communist three-man control commission which "kept the membership in line and told them what they should do and put them out if they didn't behave."

Golos ran World Tourist, a travel agency set up by the Communist Party. It was a front for his spy activities. He was Bentley's superior for five years.

While counsel protested and the court granted their motions to strike out certain conclusions, not within her personal knowledge, her story seeped through the wall of objections:

saypol Miss Bentley, had you learned what was the relation of the Communist Party of the United States to the Communist International?

bentley It was part of the Communist International and subject to its jurisdiction as such.

After Golos' death in 1943, Bentley was assigned to Amitol Gromov, first secretary of the Russian Embassy. Her chief duty continued to be the collection of information from American Communists, and to pass it on to her superiors "for transmission to Moscow." The answers became more pointed and their heat singed the defendants:

SAYPOL Well, what connection did the Communist Party membership of you and Golos have with the destination of this material to Russia?

BENTLEY The Communist Party being part of the Communist International only served the interests of Moscow, whether it be propaganda or espionage or sabotage.

She revealed the subservience of American Communist leaders to Russian dictates. The Communist International organization was based on military lines. The American head of the party, Earl Browder, was permitted no independence of judgment or action. Bentley had risen in rank so that it was she who gave orders to him directly from Russia.

BENTLEY He had to accept them. Sometimes he would fight against them, but he ended up accepting them.

Communist parties in all countries had to take their "line" from Moscow. When that line changed, they had to follow it. No deviation was permitted.

Most of the time, she used a false first name in her work. She was known as Joan, Mary or Helen. Golos was called John or Timmy. It took a year before she knew her own superior's name.

Then came the testimony linking Rosenberg with Golos and Bentley. It was circumstantial and indirect. She had, on occasion, accompanied Golos to meetings where he would meet "a contact."

On one such occasion in the early fall of 1942, they went to Knickerbocker Village. Golos said he had "to pick up some material from a contact, an engineer."

The court struck out this answer on the ground that it was hearsay. She was only permitted to tell what he did, not what he said.

BENTLEY Mr. Golos parked the car; left me in it; went across the street to wait on the corner for his contact to appear; paced up and down for a bit. Then the contact finally arrived. Then they went three or four doors down to, I think, a candy store to carry on their business. Then Mr. Golos returned to the car with an envelope of material which he had received from the contact.

Saypol endeavored to connect this incident with Rosenberg directly. The judge would not permit it. This resulted in a conference at the bench out of the hearing of the jury. Judge Learned Hand's decision in the Dennis case was discussed. The right to present circumstantial evidence was debated back and forth. Finally, the court defined the limited areas of testimony he would permit.

The lawyers returned to their battle places. But the moment another question was put, objection was made. Would Bentley be able or permitted to identify Julius Rosenberg as a spy whom Golos had contacted?

SAYPOL Miss Bentley, referring to this occasion when you accompanied Mr. Golos to the vicinity of Knickerbocker Village and you saw him in conversation with a man. Do you recall that?

BENTLEY Yes.

SAYPOL Can you describe the characteristics of that individual to whom Golos talked? What did he look like?

E. H. Bloch would not permit her to answer. He contended that the question referred to 1942 whereas the indictment covered a period beginning in 1944.

COURT I am going to sustain the objection to that particular assertion.

SAYPOL Well, then, if that is so, I will abandon that line of inquiry, if the Court please.

However, he did not do so. He approached from another direction.

SAYPOL Subsequent to the occasion when you went to the vicinity of Knickerbocker Village with Mr. Golos and saw him in conversation with a person, and continuing until November 1943, did you have telephone calls from a person who described himself as Julius?

BENTLEY Yes, I did.

SAYPOL Did you then have conversations with Golos regarding the telephone calls from the person describing himself as Julius?

BENTLEY That is correct.

SAYPOL And thereafter, having conversed with Golos about the telephone call from Julius, in the first instance, would you immediately thereafter receive further telephone calls from the person describing himself as Julius?

BENTLEY Yes.

E. H. BLOCH Same objection, your Honor.

COURT Overruled.

When the prosecutor sought to establish "Julius' occupation," the court would not permit him to do so.

Again, Saypol persisted.

SAYPOL May I have one further question, if you will allow me? Then I will drop it.

COURT Yes.

SAYPOL From your conversations with Julius and with Golos, did you come to learn in what vicinity Julius resided?

BENTLEY Yes.

(181)

E. H. BLOCH   I object to it, your Honor, upon the same grounds.
COURT   Overruled.
E. H. BLOCH   I respectfully except.
BENTLEY   Yes, he lived in Knickerbocker Village.

The judge tested her knowledge of Knickerbocker Village. She described it accurately, as being "past the Allen Street Public Markets," and that it had "narrow streets and indoor markets."

When he asked what functions she performed in these meetings and telephone calls, she replied:

BENTLEY   My part was that I took messages from Julius to Golos and told Golos that he wanted to meet him, and so on. I was a go-between.
COURT   I see. Very well.
SAYPOL   I think that is all.
        You may examine.

Elizabeth Bentley had filled in the mosaic of Russian control of the American Communist movement, thus forging a link between being a Communist and "aiding a foreign nation," which was part of the indictment. Also, despite evidentiary limitations, due to a date preceding the conspiracy, and the fact that she had never met Rosenberg face to face, she identified a "Julius" who lived in Knickerbocker Village, and with whom she had telephone conversations to arrange meetings with Golos. But she had been blocked from describing "Julius'" occupation as "engineer."

The jury would later be reminded in summation of Elitcher's testimony that when Sobell delivered a can of film to Rosenberg and then drove home with Elitcher, he reported that Rosenberg was not worried about surveillance because although he had talked on the phone to Elizabeth Bentley, he didn't think she knew who he was. Also, Greenglass had testified that Rosenberg had referred to Elizabeth Bentley. So, the court ruled during one of Bloch's objections:

> It will be for the jury to determine, not for you, not for me, it will be for the jury to determine from all the evidence whether or not the "Julius" she is referring to is the defendant Julius Rosenberg on trial. The testimony is admissible, as I see it, because of the foundation which had been laid, or, shall I say, the previous testimony which came in from the lips of Elitcher, and I believe it is found on page 355 of the record. . . . It will be for the jury to infer, whether they want to give any weight whatsoever to this portion of the evidence . . . as to whether or not the Julius she spoke to in view of this previous testimony, is the defendant Julius Rosenberg.

Nevertheless, the defendants must have been relieved that the testimony was not worse. According to their belief that Elizabeth Bentley had no scruple in "fingering" Communists, they might have feared a false and unequivocal identification of "Julius" as Rosenberg, and of his active role in delivering documents to Golos. This was not her testimony. She had been circumspect in involving him.

This time the Blochs were fully prepared to tackle the witness and were determined to do so. Her prior testimony in other cases and the cross-examination to which she had been subjected on many occasions were fully spread on the record. They had studied it. Elizabeth Bentley was in for a rough time.

꞊꞊꞊꞊꞊

CHAPTER 18

The first attack on Bentley was on her morals. E. H. Bloch set out
to prove that both her service to communism and later to the FBI
was due to her love for a man.

E. H. BLOCH Now, you have referred to a man by the name of
  Jacob Golos? He was known to you also as John?
BENTLEY John was the name he used with his undercover contacts.
  His real name was Jacob Nathan Golos.
E. H. BLOCH And what name did he use to you?
BENTLEY Well, when I first met him for the first year, I knew him
  as Timmy. After that, I knew him by his real name.
E. H. BLOCH What name did you call him?
BENTLEY You mean personally?
E. H. BLOCH Yes.
BENTLEY I called him Yasha.
E. H. BLOCH You were pretty friendly with him, weren't you?
BENTLEY I think I have said this in other trials; I was in love with
  Mr. Golos.
E. H. BLOCH And you not only were in love with him, but you lived
  with him, did you not?
BENTLEY Yes, I did and, as I have explained at each and every
  trial, that was a Communist—
E. H. BLOCH I move to strike out "at each and every trial," your
  Honor. I think I am entitled to a direct answer.
COURT Answer the question.
E. H. BLOCH You lived with him, did you not?
BENTLEY I lived with him in what was the Communist conception
  of marriage. The Communists didn't believe in bourgeois mar-
  riage.

E. H. BLOCH   And you didn't believe in bourgeois marriage?

BENTLEY   Since I was a Communist, I didn't.

E. H. BLOCH   And you lived with him, did you not?

BENTLEY   I certainly did. . . .

E. H. BLOCH   Did you know that Golos was married at the time you started to have relations with him?

BENTLEY   Mr. Golos was never legally married to any woman in his life. Any other women had the same relationship I had. He did not believe in bourgeois marriage. He was a Communist.

E. H. BLOCH   Would you characterize your relationship with Mr. Golos as your being the mistress of Mr. Golos?

BENTLEY   I don't feel I am called upon to characterize it. That is up to you.

E. H. BLOCH   I am asking you now.

COURT   No, I am going to sustain the objection. I think she is giving you the facts. Characterization is unimportant. . . .

E. H. BLOCH   Did you know that Mr. Golos had a child when you started to have relations with him?

BENTLEY   I knew that Mr. Golos had lived with a woman previously, who had gone back to the U.S.S.R. two years before, and that he had had a child by her, yes.

When Golos died, she took up with a captain in the American Army. It was then that she went to the FBI to confess her espionage activities. The inference was that her political loyalties were controlled by her sexual attachments. Bloch began his cross-examination with questions about "this captain." What he was driving at could not have been clear to the jury at that time. His first questions were:

E. H. BLOCH   Did you go to the FBI and inquire about a certain captain?

BENTLEY   I went to the FBI to tell them my story. . . .

E. H. BLOCH   Did you inquire of the FBI about a certain captain at that time?

BENTLEY   Yes. In the course of telling them things I inquired about the captain, yes.

E. H. BLOCH   And that captain was a friend of yours, was he not?

BENTLEY   Yes, I think he was an acquaintance of mine.

E. H. BLOCH   And you met him before you went to the FBI?

BENTLEY   Yes, I would say I had met him maybe three months before, something of the sort.

E. H. BLOCH   He had taken you out socially?

BENTLEY   Yes, rather, on and off, yes.

E. H. BLOCH   Did you go down to the FBI for the purpose of disclosing your Communist Party activities?

BENTLEY   Certainly. I was working with the Russian secret police;

(186)

I was going with the FBI to work with them; I was being taken out socially by a man who told me he was doing undercover work for the United States Government. That made a very dangerous situation.

Bloch turned to her espionage activities. She said she had thirty contacts from whom she obtained information which she passed on to Russia. She met about twenty of these personally. The court had previously ruled that names would not be permitted. This was the difference between a court proceeding which protected people, who had no opportunity to defend themselves from calumny, and congressional hearings, where men and women were pilloried and defenseless, when their names were entered into the record.

Of course, Bentley admitted freely that before she went to the FBI she had personally engaged in espionage work:

E. H. BLOCH   Have you ever been arrested for committing the crime of espionage or conspiring to commit espionage?
BENTLEY   No, I haven't.
E. H. BLOCH   Have you ever been indicted? There is a distinction, Miss Bentley, between an arrest and indictment, I am sorry.
BENTLEY   No, I have not been indicted, nor have I been arrested for anything.

Like Ruth Greenglass, who also confessed to espionage and was never charged or punished, Bentley remained untouched. Ruth had rendered her expiating service in the Rosenberg trial, Bentley in FBI service and in a number of trials. She had several advantages over Ruth. She had no husband to lose to jail or children to be deprived of their father. Far from being devastated, she had become a public figure and even honored for her turnabout. She was the darling of congressional committees who wanted the facts right from the bear's mouth.

Finally, Bloch risked an attack on Bentley's indirect identification of "Julius" as Rosenberg.

E. H. BLOCH   Did you recognize the voice of the man who you say called you up and said, "This is Julius"?
BENTLEY   What do you mean recognize?
E. H. BLOCH   Are you a college graduate?
BENTLEY   Well, I mean—
E. H. BLOCH   Did you recognize whose voice it was who called you up and said—
BENTLEY   I don't understand, your Honor. I have heard the man over a telephone, that is all. I have heard no other voices. What does he mean?

Saypol tried to head off the answer. The court ruled him out and himself put the question which aided the defense:

SAYPOL Just a moment. I object to the question as to form. It depends upon whether Mr. Bloch addresses himself to the first call from Julius or to subsequent calls. I hardly think—

COURT No, no. Did you ever meet a person, did you ever meet anybody in person, whose voice you heard, and you can now say is the voice of the man who identified himself as Julius on the telephone?

BENTLEY No. I have never met anyone whose voice I heard, whom I could identify as Julius.

Encouraged, Bloch gambled further, mixing morals with his search for mendacity:

E. H. BLOCH How many times in all do you say this person who called you up and said, "This is Julius"—

BENTLEY It might have been five or six; it may have been more.

E. H. BLOCH And during what period of time was this?

BENTLEY I think I have stated that. It was from the fall of '42 to about November of '43.

E. H. BLOCH Can you tell us more specifically when these calls came in?

BENTLEY Yes, they always came after midnight, in the wee small hours. I remember it because I got waked out of bed.

E. H. BLOCH You were living at that time in Mr. Golos' apartment?

BENTLEY I have just informed you, I think twice, that I did not live with Mr. Golos. I lived at 58 Barrow Street, by myself.

E. H. BLOCH When you say these calls came in in the wee hours of the morning, was that at Mr. Golos' house at which you received these calls?

BENTLEY I have just told you, the calls came to my house at 58 Barrow Street. Mr. Golos was living some other place.

E. H. BLOCH Was Mr. Golos with you at your house at 58 Barrow Street when these calls came in?

Again, Saypol intervened to no effect.

COURT The question was whether Mr. Golos was with you at 58 Barrow Street at the time when any of these calls came in.

BENTLEY Yes, on one occasion he was.

E. H. BLOCH And on that one occasion, did you answer the phone?

BENTLEY I always answered the phone.

E. H. BLOCH Did you always ask the people who called you their names?

BENTLEY If I didn't get the voice right off, but this particular party always started his conversation by saying "This is Julius."

E. H. BLOCH "This is Julius"?

BENTLEY Yes.

E. H. BLOCH That was on six or seven occasions?

BENTLEY I put it at five or six. It might be seven or eight. I don't know exactly the number of them.

Bloch's final questions sought to establish Bentley's commercial interest in her new role. Yes, she had recently written a book. It was untitled, but the subject was "How a person can become a Communist and how they can be disillusioned and get out again." It was really an autobiography. She had submitted a draft to the publisher and received an advance of $3,000. She had a royalty arrangement, so obviously the success of the book would bring her more money.

She also lectured on communism for fees on some occasions. When Bentley wouldn't specify the number of times she had been paid, Bloch suddenly became a lion and engaged in an angry exchange with the judge. It seemed a minor and inappropriate place to challenge the court:

E. H. BLOCH Was it more than five times what you were paid for lecturing?

BENTLEY It was certainly more than five times.

E. H. BLOCH Was it more than ten times?

BENTLEY I really don't see where this is getting us—

E. H. BLOCH I move to strike out the answer as not responsive.

COURT Yes, I think she is absolutely right, and I think you have got enough of an answer for the subject that you are after.

E. H. BLOCH I respectfully except—to your Honor's remarks, and may I say to the Court, so that there will be no misunderstanding of the purpose of this cross-examination that I am attempting to elicit from this witness the fact that she has something to gain financially from testifying.

COURT You have done it. You have tried and I see your purpose, and it won't make any difference whether you get an answer now to ten times or an answer to fifteen times. The witness has stated that she has written a book, she expects to get royalties, she had gotten an advance and generally has stated she is lecturing, she has been paid for it. Go ahead.

E. H. BLOCH I respectfully except to your limitation of my cross-examination on this subject.

COURT I think I am giving you unusual latitude.

After conference with his father, Bloch came up with an incisive question which had great potential. It was keen because the answer could not hurt, but could help. That is ideal cross-examination, where possible injury is minimized, and possible triumph is maximized. That is why a cross-examiner's questions should be so designed that they call for no more than an answer of "Yes" or "No" or "I don't remember." Even if the question encompasses a number of facts, it should conclude with "Is that correct?" or "That's right, isn't it?" or "Correct?" If the question calls for an explanation, the hostile witness takes advantage of the open door to repeat his previous testimony, embellish it or extricate himself from an embarrassing attack. That is why a cross-examiner should almost never ask "Why?" If there is a lie to excise from the witness' mind, he must not be permitted to blunt the scalpel with wordiness.

The witness, having already told her prepared story on direct examination, was eager to return to familiar terrain. It served no purpose to permit her to do so. Cross-examination should seek new roads where the untold truth may be found. The witness must be forced to travel in the cross-examiner's direction. A yes or no answer cannot do much damage even if it is hostile. But a question such as "Why" or "Will you explain that?" would put the witness in control of the journey.

Bloch's final attack on Bentley was well conceived. In her book, submitted to the publisher, had she ever mentioned her telephone talks with a man who said, "This is Julius"?

BENTLEY Yes.

E. H. BLOCH When?

BENTLEY I haven't the least idea when that particular part of the book was written, but that was put into the book very definitely. Whether it is still in or whether it has been cut out I don't know.

The fact that she didn't know whether it was still in the draft appeared to be a protective hedge. It warranted subpoenaing the document from the publisher. The risk was not great. If "This is Julius" appeared in her script, it added nothing to her oral testimony. It still left whatever doubt there was that "Julius" was Rosenberg, since she had never seen him and couldn't recognize his voice. If "This is Julius" was not in the original script, then it would be powerful, if not indeed, conclusive contradiction of her testimony. But the defense never subpoenaed the script. So we shall never know. Bloch released the witness.

On redirect examination, Saypol demonstrated that Bentley had been subpoenaed and flew in from Puerto Rico to testify. Did anyone really believe that she would not have volunteered to be a witness?

Another question by Saypol permitted Bentley to give an insight and inside of Communist dedication. One of the reasons she wrote her book:

was to show the incredible things that Communists will go through in order to carry out their jobs because it meant that when I was called at two in the morning I often had to go out and go many blocks in the cold to get a pay telephone to call Mr. Golos.

Bloch asked for the right of recross-examination, because he had forgotten to ask one question.

The court granted it to him. He asked her about the constitution of the Communist Party. She said, "We didn't pay much attention to it, because it was one of those paper affairs." When pressed, she went further: "It was only a paper document that no one lived up to."

Bloch wanted to know whether she had told the FBI about the telephone calls from "Julius." She strengthened her previous testimony by answering that she certainly had.

Also, she denied receiving "one penny" from the government for her co-operation. Bloch had her reveal that she had testified as a prosecution witness against William Remington and Abe Brothman. The Rosenberg case was her third appearance as an accuser. But she had appeared many times before the House Un-American Activities Committee and Senator Patrick McCarran's committee.

She didn't know Harry Gold.

COURT   And wasn't it generally the policy of those engaged in this kind of work not to talk very much about the others that are engaged in similar kind of work?

BENTLEY   That is correct. I would even doubt it seriously if Mr. Golos himself knew who Mr. Gold's identity was.

Bloch's questions permitted Saypol to engage in redirect examination on a subject which otherwise might be irrelevant.

SAYPOL   Miss Bentley, Mr. Bloch asked you about Abraham Brothman. Was he one of the members of the Communist Party who supplied you as a courier with industrial information for transmission to Soviet Russia?

BENTLEY   Yes, he was.

SAYPOL   Mr. Bloch asked you about William W. Remington. Was he one of the members of the Communist Party who supplied you with information from Government sources for transmission to Soviet Russia?

BENTLEY   Yes, he was.

SAYPOL   Mr. Bloch asked you some question about a constitution. Is it not the fact that your meetings with people like Brothman and Moskowitz were held at odd places at night, deserted places?

BENTLEY   Correct.

The court, realizing the limited purpose of Bentley's testimony concerning communism, took the precaution of warning the jury against any prejudicial impact from the subject matter:

COURT This is as good a time as any to tell the jury, so that there is no confusion whatsoever as to the purpose for which this testimony was taken, that it is not to establish the guilt here of the crime charged because any of the defendants might have been members of the Communist Party, but it is to show a link, as the Government contends, exists between aiding Russia, which is an element required by the indictment, and being members of the Communist Party, just as if being a member of the Democratic Party or the Republican Party or being a member of the Elks Club or the Masons would furnish a link or give a motive or prove intent of any of the elements set forth in the indictment, and that is the only purpose for which it is taken, and you are not to determine the guilt or innocence of any of these defendants because you think they are Communists. That is not what they are charged with here.

It was on this deflating note that Elizabeth Bentley was excused as a witness.

The government tapered off its case with a witness against Morton Sobell. First, it offered a document to prove that he had not served in the Army, and therefore that his excuse to a neighbor in Mexico that he did not wish to return to the United States because he had already been in one war was false.

The judge admitted this record of Selective Service, over the strenuous objections of Kuntz and Phillips, but he cautioned the jury that "the fact Mr. Sobell did not serve in the Army should not in any way prejudice you in your deliberations in this case."

Then came the last witness. He was James S. Huggins, the immigration inspector, stationed in Laredo, Texas, where Sobell had been brought by Mexican authorities to be turned over to the FBI. Sobell had signed the document necessary to his admission into the United States. It contained a notation, "Deported from Mexico." The witness said there were Mexican security police present and also American agents.

Kuntz cross-examined him but raised no question about the legitimacy of the notation that Sobell had been deported. He gave no hint of illegal kidnapping. Later when the trial was finished, Kuntz and Phillips claimed otherwise. It was a dramatic, although belated, appeal to which I shall come.

Then came the fateful words.

SAYPOL The Government rests, if the Court please.

After formal motions to dismiss the indictment were summarily denied, the burden shifted to the defendants. It was now up to them to determine whether the Rosenbergs and Sobell would take the stand in their own behalf, and what other witnesses they would present.

CHAPTER 19

Long before the defendants took the stand, they and their attorneys had to agree upon strategy. There were two questions which were most troubling.

The first was whether Julius Rosenberg should take the stand and risk cross-examination. Bloch had already announced that Ethel would testify. Sympathy for her plight as a mother could be counted on to soften any blow struck at her. Also she was pretty and intelligent. She could be counted on to charm the jury and cope with a cross-examiner.

Julius had none of these protective elements in his factor. Nevertheless, there was no alternative but to have him testify. The incriminating evidence offered, particularly by the Greenglasses, had to be countered. It was too dangerous to rely on his right to be silent even though the law dictated that no adverse inference was to be drawn therefrom. Only his direct denial, or contrary version of some of the incidents, which I have previously set forth to contrast with the prosecution evidence, might save him from conviction. So, the first question was easily answered by the Rosenbergs and their counsel. Julius and Ethel would take the stand and defend themselves.

However, Sobell and his lawyers, Kuntz and Phillips, disagreed violently on this subject. This was later revealed to the court. Phillips thought that Sobell should testify in his defense. He feared that otherwise his flight from the country, his use of aliases, and Elitcher's testimony, all standing uncontradicted, might convict him. Kuntz an experienced criminal lawyer, differed. He thought that the government's case was too thin to overcome the presumption of innocence. He feared that cross-examination might worsen Sobell's plight. He preferred to depend on summation, to point out the remoteness of the evidence as it applied to Sobell. Phillips bowed to Kuntz's experience. It was agreed that Sobell would not testify and would put in no defense. The decision put a heavy responsibility on counsel in the event something went wrong. It accounted for the passionate tearful plea by his lawyers for a new trial on newly discovered evidence, when it was too late. I shall come to this extraordinary development later.

The Rosenbergs and the Blochs had even greater difficulty with a second question which had to be answered. What position would they take on cross-examination when they would be asked whether they were Communists? If they conceded that they were, they would be belabored with dozens of questions about their activities in the Party. They would have to reveal that they attended meetings almost nightly; that they engaged in intensive propaganda services; that they sold the *Daily Worker*, going from door to door like school children performing a chore; that they were pleased to do other menial tasks as dedicated servants of revolution; that they read Communist literature almost exclusively, most of it prepared in Russia; that they led debates on theories which denounced capitalism and, therefore, the United States; that they had advanced to the point of giving lectures to cell groups; and perhaps, perhaps the suspicious admission that they had ceased some of these overt activities. This would lead to another series of questions whether their interest in "the cause" had really diminished, or whether they had substituted secret activities for them. The implication would be created by the prosecutor that the higher the rank, the more underground the work.

Of course, the Rosenbergs, even if they admitted being active Communists, would vigorously deny any espionage. This they did and with persuasive emphasis. Nevertheless, if they were harried with fierce cross-examination concerning Communist theory and action, would the jury believe the denials? It was as if their admission of communism was a headlong drive toward betrayal, and then at the last moment they came to a screeching halt. Would the brakes hold against the enormous momentum of prejudice against communism?

The word Communist had come into such disrepute that the courts had held it was libelous.

So Emanuel Bloch urged that when the deadly question was asked by the prosecutor that Julius and Ethel should refuse to answer on the ground that it might tend to incriminate them—or, as was the morbid jest of the day, "tend to incinerate them."

Alexander Bloch reached a different conclusion. Being older and more experienced, he examined the practical consequences of "taking the Fifth."

"Don't you think," he reasoned, "that such a plea will be an admission of communism?" Of course, the jury would be told that no such inference may be drawn. But common sense could not be abrogated by constitutional theories "If you interview an applicant for a job as a teller in a bank, and you ask him whether he was ever convicted for stealing, and he refuses to answer because it might incriminate him, do you hire him? Or do you hire a sitter for your children, who asserts his privilege not to answer when you ask him if he ever molested youngsters?"

Furthermore, the problem was not as abstract as the discussion indicated. There *had* been evidence that the Rosenbergs were Communists. Elitcher and Greenglass had sworn that they had been indoctrinated by Julius. The jury was, therefore, aware of the Rosenbergs' Communist activities. A plea of Fifth Amendment against this background would surely be taken by the jury as confirmation of facts already presented to them.

Therefore, concluded the older Bloch, it would be wiser to admit their Communist beliefs, but argue strenuously that these were political, and not inconsistent with loyalty to the United States. Even if they were pummeled on cross-examination about their Communist activities, an opportunity would be afforded them to insist that at no time did their beliefs cross the line of espionage.

Their candor and forthrightness in admitting the truth of Communist affiliation would lend credence to their denial that they had anything to do with spy activities. Otherwise, their furtive attitude in "hiding behind the Fifth Amendment" might spill over to disbelief on the vital issue on which their lives depended.

Emanuel Bloch remained unconvinced. He reasoned that if they refused to answer, at least the door would be closed to an inquiry about their dedicated service to communism over many years. They would not have to reveal with whom they met. Perhaps among such pepole might be a traitor, even though they were innocent. Who knows what the government with its vast investigatory powers might have uncovered? If the defense unlocked the door, by waiving the Fifth Amendment, it might let in incriminating material which could not be overcome. The air was heavy with prejudice against Communists. It was the lawyers' duty to block off the inquiry if it could. Fortunately, the Constitution provided a bullet-proof vest against such attacks. Why take it off? It was not merely the single question "Are you a Communist?" which was involved. If admitted, new avenues of inquiry would follow inevitably. The lawyers were in the position of a doctor who is not as much concerned with the condition the patient has as with the sequelae.

The risk, argued the younger Bloch, was far greater from admitting that they were active Communists than from any improper inference drawn from the plea of self-incrimination. Particularly was this so since the judge recognized his duty to warn the jury against such an inference.

So the argument raged between the lawyers. The emotional strain of the trial, the unexpected blows, particularly of the Greenglasses' testimony, the terrible responsibility that wrong strategy might cost their clients' lives made the difference of opinion an angry exchange. At times, it was necessary for father and son to declare to each other that the harsh words and loud presentation were merely manifestations of mutual deep concern and not personal. The older Bloch was proud of his son, and Emanuel was respectful toward his father. But things were not going well and they had become involved in a contest, which was drawing international attention, and in which they felt insecure. This was evident from their uncertainty in dealing with the prosecutor and the judge. They objected hesitantly and withdrew, sometimes with apology. At other times, they stood their ground angrily. They were caught between psychological forces, asserting their rights on the record, to preserve appellate procedures, and deference toward the judge in order not to offend him. It was he who would hand out punishment, if the Rosenbergs were convicted. This concern for their clients even affected their attitude toward Saypol. It was the prosecutor who would recommend sentence, in the event of conviction. He must not be infuriated.

So, on one hand, they had to fight vigorously for the hard-pressed defendants and, on the other hand, not antagonize too much those who might hold out mercy even if the worst happened. This ambivalence was noticeable in the record.

The Blochs decided to take their disagreement to the Rosenbergs. They had a right to have a voice, indeed a decisive vote in the matter.

So the argument was transferred in the early hours of the morning from the law office to the improvised conference room in the prison underneath the courtroom. The United States marshal, at the instructions of the judge, made the prisoners available at all hours. Time was precious. A decision had to be made. It was more important than sleep. No apology was necessary. The Rosenbergs didn't have to explain that they weren't sleeping much anyway. There being no windows, the yellow electric bulbs created the illusion of decent night hours, which the haggard faces belied.

The Blochs could have saved themselves anguish from their disagreement. Julius was so certain of the answer that he was impatient with the presentation of the problem. He insisted on claiming the privilege of the Fifth Amendment. It was part of his Communist credo. He was fully familiar with his rights under the Constitution. He knew the court rulings on the subject. He considered "the plea" a proper countermeasure to the prejudice against Communists. It was the American way to overcome the obscene hostility to those who believed in another ideology.

He was ready to deny every charge of disloyalty to the United States. But he would no more entertain the possibility of waiving the Fifth Amendment privilege than of denouncing communism itself. He believed he had a right to both, and it was the United States Constitution which guaranteed them to him. Indeed, because the Fifth Amendment was part of his legitimate arsenal, he was eager to assert it. It was as if he was declaring his patriotic belief in the inviolability of the Constitution. We shall see that when he testified, he jumped to the assertion of the Fifth Amendment even when it was not necessary, or at times before it was necessary. His lawyers and even the judge could not head him off.

Under these circumstances, there was no purpose in explaining the practical considerations or the risks involved. He was as adamant as a Communist can be about his credo, that is to say, he was fanatical about it. Alexander Bloch could only shrug his shoulders. No fortress is less impenetrable than a closed mind.

Two interesting philosophical questions were presented by this incident. The first was the apparent contradiction between the theory of the Fifth Amendment and its violation in practical effect. Many studies have been made of this paradox. They range from the purist view that being a safeguard against tyranny, the privilege may not be diluted by adverse inference of any kind, to the view that the Fifth Amendment was intended to protect against self-incrimination in criminal cases, but was not intended to preclude inferences in civil matters such as an employer or the public may draw from its assertion. The latter view is that the burden on the prosecutor should remain heavy and cannot be lightened by requiring the accused to aid in his own conviction. But such extraordinary protection was not intended to relieve the defendants of all consequences in non-criminal matters. Otherwise, runs the argument, we violate common sense and make a precious rule unenforceable.

The second philosophical question was whether a client should be permitted to make a decision of strategy contrary to the judgment of his counsel. Assuming for this purpose that the Blochs had been in agreement and advised not taking the Fifth Amendment, should they have yielded to Rosenberg's contrary view? Did they owe a duty to protect him against himself? Or, as he didn't hesitate to say, "It is my life, and this is the way we'll do it!" Not easy.

I have in the past struggled with this problem. At first, I distinguished between matters which were legal, where I insisted on my view, or the client was invited to get another lawyer whose judgment he would accept, and non-legal questions such as the amount of settlement, in which instance, I offered my judgment, but permitted the client to decide. I found later regrets by the client, combined sometimes with lack of memory, as to who was responsible for the decision. So I tried recording the difference of views in writing, and stating that the client was making the decision despite my advice. Even this did not avail. When he regretted the result and was confronted with the letter, he would reply, "I know, but after all, you knew more about it than I did. Why did you let me do it?"

Perhaps he was right. I have since taken the full responsibility of decision even in non-legal matters.

But no one could have insisted that Julius Rosenberg should waive the Fifth Amendment. He considered it interwined with his liberty and his life. The Blochs could not be faulted for yielding. Their only remedy was to withdraw as counsel, if they felt strongly enough, but this was unthinkable. It would have been desertion in the midst of battle. Such option was only open to them when they were investigating the facts and interviewing the prospective clients before they accepted the retainer.

At that time, such a precondition could be and, in my opinion, should be imposed. When the McCarthy terror was at its height, I defended a number of those under a cloud (John Garfield, Margaret Webster) from his demagogic attacks. But, in each instance, I was satisfied that they were not Communists. Others sought to retain me, but when in the privacy of my office I asked, "Are you a Communist?" and the answer was "I don't intend to answer that. That is why I am here. No one has a right to ask me that question," I agreed, but then I had a right not to accept the representation, for I could not do justice to a cause for which I had no enthusiasm, even though it was technically correct to do so. Of course, this did not mean that the accused was not entitled to be defended. Even the meanest criminal is entitled to representation. Although guilty, the degree of his guilt and severity of punishment are involved and are worthy of any attorney's effort. Since such counsel is always available, the principle may be preserved, and yet the selective decision of any individual lawyer may also be respected.

This view is contrary to the accepted thesis of the American Bar Association that the evil reputation of a defendant does not rub off on his counsel, and that it is in the honored liberal tradition to take the most unpopular cases. I agree. The fact that it is unpopular may be a challenge to spur an acceptance. It is the nature of the case which gives me pause. I cannot be passionate about a cause in which I do not believe. Therefore, it is an injustice to the client to receive a diluted dedication. A lawyer has a right to choose the kind of case for which he will pour out his heart.

When I expressed this view in a lecture at Harvard Law School, there was general criticism on the theory that if such a view was commonly accepted, a hapless and despised defendant could not obtain any representation. I countered this hypothetical absurdity with the offer that if that contingency arose, I would be the first to volunteer to defend him. I was confident that others who believed as I did would make the same offer.

The argument is also made that an attorney who refuses to represent a defendant is setting himself up as judge of his own client's guilt or innocence, which is a function of the court, not his. True, but his decision is private and secret. It does not affect the determination by the court. This process of judging a client occurs in every case, civil or criminal.

The lawyer must make a discriminating judgment as to whether he will undertake the matter. He cannot and should not abdicate this responsibility.

In any event, the Blochs could not belatedly exercise this right, even if they wished to do so. Once they entered the case, their loyalty to their clients was unconditional. The Blochs lived up to this principle in full measure, indeed, far beyond the call of duty.

So it was decided that Julius would refuse to answer any question aimed at his Communist affiliation. He would claim immunity under the Fifth Amendment. Ethel went along with this strategy. If she had any doubts, they were silenced by her love and respect for Julius' vehemence concerning a matter of high principle.

We shall see the result of this fateful decision. It became the feature of cross-examination, particularly of Ethel.

CHAPTER 20

E. H. BLOCH If the Court, please, my first witness is the defendant
Julius Rosenberg.
COURT Very well.

Rosenberg arose from his chair, walked to the raised witness stand
next to the judge's bench which was flanked on the other side by the
jury box. His body was as stiff as his right hand when he raised it to take
the oath. Then he sat down. He was pale. His black mustache was shaved
to a thin line, which gave an incongruous elegant look to a plain face.
A thick flowing mustache would have been more fitting. Neither could
have hidden his years. He was thirty-three years old.

He was under close observation on the left by the judge and on the
right by the jury. His nervousness, however, disappeared the moment he
uttered his first words. Witnesses, like actors and speakers, experience
this calm when the performance starts. Concentration on the immediate
task excludes self-conscious anxiety. That is why stutterers can speak or
sing fluently from a stage. It is also why a stutterer who is directed to
press his thumb against a different finger of his hand at each syllable he
pronounces will have no difficulty in speaking. His attention is diverted
to touch and his tongue is freed.

Bloch put him at ease with a friendly request to keep his voice up.
"Don't make the same mistake some of the witnesses made and lower
it as you go along."

Rosenberg gave his educational background. He attended schools on
the lower East Side and also Hebrew School. After he graduated from
Seward Park High School, he entered the School of Technology at the
College of the City of New York and received a degree of Bachelor of
Electrical Engineering in February 1939.

He had married at the age of twenty-one and he pointed out Ethel as his wife. She smiled at the formality of identification. They had two children, aged eight and four.

He remembered the precise date he was arrested, July 16, 1950. Until then, he was living with his wife and children in a $51-a-month apartment consisting of three rooms and a bathroom.

Rosenberg offered detail of his extremely modest standard of living. It was an indirect way of negating Greenglass' story of Rosenberg's largess with Russian money. Would not some of it have rubbed off on him for his services?

His furniture was supplied by a friend who moved to California and wanted to save storage charges. At times he would see advertisements in the *Knickerbocker Village News* by tenants who wanted to dispose of secondhand furniture. He picked up a secondhand piano for $25, and two small chests for the children's room for $5.

E. H. BLOCH Did you come into court with a coat?
ROSENBERG Yes, sir.
E. H. BLOCH When did you buy that coat?
ROSENBERG I would say it was either 1941 or 1942.
E. H. BLOCH Did you ever buy a winter overcoat since then?
ROSENBERG No, sir, I did not.
E. H. BLOCH How much did you pay for that coat?
ROSENBERG Well, I estimate it was somewhere about $55.

In eleven years, he had bought five suits, each costing about $55. Then came the answer to the accusation that the console table had been given to him by the Soviet Union so that he could use its inner compartment for secret photography.

ROSENBERG Only once did I purchase a new item.
E. H. BLOCH What item was that?
ROSENBERG A console table.
E. H. BLOCH And when did you purchase that?
ROSENBERG I would say it was either in 1944 or 1945.
E. H. BLOCH And from where did you purchase that console table?
ROSENBERG From R. H. Macy & Company.
E. H. BLOCH And how much did you pay for that console table?
ROSENBERG It was somewhere about $21.

He traced his jobs. Ethel had to work too. She obtained a position with the Census Bureau in Washington. He was able to join her when he passed an examination and became a junior engineer in the Signal Corps of the United States. They managed to be transferred to New York, where they lived with his mother for a while and ultimately set up their own small apartment. He rose to assistant engineer, his salary being promoted too, from $2,000 to $3,200 a year.

E. H. BLOCH Now, were you then separated from your job with the United States Government?
ROSENBERG I was.

This was delicate treatment of an embarrassing incident. The prosecutor was bound to delve into the reason for his "separation." Here again, a trial lawyer is faced with a difficult decision. Should he omit the question entirely and await the attack on cross-examination? If he does raise the subject, isn't it better to take the wind out of the prosecutor's sails by revealing the unpleasant truth on direct examination? This is usually the best tactic. It affords an opportunity to bathe the matter in the softest light, and it has the virtue of candor, which lends credibility to the rest of his testimony.

He became an engineer at Emerson Radio Corporation in 1945, earning $5,000 a year, but when they curtailed their staff, he formed a company of his own. His partners were David Greenglass' brother, Bernard, and a neighbor. They bought and sold surplus hardware—screws, nuts, bolts and wrenches. This business failed and he went into another, David Greenglass joining him. He traced its fortunes, which were mostly ill.

Up to this point, there was nothing fascinating in Rosenberg's story. The interest was in observing him. Every witness gives off emanations, which have little to do with the words he utters. Newspaper and other reports indicate that he was self-assured, but such confidence, unless leavened with sincerity and forthrightness, might create an unsympathetic reaction. Only the jury could obtain impressions of his veracity and sincerity.

It is impossible to form a comprehensive and reliable judgment from merely reading the cold print in the record. Some day, instead of a court stenographer, we may have a tape made of the trial which will reproduce the scene visually and orally. In some Appellate Courts, as, for example, in the Federal Court in Pennsylvania (the Third Circuit) sound recordings are made of the lawyers' arguments (no witnesses are heard on appeal). These are available only to the judges in their conference room. They not only serve to refresh their memory of what was said, they also convey the emotion and specific phrasing of the advocate. Though less important than the inflections of a witness, they have a persuasive power beyond the mere words in the printed briefs. An argument well made is much stronger than the same argument poorly made. "Form is not a protuberance on substance," wrote Judge Cardozo. "It is substance."

I have always opposed cameras or microphones in the courtroom. The witness is self-conscious enough, without placing the burden of lights, mikes and the terror which one experiences when he "is on stage." Furthermore, there is a temptation to strike postures for the recording. All one has to do is watch anyone preening himself or herself for a snapshot, to know that the pursuit of truth is more difficult in such atmos-

(205)

phere. It tends to antics and affectation. Our objective is to achieve the very opposite—a serious mood, in which revelation can prosper.

But with the new technology of unobserved cold light and hidden silent cameras, the witness, not being put in a spotlight, may become as unaware of the recording as he is of the stenographer who sits under his nose.

—→×←—

Even though the overture of Rosenberg's recital was dull, his testimony now approached an exciting theme. What did he have to say about accusations spelled out in so much detail?

The Blochs had made a list of them and now put the direct questions. Were they true? Would he deny them in every respect?

E. H. BLOCH Now, Mr. Rosenberg, are you aware of the charge that the Government has leveled against you?

ROSENBERG I am.

E. H. BLOCH Do you know what you are being charged with?

ROSENBERG Yes.

E. H. BLOCH What are you being charged with?

ROSENBERG Conspiracy to commit espionage to aid a foreign government.

E. H. BLOCH And you have been here all the time that the witnesses who appeared for the prosecution testified?

ROSENBERG Yes, sir, I have.

E. H. BLOCH And amongst those witnesses did you hear your brother-in-law Dave Greenglass testify?

ROSENBERG Yes, I did.

E. H. BLOCH And did you hear your sister-in-law Ruth Greenglass testify?

ROSENBERG I did.

E. H. BLOCH Now I want to direct the following questions and try to have you focus your attention upon your recollection of their testimony.

Mrs. Ruth Greenglass testified here, in substance, that in the middle of November 1944, you came over to her house or you invited her to your house and you asked her to enlist her husband, Dave Greenglass, in getting information out of where he was working and deliver or convey that information to you.

Did you ever have any conversation with Mrs. Ruth Greenglass at or about that time with respect to getting information from Dave Greenglass out of the place that he was working?

ROSENBERG I did not.

E. H. BLOCH Did you know in the middle of November 1944 where Dave Greenglass was stationed?

ROSENBERG   I did not.

E. H. BLOCH   Did you know in the middle of November 1944 that there was such a project known as the Los Alamos Project?

ROSENBERG   I did not. . . .

E. H. BLOCH   Did you ever give Ruth Greenglass $150, for her to go out to visit her husband in New Mexico, for the purpose of trying to enlist him in espionage work?

ROSENBERG   I did not.

E. H. BLOCH   Did you ever give Ruth Greenglass one single penny at any time during your life?

ROSENBERG   I did not.

E. H. BLOCH   Now, Ruth Greenglass testified in substance, that she went out to visit her husband, and when she came back here she conveyed certain information which she had received from her husband, and I refer specifically to the names of certain scientists like Dr. Niels Bohr, Dr. Oppenheimer, Dr. Urey. Did you ever have a conversation with Ruth Greenglass in the month of December 1944, in which any of those names were mentioned?

ROSENBERG   I did not have such a conversation. . . .

E. H. BLOCH   Did you know of the existence of the Los Alamos Project in December 1944?

ROSENBERG   I did not.

E. H. BLOCH   Dave Greenglass and Ruth Greenglass testified that about two days after Dave came into New York you came over to their house one morning and you asked Dave for certain information. Did you ever go over to the Greenglasses' house and ask them for any such information?

ROSENBERG   I did not.

In the same absolute and unequivocal manner, he denied asking for a sketch of the bomb or receiving it from Greenglass. He was shown the exhibit which was a drawing of the bomb, supposedly given to him and forwarded to the Russians. "I never saw this sketch before," he replied.

He never realized that David Greenglass was working on an atomic bomb project. When Saypol objected to this conclusion, the court overruled him.

COURT   No, no, that is the only way he can answer the charges. We have got to find out what was in his mind.

SAYPOL   True.

There had been testimony that Rosenberg had described an earlier version of the atomic bomb to Greenglass. He denied it and asserted that he could not even repeat the description he had heard in the courtroom.

He had never taken a course in nuclear physics when he was in college.

(207)

COURT   At any time prior to January 1945, had anybody discussed with you, anybody at all, discussed with you the atom bomb?

ROSENBERG   No, sir; they did not.

COURT   Did anybody discuss with you nuclear fission?

ROSENBERG   No, sir.

COURT   Did anybody discuss with you any projects that had been going on in Germany?

ROSENBERG   No, sir.

COURT   On the atom bomb?

ROSENBERG   No, sir.

A recess was declared until the next morning, March 22, 1951, at 10:30 A.M.

Apparently, during the night's preparation, it was thought advisable to make a correction. The next day, Rosenberg admitted something had slipped his mind in describing his residences. He had lived for a year with a former classmate, Marcus Pogarsky, also known as Page. Since the prosecutor later suggested that he, among others, was a Communist, it was important not to permit the accusation that the omission was deliberate.

Thereafter, the flood of denials continued. A photograph of Yakovlev was shown to him:

ROSENBERG   I have never seen this man in my life.

COURT   Did you know anybody at all in the Russian Consulate office?

ROSENBERG   I did not, sir.

Bloch repeated Greenglass' accusation that Rosenberg drove to First Avenue and about 50th Street, where a Russian got into the car to query him about the bomb.

E. H. BLOCH   Did any such incident occur?

ROSENBERG   That incident never occurred, sir.

Bloch continued to feed questions for denial when the examination suddenly took another turn involving Rosenberg's general philosophy. It was the judge who gave Rosenberg a chance to explain himself.

COURT   Did you ever discuss with Ann Sidorovich the respective preferences of economic systems between Russia and the United States?

ROSENBERG   Well, your Honor, if you will let me answer that question in my own way I want to explain that question.

COURT   Go ahead.

ROSENBERG   First of all, I am not an expert on matters on different economic systems, but in my normal social intercourse with my friends we discussed matters like that. And I believe there are merits in both systems, I mean from what I have been able to read and ascertain.

COURT   I am not talking about your belief today. I am talking about your belief at that time, in January 1945.

ROSENBERG   Well, that is what I am talking about. At that time, what I believed at that time I still believe today. In the first place, I heartily approve our system of justice as performed in this country, Anglo-Saxon jurisprudence. I am in favor, heartily in favor, of our Constitution and Bill of Rights and I owe my allegiance to my country at all times.

Bloch kept the favorable momentum going:

E. H. BLOCH   Do you owe allegiance to any other country?

ROSENBERG   No, I do not.

E. H. BLOCH   Have you any divided allegiance?

ROSENBERG   I do not.

E. H. BLOCH   Would you fight for this country—

ROSENBERG   Yes, I will.

E. H. BLOCH   —if it were engaged in a war with any other country?

ROSENBERG   Yes, I will, and in discussing the merits of other forms of governments, I discussed that with my friends on the basis of the performance of what they accomplished, and I felt that the Soviet Government has improved the lot of the underdog there, has made a lot of progress in eliminating illiteracy, has done a lot of reconstruction work and built up a lot of resources, and at the same time I felt that they contributed a major share in destroying the Hitler beast who killed six million of my co-religionists and I feel emotional about that thing.

E. H. BLOCH   Did you feel that way in 1945?

ROSENBERG   Yes, I felt that way in 1945.

E. H. BLOCH   Do you feel that way today?

ROSENBERG   I still feel that way.

COURT   Did you approve the communistic system of Russia over the capitalistic system in this country?

ROSENBERG   I am not an expert on those things, your Honor, and I did not make any such direct statement.

E. H. BLOCH   Did you ever make any comparisons in the sense that the Court has asked you, about whether you preferred one system over another?

ROSENBERG   No, I did not. I would like to state that my personal opinions are that the people of every country should decide by themselves what kind of government they want. If the English want a king, it is their business. If the Russians want communism, it is their business. If the Americans want our form of government, it is our business. I feel that the majority of people should decide for themselves what kind of government they want.

E. H. BLOCH Do you believe in the overthrow of government by force
and violence?

ROSENBERG I do not.

E. H. BLOCH Do you believe in anybody committing acts of espionage
against his own country?

ROSENBERG I do not believe that.

Rosenberg was scoring heavily. Unless the jury simply disbelieved that
he meant what he said, and that he was lying in his teeth, his answers
were impressive assertions of a credo which rejected the government's
entire case against him.

However, in law as in life, triumph is often followed by defeat. It was
Rosenberg himself, who created the shock which must have swept
through the courtroom.

COURT Well, did you ever belong to any group that discussed the system
of Russia?

ROSENBERG Well, your Honor, if you are referring to political groups—
is that what you are referring to?

COURT Any group.

ROSENBERG Well, your Honor, I feel at this time that I refuse to answer
a question that might tend to incriminate me.

COURT Well now, I won't direct you at this point to answer; I will wait
for the cross-examination.

It often happens in cross-examination that a witness who has established a definite personality is suddenly revealed to be something else
than his appearance and answers have indicated. It is as if a veil was
lifted and the true person glimpsed for the first time. Sometimes it is a
flash of anger and a vicious gesture which undoes the benign character
he had been presenting; or it may be an explosive unwarranted burst of
laughter which exposes his neurotic character. The cross-examiner seeks
to take the witness off guard, so that he may reveal himself.

Rosenberg's answer may well have had this effect on the jury. He had
sounded candid, intelligent and unequivocal in his answers. Then, his
refusal to answer because it might "incriminate him"—those awful words
—probably cast a cloud on everything he was saying. Instead of forthrightness, there was furtiveness. Instead of uninhibited truth, there was
legalism. Instead of courage which he had exhibited by praising what he
liked in Russia, there was fear. He was entitled to his constitutional right
not to give an answer which might help prove him guilty of a crime, but
what effect would his concern have on the jury, despite the instruction
that no adverse inference must be drawn from the exercise of his
privilege? The jury system is susceptible of psychological forces which
beat upon it, and they cannot be ignored in the process of persuasion.

Bloch resumed his journey on the prior path of denials, but it is doubtful that the jury could take its mind entirely off the Fifth Amendment plea, and its effect on his credibility.

Rosenberg was asked whether he had ever cut the side of a Jell-O box to use as a recognition signal. He denied he ever did.

E. H. BLOCH   Did any such incident ever take place?

ROSENBERG   It never did.

He never commented that "the simplest things are always the cleverest." Neither he nor Ethel ever typed material for transmission to Russia.

When Greenglass came to New York, Rosenberg never discussed the atomic bomb with him. He did not even know that Greenglass was working on a secret project, and he knew nothing about an atomic bomb at that time.

E. H. BLOCH   Did you discuss politics with Greenglass that night?

ROSENBERG   Well, as every intelligent American did in those times, we discussed the war.

SAYPOL   May I ask to have the answer stricken as not responsive?

E. H. BLOCH   I consent.

SAYPOL   I don't want this man set up as a standard for intelligent Americans.

E. H. BLOCH   Now, I move to strike out Mr. Saypol's statement.

COURT   Disregard Mr. Saypol's statement and strike from the record "intelligent Americans."

E. H. BLOCH   Never mind about any intelligent American. We are asking you whether you and your wife and sister-in-law and brother-in-law discussed politics?

ROSENBERG   Yes, we discussed the war.

E. H. BLOCH   Was that unusual for you to discuss politics with your family or friends?

ROSENBERG   No, it was not.

E. H. BLOCH   Have you any independent recollection of what specific subject you discussed that night with Dave and Ruth?

ROSENBERG   Well, we were talking about the effort all the different Allies were making in the war and we noted that the Russians were carrying at that particular time the heaviest load of the German Army.

The court asked whether he had expressed the opinion that the Russians were not getting the co-operation from the Allies to which they were entitled. "No, I didn't express that opinion, sir," he replied.

The court pursued this by asking whether he hadn't by that time already met Elitcher. Bloch offered to go into the Elitcher matter and the court invited him to do so whenever he wished.

Bloch proceeded first to tackle the lengthy testimony of Ruth Greenglass that Julius visited her, ordered her sister, Dorothy, into a bathroom, and talked to her about espionage.

I have already set forth his contrary version that it was Ruth who called him to express her distress because David was in some sort of trouble for stealing at Los Alamos. What went unnoticed by the cross-examiner was a curious comment Rosenberg made in describing this incident. Bloch asked him:

E. H. BLOCH Did you see Dorothy Printz here on the stand?

ROSENBERG Yes, and that is how I recalled the incident, because when she testified here in court I remembered being at her house.

A cross-examiner should have sensitive antennae to unnatural or illogical answers. Is it likely that Rosenberg would have been reminded of this incident in Ruth Greenglass' home only because he saw Dorothy Printz on the stand? According to his own testimony, he had been so oppressed by Ruth's worry about David's misfeasance, that he consulted Ethel about it. Psychologically, wasn't his reference to Dorothy on the stand, a possible giveaway that this was one meeting he could not deny?

Rosenberg denied ever having met Harry Gold. He did not know of his activities until he "read about it in the newspapers." Of course, then he did not know of Gold's visit to Albuquerque, the delivery to him of the atom sketches or the $500 given to David at that time. He categorically denied ever arranging meetings between the Greenglasses and a courier, or receiving any written material from David, secret or otherwise, or knowing Jacob Golos or Elizabeth Bentley. He never telephoned Bentley or used the signal "This is Julius." He was known among his friends as "Julie." Ethel never typed up information about the bomb. He didn't know any Russians at all. He never gave Greenglass $1,000 or $4,000, nor had he ever seen the brown wrapping paper in which the money was delivered.

E. H. BLOCH Now there is Scotch tape there. Did you ever put any Scotch tape on a wrapper like that?

ROSENBERG No, but I have used Scotch tape.

This was another answer which invited cross-examination. The defensive comment that he had "used Scotch tape" was not called for by the question. It could have been a psychological hedge or sensitivity, not unlike that which a lie detector records. Certain words register pulse reactions because of their association with events about which the subject otherwise denies having any knowledge. However, the prosecutor never pursued the strange answer.

Bloch continued to cite Greenglass' testimony in order to elicit specific denials. No, Rosenberg never suggested that Greenglass go back to Los Alamos to continue espionage contacts; nor go to universities to learn about nuclear physics, better to absorb information from his contacts.

Indeed, the opposite was true. Greenglass under the GI bill, went to school three nights a week. Rosenberg complained that he was not supervising the employees in their business. He told him:

"Look here, Dave, you are shirking on the job. You are not doing your work. The fellows aren't getting stuff out," and we had discussions over that, and we had arguments about that, and finally David quit school because of that.

E. H. BLOCH   Is it fair to say that you objected to his continuing his education at that time?

ROSENBERG   I certainly did.

Rosenberg challenged Ruth Greenglass on this point too. He testified:

Ruth said, "You are taking advantage of my husband. After all you have an education, he should have an education and he is contributing more than you are to the business anyway, because he produces the work and you just get it, and if he gave you four hours a day, that is enough for you. You should let him go to school."
Well, I did not see eye to eye with her on that and we argued about it.

E. H. BLOCH   Did you ever mention to Davey that you would support him or get the Russians to support him if he continued his college education?

ROSENBERG   I did not.

Rosenberg didn't have "students attending American universities who were subsidized by the Russians" nor did he have espionage contacts in Cleveland and Schenectady. He had never been in either of these cities in his life. He never had any contact with any employee of General Electric. Once more, the judge interrupted the flow of innocence with a piercing question.

COURT   Did you know anybody working there?

ROSENBERG   Sure I did.

COURT   Whom did you know working there?

ROSENBERG   Morton Sobell.

COURT   How long had you known Sobell?

ROSENBERG   I went to school with him.

COURT   And you had known him continuously right up until the present day?

ROSENBERG   Well, sporadically for a time and then—

COURT   Rather close?

ROSENBERG   Well, he was a friend of mine.

Bloch referred to the charge that Rosenberg had revealed the Sky Platform Project back in 1947.

(213)

I would like to explain that. I don't remember the specific incident but at that time in the popular science magazines and in the newspapers there was some talk about the Germans had done some work on some kind of suspended lens in the sky to concentrate the rays of the sun at the earth, and that is what I believe was the discussion we might have had at that time. Greenglass used to read the *Popular Mechanics* and the *Popular Science* and he always talked about things like that at the shop.

COURT Did you read it too?

ROSENBERG No, I didn't.

He never communicated with Russians by putting microfilm in an alcove of a motion picture theater. He never knew Gromov, Elizabeth Bentley's superior after Golos died. He had never told Greenglass that he had learned about an atomic-energy-driven airplane. It was not true that he had encouraged Greenglass to get out of the country, citing as an example Joel Barr's successful escape. As far as he knew, Barr had gone to Sweden to study music. He admitted knowing Joel Barr from college days. They had continued their friendship and visited each other.

The jury had previously been given the impression by Saypol that Barr was a fleeing Communist. Therefore, Rosenberg's admission of his intimate friendship with Barr was another illustration of the ineffectiveness of the Fifth Amendment plea in the face of other testimony that Rosenberg was a Communist.

Bloch then took Rosenberg over a tortuous road of his business relationship with Greenglass. The judge tried to speed the testimony to more relevant areas.

E. H. BLOCH I would like to ask a question, your Honor, but I know Mr. Saypol might object, and I am trying to speed it up. I will ask the question.

COURT This is the first time I ever heard a lawyer worry about asking a question before asking it.

Rosenberg recited his purchase of Greenglass' stock for $1,000. When he came to get the stock and resignation, Greenglass took him for a walk. This was the occasion when Greenglass, trapped and tormented, demanded $2,000. In the alternative, he asked Rosenberg to provide him with a certificate of smallpox vaccination. I have previously set forth this incident to contrast it with Greenglass' story that on that walk in the park, Rosenberg told him how to get to safety behind the Iron Curtain.

The judge again anticipated the prosecutor's cross-examination by asking why, if they were quarreling in their business, Greenglass "would come to you and confess and ask you to help him out instead of going to somebody else?" He replied, "I have no idea why he came to me."

He admitted asking Dr. Bernhardt on behalf of "a person" about vaccination requirements to enter Mexico. He denied coming to Greenglass' home in a state of alarm because the anonymity of Harry Gold had been broken spectacularly on the front page of a newspaper, where Gold's face and name were featured as an arrested spy. He never urged Greenglass to flee the country, nor did he give him $1,000 or later $4,000. He went on to demonstrate that he had no such money in his bank account.

COURT Well, Mr. Rosenberg, if it was the purpose that Mr. Greenglass had testified it was for, then it would be fair to suppose that the money would never come out of a bank account; isn't that so?
ROSENBERG Well, it is not for me to say, sir.
COURT All right.

Then he gave his version of the walk with Greenglass on the occasion when the Einsohns were met. Greenglass "with a wild look in his eyes" changed from entreaty to threat, if Rosenberg didn't get $2,000 for him. Rosenberg considered this "blackmail," a word, as we have seen, with unhappy implications.

Rosenberg never got a citation nor a watch nor did Ethel from the Russian Government. Ethel did have a watch, which he had given her, as a birthday gift. It cost $30. He didn't remember whether she had another watch. The denials, like bowling balls knocking down the prosecution's pins, finally stopped rolling. Bloch turned to affirmative testimony. It is always more difficult to construct than to destroy. Rosenberg was now ready to describe his relationship with the FBI after Greenglass' arrest. It was a curious cat-and-mouse game for a while. He was not immediately accused. Rather, he was questioned and even released. There was a suspended period which is more cruel punishment than incarceration. For no man is free who anticipates the limited time of his freedom. Tyrants considered fear of impending doom a most effective form of torture for the victim. Yet Rosenberg insisted on the stand that his innocence fortified him against any anxiety. It was impressive testimony, and he built it in considerable detail. Would the jury believe that his stoicism stemmed from inner peace, rather than simulated courage?

He began by describing the first visit to his home of three FBI men. They wanted to talk to him. Julius consulted with Ethel.

ROSENBERG Do you think I ought to talk to these gentlemen?
ETHEL ROSENBERG You know, if Davey is in some sort of trouble, if you can help my brother, talk to them; maybe you can be of some assistance to them.

The impression he thus gave was that neither he nor Ethel even suspected that they were involved. She made breakfast. He shaved. Then he was ready to talk but Harrington, one of the FBI men, said:

"We can't talk here. Would you like to come down to our office and we will drop in and have a cup of coffee?"

They drove to the Federal Building at Foley Square and went to the twentieth floor. The FBI were coy. They pretended to ask information only about Greenglass, but finally they revealed their real purpose. Rosenberg felt he had been tricked. He exploded. This is his description of the incident:

ROSENBERG   Well, there was a Mr. Norton in the room sitting at a desk with a pad in front of him, and Mr. Harrington sat on the other side of the table. I sat down on the front side of the table and another member of the FBI came in and sat behind, and they started asking questions about what I knew about David Greenglass. First they tried to get my background, what relations I had with him. I gave them my school background, work background and I told them whatever I knew about David Greenglass' education and his work background.

E. H. BLOCH   Did you tell them that you had formerly been employed by the Government of the United States?

ROSENBERG   Yes, I told them, and at that point they said to me—they questioned me and tried to focus my attention to, as I notice now, certain dates in the overt acts listed in this indictment. They asked me questions concerning when David Greenglass came in on furlough. I didn't remember. I helped them as much as I could in what I could remember. At one point in the discussion, I would say it was about two hours after I was there, they said to me, "Do you know that your brother-in-law said you told him to supply information for Russia?"

So I said, "That couldn't be so." So I said, "Where is David Greenglass?" I didn't know where he was because I knew he was taken in custody. They wouldn't tell me. I said, "Will you bring him here and let him tell me that to my face?" And they said, "What if we bring him here, what will you do?"

"I will call him a liar to his face because that is not so."

And I said, "Look, gentlemen, at first you asked me to come down and get some information concerning David Greenglass. Now you are trying to implicate me in something. I would like to see a lawyer."

Well, at this point, Mr. Norton said, "Oh, we are not accusing you of anything. We are just trying to help you."

I said, "I would like to get in touch with the lawyer for the Federation of Architects and Engineers." I asked the FBI to please call him. Well, at this point Mr. Norton said, "Have a smoke, have a piece of gum. Would you like something to eat?" And the language he used in his actions were what the fellows at West Street would call conning and we discussed around the point. Mr. Norton asked me again, "Did you ask David Greenglass to turn over information for the Russians?" And I said, "No." I denied it. And then we discussed again what periods of time David Greenglass came in. I didn't recall too well and I kept on asking Mr. Norton, "I want to get in touch with my lawyer."

Finally, some time after lunch, it was probably between 12 and 1, my wife reached me at the FBI office and I told her that the FBI is making some foolish accusations, to please—

SAYPOL   May that—

E. H. BLOCH   Never mind what you told your wife—

SAYPOL   No, no, I do not mind what he told his wife but I mind his characterization about what the charges were.

COURT   Oh, now, wait a minute, Mr. Saypol; that objection doesn't mean anything. You are either going to object to what he told his wife—if that is what he told his wife—he has a right to repeat it here.

SAYPOL   I do not object to what he told his wife.

COURT   Then he can go right ahead.

Finally, another FBI agent, Mr. Morton, called Rosenberg's attorney and permitted him to talk to him.

ROSENBERG   I told him I was down at the FBI, and he said, "Are you under arrest?" I said, "I don't know."

He said, "Ask the FBI if you are under arrest."

And I asked Mr. Norton, "Am I under arrest?"

He said, "No." Then he said, "Pick yourself up and come down to our office," and I said, "Good-bye, gentlemen," and I left the FBI office.

Despite this incident, Rosenberg's conviction that he was in the clear continued unshaken. He went about his business in "routine" fashion. Perhaps such self-confidence was stretching credibility too much. Even an innocent man would be nervous about the misunderstanding of a powerful government agency. His depiction of himself as carelessly unconcerned, therefore, provoked querulous questions from the judge, even before Saypol could get at him.

In demonstration of his innocent frame of mind, Rosenberg testified that he did not attempt to remove any articles from his home "or do anything to conceal any material or information from the Government authorities." He continued to maintain his same apartment and to go to business every day.

COURT   Did you know whether you were under surveillance by the FBI at that time?

ROSENBERG   No, I didn't know.

(217)

COURT Did you think you were?

ROSENBERG It didn't matter.

COURT Did you think you were?

ROSENBERG I didn't know.

COURT I am asking you whether you thought you were.

ROSENBERG I don't know, your Honor.

When Bloch, apparently unhappy with this answer, asked whether in view of the FBI's statement that Greenglass "had accused you of espionage, didn't it occur to you that they were going to watch you very closely?" Rosenberg refused to accept the hint that he should make a more believable answer. He held his ground, but the judge pursued the matter and he finally yielded.

ROSENBERG It occurred to me that they would have arrested me if they suspected me.

COURT The answer is you didn't think you were under surveillance?

ROSENBERG There was a possibility I could have been under surveillance.

COURT Did you think there was that possibility?

ROSENBERG Yes, it entered my mind.

Bloch returned to denials. Rosenberg owned only one camera, which the Kodak Company had given to him free because his birthday "coincided with their anniversary." He had never used it for microfilming. When he went on vacation, he would borrow a camera from Bernard Greenglass.

The prosecution's testimony that he had spent $50 or $75 a night entertaining in nightclubs, in accordance with the melodramatic notion that that was a working site for espionage, he termed ridiculous. He had only been in a nightclub once in his life when the Federation of Architects gave a dinner party at Café Society.

E. H. BLOCH Now, were you in the habit of going to high class restaurants?

ROSENBERG I don't know what you mean by high class, Mr. Bloch.

E. H. BLOCH All right. Did you ever go to restaurants where the prices were expensive?

ROSENBERG Yes, I did.

E. H. BLOCH How many?

ROSENBERG Well, once when I was taking my wife out, to a place near Emerson Radio called Pappas, and on another occasion I have eaten at a place called Nicholaus on Second Avenue.

E. H. BLOCH Did you ever eat at Manny Wolf's?

ROSENBERG Yes, I remember eating there once.

E. H. BLOCH With whom?

ROSENBERG When I was working as an inspector for Jefferson Travers

Radio, they had a dinner party and they invited the inspectors down to Manny Wolf's for dinner and for a show.

As for Sobell, he never delivered "any information relating to the national defense." When Rosenberg visited Elitcher in Washington, he did not do so on Sobell's advice.

Since Elitcher had testified that Rosenberg solicited him to join the spy brigade and had bragged that Sobell was a member of it, Bloch tackled both propositions at one time. Rosenberg was not close to the Sobells. They had visited each other only "once or twice a year" in 1946 and 1947. He had not approached Elitcher at Sobell's "instructions." He had called him because "I was lonesome and I looked up in the telephone book for Elitcher's number." He was invited to come over and they chatted about their jobs and about the war and Russia's major contribution, but there wasn't a single word spoken about espionage.

Later Rosenberg was dismissed from his government job. He went to Washington to see his congressman, Samuel Dickstein, about his appeal from the dismissal. While on this mission, he visited Elitcher, who took him to the Federal Workers Union headquarters. There was no discussion of espionage.

Rosenberg wound up with two succinct, important denials. He had never asked Greenglass to get six sets of passport photos of which he received five sets.

E. H. BLOCH   Just one last question. Did you ever have any arrangement with Dave Greenglass or Ruth Greenglass or any Russian or with your wife or with anybody in this world to transmit information to the Soviet Union or any foreign power?
ROSENBERG   I did not have any such arrangement.
E. H. BLOCH   I think I am through, your Honor.

Before the government could begin its cross-examination, Bloch was nudged by memory.

E. H. BLOCH   I am sorry, your Honor, I forgot to cover two incidents in connection with the testimony of Elitcher.

He drew a denial from Rosenberg that he had ever met with Elitcher and Sobell at 42nd Street and Third Avenue and then ate with Elitcher at Manny Wolf's. Nor did Sobell bring him a microfilm on the evening that Elitcher arrived from Washington in a jittery state because he had been followed.

This time Bloch was really through. The acquiescent atmosphere of direct examination was about to be replaced by hostile probing. The court declared a brief recess, as if a time interval would more properly set the stage for the cross-examination drama which was about to be enacted.

CHAPTER 21

If a trial was heard as a symphony, dissonances and all, the repeated theme of Julius and Ethel's cross-examination would have been the Fifth Amendment.

Within minutes after Saypol began his questioning, Rosenberg actually thrust the Fifth Amendment at him when it was not necessary to do so. Indeed, in fairness to the judge and prosecutor, they tried to head him off. However, he was so eager to spout his constitutional privilege that he volunteered information which was irrelevant in order to say that he would not permit himself to be questioned about it.

Saypol's first question was:

> Mr. Rosenberg, tell us a little bit about your associates when you were at City College. Who were they?

His answer reminded the jury how many of them had already been mentioned as Communists. There were Sobell, Pogarsky, Joel Barr and Elitcher. He remembered no others. Then followed the remarkable incident in which Rosenberg could not be stopped by the judge or a team of horses from dragging in the Fifth Amendment.

SAYPOL Was there a man or a boy by the name of Perl or Mutterperl?
ROSENBERG Your Honor, I read in the newspapers about—
COURT You had better not say anything you think may hurt you.
ROSENBERG Yes, sir, that is what I want to say. I read in the newspapers about a man being arrested for perjury—
SAYPOL Before you tell us that—
ROSENBERG Wait a second. I would like to finish my statement.
COURT Let him finish, Mr. Saypol.
ROSENBERG My name was mentioned and I feel that I refuse to answer any questions that might tend to incriminate me.

Saypol protested that Rosenberg raised "a question of incrimination" of his "own making."

The reason that the mere mention of Perl's name set Rosenberg off on his course, was that newspapers had just reported the indictment of William Perl for perjury, because he had denied knowing Rosenberg, Sobell, Elitcher's wife, Helene, or the Sidoroviches. Perl taught physics at Columbia University. He was an expert on aerodynamics and had done research on this subject for a government agency in Cleveland. He had once sworn falsely in a questionnaire of the National Advisory Committee for Aeronautics that he had married and was divorced, presumably to hide an immoral relationship. Whatever the particulars were of the indictment, the New York *Times* had a front-page story headed "COLUMBIA TEACHER ARRESTED, LINKED TO TWO ON TRIAL AS SPIES." The subheading read "Physicist Called Perjurer in Denying that He Knew Rosenberg or Sobell."

Even though the jury was locked up every night (a humorist once commented that the United States is the only country where the jury is locked up and the defendant goes home), and precautions were taken against reading newspapers or listening to radio or television, the danger always existed that there would be a leak. So defendants' counsel were understandably alarmed by the possibility that the jury would be prejudiced. They rushed to the judge's bench to protest the incident. Kuntz was so excited that the judge cautioned him to keep his voice down, lest the jury learn about the headline from the very argument against it.

Since there was no indication that the jury knew or had been "poisoned" by the item, the matter blew over. But the higher court condemned the "timing" by the prosecutor in breaking the Perl story in the midst of the Rosenberg trial as "wholly reprehensible," and it "condemned" such tactics in the future.

It was counsel's duty to object and preserve any right of reversal because of prejudicial error. At the same time, it was important to guard against revealing the outside event to the jury. If Rosenberg was responsible for informing the jurors of the forbidden newspaper story, then he was a participant in the wrong and he could not complain about it. Yet that was exactly what he did. He was so eager to announce that he would claim privilege against answering any question about Perl that it was he who announced, "I read in the newspapers about ——." The judge would not let him continue, but Rosenberg insisted. "I want to say I read in the newspapers about a man being arrested for perjury—." Now Saypol tried to head him off. It was no use. Rosenberg complained, "I would like to finish my statement . . . My name was mentioned and I feel that I refuse to answer any questions that might tend to incriminate me."

A similar incident occurred in the Charles Manson murder trial.

President Nixon, unmindful of the legally prejudicial nature of his comment, expressed indignation that so much time was being spent on the Manson trial, when everyone knew he was guilty.

Since the President was a lawyer, his unawareness of the impropriety of such interference with trial procedure, naturally caused sensational headlines. If the jury learned of his statement, a mistrial would have to be declared. The judge in that case took the most careful precautions to shield the jurors from what the President admitted was a gaffe. The judge even blacked out the windows of the bus which took the jury to the courthouse, so that they would not see a newspaper headline on a stand, or in someone's hands.

But the defendant, Charles Manson, managed to smuggle a newspaper into the courtroom, and then with smirking defiance held it high above his head for the jury to read. He thus destroyed his right to complain of its prejudicial effect. The rule that one cannot take advantage of a grievance for which he is responsible is founded in common sense. It is applied, for example, in accident trials, where it is not permitted to inform the jury that the defendant is insured. Jurors may be lavish with an insurance company's money, whereas their judgment should be based on the defendant's negligence. So if the plaintiff slips and mentions "insurance company," a mistrial is granted. However, if it is the defendant for whose benefit the rule exists, who in a moment of forgetfulness testifies about the "insurance company investigator" giving him a report, then he loses his right to object that the jury has been prejudiced thereby.

Saypol continued to goad Rosenberg with questions about his friends and associates. Did he and they have any "common activity" which brought them together as a group? Did they belong to any club or society? Rosenberg said he was a member of the American Student Union. While the prosecutor was fumbling around the subject, Rosenberg again obliged him by plunging ahead into a Fifth Amendment plea.

ROSENBERG Can I state something, sir?

COURT Yes.

SAYPOL You will in a minute.

COURT Let him state.

ROSENBERG I would like to state, on any answer I made on this question, I don't intend to waive any part of my right of self-incrimination, and if Mr. Saypol is referring to the Young Communist League or the Communist Party, I will not answer any question on it.

COURT You mean, you assert your constitutional privilege against self-incrimination.

ROSENBERG That's right.

(223)

There is such a thing as atmosphere in a courtroom. The many conflicting words and personalities create uncertainty and even confusion. Who is telling the truth? How can the issue be resolved? But at some point, the blur of events begins to dissipate itself. An atmosphere makes its presence in favor of one side. It is a mysterious occurrence. But one suddenly knows it is there. It is as if an invisible hand caused the tottering scales to tip. I do not mean to sound metaphysical. There is probably some revelation which has cast a new light and made the truth visible. Every lawyer knows this experience. One can feel that the tide has turned. Only those in the courtroom can sense it. It cannot be divined by reading the record. But I imagine that the prosecutor, even in those first few moments of cross-examination, felt Rosenberg's emphatic, unqualified declarations of innocence had somehow lost their effectiveness.

Saypol pressed on with an attack on Rosenberg's explanation of his visit to Elitcher. Did he seek him out in Washington to solicit him in espionage? I have already set forth the cross-examination on this point immediately after Elitcher's testimony; his not having seen Elitcher for four years except for a minute at a swimming pool; his sole reason for contacting him being that he was "lonely"; the judge's pummeling him about looking in the telephone book to find a name he could recognize, "You mean, you started with 'A'?" The debacle when he was asked whether he knew of Elitcher's activities in the Young Communist League and Bloch objected because there was no proof of it, but admitted there was and withdrew his objection.

When Rosenberg said that he and Elitcher discussed the war, the judge drew an opinion out of him which was suspiciously close to Greenglass' version of how he had been induced to steal the bomb.

COURT Well now, did you feel that if Great Britain shared in all our secrets that Russia should at the same time also share those secrets in 1944 and 1945?

ROSENBERG My opinion was that matters such as that were up to the Governments, the British, American and the Russian Governments.

COURT You mean the ultimate decision?

ROSENBERG Yes.

COURT Well, what was your opinion at that time?

ROSENBERG My opinion was that if we had a common enemy we should get together commonly.

Saypol pursued the lead.

SAYPOL Well, what did you know about the subject to express an opinion? Did you talk about it with others?

ROSENBERG I read about it in the newspapers.

SAYPOL Did you talk about it in groups?

(224)

ROSENBERG   Socially, when people came over to the house.

SAYPOL   Did you talk about it perhaps in any Communist unit that you might have belonged to?

ROSENBERG   I refuse to answer that question on the ground that it may incriminate me.

Once more, the judge took the precaution of protecting Rosenberg from an improper inference.

COURT   I want the jury to understand that they are to draw no inference from the witness' refusal to answer on his assertion of privilege. Proceed.

When the FBI searched Rosenberg's home, they came away with a physical object, which the prosecutor thought would trap Rosenberg in a lie. Saypol now prepared the ground for its use. After drawing from the witness the statement that "I didn't do anything but express my opinion," Saypol asked him whether he had ever made contributions to the Joint Anti-Fascist Refugee Committee? Rosenberg admitted he had.

SAYPOL   That is known to be an organization deemed subversive by the Attorney General.

E. H. BLOCH   I object to the question upon the ground that it is improper; it is inflammatory and has nothing to do with the issues.

COURT   I sustain the objection.

SAYPOL   May I submit to the Court that pursuant to Presidential Executive Order No. 9835 it has been so classified by the Attorney General.

COURT   I don't think that is a subject matter that you ought to go into.

Had he gone out and collected money for that committee? He didn't recall doing this. Saypol then showed him a can labeled "Save Spanish Republican Child, Volveremos. Return to Joint Anti-Fascist Refugee Committee, 192 Lexington Avenue, Suite 1501." It was a can found in his home. Bloch did not object to its admission into evidence. "So that perhaps you did a little more than just contribute?" asked Saypol. Rosenberg was eager to reply:

The date on this can is May 20, 1948. I hold insurance in the International Workers Order, and they sent this can to me to ask me to solicit funds. I never solicited funds. I just made a contribution to them.

Was not that International Workers Order "exclusively" a Communist organization? After objection was withdrawn, Rosenberg said he didn't believe it was. He didn't remember how he joined it, or who invited him to join. It was an insurance organization, in which he held a five-thousand-dollar life insurance policy. Saypol demanded that the policy be produced. Bloch explained that it could not be "at home."

The Rosenbergs lived at 10 Monroe Street, and after Mrs. Rosenberg's arrest their home was abandoned. At any rate, I had the lease canceled and their furniture was disposed of.

This explanation turned out to have critical importance later on, when the issue of the console table came front stage. Bloch promised to search his papers, which might contain the policy. Saypol was brusque. "That is all I ask for, the policy, not a speech." Bloch turned the other cheek:

E. H. BLOCH Well, I don't want any implication that this witness was trying to conceal from this Court and the jury the policy itself.

It was apparent that the collection can had not turned out to be the cross-examination bomb which the prosecutor had thought it would be.

I recalled another incident involving a similar organization. When John Garfield, the motion picture star, was being harassed by Senator Joseph McCarthy's committee, it found that he had helped "finance a Communist front." In preparation for Garfield's appearance, I found a check in his papers for $200 made payable to the American Committee for Yugoslav Relief, designated a Communist front by the Attorney General. He had no recollection of having made the gift. It turned out that on a USO tour during the war, Garfield had been taken in the dark of night to the Yugoslav front to entertain the partisans.

After the war, the State Department arranged with Tito to receive his committee, which happened to be headed by the colonel whose troops Garfield had visited. On a visit to Hollywood, the committee went to the Warner Brothers Studio, where the colonel greeted the bewildered Garfield effusively. After he identified himself and explained his mission to raise funds for Yugoslav orphans, Garfield had his manager make a contribution. This was the extent of his Communistic activity. Of course, the accusation evaporated, but for months before the hearing, he suffered indescribable torment. Items appeared regularly (I know they were planted) that he might be indicted for perjury because he had denied being a Communist. Titillating questions, a favorite column device, asked, "What famous Hollywood star is going to jail for denying he is [a Communist]?" Garfield could not obtain work. He was distressed to the point of heartache. I am sure his anguish contributed to his early death at the age of thirty-nine.

The collection can taken by the FBI from Rosenberg's home, considered alone, was as devoid of significance as Garfield's check. But the facts of Rosenberg's Communist activities were seeping out, despite the Fifth Amendment.

The prosecutor sedulously directed new rivulets into the stream. He read Rosenberg's testimony that he had "been separated" from his job with the United States Government in 1945. Did Rosenberg think he could evade the facts with such an elliptical answer? Then he under-estimated the elementary purpose of cross-examination.

SAYPOL   What really happened to you, you were dismissed were you not?

ROSENBERG   I was suspended.

SAYPOL   Were you then dismissed?

ROSENBERG   That is correct.

SAYPOL   And what was the reason?

ROSENBERG   It was alleged that I was a member of the Communist Party. . . .

SAYPOL   Is it not a fact that on March 28, 1945, you were summoned and in the presence of another officer of the Army, Captain Henderson advised you of the action that was being taken against you to separate you from the service because of information reaching the office that you were a Communist Party member?

ROSENBERG   I can't recall the date exactly.

SAYPOL   Can you recall the fact of being advised that that information that you were a member of the Communist Party was imparted to you?

ROSENBERG   I was down at Captain Henderson's office on one occasion.

SAYPOL   Is it not a fact that on that occasion you were told you were being removed from Government service because of the fact that information had been received that you were a member of the Communist Party?

E. H. BLOCH   If Mr. Saypol wants a concession I will concede right now that this witness was removed from Government service upon charges that he was a member of the Communist Party.

COURT   All right.

SAYPOL   Were you a member of the Communist Party?

ROSENBERG   I refuse to answer on the ground that it might incriminate me.

SAYPOL   Is it not a fact that in February 1944 you transferred from Branch 16-B of the Industrial Division of the Communist Party to the Eastern Club of the First Assembly District under Transfer No. 12179?

ROSENBERG   I refuse to answer.

SAYPOL   Is that one of the charges Captain Henderson read to you?

ROSENBERG   That is.

SAYPOL   Did Captain Henderson advise you at that time that information had been received that while a student at City College you signed a petition for the granting of a charter to a chapter of the American Student Union, which has been reported to be or had been under the influence of Communists?

ROSENBERG   He informed me.

SAYPOL   Is that the fact?

ROSENBERG I don't remember.

COURT Mr. Saypol, I suggest that you get to your destination on this. I don't think that we ought to pursue this particular line in view of the witness' expression that he is going to assert his privilege on the entire line.

The prosecutor resorted to repetition, which is the moving belt of persuasion. The judge helped to contain the concession which in the confusion he thought the defendant was making.

COURT Is it not the fact that you were removed from that position for that reason—for these reasons, that you were a member and you were active in the party?

E. H. BLOCH I have so conceded, your Honor.

COURT Wait, let us get this clear. You did not concede, as I understand it, that he was removed because he was a member. You concede, as I remember, that he was removed because of the charges.

E. H. BLOCH That is correct.

COURT Well, you just said that you will concede that he was a member.

E. H. BLOCH Oh, no, I do not mean that at all. I cannot make any such concession at all.

COURT I just want to make sure that you understood what you are conceding.

E. H. BLOCH Well, I am conceding this, that this witness was removed from Government service upon certain charges that were preferred against him under the authority of the Secretary of War.

COURT I understand that.

Rosenberg had written a reply to the charge filed against him when he was dismissed from government service. Saypol read from it:

SAYPOL And then you go on to say: "I am not now, and never have been a Communist member. I know nothing about Communist branches, divisions, clubs or transfers. I never heard either of the Division or the Club referred to. I had nothing to do with the so-called transfer. Either the case is based on a case of mistaken identity or a complete falsehood. In any event, it certainly has not the slightest basis in fact."

Did you make that answer to those charges, yes or no?

ROSENBERG I refuse to answer a question on the contents of that letter.

SAYPOL I ask you whether you made that answer to those charges as I have read them to you?

E. H. BLOCH May I advise the client, your Honor, that he should answer that question yes or no.

(228)

COURT Very well.

ROSENBERG Yes, I sent the letter in answer to those charges.

SAYPOL Was that answer true at the time you made it?

ROSENBERG I refuse to answer.

A legal argument ensued as to whether the Fifth Amendment was applicable to a collateral charge of perjury. It being Friday afternoon, the court decided to recess until Monday morning, so that the lawyers could research the point. The jury was dismissed with wishes for "a very Happy Easter and a pleasant weekend."

At the opening of court on Monday, Saypol announced that he withdrew his request to direct the witness to answer whether he had written the truth when he denied being a Communist. He would permit Rosenberg to refuse to answer the question on the ground of self-incrimination.

Apparently, the prosecution's research over the weekend had convinced it that it might be reversible error, if Rosenberg's privilege was disregarded and the court ruled he must answer whether he lied when he wrote that he was never a Communist.

This is a good illustration of built-in protective devices to insure a fair trial. A prosecutor who overpresses his rights may obtain a verdict of guilty, but also assure its reversal because of a substantial legal error. In this way, a prosecutor's zeal to convict is curbed by his awareness that he is endangering the very verdict he seeks.

The FBI had provided the prosecution with a list of names of alleged Communists who they believed were close to Rosenberg and were working with him. Saypol hoped to unnerve Rosenberg by questioning him about these "friends," and obtaining admissions from him. But Rosenberg stalwartly denied any relationship with them of an unusual nature. Vivian Glassman "was Joel Barr's sweetheart," and when he left the country, she would visit the Rosenbergs and once, Rosenberg's shop. What did they talk about?

ROSENBERG Well, she is a social worker and my oldest boy has been very emotionally disturbed for quite a number of years, and she used to work at the Jewish Board of Guardians, and I discussed the problem of my oldest boy with her.

He never gave her $2,000. He never sent her to Cleveland. He was positive of it. He might have read about it in a newspaper, but it wasn't true.

He also knew a man called Alfred Saurent. He had visited his home. He had borrowed $400 in cash from him and still owed that money to him. He had been introduced to Saurent by Joel Barr. When he didn't remember Saurent's address, Saypol suggested 65 Morton Street. Rosenberg said, "That is the place, Morton Street." "You

(229)

couldn't remember that, could you?" sneered Saypol. When Rosenberg didn't know where Saurent was now, Saypol asked, "Don't you know that he is in Mexico?"

A storm of indignation at the prosecutor's tactics broke upon the courtroom.

E. H. BLOCH I object to that upon the ground that it is incompetent, irrelevant and immaterial, and highly inflammatory. I move for a mistrial.

COURT Denied.

E. H. BLOCH I respectfully except.

KUNTZ We join in that application, if your Honor please.

COURT Both motions are denied. I don't know what the excitement is over, asking whether a witness is in Mexico.

KUNTZ Now all I have heard so far, although it hasn't concerned us actually—I mean directly—is that by implication, "Do you know this one, did you meet that one, did you see that one"?

Now I might have met Costello and seen him and it doesn't mean a thing—

COURT And then again it might mean something, too.

KUNTZ Well, I know, but I say a question of that kind is clearly prejudicial. A person says "Do you know he is in Mexico"?; especially when there is no evidence in this case that he is in Mexico.

COURT There is rarely a question that can be asked that isn't prejudicial.

On the day Greenglass was arrested, Rosenberg had been pulled in too, but he was released. One month later he was arrested and incarcerated. During that intervening month did he believe he was under surveillance? He didn't know whether he was or not, even though he saw the FBI men outside his shop. This opened the door to sarcastic cross-examination.

There are certain kinds of questions not important in themselves, but valuable in their effect on credibility. The witness usually creates the opportunity for such cross-examination by the improbability of his answers. Often the admission sought may be quite harmless, whereas the denial makes him look like a liar. Why play such an uneven game?

Rosenberg's insistence that he didn't know that he was under observation led to the following:

SAYPOL Did you think it was unusual to see an agent of the FBI, after he had talked with you at an interview, looking up at your shop?

ROSENBERG That is his business, Mr. Saypol, not mine.

SAYPOL   What did you think about it?

ROSENBERG   The possibility he was looking for something.

SAYPOL   Somebody else?

ROSENBERG   I have no idea, sir.

SAYPOL   Not for you?

ROSENBERG   I have no idea what he was looking for.

SAYPOL   You were not concerned about his presence outside your shop?

ROSENBERG   No, I wasn't concerned, Mr. Saypol, because I wasn't guilty of any crime.

COURT   The question is, did you think about what he was doing there?

ROSENBERG   No, it didn't enter my mind. It was his business.

COURT   The fact that you say an FBI agent looking into your place of business—

ROSENBERG   He wasn't looking; he was across the street from the Pitt Machine works and he was walking by nonchalantly looking in.

COURT   That was the same agent who had talked to you?

ROSENBERG   Yes.

COURT   You say it made no impression whatsoever upon you?

ROSENBERG   It didn't concern me.

COURT   I say, it made no impression on you?

ROSENBERG   I knew he may have been looking for something.

COURT   You didn't think it had anything to do with you?

ROSENBERG   It might have and it might not have, but it didn't concern me.

COURT   I am asking you whether you thought it had anything to do with you.

ROSENBERG   Maybe yes and maybe no. It didn't enter my mind as to what his purpose was.

COURT   Is that the best answer you could give?

ROSENBERG   Yes.

COURT   Maybe yes and maybe no?

ROSENBERG   Yes.

—————>←—————

"Let us have a little talk about this console table," said Saypol, opening up a new area of cross-examination. Both sides had invested much on this issue. The government had presented evidence that the table was a gift from the Russians to expedite Rosenberg's spy activities. It claimed there was a hollowed-out section for microfilming, and that Rosenberg had demonstrated its use, by dousing the lights, turning the table on its side, one of its leaves acting as a shield, so that the microfilming could be done in appropriately secret atmosphere.

Rosenberg testified that it was an ordinary console table, used for eating, not photographing, and that he had bought it at Macy's for $21.

(231)

The table was a physical object which could confirm or give the lie to Greenglass' elaborate story. Where was it? It was never produced at the trial.

Had the government plunged on a theory which could be disproved and destroy its entire case?

Was it significant that the defense did not offer evidence, that it had moved heaven and earth to find the table in order to produce it triumphantly as a conclusive demonstration that the Greenglasses had indulged in fantasy, not fact?

Instead, the battle was fought on Macy's grounds. Rosenberg claimed that Macy's records, if they were still available, would show that he had purchased the table for $21. The government claimed that there were no such records, and that the absence of proof was no contradiction of its affirmative detailed oral evidence of the hollowed-out equipment disguised as a console table.

So the table became the center of a little trial all of its own. At the very end of the trial, a new and unexpected witness appeared, who gave extraordinary testimony on this issue. It was one of the surprises of the case, but then, was there ever a trial in which unforeseen dramatic events did not occur? We shall come to this one later.

In the meantime, the battle of Macy's began as Saypol opened his cross-examination on this subject. He had Rosenberg describe the table in detail. When it was opened, six people could sit around it. In the last four years, it was used for eating. Then Saypol showed him pictures of different models of console tables, and he picked the ones which resembled it most. They were marked as Exhibit 78.

Rosenberg was prepared for the attack. The moment he was asked about his purchase at Macy's for $21, Bloch asked to make a statement. The court would not permit him to interrupt cross-examination, but Rosenberg stepped in.

ROSENBERG   Mr. Saypol, could I say something on that? I have asked my attorneys to have the Macy's people go through their records and files, and I am sure if the Government request them they will find a sales slip with my signature on it, when I signed in Macy's in 1944 or '45, for that console table, and I believe I bought something else at that time, too. It was shipped to my house.

COURT   What did you have, a D. A. Account or cash?

ROSENBERG   No, I had to pay cash.

COURT   Why would your name be on a sales slip?

ROSENBERG   Because I had to give him the money, and there was—I had to have some notation like a receipt, that I paid the money. I believe the salesman brought over one of these folding booklets, and I signed one of these folding booklets.

(232)

COURT Was it delivered, or did you take it with you?

ROSENBERG It was delivered. It was too big for me to take with me.

The atmosphere was tense, and produced an immediate shouting match between counsel in which Rosenberg joined.

SAYPOL Do you know, Mr. Rosenberg, that we have asked Macy's to find that slip and they can't find it?

E. H. BLOCH That is not so, your Honor. That is the statement I was going to make.

SAYPOL I am responding to what Mr. Bloch said and what the witness has volunteered.

COURT Mr. Bloch, please be seated. You will have your chance on redirect.

ROSENBERG Your Honor, I have requested my attorneys to find that receipt.

COURT You said that before.

ROSENBERG And my attorneys told me that Macy's cannot find the receipt unless I gave them a number or copy of receipt that I had, because it is filed by number.

COURT All right, go ahead.

ROSENBERG Now, I feel that if somebody looks through all the numbers through those years, they will find one for Julius Rosenberg, and it is worth finding if it is such an important issue.

Where was the table kept in the apartment? The prosecution had a blueprint of the layout, showed it to Rosenberg, and had him mark the spot near the kitchen where it stood against the wall. When it was used for eating it was moved out so "we could sit behind it." The blueprint was admitted into evidence as Exhibit 79. Although the furniture was shifted around at times, the console table "was always in the living room."

SAYPOL When did you see it last in the living room?

ROSENBERG When I was arrested, sir.

Rosenberg stated that he had bought this table "in 1944 or 1945" during the war. Saypol claimed tables were scarce and expensive at that time.

SAYPOL Did you have any trouble finding any furniture at that time?

ROSENBERG That was on the floor of Macy's. There was a big display, many little tables were on the floor.

SAYPOL The place was full of little tables?

ROSENBERG That's right.

SAYPOL Don't you know, Mr. Rosenberg, that you couldn't buy a

(233)

console table in Macy's, if they had it, in 1944 and 1945, for less than $85?

ROSENBERG I am sorry, sir. I bought that table for that amount. That was a display piece, Mr. Saypol, and I believe it was marked down.

So the record stood, as the prosecutor turned to other subjects. But the smoldering issue of the console table was to burst aflame before the trial was over, and indeed in unusual proceedings after the trial.

———→←———

Rosenberg denied that he ever had or used a Leica camera.

As for the watches, the presumed gifts for him and Ethel from the Russians, he bought a watch for Ethel in 1945 "from a peddler who used to come around regularly when people were paid on Fridays." It was for her birthday and cost "somewhere around $30."

SAYPOL Haven't you got a brother-in-law in the wholesale jewelry business?

ROSENBERG That is correct.

SAYPOL What is his name, Sam?

ROSENBERG That's right.

SAYPOL Didn't he sell watches wholesale?

ROSENBERG Yes, that's right.

SAYPOL You didn't think of buying it from him, did you?

ROSENBERG You see, Mr. Saypol, I couldn't buy very many things from him. Every time I asked to buy something from him, he was always too busy.

As for his own watches, he never received one from the Russians. One was given to him as a present by his father. It was an Omega. Where was it? He had lost it.

ROSENBERG Well, on a vacation trip that I was taking with my wife and child, the band broke and I put it in my vest pocket, and the baby, who was sitting on my lap, picked it up and dropped it out the train. When I got off the train I remember I reported to the New York Central Lost and Found Division, the loss of this watch. It was after my father's death. I told them it was very important to me because it was something that my father had given to me. I wrote out a slip telling them what the watch was like and what it meant to me, and I never heard from them again on it.

On questioning by the court, he said this was the second wrist watch he had lost. He did not know, as Saypol suggested, that an Omega watch "costs more than $100."

SAYPOL Did your father ever buy you presents for $100 on your birthday?

(234)

ROSENBERG No, sir.

The prosecutor turned to the incident when Rosenberg visited Ruth Greenglass and asked her sister, Dorothy, to leave the room. Phillips, attorney for Sobell, who rarely had spoken, asked whether the court would not declare the ten-minute recess usually taken in midmorning, to permit jurors and counsel "to stretch their legs," a euphemism for a visit to the bathroom and a smoke. The court thought it was a bit early and commented:

COURT Is there something about this subject that suggests a recess to you?

PHILLIPS The clock showed me a recess. I turned around and looked at it.

This statement by the judge was later cited as an instance of his prejudice, and its effect on the jury. But in this instance, no motion was made for a mistrial, and as we shall see, defense counsel's effusive praise of the judge, at the end of the trial, diluted the grievance.

Rosenberg was questioned about his advice to Ruth Greenglass to warn David against stealing gasoline and "parts." He didn't remember this conversation with Ruth, until her sister, Dorothy, had testified. Still, knowing of David Greenglass' dishonesty, why did he go into business with him? The court took over cross-examination on this point.

COURT Well, didn't you question him before you went into business with him a little more thoroughly and before you put your money into that business to find out whether or not he had more than ideas about these things?

ROSENBERG It was only mentioned to me once by his wife. I had no proof that he did anything like that. I actually didn't know whether he would carry out his thought into action.

When Saypol tried to accelerate the drive on Rosenberg's credibility, he was repulsed with a most telling reply. He asked Rosenberg why he hadn't told the FBI about this incident when they questioned him.

SAYPOL Did you think you should have volunteered it to them?

ROSENBERG Well, when a member of the family is in trouble, Mr. Saypol, you are not interested in sinking him.

What a contrast with the Greenglasses' determined effort to sink Ethel and Julius!

The judge pursued the matter but Rosenberg actually strengthened his moral position.

COURT Were you trying to protect him at that time?

ROSENBERG Well, I didn't know what he was accused of, your Honor. I had a suspicion he was accused of stealing some uranium at that time.

COURT Well, in connection with that, were you interested in protecting him?

ROSENBERG I wasn't interested in doing him any harm at that particular point.

COURT Were you interested in protecting him, I asked you?

ROSENBERG Well, I felt that when a man is in trouble, the one thing his family should do is stick by the man, regardless of the trouble he is in.

COURT You are not answering the question. You were interested in protecting him?

ROSENBERG Not in protecting that act itself, but protecting the individual.

COURT To the point where you would not reveal something which you felt—

ROSENBERG Well, I wasn't asked a particular thing like that and there was nothing for me to reveal. I wasn't aware of the trouble he was in.

Unless the jury believed he was merely trying to extricate himself from his failure to tell the same story to the FBI, it must have been impressed with his decency, irrespective of the legal aspects.

The prosecutor pressed on. At the time that he learned about David's intended misconduct, did not Rosenberg know of the theft of atomic secrets from Alamos?

ROSENBERG Well, I read about the Harry Gold case.

SAYPOL You read about the Klaus Fuchs case, too?

ROSENBERG That is correct.

SAYPOL You knew that David Greenglass had been questioned in February by an agent of the FBI regarding the theft of uranium, didn't you?

ROSENBERG That is correct.

SAYPOL Where did you find that out?

ROSENBERG David told me. . . .

SAYPOL And you still say that you had no suspicion, when the agents questioned you, regarding the nature of the arrest of David Greenglass?

ROSENBERG That's right, because David Greenglass himself told me that he didn't steal the uranium after that interview, and I believed him.

The prosecutor referred to Rosenberg's direct testimony that he was willing to fight for the United States, and pointed out that he was never in the Army, obtaining deferment because he was in Signal Corps work.

(236)

ROSENBERG The Government asked for deferments for me.

SAYPOL You asked, too, did you not?

ROSENBERG No, sir; the Government asked for my deferment.

SAYPOL Didn't you join in any application, 42-A, for deferment?

ROSENBERG Well, I was told to fill the application out.

SAYPOL So you did join in them?

ROSENBERG Naturally.

The cross-examination became quarrelsome and less pointed. There were repeated attempts to trip the defendant on dates, which could not have been significant, even if he had been confused. The court became impatient and chided Saypol.

COURT I think the subject matter has been very well exhausted and I would suggest, if you have just a few more questions on it, all right; otherwise, go on to something else.

A little later:

COURT Oh, let us not have that. Get along, Mr. Saypol. . . .
Mr. Saypol, do you suppose if I declare a recess you could shorten your cross-examination?

Rosenberg was subjected to a long and rambling series of questions about his replies to FBI questions. The court interjected to ask whether he had revealed Ruth's fears that David was stealing from the Army.

ROSENBERG No, I didn't tell them, your Honor. The way I was brought up, I don't inform on my wife's brother, and whatever he did, I didn't know about and that is for him to decide, for him to answer.

SAYPOL Then what you are saying is, even if there is something to inform about, you don't inform?

ROSENBERG No, I didn't say that, sir, but since I was not aware of what troubles he was in, I would not aggravate his troubles by telling what my opinions of those troubles are.

Every cross-examiner saves a surprise question, if he can, for the end. Despite the droning and rambling nature to which the attack had descended, it was inevitable that a new live subject would conclude the questioning. It came and with it the excited exchanges of counsel, the court and the defendant.

SAYPOL Did you, in the month of June 1950, or in the month of May 1950, have any passport photographs taken of yourself?

ROSENBERG No, I did not.

SAYPOL Did you go to a photographer's shop at 99 Park Row and have any photographs taken of yourself?

ROSENBERG I have been in many photographers' shops and had photos taken.

(237)

SAYPOL Did you have any taken in May or June of 1950?

ROSENBERG I don't recall. I might have had some photos taken.

SAYPOL For what purpose might you have had those photographs taken?

ROSENBERG Well, when I walk with the children, many times with my wife, we would step in; we would have—we would pass a man on the street with one of these box cameras and we would take some pictures. We would step into a place and take some pictures and the pictures we like, we keep.

COURT He is not asking you that. He is asking you about these particular pictures in June 1950. What was the purpose of those pictures?

ROSENBERG Just—if you take pictures, you just go in, take some pictures, snapshots.

SAYPOL What did you tell the man when you asked him to take those pictures in May or June 1950?

ROSENBERG I didn't tell the man anything.

SAYPOL Are you sure of that?

ROSENBERG I didn't tell the man anything.

SAYPOL See if you can't recall. Try hard. May or June 1950, at 99 Park Row.

ROSENBERG I don't recall telling the man anything.

The questions foreshadowed the appearance of a surprise witness.

SAYPOL You mean, you might have told him something, but you don't recall it now?

ROSENBERG I don't recall my saying anything at this time.

SAYPOL What don't you recall? Tell us that.

ROSENBERG I don't know, sir.

SAYPOL Do you remember telling the man at 99 Park Row that you had to go to France to settle an estate?

ROSENBERG I didn't tell him anything of the sort. . . .

SAYPOL At the time David was talking about going to Mexico, what kind of pictures did you take and how many?

ROSENBERG I don't recall.

Rosenberg became flustered, and Saypol was merciless. There was an explosive protest at counsel table.

SAYPOL When did you find out that Sobell was in Mexico?

ROSENBERG When did I find out?

SAYPOL You heard my question, didn't you?

ROSENBERG Yes.

SAYPOL Was it a hard one?

ROSENBERG I heard that Sobell was in Mexico through the newspapers.

SAYPOL What did you have to do with sending Sobell away?

ROSENBERG Nothing.

(238)

KUNTZ I object to that, if your Honor please. There is no testimony here that he had anything to do with sending Sobell or anybody else away.

COURT You are excited, Mr. Kuntz.

KUNTZ I mean, to ask a question that way, I can convict anybody by that kind of question.

COURT The jury will please disregard that statement by Mr. Kuntz, supposedly in behalf of his own client.

The judge asked Rosenberg whether he had "anything to do with sending Sobell away to Mexico." "I certainly did not, sir," was the reply. Kuntz said he was satisfied with the answer, but Phillips demanded a ruling that Saypol's previous question was improper.

COURT Are co-counsel fighting with each other there? I don't understand it.

PHILLIPS No, we are both on the same side, except that I am a little more emphatic on the first part.

COURT Please be seated, Mr. Phillips. We have heard enough of that.

SAYPOL I have had all I want.

It was on this quarrelsome note that Saypol announced the end of Rosenberg's cross-examination.

———→←———

Sobell's lawyer had a right to cross-examine. So Kuntz put a few questions to Rosenberg to establish the innocence of his client. He referred to Elitcher's testimony that Sobell delivered a can of film to Rosenberg late at night.

KUNTZ Now, I want to know whether in July 1948 or any time from the beginning of the world to today did Sobell ever give you a can with any film in it?

ROSENBERG No, he did not.

Sobell, he said, never gave him any information belonging to the government.

Kuntz read from Elitcher's testimony that after delivering the film, Sobell returned to the car and reported that Rosenberg was not worried about Elitcher's having been followed; that he once talked to Elizabeth Bentley on the phone, but she didn't know Rosenberg. Had such a conversation ever taken place? Rosenberg replied, "No, sir, it did not." Kuntz thanked the witness and said, "That is all."

Bloch had a few questions on redirect examination. He offered in evidence a letter which proved that Rosenberg was a policyholder in the International Workers Order, and that he had requested Bloch to pay his premium.

He also refreshed Rosenberg's recollections about other "names" who were classmates and friends, presumably, without saying so, to counter the impression that he only associated with Communists.

More important, he denied telling Greenglass that he stole a proximity fuse while working at Emerson Radio Corporation, and, in fact, he had never done so.

Rosenberg stepped down. He was through with his ordeal. From then on, he would silently watch numerous defense and rebuttal witnesses take the stand. Most of them he would not know, but the one he would listen to with pride, confidence and deep sorrow was Ethel. When he was arrested, he had not dreamed that she would be involved too. When he heard on his radio in his prison cell that she had been seized and indicted, he told the guard it was the worst moment of his life. Soon he was to hear her defend him and herself, fighting off the attacks which he had just experienced.

CHAPTER 22

It is rare that defendants charged with serious crimes have no prior criminal record. The Rosenbergs had an impeccable past. They had never received a ticket for traffic violation or jay walking. Yet here they were accused of the most horrendous charge in the entire catalogue of crimes. Even more incongruous was the fact that they were supposed to have spearheaded an ingenious, foreign spy organization to accomplish a feat unprecedented in the history of espionage achievements. At the dawn of the nuclear age, when the United States had a monopoly of power, they had supposedly wrenched the secret from its guarded gates and given it to Russia. Thus, they were accused of making possible a cold war, but not so cold that there weren't sparks which lit little wars on several continents.

So when Alexander Bloch began by asking Ethel to describe her early life and education, he was not merely filling in the background of her life. He was depicting the humble and innocent antecedents which made the government's charge all the more bizarre, as if to say how could a master criminal grow full blown from such soil?

Ethel described her girlhood on the East Side. She had lived at home until she married at age twenty-three. Her youngest brother, David, was seventeen years old at the time. The mere mention of David, whom she had affectionately called "Doovey," evoked the horror of his being the star witness against her. She attended Public School 22, Junior High School 12, and Seward Park High School from which she was graduated in June 1931 at the age of sixteen.

Then she took a short secretarial course for about six months in bookkeeping, stenography and typing. As was the custom in orthodox Jewish homes, she "had a private Hebrew tutor who came to the house." She also took piano lessons for two years. This, too, was characteristic of Jewish education, combining religion with art. Boys usually studied the violin. But Ethel developed her cultural gifts in a less traditional manner. She took "voice studies" at the Carnegie Hall Studio, and she became the youngest member of the Schola Cantorum under the direction of Hugh Ross. She studied "music for children" at the Bank Street School in Greenwich Village, and also spread her musical curiosity with a course in guitar.

Later when her son Michael was two and one-half years old, she took a course at the New School for Social Research in child psychology. This was an indirect revelation of the fact that even at that early age her son had shown neurotic tendencies. Somehow, the wholesome life which knits even underprivileged families in love had failed her. At the time of the trial, her sons were eight and four years old.

A. BLOCH Where are your children now?

ETHEL ROSENBERG They are at a temporary shelter in the Bronx.

A. BLOCH Have you seen them since you were arrested?

ETHEL ROSENBERG No, I have not.

The depth of the personal tragedy was thus eloquently sketched in a few words. With similar economy, she drew the picture of a housewife, contrasting sharply with any Mata Hari concept. For nine years she lived in a modest three-room apartment at 10 Monroe Street:

A. BLOCH Did you do all the chores of a housewife?

ETHEL ROSENBERG Yes, I did.

A. BLOCH Cooking, washing, cleaning, darning, scrubbing?

ETHEL ROSENBERG Yes, I did.

A. BLOCH Did you hire any help throughout that period?

ETHEL ROSENBERG On occasion for brief periods. I know that when I came from the hospital after the birth of the first child I had some help for the first month, and then upon the time that the second child arrived, I had help for about two months, and there was a period when I was ill and that started about November 1944, I had to have help, right up to about the spring of 1945.

A. BLOCH Now, outside of these three periods you last mentioned, you did all the housework yourself?

ETHEL ROSENBERG That is right.

A. BLOCH Your laundry and everything?

ETHEL ROSENBERG That is correct.

Her furniture came from friends, Harry and Sylvia Steingart, who moved to California, and saved storage charges by leaving it, temporarily, with the Rosenbergs.

Aside from the "rickety bridge table" and two others, Ethel said that she acquired a console table that my husband purchased at R. H. Macy. A very inexpensive table, with a back that you could—sometimes it would stand up, and other times if we wanted to use it for eating purposes, it folded down.

COURT Were you with him when he purchased it?

ETHEL ROSENBERG No, I was not.

A. BLOCH Were you at home when it was delivered?

ETHEL ROSENBERG Yes, I was.

A. BLOCH And did you see who delivered it?

ETHEL ROSENBERG Just the usual delivery person.

A. BLOCH And can you recollect the year during which the table was acquired and sent to your home and received in your home?

ETHEL ROSENBERG Well, it was somewhere between, somewhere either in 1944 or 1945.

COURT Do you remember whether you signed for it when it came or did your husband sign for it?

ETHEL ROSENBERG Oh, I think I signed for it when it came. It came during the day and I was home.

She also obtained a "rather battered, secondhand piano for a very small cost from a neighbor in Knickerbocker Village." At the time of her arrest all this, including the console table, was in the apartment.

Once more, the testimony sent up a question mark, "Where was the console table?" Was it provided by Russia for microfilming, or was it an ordinary Macy table? The questions awaited an answer.

COURT Did your husband do any other shopping by himself for furniture on any other occasion?

ETHEL ROSENBERG He did buy something else. At the time I believe he bought a table.

COURT At the same time?

ETHEL ROSENBERG Yes.

COURT Was another piece of furniture purchased then?

ETHEL ROSENBERG I believe it was about the same time.

COURT What was that piece?

ETHEL ROSENBERG I am not sure.

A. BLOCH If I should suggest a lamp, would that refresh your recollection?

ETHEL ROSENBERG It might have been. I remember there was some other item, but I couldn't—

SAYPOL Well, I object to the suggestion. He might as well suggest a refrigerator.

COURT All right. We will take it as a suggestion and the jury will understand where it came from.

COURT Did you know that he was going to make that purchase when he did make it?

ETHEL ROSENBERG Oh, yes, we had decided that we really needed a decent piece of furniture, at least a table, and so we did decide to make that expenditure.

COURT As far as you know, how much was that expenditure?

ETHEL ROSENBERG It was about $20 or $21. I remember that.

COURT Was there any sale on at the time?

ETHEL ROSENBERG Yes. He came home and told me he really made a good buy; that it was—

COURT Did you know in advance? Was there something advertised in the paper? Was there a sale at Macy's?

ETHEL ROSENBERG I couldn't say. I really couldn't recall at this time whether I had noticed a sale or not. We had just decided we needed a table and he stopped in to Macy's and found a buy.

She was growing weaker. Bloch asked her to keep her voice up.

Ultimately, she disposed of the other tables, by sending one back to the Steingarts in California, and selling the tables (not the console table) for $5.00 to a secondhand furniture dealer.

She filled out the description of her modest, almost impoverished style of living by stating that her rent was $41 a month, raised to $45. Julius had said it was $51, but the discrepancy was not important. All this detail served to contradict the theory that she and her husband were entrusted by the Russians with thousands of dollars to enlist and pay off couriers. Why, in view of their own alleged service, were they not entitled to more comfortable operating quarters? Or was the jury asked to believe that this was one more sacrifice they had to make in the interest of non-identity?

The typewriter taken from her home at the time of her arrest had been acquired by her when she was eighteen years old. She bought it for $30 from one of the actors of the Clark House dramatic group.

She met Julius in 1936 while he was at City College. She typed papers for him while he was attending college, and after they married, his business letters, like "bids for various Government surplus material" and "letters in regard to reinstatement after he was dismissed by the Government."

The moment Bloch put his first question on the merits, the atmosphere changed. Within seconds, Ethel was claiming Fifth Amendment privilege.

A. BLOCH Did you at any time type any matters that may be called information concerning anything relating to our national defense?

ETHEL ROSENBERG No, I did not.

COURT Did you know anything about the charges that had been leveled against your husband by the Government in '45?

ETHEL ROSENBERG Oh, you mean the time that the Government dismissed him?

(244)

COURT Yes.

ETHEL ROSENBERG Well, it was alleged that he was a member of the Communist Party.

COURT And he was dismissed for that reason?

ETHEL ROSENBERG I refuse to answer on the ground that this might be incriminating.

COURT No, no, no. I say, the Government dismissed him for that reason? I am not asking you whether he was. I am asking you whether the Government gave that as a reason for his dismissal.

A. BLOCH May I advise the witness to answer that question?

ETHEL ROSENBERG Well, they gave that as a reason, that is right.

COURT Now, you typed the reply for him; is that right?

ETHEL ROSENBERG Yes.

COURT And the reply which you typed denied that he was a Communist; is that correct?

ETHEL ROSENBERG I refuse to answer on the ground that this might be self-incriminating.

A. BLOCH I advise you to answer.

ETHEL ROSENBERG Yes.

Bloch returned to less stormy waters. Ethel recited the various jobs she had held before marriage. She also did professional singing. What did she do with her earnings? "Except for carfare and lunches, it was turned into the family." She had a "scholarship to take dramatic courses and modern dancing" and she pursued it at the dramatic group of the Clark House (Settlement). There was understandable omission of her mother's disapproval of her artistic bent and the resulting animosity between them.

After her marriage, she turned to more prosaic activities. She was a member of the Ladies Auxiliary of the Federation of Architects and Engineers, Julius' union, "and I did a lot of typing for them." She was also secretary of the East Side Defense Council, a neighborhood branch of the official Civilian Defense Organization "and that entailed a lot of typing." All this demonstrated that her typewriter and her skill in using it were employed in other than spy activities. She had been a member of the International Ladies Garment Workers' Union and another union, when she worked in those industries.

Bloch requested an adjournment before going "into the main part of my direct examination." The court suggested that there was a loose end left of Julius Rosenberg's testimony, which might be cleared up first. So Ethel stepped off and Julius replaced her.

—>←—

The government had produced a batch of photographs taken from their home for which E. H. Bloch had called. His purpose was to confirm Julius' testimony that he often stopped off to take snapshots. Bloch offered them in evidence. Saypol objected. The court sustained him: "We are not interested in seeing a lot of photographs of people that might have nothing to do with the case." Bloch had no other question but the prosecutor and the judge did.

SAYPOL Are the photographs in that batch, which you took May 1950, at 99 Park Row, which I described as passport photographs?

ROSENBERG There are a lot of photographs that aren't here, that we have taken.

COURT Well, he is asking you whether those photographs are there, those that you took in May or June?

ROSENBERG No, I don't see any photographs that I took in May or June 1950.

COURT Are the photographs there that David Greenglass says he took for passport photographs, that he says he gave to you?

ROSENBERG I don't notice any photographs there.

Then Saypol saw to it that before Julius stepped off the stand, he would have one more opportunity to claim self-incrimination.

SAYPOL One question if I may ask it? Is or was your wife a member of the Communist Party?

ROSENBERG I refuse to answer on the ground it might tend to incriminate me.

SAYPOL Very well, I don't intend to press it.

COURT Wait a minute. You are not going to press for an answer?

SAYPOL No, I don't think so.

COURT You may step down.

(Witness excused.)

The reason that the judge was surprised at the prosecutor's restraint was that there was no self-incrimination involved in admitting that his wife was a Communist. If it was followed with the question as to whether he, Julius, was too, that would be different. Either Saypol was unaware of the distinction, despite the judge putting a finger in his eye, or he appraised the Fifth Amendment plea more damaging than an answer. It was another aspect of the over-all strategy whether it would not have been more advantageous for the Rosenbergs to admit that they were Communists and fight the battle on the issue of espionage, rather than to resist on the issue of communism, and thus make it appear that they did so because communism and espionage could be equated.

The next morning, March 27, 1951, E. H. Bloch and Saypol advised the court that Macy's attorney, Mr. Kelly, was in court ready to say that further search revealed that Macy, and not United Parcel Service, delivered merchandise in 1945, as well as 1944, and that since the records for those years had been destroyed, it was impossible to trace the purchase or delivery of a console table which might have been bought in either of those years.

It was agreed that Mr. Kelly would so testify and he was excused. But not before Saypol requested Bloch's agreement that if asked on cross-examination whether "anybody can walk into R. H. Macy now and make inquiry of the facts testified to by Mr. Kelly, and ascertain that those records are non-existent for the years 1944 and 1945":

E. H. BLOCH I don't understand the import of the statement, but inquiries were made by the defense and R. H. Macy was subpoenaed.

SAYPOL Is that acceptable, though?

E. H. BLOCH Yes, sure.

COURT All right.

Of course the import was that since the non-availability of the records could be established by prior inquiry, the defendants had gone through an act of subpoenaing records which they knew could not be found. It was an insidious inference, and in view of Kelly's doubts and further research to determine the facts, an unlikely one.

———→←———

The witness chair was still empty. Ethel Rosenberg filled it as she resumed her testimony. Emanuel Bloch's father again stepped forward to give paternal guidance as he took her through a detailed series of denials of the Greenglass testimony. The smooth journey of friendly questioning was interrupted by the judge's questions, even before the prosecutor could begin his cross-examination.

Bloch began by asking her whether she had ever attempted to persuade Ruth Greenglass to approach David to steal the secrets of Los Alamos. "I did not," she replied. Nor was there any conversation on that occasion that she and Julius had ceased open Communist work because they had reached a more important plateau of service to Russia. Nor had Julius said on that occasion that he knew David was working on the atomic bomb.

COURT Did you know that your brother was working on the atomic bomb project?

ETHEL ROSENBERG No.

COURT When did you find out about that for the first time?

ETHEL ROSENBERG Oh, when he came out of the Army.

COURT You mean in 1946?

ETHEL ROSENBERG Yes.

COURT Did you know that he was working on a secret project while he was in the Army?

(247)

ETHEL ROSENBERG Well, he told us that when he came in on furlough.

COURT When?

ETHEL ROSENBERG At my mother's house.

COURT In January 1945 or in November 1944?

ETHEL ROSENBERG I don't know the exact date of the furlough, but the first time.

A. BLOCH May I ask you to keep your voice up, please?

ETHEL ROSENBERG Yes, I am sorry.

Alexander Bloch held the record of Greenglass' testimony in his hand, read out the page from which he was reading, and continued to draw denials from Ethel.

No, Julius did not say on that occasion that the atomic bomb was a most destructive weapon, had dangerous radiation effects and "that he felt that the information should be shared with Russia who was our ally at the time, because if all nations had the information then one nation couldn't use the bomb as a threat against another." There was no such conversation at any time in any place.

The court interrupted the recital again.

COURT Well, what were your own views about the subject matter of the United States having any weapon that Russia didn't have at that time? That is, in 1944 and 1945?

A. BLOCH May I respectfully object to your question?

COURT Yes. Objection overruled.

A. BLOCH As incompetent, irrelevant, and immaterial.

COURT It is most relevant. It goes to the matter of the state of mind, and intention has to be established in this case.

A. BLOCH I except.

(Last question read at the request of the Court.)

ETHEL ROSENBERG I don't recall having any views at all about it.

COURT Your mind was a blank on the subject?

ETHEL ROSENBERG Absolutely.

COURT There was never any discussions about it at all?

ETHEL ROSENBERG Not about that, not about the weapon.

COURT Was there any discussion at all as to any advantages which the United States had to make warfare that the Russians didn't have?

ETHEL ROSENBERG No, nothing of that sort.

COURT You never heard any discussions that there should be some equalization between Russia and the United States?

ETHEL ROSENBERG No, sir.

Bloch continued as if his effort was not punctuated by skeptical intercession. Had Julius on that occasion outlined the information Ruth should seek from David when she visited him? Ethel said she was never "present at any such conversation," nor did she ever discuss transmitting information to Julius or to "any of his emissaries."

Bloch announced the next page of the record, which set forth the meeting at Rosenberg's home when David returned on his first furlough and Ann Sidorovich was present. Was a plan discussed of having Ruth and Ann exchange purses in a theater in Denver? Definitely not.

A. BLOCH Do you recall whether on that occasion Ann Sidorovich was present in your home?

ETHEL ROSENBERG She may or may not have been. I really don't recall that.

Bloch then repeated the Greenglasses' testimony about the Jell-O box, and how Julius had said:

A. BLOCH "This half will be brought to you by another party and he will bear the greetings from me and you will know that I have sent him"; was there any such thing?

Did you ever hear of any such thing as a Jell-O box being cut in two in order to be a means of identification of any emissary or agent to be sent by your husband out West in order to get information from the Los Alamos Project?

ETHEL ROSENBERG Outside of this courtroom, I never heard of any such thing.

COURT Incidentally, did you have any Jell-O boxes in your apartment?

ETHEL ROSENBERG Oh, yes.

She denied that Julius had commented "the simplest things are always the cleverest." Nor was it true that David and Julius discussed how the bomb was detonated; nor that she had explained her tiredness, as being due to typing secret reports for Julius; nor had she ever copied information about the bomb, sent by David. Neither Julius nor she ever gave Ruth Greenglass $150 to go to Albuquerque.

A. BLOCH Now, your sister-in-law testified, in substance, that she had a miscarriage some time after she had been living with her husband in Albuquerque, and that she had written you a letter in which she informed you of the fact that she had had a miscarriage, and that thereupon she received a response from you in the shape of a letter, in writing, in which you said, in substance, that soon a relative will come to visit her, and insinuated that that was a sort of a signal, or that the word "relative" had some meaning, transmitting to her the idea that somebody was going to come to see her and receive information; did you ever write a letter containing a phrase that a relative would come to see her?

ETHEL ROSENBERG No, I did not.

(249)

A. BLOCH   Did you ever make an arrangement with her, or did your husband in your presence, that if the phrase "relative" would be used in any letter, it would mean as an identifying mark, and that it would refer to somebody, an emissary of yours or your husband's coming over to get information?

ETHEL ROSENBERG   There was never any such talk.

Ethel wrote occasionally to Ruth. Formal questions evoked poignant answers.

A. BLOCH   Did you also communicate with your brother?

ETHEL ROSENBERG   Yes, I did.

A. BLOCH   Now, your brother Dave was the youngest in the family?

ETHEL ROSENBERG   That's right.

A. BLOCH   And you were six years older than he was; and what was the relationship between him and you throughout the period of your living together in the same household, until you married and after you married?

ETHEL ROSENBERG   Well, he was my baby brother.

A. BLOCH   Did you treat him as such?

ETHEL ROSENBERG   Yes, that is exactly how I treated him.

A. BLOCH   Did you love him?

ETHEL ROSENBERG   Yes, I loved him very much.

The court turned her intended point around. Was David so susceptible to her and Julius that he would do their bidding, even if distasteful to him?

COURT   Did he sort of look up to you?

ETHEL ROSENBERG   Yes.

COURT   And your husband? Before the arguments that were discussed here in court?

ETHEL ROSENBERG   He liked us both. He liked my husband.

COURT   Sort of hero worship?

ETHEL ROSENBERG   Oh, by no stretch of the imagination could you say that was hero worship.

COURT   You heard him so testify, did you not?

ETHEL ROSENBERG   Yes, I did.

Ethel's mother couldn't write English "very well," and so Ethel wrote letters for her to David, but they were chatty, innocuous letters, not disguised spy epistles.

A. BLOCH   Now can you give us an idea of what you wrote about when you did write to your brother and to your sister-in-law?

ETHEL ROSENBERG   Well, I wrote the usual "How are you? We are all right," and "Take care of yourself," and "This one had a baby," or "The other one got married," and things of that sort.

She never knew Yakovlev, Golos, Bentley, Gold or Dr. Fuchs. She read about them in the newspapers. She never knew a Russian, nor did Julius ever introduce one to her:

A. BLOCH Did your husband at any time ever mention to you that he was engaged in any spying or espionage work or transmitting information received from various sources or from any source to the Russians?

ETHEL ROSENBERG He wasn't doing any such thing. He couldn't possibly have mentioned it to me.

Bloch then proceeded to show Ethel's illness during the period she was supposed to be active in espionage activities in 1944 and 1945.

ETHEL ROSENBERG Well, it so happens that I have had a spinal curvature since I was about thirteen and every once in a while that has given me some trouble, and at that time it began to kick up again, and occasionally I have to get into bed and nurse a severe backache. Through the bargain, I developed a case of low blood pressure, and that used to give me dizzy spells, sometimes to the point where I almost fainted. I also had very severe headaches, and it finally got so bad that I went to visit my doctor.

A. BLOCH Who is your doctor?

ETHEL ROSENBERG Doctor Max Lionel Hart of Rego Park, Long Island.

A. BLOCH Is Dr. Hart one of the witnesses listed as a Government witness in this case?

ETHEL ROSENBERG Yes, he is.

COURT What is the point there? Why ask her that question? What is the relevancy of that?

A. BLOCH Why not?

COURT You mean to say that the Government has to call every witness listed on that?

A. BLOCH I didn't say anything of the kind. I am just identifying the man. That is all.

COURT All right. Go ahead.

A. BLOCH And how long between that period, between the fall of 1944 and the middle of 1945, were you under Dr. Hart's care, professional care?

ETHEL ROSENBERG Well, I used to go for iron injections once or twice a week, at least once a week, and very often twice a week regularly.

A. BLOCH And that was during the period in which they claim you participated in this espionage plan?

ETHEL ROSENBERG Well, that was the period between the fall of 1944 and the spring of 1945.

(251)

The court would not permit the reference to go unchallenged.

COURT But you saw your brother, didn't you, when he came in on
    his furlough in January 1945?
ETHEL ROSENBERG Yes, I did.

Ethel added her son's infirmity to her own as an indication that
her troubles precluded activities on an espionage front.

A. BLOCH And what was the condition of your child's health?
ETHEL ROSENBERG The condition of my child was very poor. I had
    had a very difficult time ever since his birth, I mean, with him.
    He was given to severe colds and sore throat with high fever. It
    wasn't the usual thing of where a baby gets sick occasionally.
    It was practically every week in and week out. By the time he
    was a year and a half old, that winter was extremely severe.

The process of citing the page of the record and reading Greenglass'
testimony in order to draw a denial of it continued.

It was as if a tape recording was played back of the government's
case, except that Bloch's voice substituted for that of the witness. This
is a dilemma which every defense lawyer faces. He must enter denials
in the record of the accusations, but he shudders at repeating the
charges and revivifying their impact on the jury. The solution is to
paraphrase the original testimony so carefully as to deprive it of emotional sting; to leave out colorful detail which gives it verisimilitude,
and yet state enough so that the denial is complete. The risk is that
the answer will be what the law calls "a negative pregnant." For
example, if the accusation was that "he sat down and typed the
material speedily," the denial may only mean that he didn't type it
speedily—he just typed it. This, of course, would be an evasion rather
than a refutation. It would be a "negative pregnant," a denial whose
belly is filled with admission.

Avoiding this trap, it is best to so characterize the testimony which
is to be denied, that it lacks the venomous connotations of a hostile
witness, or even its persuasive formulation, and yet is complete enough
to make the denial all pervasive. The easy path of just reading the
testimony is not the best way of accomplishing this objective.

Bloch turned to Greenglass' second furlough when he said he brought
a sketch of a cross-section of the bomb and twelve pages of instructions.
Julius studied the invaluable revelation and, hiding his elation with
modest evaluation, announced that he was very pleased. He asked
Ethel to type the material at once. Did any of this happen? Ethel
answered it never did. She did not set up a bridge table and type the
material, while David helped decipher his scribbled notes, and Julius
and Ethel smoothed the grammar. Nor did Julius burn the original

(252)

notes and flush the ashes in a bowl. Nor was $200 passed to David. None of this ever happened, she swore.

When David got out of the Army, Ethel and Julius invited him and Ruth to live in their home, while they went on a ten-day vacation at Rivercrest Inn on the Hudson. So the Greenglasses were pictured as biting the hand of those who not only fed but sheltered them.

In every drama, humor inserts itself, even unwittingly, as if to relieve the tension and balance the emotions. Therefore, in every trial, one finds unintended witticism. The judge was pushing Bloch to be briefer. He commented that lawyers "like the sound" of their voice and "take double the time" necessary to make their point. To soften the criticism, he said that "I was probably guilty of it myself when I was practicing law."

Alexander Bloch eager to accommodate the judge replied in a spirit of good will, "I know you were." The judge could have stood without such ready agreement.

Once more the missing console table became the center of attention. Bloch gave it the full treatment by reading the precise accusation.

A. BLOCH Your sister-in-law testified that on a certain occasion in 1946, or at least she thought it was in 1946—that is page 1013 —your sister-in-law visited you at your home and that she noticed a piece of furniture and that that piece of furniture was a mahogany console table; and that she had a conversation with the Rosenbergs—that means you and your husband—concerning the table; that she said that she admired the table and she asked you "when she bought a new piece of furniture," and that "she said she had not bought it, she had gotten it as a gift"; that she said "it was a very nice gift to get from a friend," and that "Julius said it was from his friend and it was a special kind of table," and thereupon your husband, Julius, "turned the table on its side to show us why it was so special"; did any such thing ever occur?

ETHEL ROSENBERG No, it did not.

A. BLOCH She further testified that "there was a portion of the table that was hollowed out for a lamp to fit underneath it so that the table could be used for photograph purposes," and that your husband said that "when he used the table he darkened the room so that there would be no other light and he wouldn't be obvious to anyone looking in"; did you hear any such conversation, at any time, either in 1946 or 1947, or at any other period?

ETHEL ROSENBERG I never heard any such conversation.

A. BLOCH Did your husband ever use any table, console table or any other table, for photograph purposes?

ETHEL ROSENBERG No, he did not.

(253)

A. BLOCH Did your husband ever photograph on microfilm or any other substance anything pertaining to any information or secret concerning the national defense, or anything else at all?

ETHEL ROSENBERG No, he did not.

Bloch read from page 1015 that Julius urged David to return to Los Alamos as a civilian in order to utilize his expertise in espionage. Ethel never heard such a conversation.

Saypol, having been referred to the precise page, objected that Ethel was not mentioned as being present on that occasion. Ruth had said that only David and Julius were present with her. "Obviously," said Saypol, "this witness could have no knowledge of the conversation that transpired at the time."

Ethel denied that Julius had ever said he was arranging for students to be subsidized by the Russian Government so that they could become useful to it, nor that he urged such a program on David.

The next question gave Ethel an opportunity not merely to deny but to give her version of an incident. Julius had come home to report Ruth's concern about David's misconduct. What did he say?

ETHEL ROSENBERG When he came home and he said that Ruth was kind of worried about some crazy notions that Dave had about making some money, about taking some things, and I said, "Well, what did you tell her? Did you make sure to tell her to warn him about it, not to do it?"

He said, "Yes," that he had.

So then I asked, "Well, did Ruthie say that she would do that, that she would warn him?"

And he said, "Well, she kind of nodded her head at me and I got the feeling that she agreed with me."

And I said, "Well, all right, then I guess there is nothing to worry about."

Later, as Julius had testified, David demanded $2,000 from him. It was not an entreaty. It was accompanied by an ugly threat. Did Julius report this incident to her?

ETHEL ROSENBERG Well, the first time he said that Davey had demanded $2,000 from him and had seemed pretty upset, and that when my husband told him that he had no such amount of money, he couldn't raise any such money for him, he said, "Well, could you do me another favor? Could you at least find out if your doctor will give me a vaccination certificate?"

COURT Did he add why he wanted that vaccination certificate?

ETHEL ROSENBERG No, I don't recall my husband telling me anything of any reason for it. Except that Dave said that he was in a jam, he was in some trouble.

A. BLOCH   Were you worried about it?

ETHEL ROSENBERG   Yes, I was.

COURT   Well, forget whether you were worried about it; what did you do about it?

ETHEL ROSENBERG   Well, I said to my husband, "Well, doesn't he know the kind of financial situation we are in? Didn't you tell him you can't give him money like that?" And then I remember saying something to the effect that "If Ruthie doesn't stop nagging him for money, she is liable to give him another psychological heart attack like he had in the winter."

Still later, Julius told Ethel about another meeting.

ETHEL ROSENBERG   Well, this time my husband told me that Davey really must be in some very serious trouble, that he was extremely nervous and agitated and that he began to talk wildly, threatened that he would be sorry if he didn't—my husband said that David threatened him, that he, my husband, would be sorry if that money wasn't forthcoming.

A. BLOCH   What did you say or do about it?

ETHEL ROSENBERG   Well, I told my husband that I thought I should call the house and find out if everything is all right, and my husband said, "Well, the only thing is, Dave may be working, he may not even be home and I have no way of knowing just how much of this Ruthie knows about," and she has really had her hands full between her burns and having given birth to a child, and perhaps it would be wiser if he took it upon himself to see him at the earliest opportunity he could.

Bloch then read Ruth Greenglass' vivid testimony of Ethel's appeal to her, to instruct David not to talk, and even to go to jail for a year or two, to prevent a disaster from full revelation.

Ethel was invited to give her version of "the walks around the block." I have previously set it forth, immediately after Ruth's testimony, to provide an immediate opportunity for comparison and contrast. It was the sharpest kind of difference imaginable. Ethel had simply inquired whether David and Ruth were really "mixed up in this horrible mess." She offered to stand by them. Ruth resented the doubt of their innocence, and angrily asserted that they had hired a lawyer "to fight this case because we are not guilty. Did you think we were?" she asked defiantly.

Now Bloch elicited the important denial.

A. BLOCH   Did you at any time either on that occasion or any other occasion, either in words or in substance ask her to get an assurance from Dave that he was not going to talk, that he was going to claim he was going to be innocent, or that he was

(255)

innocent and that if he does that, everybody will be okay and satisfied?

ETHEL ROSENBERG No, I never said any such thing.

The last questions on direct examination were addressed to the watches Russia was supposed to have given Ethel and Julius in appreciation of their timeless service.

Bloch called for a watch taken by the FBI from their home when they seized all objects which might be incriminating. The prosecutor Lane produced it. Ethel stated that it was her wrist watch, given to her by Julius on her birthday, September 28, 1945. No one had ever "intimated" to her that it came "from the Russians," or was paid for by them.

Then she was asked about Julius' wrist watch. On the train ride home on the east shore of the Hudson to New York, after visiting Plattekill, Julius lost it.

ETHEL ROSENBERG Well, we were in the taxicab on the way home and I said, "You know, you really should have put in a claim." He had gone back and asked for it through the train when he discovered that it was gone and had been unable to find it. He left the taxicab. I sat there with the children, and he went back to the inside. We were right outside the terminal; and he put in a claim for the wrist watch.

A. BLOCH He reported it to the people there?

ETHEL ROSENBERG Yes.

A. BLOCH In the office?

ETHEL ROSENBERG That's right.

A. BLOCH That is all as far as I am concerned.

He sat down. His son, representing Julius, arose for brief "cross-examination." He was emotional, because he was defending himself, too, from the charge that "her lawyer" had asked Ethel to appeal to Ruth for David's silence.

E. H. BLOCH Did I ever advise you to go to see Ruthie Greenglass and tell Ruthie Greenglass to tell her husband to keep his mouth shut?

COURT What has that got to do with it? There has been no accusation hurled at you.

E. H. BLOCH But Ruthie Greenglass testified that Ethel Rosenberg said her lawyer sent her down.

COURT All right, go ahead.

ETHEL ROSENBERG No, you never told me to do any such thing.

E. H. BLOCH Well, what did I tell you to do with respect to the Greenglass family?

ETHEL ROSENBERG You told me to stay away from them.

E. H. BLOCH Did I tell you I believed that they were your enemies?

ETHEL ROSENBERG Yes, you told me that.

E. H. BLOCH That is all.

Kuntz had no cross-examination on behalf of Sobell. So Ethel was left to face Saypol in a lengthy and grueling cross-examination.

CHAPTER 23

He began with her very last answers.

SAYPOL Your lawyer asked you about the place where the lost watch was reported and you said in the office. In which office did he report it?

ETHEL ROSENBERG I didn't say in the office. I don't recall saying anything about an office.

SAYPOL Didn't you hear your lawyer a few minutes ago say did you report it in the office and didn't you say yes? Didn't you answer that?

A. BLOCH If your Honor please, she didn't say so at all. She said her husband reported it and she remained in the taxicab.

COURT Well, I don't remember what she said exactly.

The fact was that seconds before, Bloch had asked her whether Julius reported the loss of a watch.

A. BLOCH In the office?

ETHEL ROSENBERG That's right.

Since the court, too, didn't remember this answer, she might be forgiven for the lapse. Saypol did not insist on reading back her testimony to demonstrate her contradiction, which was not important in itself, but as a psychological unnerving of the witness at the very start of her cross-examination.

There was another possible contradiction. Julius had testified about his watch that while on the train, "the band broke and I put it in my vest pocket, and the baby who was sitting on my lap, picked it up and dropped it out of the train." Yet Ethel testified that Julius "asked for it through the train when he discovered that it was gone and had been

(259)

unable to find it." Why would he inquire among the passengers for a watch the baby had dropped out of the window—or was it only the band? The entire incident may have had no significance, but if the prosecution's aim was to create suspicion that the "lost watch" theory was concocted in order to avoid producing the watch, then the government might have addressed itself to the possible contradiction.

Saypol immediately moved to his most promising subject matter. Ethel had testified before the grand jury. She admitted having been warned of her "constitutional rights against incrimination." He showed her the minutes of her testimony on that occasion. She admitted her signature. It was offered in evidence. Bloch had no objection but a moment later changed his mind.

A. BLOCH   My son has just called my attention to the fact that it covers the question of alleged communism, and I therefore object to the introduction of this paper in evidence on the ground it is incompetent, irrelevant and immaterial.

At first, the court upheld him. It bore her signature, "but what is the relevancy to the case? She may have signed a lot of papers." Soon, the relevancy became evident, and the judge permitted the document to be marked in evidence. Bloch continued to object.

E. H. BLOCH   I am concerned whether or not I was remiss in my duty in not advising this witness, prior to the time that she was shown this document, whether or not to answer the question whether or not it was her signature, but it is in, and I just want to assert my thoughts with respect to any further questioning.

On Ethel's appearance before the grand jury she was asked whether she had ever signed a Communist Party nominating petition. She answered that she had. When Saypol asked her whether she had made that answer, she replied, "I refuse to answer on the ground that this might tend to incriminate me."

There followed an involved legal discussion among counsel and the court concerning her right to claim privilege. Finally, the court asked Ethel:

COURT   Let me ask you this: Did you tell the grand jury the truth and the entire truth when you testified?

ETHEL ROSENBERG   Yes.

The prosecutor harked back to Julius Rosenberg's correction of his testimony:

SAYPOL   I say 111 South 3rd Street is the address where you lived with your husband and about which he forgot to testify or tell us the first day of his testimony.

(260)

ETHEL ROSENBERG That is right.

SAYPOL Whom did you live with there?

ETHEL ROSENBERG We lived with a couple by the name of Pogarsky.

SAYPOL Also known as Page?

ETHEL ROSENBERG Yes.

SAYPOL Were they members of the Communist Party?

ETHEL ROSENBERG I refuse to answer on the ground of self-incrimination.

The court sought to obtain her real purpose in claiming privilege. It was obvious that she was plunging blindly into a maze which legal experts would have difficulty traversing.

COURT Well now, Mrs. Rosenberg, do you feel it would incriminate you if you answered whether the Pages or Pogarskys were members of the Communist Party?

ETHEL ROSENBERG Well, I am apprehensive of self-incrimination.

COURT Do you feel that it might affect you in this case or do you feel that you might be prosecuted because of an answer that you might make in another case?

ETHEL ROSENBERG Whatever I might feel, I refuse to answer on the ground of self-incrimination.

The judge realized that steering through the jungle of intricacies concerning the precious rights of the Fifth Amendment and its sensitive limitations was hazardous. He took the precaution again of warning the jury:

COURT I want to say to the jury in the absence of a direction by the Court, you can't draw any inferences from the refusal to answer by the witness.

SAYPOL And I should think the Court would add to that the guilt or innocence on the main issue, that the jury should take into consideration ultimately when the question reaches it—

COURT I will charge them properly.

SAYPOL The causal relation.

COURT You can't infer that the witness has admitted anything from the refusal to answer. That is all.

When Saypol asked her whether she hadn't spent the summer of 1944 with the Sidoroviches, she denied it, and fought back angrily at his "supporting" proof.

SAYPOL Isn't that the summer you sprained or strained your back because you were lugging water from the well?

ETHEL ROSENBERG First of all, I didn't strain my back at any time. I had a spinal curvature from the time I was thirteen, and second of all, I didn't spend the summer of 1944 with the Sidoroviches.

SAYPOL   Well, did you ever tell anybody that you strained or sprained
    your back lugging water from the well?
ETHEL ROSENBERG   I don't recall saying any such thing.

Through a series of questions he elicited the fact that the name of her
maid in 1944 was Evelyn Cox and that "she cleaned and polished the
furniture." "Did you part good friends?" he asked. "Yes," she replied.
Had these questions something to do with the console table?

Pounded at with shifting questions, it might not have occurred to
Ethel that the maid would be a government witness. Or did it add to
her apprehensions and dry her throat with fear, so that repeatedly the
court, Bloch and Saypol requested her "to speak up," each with different
intonations of sympathy, goading or warning?

The prosecutor's turning to the console table next might have revealed
an unconscious association with the maid. He showed Ethel pictures of
various tables and asked which one most resembled the console table.
Where was it kept in the house? In many different places "because we
switched around the furniture to suit our needs." She was reminded of
Julius' testimony that it stood on the side of the wall opposite the
kitchen. She confirmed this. However, she didn't remember whether it
was ever put in a closet. She may have put it there.

SAYPOL   Did you ever tell any one that that table was a present?
ETHEL ROSENBERG   No, I never did.
SAYPOL   You are sure of that?
ETHEL ROSENBERG   I am sure of that, yes.

The inordinate concentration of the government on the console table
would have alerted the most astigmatic defense counsel of an impending
crisis. The Chinese compose words out of several words. The word
"crisis" is constructed by combining "danger" and "opportunity." The
table presented both. If it was not produced, the testimony of its special
construction, contradicting its Macy origin, strengthened the credibility
of the Greenglasses and discredited that of the Rosenbergs correspond-
ingly. However, if the table could be found and produced to demonstrate
its $21 innocence, would it not be a fatal blow to the prosecution? We
shall see that after the trial ended Bloch contended in court that he had
not searched for the table because "Frankly, I didn't consider the
Greenglasses' testimony on this point very significant."

When the FBI searched the Rosenberg apartment, they found equipment for developing film. Ethel had to face cross-examination in which
she asserted its innocent nature.

SAYPOL   Did your husband ever do his own developing and printing at
    home?
ETHEL ROSENBERG   He never did. He made one attempt in 1950 to
    develop some films and he did such a poor job of it that he decided
    that that kind of a hobby wasn't for him.

(262)

SAYPOL In that the first time he ever tried to develop some film?

ETHEL ROSENBERG That's right; first time.

SAYPOL What kind of material, what kind of equipment did he have and did he use in connection with his attempt to try to develop some films?

ETHEL ROSENBERG I don't think I could even describe it or name the stuff. It was just some developing developer, whatever you call it.

SAYPOL Did he have trays?

ETHEL ROSENBERG What did you say?

SAYPOL Did he have trays, enamel trays, that he used for developing and printing photographs?

ETHEL ROSENBERG Not that I can recall.

SAYPOL Did he have chemicals?

ETHEL ROSENBERG I think he had some kind of chemical.

SAYPOL Did he have what is known as a daylight developing tank?

ETHEL ROSENBERG I never even heard of those words until you just said them.

SAYPOL Don't you know that when he was arrested, the agents of the Federal Bureau of Investigation took away from your home some photographic equipment, including a developing tank and some trays?

A. BLOCH I will object to it upon the ground it is assuming something that has not been proven. It may not be proven, and it is in the record.

COURT Overruled.

A. BLOCH Exception.

ETHEL ROSENBERG Well, as I told you, I know there was some kind of developer around, but I wouldn't know what you call these things.

The government attacked from all angles. Suddenly, Ethel was beset with questions about passport photos. In view of the Greenglasses' testimony that they were importuned by the Rosenbergs to flee the country, and were given sums of money to do so, and also that Julius too intended to flee and meet them in Mexico, cross-examination on this point presented ominous possibilities.

Ethel denied ever having any passport photos made. But she admitted having family photos taken. The question was whether these occurred after the atom spy revelations broke.

COURT Well now, you remember the month of May very well, don't you?

ETHEL ROSENBERG Yes.

COURT You remember the month of June 1950 very well?

ETHEL ROSENBERG Yes.

COURT You remember all the incidents that have occurred?

ETHEL ROSENBERG Yes.

(263)

COURT Did you have any pictures taken for any purpose whatsoever in May or June 1950?

ETHEL ROSENBERG We may have; we may have.

COURT Do you remember where?

ETHEL ROSENBERG No, all I remember was some commercial photographer.

COURT How did you happen to go to that particular commercial photographer?

ETHEL ROSENBERG Well, I didn't say I went to any particular commercial photographer.

COURT Well, you just remembered posing before a camera?

ETHEL ROSENBERG Yes.

COURT How did you happen to get before that camera?

ETHEL ROSENBERG Well, my older boy happens to be very much interested in machines of any kind.

Saypol eagerly followed the judge's questions and added heavy sarcasm to it. Ethel fought back determinedly against the combined attack.

SAYPOL Is that the eight-year-old boy?

ETHEL ROSENBERG That's right. He is very precocious.

SAYPOL So you took him in to play with the photographer, is that the idea?

COURT Just a moment.

E. H. BLOCH I submit that the witness—

SAYPOL Well—

COURT Mr. Saypol, will you wait until I am through?

E. H. BLOCH I move that Mr. Saypol's remarks be stricken from the record.

COURT They will be stricken.

I asked you how did you happen to get to that particular photographer? Who recommended that particular photographer?

ETHEL ROSENBERG Nobody ever recommended any particular commercial photographer to us.

COURT How did you happen to go to that particular one?

ETHEL ROSENBERG We, as I tried to explain, my older child was interested in machines, among other things. We, it was our wont to go for walks with them and to stop and look at anything of interest, anything that might be of interest to the children, and very often, as we took these walks, the older child particularly would ask, "Oh, come, let's go in here and get our pictures taken." That is—I think kids generally do that kind of thing.

COURT How many times would you say he had done that?

ETHEL ROSENBERG Oh, several times. We happen to be what you would call "snapshot hounds" and that bunch of pictures that you saw there doesn't nearly represent all the snapshots and all the photos that we have had made of ourselves and the children all through our lives.

COURT Then you remember, you say, having had some photographs taken in May or in June?

ETHEL ROSENBERG It may have been that time. I am really not sure. There were so many frequent occasions when we dropped into these places.

COURT I am talking about the very last ones that you had taken.

ETHEL ROSENBERG Well, I can't say what I don't recall and I really don't recall specifically.

SAYPOL Well, we have it now at least that the photographer, the commercial photographer, was within walking distance of your home at 10 Monroe Street; is that right?

ETHEL ROSENBERG Well, there were times we took walks and took photographs elsewhere.

SAYPOL We are now talking about the time that you last remember, within the two years, when you went with your family to a commercial photographer to have a picture taken or pictures?

ETHEL ROSENBERG But I didn't say that we took a walk this particular time to this particular place.

SAYPOL Where was it?

ETHEL ROSENBERG I wouldn't know.

COURT Is this a convenient place to recess for lunch, Mr. Saypol?

SAYPOL All right.

COURT We will recess until 2:20.

—→←—

It is unlikely that Ethel, Julius and their counsel could eat much during the brought-in-sandwich lunch provided in the prison conference room underneath the courtroom. If there was any solace, it was the possible sympathy which the remorseless attacks on Ethel might be creating for her with the jury.

There are subtle psychological elements which make overbearing cross-examination counterproductive. Jurors do not like to see a witness, and especially a woman crushed, unless she has already been proven so venal that no punishment is too much for her. Ethel hardly fitted that category. She was a sweet-looking, simple woman, a mother of two young children, of artistic bent, denying all complicity in a scheme of which she was accused by her own feelingless brother.

When the powerful forces of the court and the government combined to attack her, and the prosecutor unchivalrously sneered at her in the bargain, there was the possibility that the jury would symbolically put a protective arm around her. I have seen this happen many times.

The human aspects of jury reaction are not to be underestimated. They are based on the same moral precepts as our laws, but they are not codified. Unlike precise statutes, they are the responses to individual stimuli, based upon general rules of "fair play."

We instruct juries not to permit sympathy or prejudice to sway them, but we know that the ideal is not attainable any more than in any other realm. The stricture is intended to curb and minimize feelings which cannot be eradicated entirely. In a way, the forbidden residue leavens the process of justice.

The man who demands his symbolic pound of flesh because it is in his bond is not admired, and judges as well as juries delight in finding some technical flaw to defeat him. Similarly, juries lean against arrogant or rude witnesses. They translate their feelings legally in terms of credibility. They won't believe such a witness, so that they can decide against him. And who can say they are wrong?

The courtroom is, therefore, not a mere arena for rational combat. It seethes with psychological variants, and the lawyer who is unaware of them is wandering about blind to the forces which swirl around him.

That is why a witness should not only be prepared to know the complicated facts. I instruct him what to wear and how to behave in the unaccustomed surroundings of the courtroom. I insist that no matter how he is badgered on cross-examination, he must be polite to his tormentor. He can strike back by emphasizing the facts, but not by sarcasm or anger toward the adversary. He must neither fawn nor fret, flatter nor foment. The jury is better disposed to a gentleman, not because of his manners, but because of an aura of decency which sincere good behavior projects. For the same reason, a jury may resent vicious cross-examination or rudeness on the part of the prosecutor. The lawyer whose duties are manifold must keep a lateral gaze at the jury. If they wince as the witness is crushed, it is best to let up, since the triumph may be so complete that it turns into defeat. Only when the witness has been demonstrated to be evil, and the jury enjoys his discomfiture, may the stops on cross-examination be let out.

Unless the jury was firmly convinced by the prosecution evidence, despite Julius' and Ethel's denials, she hardly fitted the picture of base criminal at this stage of the trial. But what was still to come?

After the lunch recess, questions concerning possible passport photos continued to pour on Ethel. She insisted that she had "usual little snapshots" taken, once at a photographer's store on Clinton Street. They were inexpensive, "nothing like $9 or $10." Why had the prosecutor mentioned this sum? Was he fishing or was there a surprise in store? Once Ethel had a picture taken of her two growing children at a studio at Fifth Avenue and 39th Street. She paid $1.00.

SAYPOL Those weren't passport photographs, were they?

ETHEL ROSENBERG I never took any passport photographs.

The prosecutor dropped the subject abruptly, upon drawing this absolute denial.

He turned to the subject of Ethel's conduct, when she learned that David Greenglass was stealing from the Army—uranium of all things. Did she speak to anybody in the family about it?

ETHEL ROSENBERG No, I didn't. I was quite certain that he and his wife could handle their own affairs.

There came a time when she learned that the FBI was questioning David about stolen uranium. She talked to Julius about it. Was anything said "concerning the fact that that might have to do with the atomic bomb"?

"Not that I can recall," she replied, even though at that time she knew "that Davey had been working on the atomic bomb."

Even when Julius told her that Davey "had dropped the word 'Mexico,'" she didn't talk to anyone in the family about it.

Saypol took it upon himself to defend his witnesses even against slurs which were not material to the case. Ethel had testified that when Julius told her how desperate David was, she commented that Ruth was probably nagging him about money, and that if she continued to do so, she would provoke another psychological heart attack.

SAYPOL Well, at the time you said Ruthie was nagging him for money, Ruthie had been in the hospital and had a baby, hadn't she?
ETHEL ROSENBERG Possible.
SAYPOL She had been in the hospital before because of some serious burns?
ETHEL ROSENBERG That is right.
SAYPOL What was it that made you suggest that maybe Ruthie was nagging him for money? Did you think she wanted it for a hospital bill?
ETHEL ROSENBERG Whatever she may have wanted it for, it was common knowledge that Ruthie always nagged Davey about money.

If Ethel's understandable purpose was to strike back at Ruth and hurt her, this was a most effective way of doing so. I doubt that any other testimony in the trial got under Ruth's skin as much as this did. People are often more sensitive about reflections on their personality, sex appeal or idiosyncratic habits than to serious generic accusations. For example, I remember a husband in a matrimonial case sitting quite unperturbed during a description of his philandering, but going into a frenzy when the wife stated that he was stingy and always gave inadequate tips. Similarly, a woman in a contract dispute may take calmly testimony about her breach of the terms of employment, but becomes a tigress when a hostile witness comments parenthetically that she usually looked "dowdy." Vanity has a lower boiling point than honor.

(267)

There is a parlor game, which I advise no one to play if he or she desires to retain lifelong friendships, in which all the participants rate each other from 1 to 10, on a piece of paper, for brilliance, intelligence, beauty, sex appeal, good mate, honesty, sense of humor, neatness, etc. Watch the face of the victim who has won the highest laurels in most categories but only scores 4 in sex appeal or sense of humor. Conversely, watch the look of satisfaction on those whose score is reverse.

Saypol was therefore psychologically sound in attempting to counteract the charge that Ruth "nagged" David by demonstrating that perhaps Ruth needed money for her hospital expense. This might change the coloration of the "nag" from greed to necessity. What is the Chinese proverb "Some people call insistence on the truth, nagging"?

A prosecutor is fortunate if he can defend the character of his witnesses. Often, this is impossible. He must present criminals to prove his case. This was the situation here. Greenglass pounded his chest with *mea culpa,* so loud that it could be heard around the world. Gold revealed the insidious workings of the Russian spy system, exposing himself readily as an important cog. Bentley had reformed, but her past was, according to her own words, traitorous. Even Ruth conceded to being a carrier of espionage germs, and then a courier of the corrupted results. Still, it might be helpful not to be depicted as a witch or bitch toward her husband, because the jury, like she, might be more affected by such heartlessness than by her acquiescent intrigue.

SAYPOL Did you help him join the Communist Party?

Ethel interrupted Bloch's advice that she could claim the Fifth Amendment by blurting out firmly—"I refuse to answer."

SAYPOL She knows the answer.

E. H. BLOCH She is a better lawyer than I am, no doubt.

SAYPOL Go ahead.

ETHEL ROSENBERG I am going to refuse to answer on the ground of self-incrimination.

SAYPOL Now that your lawyer has interrupted, do you so refuse?

ETHEL ROSENBERG That is right.

The next questions seemed innocuous, but they laid the foundation for the main attack upon her. Shortly after Julius was questioned by the FBI he and she had retained Bloch. Thereafter, they confided in Bloch whatever they knew about the matter. They told him the truth. They withheld nothing.

Whatever her feelings were about David, while she sat on the stand, from which for hours he had pointed an accusing finger at her, she insisted that she always bore nothing but affection for her brother. When he was arrested, she "plied" Ruth with questions about his health and how he was "standing up in jail."

SAYPOL   You mean, was he talking about you and your husband? Is
    that what you meant when you asked that?
ETHEL ROSENBERG   Of course not.
SAYPOL   Did you talk at that time about the possibility that perhaps
    Davey was going to implicate you in this?
ETHEL ROSENBERG   Well, we did recall that the FBI had mentioned,
    had spoken to my husband in terms of my brother having impli-
    cated us, but frankly we didn't believe them.

Having been rebuffed, Saypol immediately turned to the sure opportunity provided by the Rosenbergs' decision to claim self-incrimination.

SAYPOL   You were completely frank with Mr. Bloch and you told him
    the truth?
ETHEL ROSENBERG   That is right.

Why had the prosecutor suddenly turned so benign and helpful?
It soon became apparent that a trap had been laid. It was so deep
that Ethel struggled for hours to climb out of it. Even the judge's
help could not lift her above it. It was the only time in her appearance on the stand that she conceded she could not explain why
she had done what she did.

It all revolved around her appearance before the grand jury. Time
and again she refused to answer questions put to her there, on the
ground that to do so might incriminate her. Yet at the trial, when
the same questions were asked, she answered them proclaiming her innocence. This raised a unique question under the Fifth Amendment.
She had the right to assert it and refuse to answer. But if she
believed at that time that to answer might involve her in a crime,
how much credence was to be given to her answers to the same
questions at the trial, that she had done nothing which might tend
to incriminate her?

She was caught in the vise of asserting on one hand that to answer
truthfully might prove her a criminal, and asserting on the other
hand that she could answer the identical questions because she was
innocent. It ran in a vicious circle. If innocent, why did she refuse
to answer before the grand jury?

This battle of contradictions spread across a varied series of questions.
It was punctuated by continuous objections and even motions for a
mistrial. There were numerous legal arguments of the subtleties involved
in recognizing the Fifth Amendment privilege and yet permitting the
subject of credibility to survive it under the peculiar circumstance. The
judge at one point urged Saypol to cease pouring new incendiary illustrations on the burning issue, but even he could not dislodge the
prosecutor. Above all, Ethel appeared disarmed so that she could not
offer a defense against the imputations hurled at her. Since this struggle

may well have been one of the determinative factors in the trial, I will trace the topography upon which it was fought.

Having stated that she told her lawyer the full truth, it appeared that it was on his advice that she claimed the Fifth Amendment when she appeared before the grand jury.

SAYPOL   Do you remember having been asked this question and giving this answer:
> "Q   That may incriminate, the fact that you talked with your lawyer?
> "A   That was my answer."

Was that the truth?

ETHEL ROSENBERG   All I can say, Mr. Saypol, at this time, is that I don't remember what reason I may or may not have had at that time for giving such an answer.

The court pointed out the dilemma to her and asked why she had claimed before the grand jury that to answer might incriminate her?

COURT   Now, what was the reason?

ETHEL ROSENBERG   I couldn't say at this time.

COURT   In your own interest, I think you ought to think about it and see if you can give us some reason.

ETHEL ROSENBERG   I really couldn't say.

At the grand jury she was asked whether she had "discussed this case with your brother David Greenglass." She refused to answer, claiming privilege. Was it true that to answer might tend to incriminate her?

ETHEL ROSENBERG   It was true, because my brother David was under arrest.

SAYPOL   How would that incriminate you, if you are innocent?

ETHEL ROSENBERG   As long as I had any idea that there might be some chance for me to be incriminated I had the right to use that privilege.

When the question was pursued, the atmosphere grew heated and resulted in a motion for a mistrial.

COURT   Now let me ask a question. If you had answered at that time that you had spoken to David, for reasons best known to you, you felt that that would incriminate you?

ETHEL ROSENBERG   Well, if I used the privilege of self-incrimination at that time, I must have felt that perhaps there might be something that might incriminate me in answering.

SAYPOL   As a matter of fact, at that time you didn't know how much the FBI knew about you and so you weren't taking any chances; isn't that it?

ETHEL ROSENBERG I was using—I didn't know what the FBI knew or didn't know.

SAYPOL Of course you didn't, so you weren't taking any chance in implicating yourself or your husband?

E. H. BLOCH Wait a second. I object to this entire line of questions . . .

He moved for a mistrial.

COURT I think it is proper cross-examination. Your motion for a mistrial is denied. Your objection is overruled.

Before the grand jury, she had refused to answer whether she had discussed with David the work he was doing at Los Alamos. How would an answer have incriminated her if she wasn't connected with his espionage activities? The court sustained objection. She was spared from explaining, but not for long.

When Saypol protested that he was being subjected to a baseless barrage of objections, the judge said,

COURT Now that is your version. I will now tell the jury that they will draw no inferences whatsoever from a lawyer's objection. That is his prerogative. That is what he is supposed to do if he thinks he should object.

When another illustration was given her of a claim of self-incrimination before the grand jury, she could only conjecture why she had feared criminal involvement.

ETHEL ROSENBERG Well, if I answered that I didn't want to answer the question on the grounds that it might incriminate me, I must have had a reason to think that it might incriminate me.

SAYPOL Well, that reason was based on the advice that your lawyer had given you, was it not?

ETHEL ROSENBERG My lawyer had advised me of my rights.

SAYPOL He advised you only on the basis of what you told him?

ETHEL ROSENBERG He advised me as to my rights, but he also advised me it was entirely up to me to decide, on the basis of what the question was, whether or not I thought any answer might incriminate me, and I so used that right.

SAYPOL You weren't making those answers because of a concern that you had about incriminating your brother, were you?

ETHEL ROSENBERG I can't recall right now what my reasons were at that time for using that right. I said before and I say again, if I used that right, then I must have had some reason or other. I cannot recall right now what that reason might or might not have been, depending on the different questions I was asked.

A lengthy legal argument with the judge ensued, in which Bloch tried to distinguish between Ethel's compulsory appearance under subpoena before the grand jury, and her voluntary appearance as a witness at the trial, since she did not have to take the stand if she chose not to do so. The judge couldn't see any merit in the distinction insofar as the Fifth Amendment was concerned. He pointed out that he had protected that privilege for the defendants at all times. It was she who had dropped its shield by answering at the trial.

COURT And I have given the witness every opportunity to explain, indeed I have sought an explanation if she could give it to me as to anything that occurred that caused this change.

She pleaded privilege before the grand jury when she was asked whether she had ever met Harry Gold. At the trial, however, she said she had never met him. If her statement at the trial was true, how would answering the same question before the grand jury incriminate her? The court sustained an objection because the point had been amply made and additional illustrations were not necessary. "So, Mr. Saypol, you need not ask each particular question."

Saypol replied, "I am going to go on quickly now. I just want to make the record. I know what the answer is going to be." He proceeded to multiply the illustrations of her claims of self-incrimination to questions she now said she could answer without involvement. So she had refused to answer whether she saw the sketches which Greenglass had brought from Los Alamos; whether she heard Greenglass give Julius information about the bomb; whether she knew that her husband "was affiliated with the Soviet Union"; whether she discussed with Ruth the work David was doing at Los Alamos; whether she heard David discuss the atom bomb and nuclear fission? Whether she knew Anatoli Yakovlev? "How," asked Saypol, "would saying that you did not know Yakovlev, if that was the truth, incriminate you?" She replied, "It is not necessary to explain the use of self-incrimination."

Twice more the judge tried to stop the cumulative demonstration:

COURT I think we have had enough of this subject, Mr. Saypol, and for this particular purpose, and the purpose for which it is limited, I don't see anything would be added by constant questioning and more assertion of the privilege. So I am going to ask you to go on to another topic.

Saypol summed up all the illustrations in one question, and drew another admission from Ethel: "As I said before, I can't remember now what reasons I might or might not have had to use the ground of self-incrimination then."

Content with the echo of her previous embarrassment, Saypol announced, "I have had enough questions."

At one time during these skirmishes, Ethel unexpectedly opened a window on the boiling hatreds which had developed in the family after the arrests.

ETHEL ROSENBERG Well, I remember now that when I visited my husband some time before I was myself arrested he told me that he had met my brother David at the West Street House of Detention, and in reply to some discussion about recreation periods, that is, as to when my brother wanted his recreation period on the roof and when my husband wanted his, because they intended to keep them separated—in reply to that my husband told me that David had acted very hostile toward him, and had said, "If he comes anywhere near me I will knock his head off," or words to that effect.

The prosecutor did not follow up this revelation although it raised a question as to why Greenglass was so bitter at Julius, unless he felt that he had been drawn into the disaster by him. If it was Greenglass who was involving Julius unjustly, would it not have been Julius who was fuming with rage?

E. H. Bloch tried valiantly on redirect examination to rehabilitate Ethel, by giving her an opportunity to assert that she believed she was innocent when she testified before the grand jury, and also when she testified at the trial.

COURT The point is, you answered these questions at the trial and refused to on the ground that it would tend to incriminate you before the grand jury.

ETHEL ROSENBERG As I said before, I can't remember now what reasons I might or might not have had to use the ground of self-incrimination then.

So the wheel had turned back again to where it had been.
Ethel stepped off the stand.
Bloch announced, "Defendants Julius Rosenberg and Ethel Rosenberg rest."

———→←———

Would Sobell rest without putting in a defense? Kuntz, one of his attorneys, rose to demand that the indictment be deemed in evidence so that he could read from it in summation. Tensions were increasing. There was an acrimonious exchange which was not without its humor.

SAYPOL I think I should make the observation that Mr. Kuntz shouldn't get too excited—

KUNTZ Mr. Kuntz is not excited.

SAYPOL —because we will ask your Honor to charge as to each de-

(273)

fendant in the case, that a single overt act as to any and all may be mentioned.

COURT Oh, Mr. Saypol, please. I will instruct the jury on the law. I know what Mr. Kuntz has in mind, and I will see that the jury understands fully what the law on the subject is. You need have no fear or no concern about that, Mr. Kuntz and Mr. Saypol.

KUNTZ Mr. Kuntz in all his excitement never makes a wrong statement or improper statement.

COURT Of course not, neither does Mr. Saypol.

KUNTZ I wish Mr. Saypol would do as little harm in his calmness as I do in my excitement.

COURT Let us have no more. We are near the end of this case.

Kuntz then announced that "Sobell desires to rest on the record." The court inquired whether the government had rebuttal witnesses. Indeed it did. They sent new shocks through the courtroom.

CHAPTER 24

The government called Evelyn Cox to the stand. She was the part-time maid for the Rosenbergs. One could almost see the prosecutor licking his chops as he adopted an intimate, my-dear-friend approach to the witness.

SAYPOL Mrs. Cox, will you sit right back and make yourself easy, like you do in a rocking chair.

You and I had some talk about the Rosenbergs, you remember?

EVELYN COX Yes, Mr. Saypol.

She was married and had one child. In 1944 and 1945 she worked three days a week for the Rosenbergs at their apartment in Knicker-bocker Village. She was asked to identify the defendants. She pointed to Julius who stood, then to Ethel Rosenberg, who also rose. "That's her," she said.

She remembered a new piece of furniture coming into the house. It was a console table. All the rest of the furniture was secondhand. When Mrs. Cox saw it, she admired it, and she talked to Ethel about it.

EVELYN COX I asked her where it came from. It was such a pretty table and she said that a friend of her husband gave it to him as a gift. Then she added that he hadn't seen him for a long time and it was a sort of a wedding present. That is all the talk we ever had about the table.

SAYPOL Did she ever say to you that she bought it in Macy's?

EVELYN COX No.

SAYPOL Did she ever say to you that her husband bought it and paid $21 for it in Macy's?

EVELYN COX No, she said it was a gift to her husband from a friend.

After a while this table was moved from the wall against which it always stood, into a closet. From that time on, even though it was a new and the best piece in the apartment, it remained in the closet.

SAYPOL That is the closet which is right next to the bathroom?
EVELYN COX To the bathroom.
SAYPOL So that if one opened the door to the closet, the electric light from the bathroom would shine into the closet?
EVELYN COX Yes, sir.
SAYPOL Did you ever see the table outside again in the living room—
EVELYN COX No.

There was no other furniture in the closet. Bloch was invited to cross-examine.

He suggested that perhaps the table she had in mind came from the friends in California, who had left their secondhand possessions with the Rosenbergs to save storage. No, she insisted, the mahogany console table was the only new piece in the house while she worked there in 1944 and 1945.

E. H. BLOCH Did there come a time while you were working for the Rosenbergs when one of the tables was disposed of or sold by Mrs. Rosenberg?
EVELYN COX You mean the console? That is the only table, and it wasn't disposed of because it was in the closet. Mrs. Rosenberg put it in the closet.
E. H. BLOCH When you left in 1945 was that console table that you just described still in the closet?
EVELYN COX Yes, it was in the closet. It came in 1945, she got it in 1945.

It had stood against a wall for about two or three months before being placed in the closet.

E. H. BLOCH Now while it was outside did you notice whether it was used for eating purposes?
EVELYN COX It was never used for any purposes, so far as I know, never.
E. H. BLOCH You mean it was just a decorative—
EVELYN COX It was an ornament.
E. H. BLOCH Could that console table have been opened up so that it could be used for eating purposes?
EVELYN COX Well, it had a leaf. It had a leaf, you know, that used to stay against the wall that it could have been used but I don't know that they ever used it. I never saw them using it.

There followed a long inquiry into the size and measurements of the table. Since it had a leaf which stood up, there was much confusion as to what was being measured. Saypol interrupted and offered to clear up the matter. He took the examination out of Bloch's hands, and when he was through, he said to Bloch, "Does that help you?" E. H. Bloch replied, "It does; thank you very much, Mr. Saypol."

The sudden effusion of friendly assistance, even though on an inconsequential matter, struck a strange note in the generally heated atmosphere.

Bloch tried another gambit.

E. H. BLOCH   I would just like to ask you one question: When you had a conversation with Mrs. Rosenberg about where the table came from—do you remember you testified about that? Did she or did she not say that this was a gift from her husband?

EVELYN COX   She said it was a gift to her husband from a friend who hadn't seen him for years.

E. H. BLOCH   Now is it your testimony, Mrs. Cox, that while you were working there during the years 1944 and 1945, that this console table that you have described was the only console table that was delivered or was new furniture in the Rosenberg home?

EVELYN COX   Yes.

Before concluding, he sought Mrs. Cox's opinion about Ethel.

E. H. BLOCH   May I ask you, Mrs. Cox, in the two years in which you worked for Mrs. Rosenberg, did you find Mrs. Rosenberg to be an honest woman?

EVELYN COX   Very.

Saypol objected, but he could not have received a better answer. Simple, forthright witnesses are the most persuasive. Mrs. Cox's ready praise of Ethel showed her to be objective and without guile. She was not catering to the prosecutor, or awed by the fact that she was a government witness. Her ready response that Ethel was "very" honest made everything else she testified about more believable.

The question, however, was legally inadmissible. The defendant may offer character witness, and usually does, selecting, where possible, distinguished people such as rabbis, priests or teachers. For example, Supreme Court Justice Felix Frankfurter and Secretary of State Dean Acheson appeared as character witness for Alger Hiss. They did not testify concerning the merits of the controversy. They were limited to the question whether the accused enjoyed a good reputation in the community for veracity.

The test is not what the character witness thinks. He may only state the defendant's reputation in his community. The theory is that one's neighbors get to know him and that their multiple judgment establishes his reputation. Of course, no test is perfect. There is an epigram to the effect that when a farmer sells a barrel of apples, his reputation is on top, and his character at the bottom. Reputation in the community helps to establish character.

The Rosenbergs did not produce a single character witness. Since their credibility was the essence of the case, such witnesses might have been helpful, but was there anyone who wanted to be associated with the defense?

Mrs. Cox had not lived in the Rosenberg community, and she was therefore not qualified to testify about their reputation in it. When she stepped off the stand, the mystery of the console table had deepened, but not to the defendants' advantage.

The next rebuttal witness was Helen Pagano, secretary for O. John Rogge, lawyer for Greenglass. Kilsheimer questioned her for the government, and tried to elicit the fact that Louis Abel, the brother-in-law of Greenglass, had brought approximately $4,000 in a brown paper to the office and that she recognized the brown paper which had been marked in evidence as the wrapper. Before she could identify it, Bloch conceded that:

> I am not going to be technical about it. Of course. I never disputed the fact that Mr. Abel came to Mr. Rogge and gave him $4,000 in this brown bag.

COURT He doesn't dispute it.

The witness said that the brown paper exhibit was the wrapper in which she had received the money in the law office.

The government then called the final witness of the twenty-three it presented at the trial. Although his possible appearance, like that of the maid, had been telegraphed by previous questions, it nevertheless was a surprise. Even more startling was his testimony.

———→←———

Ben Schneider stepped to the witness stand and was sworn in. He was a middle-aged, pink-faced, bald man. Before he could be asked a single question, E. H. Bloch arose to object that the name of Schneider did not appear on the government's witness list, and, therefore, the defense was surprised, and he ought not be permitted to testify.

The court pointed out that there was an exception to the rule, if the witness was unknown to the government at the time it submitted its list and was a rebuttal witness. How long ago, asked Bloch, had the government known it would call this witness? Bloch stated with his usual courtesy, "I am willing to take Mr. Saypol's statement to that." Saypol stated that one question of the witness would clear it up.

SAYPOL When is the first time in your life that you saw me as a lawyer?
E. H. BLOCH No, that isn't the question.
SAYPOL In any other way?

SCHNEIDER   Yesterday.

E. H. BLOCH   That is not it, your Honor, I mean the first time the Government, not Mr. Saypol.

COURT   Just sit down, please, Mr. Bloch. I know the point you are urging and we will cover it.

E. H. BLOCH   All right.

SAYPOL   When was the first time, Mr. Schneider, that you had any knowledge, any notice, any conversation with any human being regarding the fact of your being a witness here?

SCHNEIDER   Yesterday.

SAYPOL   What time?

SCHNEIDER   About 11:30.

SAYPOL   At that time were you visited by some agents from the Federal Bureau of Investigation?

SCHNEIDER   Yes, sir.

SAYPOL   And was it the very first time?

SCHNEIDER   Yes, sir.

All this served to create more suspense and provided a dramatic preamble to the revelations which were to come.

The first questions revealed what might be in store for the Rosenbergs and must have made their hearts pound.

SAYPOL   What is your business?

SCHNEIDER   A photographer, sir.

SAYPOL   Where is your place of business?

SCHNEIDER   99 Park Row.

SAYPOL   When you say that you are a photographer, what is the substantial part of your business, what do you do mainly?

SCHNEIDER   Passport photographs and identification photographs.

The witness was shown a photograph of his place of business taken by the FBI agents "since yesterday when they saw you for the first time." On Bloch's proper objection, he testified that the scene was the same in May and June 1950. Then it was admitted in evidence.

In May or June 1950, had he been visited by a family consisting of a husband, wife and two children? Bloch's objection that the government was bound by Julius' and Ethel's denials on a "collateral matter," was peremptorily denied. The door was open to Schneider's full story.

Schneider said the children "appeared to me to be about six and four." It was a Saturday. Did he see the man and woman in the courtroom? He pointed to Julius and Ethel, and each stood up. I reconstruct the events as he depicted them from the stand.

ROSENBERG   We want some passport photos taken.

SCHNEIDER   Certainly—you want the family?

(279)

ROSENBERG Yes. Separate shots of me and my wife, and one of my wife and the children.

SCHNEIDER Sure, step over here.

ETHEL ROSENBERG What do you charge?

SCHNEIDER Three for a dollar.

ROSENBERG We want three dozen.

SCHNEIDER (Surprised) Three dozen?

ETHEL ROSENBERG What will that cost?

SCHNEIDER Let's see, three poses, thirty-six—passport size, that will be $9.00.

ROSENBERG O.K. Go ahead.

(Schneider sat Ethel on a stool and snapped her quickly. Thereafter, he snapped Julius. Then he arranged a group of three. Ethel sat on the stool, holding the young child on her lap. The older one stood beside her.)

ROSENBERG When will they be ready?

SCHNEIDER Oh, in about twenty minutes. You can wait for them if you want to. You know, Saturday, I am not busy. I come in to fix the chemicals and clean up. I'll get to this right now.

(The children began running around the place. They were unruly. Schneider feared that they would do some damage.)

SCHNEIDER Why don't you take the kids out and come back in twenty minutes?

ETHEL ROSENBERG All right, children, come on. We'll go for a walk.

ROSENBERG I'll stay. Come right back.

(Twenty minutes later, Ethel returned with the children, who were still prancing about. Schneider was drying the photos. He showed them to Julius and Ethel.)

SCHNEIDER I hope you have a nice trip.

ROSENBERG We're going to France.

SCHNEIDER That's a nice trip with the family.

ROSENBERG Yes, my wife was left some property there, and we're going over to take care of it.

(Schneider handed the photos to Julius.)

SCHNEIDER That's $9.00.

(Julius paid.)

Thanks.

(The Rosenbergs left.)

Saypol asked Schneider, "And is that the last time you saw him before today?" "That's right," he replied. He said that the FBI agents had shown him photographs of the Rosenbergs and he recognized them.

Long after the trial was ended, it was revealed that Schneider had appeared in court the preceding morning, escorted by FBI men, to see whether he could identify the Rosenbergs as the customers who had ordered three dozen passport photos. So he had seen them "before" the morning of the trial. We shall see how the Appellate Court dealt with this "contradiction."

Schneider concluded his direct testimony by stating that the unusual nine-dollar order and the visit on Saturday had fixed the incident in his mind.

"You may cross-examine," said the prosecutor. One could almost hear the inflection of the tone, as if to say, "And what are you going to do about this?"

E. H. Bloch began by asking for the negatives. Schneider said he didn't keep them and never did in his business.

The photograph of his shop showed the inside. He was asked to describe the outside. From the questions asked, it was obvious that the defense was not unprepared. The lawyers, having heard "99 Park Row" mentioned during Rosenberg's cross-examination, had apparently visited the place, which was near the courthouse. The object of questions was to demonstrate that Schneider did not specialize in passport photos. In his window, there was a display of pictures of weddings, and brides and grooms. Being near the Municipal Building, where marriage licenses were obtained, he was available to photograph couples, who years later could look back at their slim figures. While Schneider did not have "a large sign on the outside saying 'Passport Photos,' he did have a sign in his window which read 'Family photos, passport photos.'" Another sign read "Passport Identification Engineers."

Bloch tried to get a grip for contradiction. Did Schneider keep books or any record which might show that he photographed the Rosenbergs?

SCHNEIDER   No, we generally take photographs like this, see, engineers, three for a dollar. We don't keep no records of it.

E. H. BLOCH   Haven't you any sales slips in your place of business?

SCHNEIDER   No.

E. H. BLOCH   None at all?

SCHNEIDER   No.

Schneider read all the newspapers. He had seen pictures of either Ethel or Julius "a couple of weeks ago."

E. H. BLOCH   Didn't mean a thing to you?

SCHNEIDER   I didn't think of them; I didn't think of them at that time.

E. H. BLOCH   And the first time you thought of them was when?

SCHNEIDER   When the FBI men came in and showed me a photograph, a front and side view, and then I saw it, I recognized.

E. H. BLOCH   You recognized them?

SCHNEIDER   Yes.

E. H. BLOCH   What kind of a view did you see of Mr. Rosenberg in the newspapers? Was it a front view or a side view?

SCHNEIDER   Just a front view.

He didn't recall seeing Ethel's picture in a newspaper. Bloch understandably was digging hard at the witness.

E. H. BLOCH   Did you ever see a front view of Mrs. Rosenberg in the newspapers?

(281)

SCHNEIDER No, I don't recall.

E. H. BLOCH You say you read the *News* and the *Mirror* regularly?

SCHNEIDER Yes.

Schneider "usually" came in on Saturdays.

E. H. BLOCH You didn't mean to say, did you, that you remembered this incident because you came down this particular Saturday?

SCHNEIDER Yes, I come down Saturday. I generally make up my chemicals and fix the papers for the entire week, clean up the place, you see.

COURT But you don't do any work; is that it?

SCHNEIDER No, no, unless somebody comes in. It is a very slow day, see, Saturday. During July and August, I generally take off the Saturdays, see?

Knickerbocker Village was about ten minutes' walking distance from his shop. On the Saturday that he photographed the Rosenbergs, he "must have had" one or two other customers.

Schneider fixed the Rosenbergs' visit as the middle of June 1950, at about eleven-thirty. "It was on a Saturday. That is as much as I know."

E. H. BLOCH Now there are some Saturdays when you do a rather rushing business?

SCHNEIDER Not a rushing business.

E. H. BLOCH Well, a good business?

SAYPOL Did you say "a Russian business" or "rushing business"?

E. H. BLOCH I didn't know that Mr. Saypol was a punster.

COURT You mean you haven't found it out after all these weeks?

E. H. BLOCH I have been giving him the benefit of the doubt.

KUNTZ It seems to me, Judge Kaufman, in a case like this, that humor is out of place.

SAYPOL It is not intended as humor. I just want to be clear what his language was.

COURT Let's get on. Try to restrain your desire to be another Milton Berle.

I believe Kuntz's comment was the most appropriate. Yet seconds later, he, too, had earned a mild reprimand. He leaned over to suggest a question to Bloch.

COURT Mr. Kuntz, if you want to make any suggestions, I might suggest that you do it quietly. I heard it all the way up here.

KUNTZ I am sorry. I didn't mean to do that.

There followed an exchange of which an Appellate Court later took special note.

E. H. BLOCH Did you see the Rosenbergs from the time you say they took pictures in your place, in June 1950, until the time you walked in this courtroom?

COURT He answered that question.

E. H. BLOCH I am sorry.

SAYPOL I object to it.

COURT You object because it has just been answered?

SAYPOL Yes.

COURT I understood he answered. He said, "No."

E. H. BLOCH He said "No"?

COURT That is right.

E. H. BLOCH I didn't so understand, your Honor.

Schneider recalled distinctly the poses he shot. No amount of cross-examination could swerve him. He took individual pictures of Ethel and of Julius, and one picture of Ethel, a child on her lap and the older one standing beside her. All the pictures were the same size.

Schneider said the major part of his business was "identification photographs and passports."

Did other customers tell him where they were traveling, as he claimed the Rosenbergs did?

SCHNEIDER Well, why, you get people who like to talk, and well, naturally, you have a conversation, but not often, you know, people come in and talkative, like to talk. That is about it.

The witness was excused.

COURT Any more witnesses?

SAYPOL No, that is the Government's case. The Government rests.

COURT Defense rests?

E. H. BLOCH Defense rests.

COURT Do you rest, Mr. Kuntz?

KUNTZ We rest, your Honor.

These announcements were like steel bands placed around the testimony. The jury, the judge and the Appellate Courts were bound by contents within. Nothing could be added, nothing subtracted. If, later, there was any claim of newly discovered evidence, it would have to meet severe tests, which I shall describe, in order to break the bands and enlarge the testimony. The fate of the Rosenbergs and Sobell was sealed in the record.

CHAPTER 25

There were still legal proceedings to take place, not in the presence of the jury. Counsel is permitted to make motions to dismiss the case. These are formal, to preserve constitutional arguments, and the inadequacy of the evidence to warrant a conviction.

But the Rosenberg case did not follow the usual pattern even here. An extraordinary incident occurred in which counsel accused the judge of prejudicial interference with the trial. It was the elder Bloch who spoke up, after his son had moved to dismiss the indictment and "for a judgment of acquittal upon the ground that as a matter of law, the prosecution had failed to establish guilt of these defendants beyond a reasonable doubt" (a motion which was immediately denied). Alexander Bloch addressed the court:

A. BLOCH   I would like to make a motion on behalf of the defendant Rosenberg.

COURT   Yes.

A. BLOCH   I am doing it reluctantly, but I feel it my duty to make it. I move for a mistrial upon the ground that the frequent questioning by the Court, not intending harm, of course, of witnesses, especially of the defendants, had a tendency of unduly influencing the jury to the prejudice of the defendants and depriving them of their constitutional right to a fair and impartial trial.

COURT   You never took an objection on that ground while I was questioning, Mr. Bloch.

A. BLOCH   Your questions came one at a time, Judge.

COURT   Of course, and there was plenty of time to take your objection at that time, but it may be if I thought that you in any way felt at that time that I was unduly prejudicing the jury instead of trying to keep the issues clearly before them, I may have refrained, but there was never any objection from any of the counsel on that ground, and I think it is purely an afterthought, and I think it is purely done for the purpose of putting anything in the record upon which you might be able to hang your hats in the event there should be an appeal.

A. BLOCH Not at all. It is done in good faith.

COURT Well, I question it.

At this direct charge of bad faith, the son intervened to appease the judge:

E. H. BLOCH May I say to the Court, as a statement of a lawyer, that we discussed this question very seriously, as to whether or not to make this specific motion at the end of the prosecution's case, and we refrained from making it, because, we, ourselves, were not satisfied at that time that the motion would have had any real validity.

COURT Yes.

E. H. BLOCH But you can understand, your Honor—and I want to say this for the Court, and I, for one, and I think all my co-counsel feel, that you have been extremely courteous to us and you have afforded us lawyers every privilege that a lawyer should expect in a criminal case, but if our conscience would bother us, your Honor, if we didn't make this motion, I hope that your Honor will understand that it is made in the utmost good faith and without in any way trying to impugn the Court.

COURT Very well, the motion is denied.

A. BLOCH I may add that my statement is that it was unintentional on your part.

COURT Motion denied.

A. BLOCH Exception.

But could the Blochs have it both ways? There is the legal anecdote of the lawyer who gave a supreme illustration of tact in dealing with a judge. "A year ago, your Honor decided a case identical to ours for the plaintiff, and a month ago another identical case, for the defendant. And I must say, in both cases your Honor acted most admirably."

The Blochs in their effort to raise an appealable point and still not offend the judge strove similarly to bridge the inconsistency with tact.

Now it was Sobell's opportunity to move for dismissal. His was a more arguable point, because the evidence against him was meager. Phillips, one of his attorneys, made the argument. It raised a fascinating question of law concerning the meaning and effect of a conspiracy charge, which has so troubled and confused the public and even the bar. The exchange of views during the argument presented a lucid, capsule explanation of the point, in dramatic terms.

Phillips argued that he never anticipated from reading the indictment that Sobell would be charged "with anything relating to the giving away of atomic energy secrets." He tried to demonstrate the dilemma this created, by enacting an imaginary scene with his own client. Suppose Sobell had come to him and confessed to everything which Elitcher, his only accuser, had testified to later on the stand, namely, that Sobell had solicited Elitcher to give information from his governmental department. Suppose, then Phillips had advised him to plead guilty and throw himself on the mercy of the court.

PHILLIPS Then supposing for the sake of argument at the trial there was all the additional story of giving away atom bomb secrets. Could he have said to me, "What have you done to me, Phillips? I never meant to plead guilty of giving away secrets of the atom bomb"?

COURT No, he couldn't have said that to you.

PHILLIPS Pardon me?

COURT He couldn't have said that to you because as a lawyer you should have said to him, if that had occurred, "No, before I am going to advise you to plead guilty, I want you to understand the law; I want you to understand that the law of conspiracy is this: that once you have joined in a conspiracy, the acts of your co-conspirators are chargeable to you, even, if you don't know exactly what they are doing, as long as you have the same common unlawful objective."

The next brief exchange presented a little model of the art of persuasion.

PHILLIPS I can see your Honor did not get my point.

COURT I get your point.

PHILLIPS No, I didn't make myself understood.

One never accuses a judge of not understanding. The lawyer should always assert that he didn't make himself clear. No matter how broadminded the judge, a public challenge to his comprehension is humiliating to him, if true, and inflammatory, if not. It is the persuader's duty to earn a reconsideration, by blaming himself for lack of clarity. Then, if false, the judge may appreciate the generosity of the gesture and be induced to reciprocate. If true, how big of counsel to acknowledge his ineptitude. In either event, the judge's resistance is diminished. The same holds true out of court, whether in a business negotiation or political discussion. Hypocrisy? Well, harmless, and part of the social graces, in which the brutal truth ("You don't know what the hell you are talking about") is unnecessarily offensive and hurtful. Even, if there is nothing to gain by artfulness, it has perhaps the greatest virtue of not injuring another's sensibility needlessly.

Phillips tried again:

PHILLIPS   I said supposing neither he nor I had any idea we were going to try a case of the atom bomb. Suppose all I had was this indictment in front of me and he told me the story of Elitcher, and which Elitcher does not connect him with the atom bomb.

COURT   I still say exactly what I said; it would have been your duty to say, "Look here, Mr. Sobell, you have had some relationship with Rosenberg which I didn't know about, which perhaps you do know about. I don't know. But I want to tell you this, that the law is that if Rosenberg is in this conspiracy with you and he has gone out and done some other acts, and they show that you were in the conspiracy, even if you don't know about these other acts the Government will charge them against you."

PHILLIPS   I still haven't made myself understood.

COURT   Well, let us not labor the point. I have your point very clearly. I don't want it labored any more. I think you have made your point very clearly to me.

The next time Phillips claimed he was still not making himself understood, his humility had worn so threadbare that anyone could look through it. But he did express the point differently and with more legal sagacity. Indeed, one appellate judge thought his last formulation was sound enough to have required the judge to submit it to the jury for determination, instead of ruling it out as a matter of law. It was this:

PHILLIPS   To avoid any possibility that I left anything out, I want to ask that the testimony of Elitcher does not at all bear out any state of facts of concerted action, concerted action by Sobell and Rosenberg, in connection with the trial of the facts in this case. In other words, the only concerted action, allowing every word of Elitcher's to be true, is a concerted action to secure Elitcher's knowledge and Elitcher's information for purposes which Elitcher did not go into. Anything else in Elitcher's testimony which implies what Rosenberg did, or implies what Sobell did, is consistent with a theory that each one did it all by himself and on his own and therefore no conspiracy. I don't know if I make myself clear.

COURT   You make yourself very clear, Mr. Phillips. You have a way of expressing yourself which is delightful. Only I don't agree with you.

———→←———

The court asked counsel to come in early the next morning, March 28, 1951, so that another legal procedure could be completed out of the presence of the jury.

It involved the submission by both sides of "Requests to Charge," and the court's rulings on this protective device for a fair trial which is little understood. When the judge instructs the jury concerning the law to be applied to the facts, as *they* find them, the defendants or the government may differ with him. They have the right, after he has finished, to record their exceptions on the record, and even request a different charge. The Appellate Court then has a clearly defined area for review of any errors in the judge's charge.

To afford the judge the fullest opportunity to avoid giving the jury erroneous rules, each side is invited to submit in advance "Requests to Charge." These are usually accompanied by legal authorities, which act as a guideline for what is required or is not permissible. The judge may thus learn from counsel what he should or should not incorporate in his charge.

Of course, he does his own research and writes his charge in sections as the testimony develops.

Some of the instructions to the jury are standard in every case such as who has the burden of proof, the test of guilt beyond a reasonable doubt, the interest of the witness in the outcome and its effect on his credibility, etc. But most of the instructions must be tailored to the specific situation and testimony. Many a conviction has been reversed, and the case sent back for a new trial because of the refusal to include a requested charge, or the incorporation of one not properly stated.

This is not a technical matter. If the legal yardstick, by which the defendant's guilt was measured, was wrong, he did not receive a fair trial. It is only when the error is inconsequential in the light of the overwhelming evidence to support the verdict that it is not fatal to the verdict. Another example of an error which does not require reversal is a matter which is merely corroborative, and independent evidence exists of the fact which was properly proved.

Judge Kaufman, as he said, "had pounded and hounded" counsel to submit their requests for charges in advance. One can understand why they lagged. Their immediate problem was preparation for direct and cross-examination. These were all-consuming tasks, day and night. Then toward the end of the trial, they had sought to catch up with their obligation to prepare requests for charge.

So the next morning, the judge went over the list of each side. In most instances, he announced that he had included the point in his prepared charge "either in the form requested or, substantially, in my own language." In others, that he had granted the request "with certain additions" of his own.

KUNTZ   We would suggest that your Honor charge that if the jury does not believe Elitcher or if they have reasonable doubt as to the truth of his testimony they must acquit Sobell.

(289)

COURT I am covering that. I am saying substantially the only testimony
that they must consider as to whether or not Sobell is in the conspiracy is Elitcher's, plus the flight testimony.
KUNTZ All right.

The government's requests were also reviewed.
Then the jury was summoned from the anteroom. They settled down
to hear five hours of summation.

CHAPTER 26

Since the government has the burden of proof and must present its evidence first, it is given the privilege of summing up last. So E. H. Bloch was the first to address the jury.

The art of summation is unique. There is no standard under which one may enlist. The style is as varied as men's personalities. The objective is clear, to marshal the facts in the most persuasive way for his client. To weave the diffuse threads of evidence into a discernible texture, so that what seemed separate and remote becomes part of the whole—a clear picture of the objective.

Some lawyers achieve this result by calm analysis, others by stormy attack on the opposition. The Rosenberg case presented all varieties. Whatever the method, if it is not an affectation, but derives from sincerity and inner emotion, it is effective.

Great summations have one other ingredient. They are direct communications to the jurors' minds and hearts. They are not speeches at them. They insinuate themselves through the jurors' shield. It has been described as the skill of jumping over the jury rail and climbing into the jury box. This, too, is an indefinable gift. It means colloquialism at times, a rapport of common language, used however as contrast with eloquent statement. Winston Churchill resorted to this technique. Who can forget the surprise of his shifting from Olympian heights of expression, when he referred to Hitler's threat "to wring England's neck like a chicken," and exclaimed, "Some chicken. Some neck!"

One thing is certain, the day is past when a lawyer can merely declaim or indulge in elocutional bombast. He must build his arguments on fact. Only when he has established such a foundation, can he indulge in emotional appeal. The jury must begin the journey slowly on hard evidence, and later it may be carried away unsuspectingly on a stream of passion.

As in all persuasive oral efforts, there must be a design for easy comprehension. Unlike written works, there is no opportunity to stop and reconsider, or to reread. If the oral flow is too fast or involved, then the jury cannot catch up. Attention is cut. The juror surrenders and withdraws, pretending to listen, when his thoughts are elsewhere. A speaker once said, "My duty is to speak, and yours is to listen, but if you finish before I do, please let me know." Jurors don't let you know and if the lawyer's eyes are buried in his script, he will never observe that he is not communicating.

All this is more true, because summations are long and tax the erosion quotient of the attention span. I once wrote, "If a speaker doesn't strike oil in fifteen minutes, he should stop boring." Addresses to juries are necessarily long in complicated cases. How else are hundreds of facts scattered by different witnesses and modified by cross-examination going to be pulled together meaningfully?

Emanuel Bloch used the intimate, informal approach in addressing the jury. His summation does not read as well as Saypol's, who had an eloquently worded address, which he read. But that doesn't mean it wasn't more effective. Again, as with testimony, one can judge only by seeing and hearing, not by reading the inert printed record. Also, Bloch's summation had a design, a formula, which I will analyze.

He began with a gracious tribute, whose words he was to hear flung back at him by the Appellate Courts.

E. H. BLOCH I would like to say to the Court on behalf of all defense counsel that we feel that you have treated us with the utmost courtesy, that you have extended to us the privileges that we expect as lawyers, and despite any disagreements we may have had with the Court on questions of law, we feel that the trial has been conducted and we hope we have contributed our share, with that dignity and that decorum that befits an American trial.

His generosity overflowed to the prosecutor as well.

E. H. BLOCH I would like to also say to the members of Mr. Saypol's staff that we are appreciative of the courtesies extended to us, and even though Mr. Saypol and I have engaged in a certain amount of repartee, it doesn't mean anything; it happens in every trial; and we feel, as we come here in the closing stages of this case, that as much has been done both by the prosecution and by the defense to present to you the respective sides of this controversy.

Then he made a moving appeal to eliminate prejudice against communism in deciding the case. He approached the point gingerly and then opened the throttle wide.

E. H. BLOCH   The fear that an impartial jury could not be secured was particularly important in this type of case. Now, all of you are New Yorkers or you come from the environs of New York. We are a pretty sophisticated people. People can't put things over on us very easily. We are fairly wise in the ways of the world and the ways of people and we all know that there is not a person in this world who hasn't some prejudice, and you would be inhuman if you didn't have some prejudice. But we ask you now as we asked you before, please don't decide this case because you may have some bias or some prejudice against some political philosophy.

The charge, he stressed, was conspiracy to commit espionage. There followed a virtual admission that Ethel and Julius were Communists, and a plea not to convict them because they were.

E. H. BLOCH   If you want to convict these defendants because you think that they are Communists and you don't like communism and you don't like any member of the Communist Party, then, ladies and gentlemen, I can sit down now and there is absolutely no use in my talking. There was no use in going through this whole rigmarole of a three weeks' trial. That is not the crime.

The futility of the numerous Fifth Amendment pleas taken by the Rosenbergs was thus demonstrated at the end of the trial. Counsel had to concede finally that they were Communists, and pitch his argument on the fact that this was not the charge for which they were being tried. Then why not have adopted this strategy earlier and avoided the prejudicial struggle of claiming incrimination, rather than making the same admission?

Bloch sought to cast the becoming light of his own anti-Communist beliefs upon his clients.

E. H. BLOCH   But believe me, ladies and gentlemen, I am not here, other defense counsel are not here as attorneys for the Communist Party and we are not here as attorneys for the Soviet Union. I can only speak for myself and my father. We are representing Julius and Ethel Rosenberg, two American citizens, who come to you as American citizens, charged with a specific crime, and ask you to judge them the way you would want to be judged if you were sitting over there before twelve other jurors.

He referred to the "most moving drama that any human being could concoct" which the jurors had witnessed, "a brother testifying against his sister, in a case where her life could be at stake," a drama in which "the most terrible weapon yet invented" was involved. He paid tribute to the jury system,

E. H. BLOCH . . . you sitting here in this jury box, constitute the bed-
   rock of American justice, which is founded upon the concept that
   it is the average man and woman that has the wisdom to decide
   what is a fact and what is not a fact.

Then he turned earnestly to the formula he had adopted for his persuasive effort. He explained that there were two kinds of evidence, oral
and written. He proceeded to demonstrate that all the evidence against
the Rosenbergs was oral. None of the dozens of exhibits connected the
Rosenbergs with the crime.
   Setting forth on this mission, he had before him all of the exhibits,
and he referred to each one, arguing that in itself it was no proof of
Rosenberg's guilt. So, for example, the sketches of the atomic bomb reproduced by Greenglass for the trial were not drawn by Rosenberg. It
was oral testimony of Greenglass that connected them with Julius and
Ethel. The same was true of the Jell-O box strips. Only oral testimony
bridged the gap between the Jell-O box and the Rosenbergs. The brown
wrapper in which the $4,000 was delivered was an original paper, but
it did not in itself prove that Rosenberg had handled it or delivered it.

E. H. BLOCH I am just wondering how it is that this either wasn't subjected to fingerprint analysis or that no fingerprint expert came here
   to tell us whose fingerprints were upon that wrapping paper.

So he continued with each exhibit, Yakovlev's picture, Gold's photograph, the registry entry of Harry Gold in the Hotel Hilton at Albuquerque, exhibits of Sobell's trip to Mexico and his letters, pictures of console tables, etc.

E. H. BLOCH Anything in print here from which you can say that Rosenberg was implicated in this conspiracy? Not one piece of paper,
   not one document.

Finally, he exclaimed, one exhibit did turn up which came directly
from Rosenberg's home.

E. H. BLOCH Here it is (indicating). It's a tin can. No question this
   came from Rosenberg's home. This is it, gentlemen. This is the only
   piece of documentary evidence that the Government has produced
   in this case, trying to tie up Rosenberg with this crime. And let's
   see about this terrible exhibit. It's a can. It says, "Save a Spanish
   Republican Child," and it is issued pursuant to a license from the
   City of New York, Welfare Department. And this bears a date of
   somewhere around 1948, but that is not important.
      Hollow, hollow—like the case against Rosenberg, as I think I can
   convince you after we analyze this testimony and analyze the kind
   of people who testified here and why they testified.
      Yes, they got him; they got him with the goods, with a tin can.

Tell me, what is this tin can? I don't care whether you are in favor of Franco, and I don't care whether you are in favor of the Loyalists. That has to do with a person's political beliefs, but can you tell me, and can you tell anybody, and most important, can you tell yourselves in your consciences, that there is anything in this can from which you can state or infer that Rosenberg was guilty of conspiracy to commit espionage?

He referred also to the nominating petition signed by Ethel in 1941.

E. H. BLOCH Does this tie Ethel Rosenberg up with a conspiracy to commit espionage? Ask yourselves that.
And of course I know you are going to be honest with yourselves and admit very readily—not out loud, but very readily—that there isn't one piece of documentary evidence in this case to tie the Rosenbergs up with this conspiracy.

He praised the efficiency of the FBI and concluded that they couldn't "find some piece of evidence that you could feel, that you could see, that would tie the Rosenbergs up with this case."
So he concluded if the case depended on documentary evidence, "you would go into the jury room, you might light a cigarette, you would come back in half a minute and you would acquit the Rosenbergs. And, of course, the case is not as simple as that."
He pursued his syllogism. "This case, therefore, against the Rosenbergs depends upon oral testimony." He called upon the jury to apply the wisdom gained from ordinary experience in dealing with people in judging their trustworthiness.

E. H. BLOCH . . . it is not only what they said—it is who said it. Is the person who said it capable of belief ordinarily? Would you believe a perjurer in your ordinary dealings? Ordinarily, would you believe a crook in your dealings, in your private life?

In passing, he paid another compliment to the judge.

E. H. BLOCH . . . you have been fortunate, because the Judge has been fairly lenient in permitting counsel to develop for you the kind of people who testified here.

Credibility, believability—that was the issue.

E. H. BLOCH You know, you could teach a parrot to get up there and tell a story, but you wouldn't believe a parrot. You can teach anybody—anybody, to get up there and tell a story. That doesn't mean that you can believe him. Before you believe anybody who was willing to swear away the life of somebody I think that justice dictates that you consider the type of person testifying.

(295)

The main actors in the drama were four: "Dave and Ruth Greenglass —that is one team; on this side and in the other corner of the ring there are Julius and Ethel Rosenberg. This is a case of the Greenglasses against the Rosenbergs. That is what this case reduces itself down to."

Then he launched a verbal attack on David Greenglass, which gained force from its colloquial wording. No highfalutin formal phrases such as Saypol later used; it expressed the pent-up feelings of the Rosenbergs and their counsel. Greenglass was a traitor not only to his country but to his family. Bloch's explosive indignation was all the more eloquent because it was an outcry rather than a polished argument.

E. H. BLOCH Now, let us take Dave Greenglass. This didn't come out of my mouth. This came out of his mouth. Is he a self-confessed spy? Is there any doubt in any of your minds that Dave Greenglass is a self-confessed espionage agent? He characterized himself that way. What did this man do? He took an oath when he entered the Army of the United States. He didn't even remember what the oath was. That is how seriously he took it. But, in substance, he swore to support our country. Is there any doubt in your mind that he violated that oath? Is there any doubt in your mind that he disgraced the uniform of every soldier in the United States by his actions?

Do you know what that man did? He was assigned to one of the most important secret projects in this country, and by his own statements, by his own admissions, he told you that he stole information out of there and gave it to strangers, and that it was going to the Soviet Government. Now, that is undisputed. I would like Mr. Saypol or anybody who is going to sum up on the part of the Government to refute that. Is there any doubt in your mind about that?

You know, before I summed up, I wanted to go to a dictionary and I wanted to find a word that could describe a Dave Greenglass. I couldn't find it, because I don't think that there is a word in the English vocabulary or in the dictionary of any civilization which can describe a character like Dave Greenglass.

But one thing I think you do know, that any man who will testify against his own blood and flesh, his own sister, is repulsive, is revolting, who violates every code that any civilization has ever lived by. He is the lowest of the lowest animals that I have ever seen, and if you are honest with yourself, you will admit that he is lowest than the lowest animal that you have ever seen.

This is not a man; this is an animal. And how he got up there, and how he got up there. Did you look at him? I know you did; you watched him; all your eyes were fastened on him, just as people are fascinated by horror; and he smirked and he smiled and I asked him a question, so that it would be in the cold printed record, "Are you aware of your smile?" And do you know the answer I got? Do you remember it? "Not very." Listen to that answer, "Not very."

Well, maybe some people enjoy funerals; maybe some people enjoy lynchings, but I wonder whether in anything that you have read or in anything that you have experienced you have ever come across a man, who comes around to bury his own sister and smiles.

Tell me, is this the kind of a man you are going to believe? God Almighty, if ever a witness discredited himself on a stand, he did. What kind of a man can we disbelieve if we are going to believe Dave Greenglass? What is the sense of having witness chairs? What is the sense of having juries subject witnesses' testimony to scrutiny and analysis? Is that the kind of a man that you would believe in your own life or would you punch him in the nose and throw him out and have nothing to do with him because he is a low rebel? Come on, be honest with yourselves, ladies and gentlemen, is that the kind of testimony that you are going to accept?

I can imagine the satisfaction which Julius and Ethel got from this tirade. Guilty or innocent, they must have ached for retaliation. The Greenglasses had turned on them viciously, and now their attorney was expressing their pain and frustration in simple words suitable to their deep emotions. Could they have denied themselves a glance at David Greenglass, sitting at the other end of the table and watching him wince as he was denounced?

Bloch had only begun.

E. H. BLOCH   And he was arrogant; he was arrogant. He felt he had the Government of the United States behind him. He had a right to be arrogant; he had a right to be arrogant, because I want to say right now that the Greenglasses put it all over the FBI and put it all over Mr. Saypol's staff, and I submit that they are smarter than the whole bunch. They sold them a bill of goods. Every man sitting over here is an honest man. The FBI representatives, Mr. Saypol and his staff, every man of them, they are doing their duty, but you know, even the smartest of us can be tricked, and do you want me to show you how they were tricked?

Ruth Greenglass admitted here that she was in this conspiracy. Is there any doubt about that? Is there any doubt that in the middle of November she came out to Albuquerque and tried to induce her husband to sell secrets? Is there any doubt that she grabbed Gold's money and deposited it in the bank? Is there any doubt that she gained by the illegal fruits of her husband's venture? Is there any doubt that she knew all about it?

Ruth Greenglass has never been arrested. She has never been indicted. She has never been sent to jail. Doesn't that strike you as strange? If this is such a terrible crime, and I tell you, gentlemen,

(297)

it is a serious crime, a most serious crime, don't you think that the Greenglasses put it over the Government when Ruth Greenglass wasn't even indicted? Something peculiar, and I am not attributing anything wrong to the FBI or the prosecutor's staff, and let us get that straight right now. With all due respect I think the Greenglasses sold you a bill of goods. . . .

Ruth Greenglass got out. She walked out and put her sister-in-law in. That was a deal that the Greenglasses planned and made for themselves, and they made it—they may not have made it by express agreement with the Government, and I don't think the Government would countenance anything like that, but tell me, do actions speak louder than words? Is the proof of the pudding in the eating? Is Ruth Greenglass a defendant here?

To establish a motive for Greenglass' "fingering" the Rosenbergs, Bloch found at least one virtue in Greenglass' corrupt character. He loved his wife.

E. H. BLOCH   And, ladies and gentlemen, this explains why Dave Greenglass was willing to bury his sister and his brother-in-law to save his wife. Yes, there were other factors of course. He had a grudge against Rosenberg because he felt that Rosenberg had gyped him out of a thousand dollars, but that would not have been enough to explain Greenglass' act.

Bloch strewed more condemnatory adjectives on Greenglass along the path of his argument. He called him "crafty" and "tricky." He contended that Greenglass must have "snooped around" long before he gave Ruth information about the scientists at Los Alamos. How else could he have had so much data ready?

He heaped ridicule upon Greenglass' story that he had decided immediately to co-operate with the FBI out of a sense of belated honor. Why then did he take six sets of passport photos? He was trapped. He was trying to get out of the country. "Do you believe that cock-and-bull story that Rosenberg told him to take passport photos and he gave him five sets and they kept one set?"

He argued that their hiding the $4,000 they received (from Russians, not as they said, from Rosenberg) was inconsistent with "coming clean" with the government. And if they intended to confess and not resist, why had they hired Rogge and paid him the $4,000?

The court asked Bloch whether he would like a five-minute recess. He welcomed it. When he returned, he had new words for Greenglass' infamy.

E. H. BLOCH   Not only are the Greenglasses self-confessed spies but they were mercenary spies. They spied for money. . . .

They would do anything for money. They would murder people for money. They are trying to murder people for money.

Bloch tried to reach the jurors' minds with plain, non-lawyer language, tinged with slang. For the first time, he combined Greenglass' venomous selfishness with the Rosenbergs' vulnerability, because they were "alleged" to be Communists. He described the change of atmosphere from 1944 to the McCarthy committee days of the 1950s.

E. H. BLOCH Now I will tell you what the plot of the Greenglasses was here. Two-fold. Greenglass figured that if he could put the finger on somebody, he would lessen his own punishment; and he had to put the finger on somebody who was here in the United States, and he had to put the finger on somebody who was a clay pigeon; and that man sitting there (indicating defendant Julius Rosenberg) is a clay pigeon, because he was fired from the Government service, because it was alleged that he was a member of the Communist Party; and he was a guy who was very open and expressed his views about the United States and the Soviet Union, which may have been all right when the Soviet Union and the United States were Allies, but today it is anathema; and you heard him testify, and he said it openly here, he didn't try to conceal it, "Yes, I thought that the Soviet did a lot for the underdog and they did a lot of reconstruction work" and he went on to recount one or two other things that he felt should be to their credit. Well, that is the kind of philosophy that was expounded in the New Deal days by Franklin Delano Roosevelt and by these gentlemen of the press, sitting here. But, boy, when you do that today, it is different; and in 1950 we had the same kind of climate that we have now. This man was a clay pigeon.

He grew confidential with the jury, although his words were being sped throughout the world.

"Entre nous," he said, it was Ruth "who was the smarter of the two," and it was she and not David who "hatched" the plot to involve Julius, because he was "a perfect target."

He turned to a description of Julius, utilizing heavy sarcasm and ridicule.

. . . this terrible spy, this big racketeer, who had a thousand dollars and $4,000 to hand out, who educated students at universities with Russian money and was paid out untold sums of money.

What kind of a man was this? Is this a Costello? Is this your concept of a racketeer? Is this your concept of a pay-off man, a man who lived in a Knickerbocker Village apartment at $45 a month, and finally his rent was raised after many, many years, was raised to $51 a month, whose wife did scrubbing and cleaning and who had two kids, and they had a terrible struggle and they had to go and borrow money, and he scraped together $1,000 in May 1950 to buy stock in the Pitt Machine Company, and he had to give notes for $4,500 for the balance of the purchase price; tell me, does that square with your idea of a pay-off man?

By this time, he could indulge safely in the "look at my client's innocent face" technique, hurling a few choice epithets at Ruth, which must have done Ethel's heart good.

Now, look at that terrible spy (pointing to the defendant Ethel Rosenberg). Look at that terrible spy and compare her to Ruthie Greenglass, who came here all dolled up, arrogant, smart, cute, eager-beaver, like a phonograph record.

Bloch then referred to the striking similarity between Ruth's direct testimony and her repetition of it, when invited to do so on cross-examination.

. . . you will find that repeated, almost word for word, if not word for word, the whole business; and she wants you to believe that she didn't rehearse this story with Dave and Dave Greenglass didn't rehearse this story with her. Cute, cute. Maybe some of you are more acute in sizing up women than others, but if Ruth Greenglass is not the embodiment of evil, I would like to know what person is?

Is Ruth Greenglass the kind of person that can be trusted? Let me tell you something, she is so acute that she wriggled out of this. That is how smart she is. She wriggled out of it. She squirmed through that needle's eye. Well, if she can fool the FBI, I do hope that she won't be able to fool you.

The family touch pervaded the courtroom, even among the attorneys. Emanuel Bloch told the jury that his father told him during recess "that he feels I am covering the testimony relating to Ethel Rosenberg sufficiently, at least to his satisfaction that he won't have to sum up to you." While the father's confidence in his son's summation was not misplaced, it deprived the defense of an emotional facet of the finely cut concluding argument. Even if only for five minutes, the appearance of the seventy-five-year-old Alexander Bloch, pleading for Ethel's freedom so that she could go back to her children, whom she had not seen for months, might have had a great impact upon the jury. For, as I have indicated, such sympathetic considerations survive formal instruction against the influence of sympathy. Also, a fatherly, quiet tone might have added a dimension to the hard-hitting attack which Emanuel Bloch was making.

Quite aware of the human aspects involved, even though their weight in the judicial scales was zero, Bloch kept pressing the issue of loyalty to one's own. He referred to Ethel's testimony that she approached Ruth in an effort to help David (not to seek his silence). He worked himself into Jewish slang.

> . . . whether her brother did anything wrong or right, she wanted to help him. That is human. Can we condemn every member of a family who wants to stick to another member of the family? What is so terrible? Wouldn't you do it, and wouldn't I do it? And here is a man who had had a fight with Davey to get his stock. And when Davey came around and said he was in trouble, like a schnook—that is a Jewish word; it means this—I am trying to get the exact translation—well, a very easygoing fool. He goes to his doctor to try to get a false certificate for Davey.

COURT Is the word stooge what you are looking for?
E. H. BLOCH Stooge? Stooge.

The role of informer was denounced unqualifiedly. Even if Rosenberg "knew that Davey was guilty of the most terrible crime, he would never have squealed on him." Thus, the jury was confronted with another moral dilemma. Was the underworld code against squealing on one's own to be adopted by honest people, too?

At last, Bloch took his teeth out of Greenglass' hide and turned to other witnesses. Harry Gold was a "pathetic figure. Hope is abandoned with him."

> He got his 30-year bit and he told the truth. That is why I didn't cross-examine him.

But, he argued, that Gold, "one of the top conspirators, never saw Rosenberg, never met him, never had any transaction with him."

Gold got his half of the Jell-O box signal from Yakovlev. Therefore, contended Bloch, it could be assumed that David Greenglass got his half also from Yakovlev and not from Rosenberg, as he testified.

Bloch's attack on Elizabeth Bentley was savage.

> Bentley is a professional anti-Communist. She makes money on it. I am sure the Government doesn't pay her any money. She writes books, she lectures. This is her business; her business is testifying.
>
> Now, what did she say? Let us hear what this great authority said, this intellectual moll, this Puritan little girl from New England. Did she ever meet Rosenberg? She was a top gal. She gave orders, she says, to Earl Browder.

He challenged her testimony about talking to a man whose voice she couldn't identify and who said, "This is Julius." If all names were disguised, why, he argued, should "Julius" be authentic?

When he got to the testimony that Russia had given a citation to

(301)

Julius for his great achievement is espionage, Bloch virtually threw up his hands in disgust at the "incredible story."

> Now, for God's sake, you are intelligent people. Do you believe, or have you ever heard that a Government cites somebody without making public the citation? And do you believe that this little guy (indicating), with a little business, this terribly wealthy man who hasn't got a dime to his name, that he was cited by the Russian Government? If you believe that, for God's sake, convict the Rosenbergs and let's get an end to this case; but if you don't believe it, then take a lot of the other things with salt that these Greenglasses said in their anxiety to bury the Rosenbergs.

His reference to the watch supposedly given him by Russia was fleeting. It was certain that the prosecutor would take note of it. He merely commented on the loss of the watch on the New York Central and concluded with a rhetorical question, "That is supposed to be the watch, I suppose, that the Russians gave him."

"Now, let us get to the console table, because that may be disturbing you." He contended that if the table had had a "hollowed-out" space underneath for a lamp, that Mrs. Evelyn Cox, the maid, would have noticed it. He did not challange her veracity (which involved her statement that the Rosenbergs never said they bought the table at Macy's, but rather that it was a gift from a friend). Indeed, he praised her effusively:

> There is no doubt in my mind that Mrs. Evelyn Cox wanted to tell the truth, the whole truth and nothing but the truth. I don't think that woman would lie for anybody.

While it was good tactics not to attack such an honest witness, where did that leave the defense on her corroborating testimony of the Greenglass story?

Bloch recalled his earnest efforts to find Macy's records, which would confirm Rosenberg's testimony of purchase.

The court, acting as timekeeper, told Bloch that he had twenty-five minutes left of summation time. Later, he called out fifteen minutes. It was like a countdown, but would the missile of persuasion take off triumphantly?

Bloch referred to two tiny "slips" which he urged were significant. The first was that Greenglass didn't recognize Gold's picture in the newspaper when Rosenberg brought it to him. Bloch had offered the newspaper in evidence and asked the jury, whether that was the truth, in view of the meeting with Gold in Albuquerque.

The second "slip" was Greenglass' testimony that Rosenberg visited him early in the morning. If true, why hadn't the government produced a late or absent record in the government office where he then worked?

As to Elitcher:

> . . . do you believe that a man who hasn't seen a classmate of his for six years will walk into his house and before he is even there an hour he will say to the man, "Get your wife out of the room," and then right there and then make an offer to him to commit espionage?

Finally, Bloch dealt with what he called "the Hollywood finisher," the testimony of the photographer Ben Schneider. He called it "the vulgar, tawdry part of the trial"—no negative, no bill, no record which might be tangible. He argued that passport photos would not have a mother and two children in one pose. He pointed out that the sign "Passport Photos" was not prominent, and that the Rosenbergs simply took snapshots of the family.

Bloch contended that the case was to last months and "petered out" in three weeks. Why hadn't the government called witnesses on its list, like Ann Sidorovich and the wife of Saurent?

As the announcement was made that his time was up, Bloch made his peroration.

> Now, I want to conclude very simply. I told you at the beginning and I tell you now that we don't come to you in this kind of charge looking for sympathy. Believe me, ladies and gentlemen, there is plenty of room here for a lawyer to try to harp on your emotions, especially so far as Ethel Rosenberg is concerned; a mother, she has two children, her husband is under arrest.
>
> No, because if these people are guilty of that crime they deserve no sympathy.
>
> No, we want you to decide this case with your minds, not with your hearts, with your minds. . . .
>
> I say that if you do that, you can come to no other conclusion than that these defendants are innocent and you are going to show to the world that in America a man can get a fair trial.

>—><—

Kuntz summed up for Sobell. His style and strategy contrasted sharply with those of Bloch. He acted the old war horse, referring immediately to his experience of thirty years, "which you can see by these hairs." His was the audacity of age. We have already observed that he was loud, so loud that the court had warned him during the trial that his whispers were shouts. Above all, his technique was to attack everyone in sight, particularly Saypol. No namby-pamby courtesy. This was a war. He had received no quarter from the prosecution and he was giving none.

He began by referring to the "overt acts" to accomplish the conspiracy, which was set forth in the indictment. "I defy Mr. Saypol and I defy you to find anywhere outside of what I read to you the name of Morton Sobell."

He was not given to moderate statement.

KUNTZ I saw the most amazing experience in my court life in this case. I saw my good friend Mr. Harrington and Mr. Norton and Mr. Branigan and Mr. Lane and Mr. Cohn and Mr. Kilsheimer and Mr. Saypol, all of them, like the mountain, they labored and labored and labored, and they brought forth a mouse—Elitcher.

Did anybody else say a word about that part of the conspiracy? Oh, I will come to Mexico. But if you take Elitcher out of this case, are we part of the conspiracy?

He announced, "I am not going to be charitable like Manny Bloch." Why should he be charitable, he asked, when a man's life depended on what he did? He hadn't slept throughout the trial.

He took Elitcher apart. He was a miserable liar and a perjurer, "who will kill another man to save his own miserable skin."

The first time that Sobell's name was even mentioned in the record was on page 315. Even then he was referred to incidentally; Rosenberg was supposed to have visited Elitcher, invited him into an espionage ring and said, "Sobell is also in." If the jury took out those few words, there was no evidence of conspiracy up to that time. Sobell had been close to Elitcher. If he was to be solicited for spying, why would not Sobell have made the approach, if he was really involved? Why would a virtual stranger like Rosenberg have performed the mission?

He claimed that Elitcher was frightened, because he had committed perjury, as he admitted, and therefore did the government's bidding to gain immunity for himself.

Kuntz claimed that the other links which Elitcher forged to Sobell were just as tenuous. When Elitcher reported Rosenberg's approach to him and cited Sobell as a conspirator, "Sobell became angry." That would be consistent with innocence. But then there were the few extra words, "Rosenberg should not have mentioned my name."

Kuntz again appealed for a deletion of what he claimed was an artificial addition. "Take that part out," he urged, "and you still have no conspiracy."

By this time Kuntz had worked himself into a rage at Saypol.

KUNTZ I am going to point my finger at this man (indicating Mr. Saypol), because that is all he is in this case, just like me; just as this man (indicating), as that man (indicating), that man is that man (indicating). He happens to be a lawyer with a Government job now, and that is all to me.

And when I see what is going on with some of our Government officials, please excuse me if I don't put a halo around him or anybody else, please excuse me; I have been living in this country too long to see what is going on.

Now, let us see what I mean, and I point the finger at Saypol.

He referred to the tactics of Saypol in asking Elitcher whether he had ever seen Sobell take any paper or documents, when he worked for the Reeves Instrument Company. Elitcher replied that Sobell had a brief case "and he took material out, but what it was, I don't know."

Kuntz sputtered with indignation.

KUNTZ Is that a poisonous question by Saypol, the man who is working for us, for me? Yes, for me.

I don't like that kind of stuff. I want to tell you that I am more concerned with the safety of our country than he is, because I tell you, ladies and gentlemen, you injure the liberty or life of one citizen and you wipe the foundation out of our country. We don't do things like that. We don't like them done. I don't like them done.

Of course he took documents. The man had an important job; going out to Roosevelt Air Field. His job was communication, as Elitcher said.

It had to do with air flight and so on.

What do you think he took out, postage stamps? The man was doing experimental work at Reeves. He had people under him.

The other Elitcher testimony which involved Sobell was his recital of coming from Washington to stay temporarily with his friend. When he reported his fear that he was being followed, Sobell again was angry. "Max, you shouldn't have come here. I have dangerous material." Just another addition of a few words, claimed Kuntz, or again there would not be a scintilla of evidence of conspiracy. The dangerous material turned out to be a can in which there was supposed to be film. There was no proof of its contents.

There was not one word in the record that Sobell was involved with atom bomb secrets. Greenglass never mentioned his name. He didn't know him.

Then he turned to Sobell's "flight to Mexico," which he called the government's "killer-diller."

KUNTZ Well, let's see, let's see about that Mexican trip. I say that Sobell and his family went down to Mexico by airplane in his own name—how do you like that? I dare him deny that. I dare Saypol to deny that.

So up to that point there is no flight, is there, if I go to Mexico in my own name, with my family? Nothing wrong.

I would like to see Saypol try to stop me.

Sobell and his wife took an apartment in their own names in Mexico City. True, Sobell then flew to Tampico and Vera Cruz.

KUNTZ I don't care what kind of a brainstorm Sobell might have had. I don't care either if he had read in the newspapers something about Rosenberg or friends of his being involved. I don't care why. That is his own business.

He recalled reading that Saypol has gone down to Mexico himself "to dig up this poison. Just take those two things out and you have no active conspiracy, have you?" Kuntz insisted that Sobell had not concealed himself, because he lived under his own name in Mexico. He referred vaguely to Sobell's aliases as a "brainstorm."

His final attack was on the notation on an exhibit that Sobell "had been deported from Mexico." He argued that the witness Huggins who produced the exhibit conceded that he made that entry "from his own observation." He condemned "Saypol's poison" again. Why hadn't the prosecutor brought in a court record or other authentic proof of deportation?

There was a loud reaction from the audience in the packed courtroom.

COURT May I say to the audience that they will have to desist from any further demonstration. Proceed.

KUNTZ And you and I have to watch out for these things. I say every little citizen must be protected or we undermine the very foundations of our country.

I was born here. I love this country. I do not coddle with anybody that will attempt to injure, even if that person happens to enjoy the office of the United States Attorney and he uses methods that we don't like; we are going to tell him so. Because we can take care of our criminals with decent methods and decent procedure so that you and I are protected at the same time, because tomorrow, who knows, one of your Elitchers might get on and point the finger at you and just add a word here and add a word there to save maybe his own skin.

He concluded that "Mort Sobell has walked with dignity all his life and he has raised his family and I tell you no matter what happens here, he will continue to walk with dignity. Then we will leave little miserable Elitcher to his own conscience."

CHAPTER 27

The government's summation was pitched on a high plane. Its polished language and finely constructed sentences clearly indicated that it was read from a carefully edited script. It was not interspersed, as was the defense summations, with continuous rhetorical questions and "You remember that, don't you" interpolations to catch one's breath and thoughts. It had no colloquial language or slang to make informal contact with the jurors. It talked up, not down to them, and it was devoid of passionate appeals. On the contrary, it emphasized an intellectual approach and set forth the prosecutor's duty to protect the innocent as well as to convict the guilty. It belonged to that genre of summation which is delivered calmly, and aims toward reason: Its eloquence stemmed from its well-spun, literary expression and assertion of principle.

So the jurors were subjected to three different types of summation; Bloch's, a blend of emotion, informality and courtesy; Kuntz's, a fighting, wild-swinging harangue; and Saypol's, a reasoned, dispassionate analysis.

However, Saypol was stung by Kuntz's personal attack and he addressed himself to it, before he proceeded with the evidence.

SAYPOL We who have worked in these courts know that lawyers for defendants pursue certain well-defined courses. If a defendant can prevail on the law, that is what his counsel does; he pursues the issues on the law. If the facts are with him, what else need he do but show the facts? But when the lawyer, when some kind of lawyer has neither facts nor law, they have a game that they call kicking the prosecutor around, and that is the amazing thing that you have seen here this morning.

That is so well known that our courts have had the occasions to discuss it, and this Court has said as follows about that practice: "The attempt to turn this trial of men, whose guilt was abundantly proved, into a trial of Government's counsel, though a not infrequent expedient of defendants who have no other recourse, ought not, in our opinion, to succeed."

He also answered the charge that the FBI had been duped.

SAYPOL   The FBI never prosecutes anybody. The FBI never makes any complaint against anybody. The activities of the FBI are confined solely and exclusively to gathering the evidence and submitting it to the prosecutor for his decision as to whether or not it warrants submission to the consideration of a grand jury, citizens like you, for their evaluation and for their conclusion as to whether or not there should be a prosecution, and if there be, in the form of an indictment, as you have one here.

Then he struck a note of high principle.

SAYPOL   My only fear is that in a case like this, your prejudices shouldn't be so aroused as to be exercised unfavorably toward the clients they represent. I beg you, judge them for the guilt, as charged in the indictment. Don't judge the defendants by their lawyers' bad taste or bad manners. That is not the thing I want you to do.

He descended from the heights for a moment. Because he was puzzled by "the vitriol" of the attack, he said he looked up another law book and found the motive for Kuntz's personal attack on him. He pointed out that in 1936, Kuntz was a candidate for election to the Court of General Sessions, the highest criminal court of New York. There was an uproar.

KUNTZ   Wait a second. What has this got to do with this case?
COURT   No, let us not go into that.
SAYPOL   I think I have the right to explain the personal—
KUNTZ   All right, I will let him state what I was a candidate for.
E. H. BLOCH   If your Honor please, I may not have anything to do with this, but I believe any discussion about Edward Kuntz in any of his political ideas. or candidacy might prejudice my client.
COURT   Excuse me, gentlemen. I would rather not have you go into it.
KUNTZ   I am not worried about it.
COURT   I say I would rather not have him go into it.
SAYPOL   The most I shall say is that it appears to me that there may have been a motive to get even with me, but I emphasize, and

I emphasize and I beg of you, no matter how offensive that may have been to you, please do not fasten guilt for that intemperate, that improper attack on these defendants, because if you do it will not be right.

Now, let us get on with light and without heat.

Knowing that there was confusion about the legal significance of a conspiracy, Saypol analogized it with a business partnership to give it common understanding.

SAYPOL All of the partners and employees of the firm do not do the same thing at the same time. While one partner talks to a customer, another may be negotiating with another prospect. . . . Each act by each party, by each employer in the course of business is an act performed for the benefit of the firm and for the benefit of his fellows.

Imagine a wheel. In the center of the wheel, Rosenberg, reaching out like the tentacles of an octopus.

Rosenberg to David Greenglass. Ethel Rosenberg, Ruth Greenglass; Rosenberg to Harry Gold; Rosenberg, Yakovlev. Information obtained, supplied. Rosenberg, Sobell, Elitcher—always the objective in the center coming from all the legs, all the tentacles going to the one center, solely for the one object: The benefit of Soviet Russia. The sources, Government sources, Los Alamos, atomic information.

Sobell, Elitcher, information from the Navy, relating particularly to gunfire control; always secret, always classified, always of advantage to a foreign government.

When he proceeded to analyze the evidence he did so mostly in broad general strokes, stating conclusions. He was like some judges, described by Cardozo, whose opinions read as if they were thunderous pronouncements from Mount Sinai. They do not struggle with the conflicting views, but rather assert the conclusory facts.

SAYPOL The association of Rosenberg and Sobell began at City College, and it continues until today. They have been held together by one common bond: Their mutual devotion to communism and the Soviet Union, and their membership in this conspiracy to commit espionage for that Soviet Union. That is why their classmate, Max Elitcher, was asked to join the Young Communist League when they were at college. That is why Sobell and Rosenberg joined in the concerted action to recruit Elitcher into their Soviet espionage ring.

While Sobell was chairman of his Communist Party unit in Washington, delivering to its members weekly directives concerning worship of the Soviet Union, Rosenberg was working his way up in the Communist Party underground.

He referred to Elizabeth Bentley's description of the allegiance which American Communists gave to the Communist International. He pointed out that the same day that Rosenberg told Sobell he had talked to Elizabeth Bentley, she had appeared before the United States Senate and "made a full disclosure." This was long before she wrote any books. "You may infer," he told the jury, "whether that wasn't the thing that made Rosenberg apprehensive about possible detection."

SAYPOL   Rosenberg told Elitcher at Manny Wolf's that night in 1948, just as Rosenberg and Ethel Rosenberg had told Ruth Greenglass that night in November 1944, how he had realized the ambition of his life. He told them how he had gone from one Communist Party contact to another until he had achieved the coveted status of a Communist Party espionage agent . . . when Golos was Rosenberg's Communist espionage superior, Rosenberg became known to Elizabeth Bentley.

We know of Golos' clandestine meeting in which he received information from Julius, the engineer who lived in Knickerbocker Village. We know this from the telephone calls Miss Bentley received from this engineer, from Knickerbocker Village, Julius, as an intermediary, arranging clandestine meetings between Julius and Golos, his Communist espionage superior. But most important all we know of Rosenberg's dealings with Bentley from statements made by Rosenberg himself to Max Elitcher and David Greenglass.

Saypol stated that the identity of "other traitors who sold their country down the river with Rosenberg and Sobell remains undisclosed." It could be inferred from Rosenberg's boasts to Greenglass that he had a network of informants, and that others were being shielded by him. This was the first clear indication that the government hoped to widen the breach in the solidarity of the espionage personnel. The implosion chain of confession had led from Fuchs to Gold to Greenglass to Rosenberg. But Ethel and Julius had stopped the crack from widening. They had proclaimed their innocence. The government was frustrated and determined to learn more. We shall see how this effort continued to the very end.

Saypol put a question which he was eager to answer. Why weren't the original sketches of the bomb produced in court? Because they were "far away on the other side of the ocean behind the Iron Curtain."

He denounced the Rosenbergs for adding "the supreme touch to their betrayal of this country . . . by lying and lying and lying here brazenly in an attempt to deceive you, to lie their way out of what they did."

Prosecutors are experienced in meeting attacks on disreputable witnesses through whom they have established certain facts. Saypol gave an excellent illustration of the technique:

SAYPOL   There is no condonation for the activities of the Greenglasses in 1944 and 1945. David Greenglass is a confessed member of the Rosenberg espionage ring. . . . By his own plea of guilty, by his own voluntary act, without weaving a web of lies in an attempt to deceive you, he has made himself liable to the death penalty, too. The spurious defense that Greenglass, or the Greenglasses, in order to satisfy a business grudge, a business dispute against the Rosenbergs, has concocted a story about espionage, making himself liable to the capital penalty by his plea of guilty because of the business disagreement, is as much of a concoction as the story of the defendants that Greenglass went to his worst enemy, Julius Rosenberg, for help when he wanted to flee the country.

He turned the sword of scorn around and pointed it at the Rosenbergs.

SAYPOL   Greenglass' relations toward his older sister, Ethel, and her husband, Julius, were such that he was willing prey to their Communistic propaganda. He committed this crime because they persuaded him to do it.

The breach of family loyalty, he argued, was not committed by David testifying against his sister, Ethel, but by the older Rosenbergs "dragging an American soldier into the sordid business of betraying his country for the benefit of the Soviet Union." He contrasted their attitudes, the Greenglasses making amends for their sins by telling the truth and taking the consequences, whereas the Rosenbergs had magnified the betrayal of their country by lying.

In his summation, Bloch had asked why the government had not produced Ann Sidorovich. Saypol hinted that she, too, had fled the country.

SAYPOL   A query has been thrust at me from you. Where is Ann Sidorovich? They know why I can't say, but I say Ann Sidorovich was their friend. I ask where is Ann Sidorovich? So far as I know she is still their friend.

Even on the night she was at the Rosenberg home, it was anticipated she "might not be available" to make the trip to Albuquerque. That is why the Jell-O box signal was given to another courier.

He recalled Rosenberg's phrase, that the simplest things are always the cleverest, and applied it to selecting a photographer for passport photos "right behind this" courthouse, at 99 Park Row, and "right under" the nose of the FBI. That evidence was presented by Schneider and was obtained at the very last moment. Without elaborating it, the inference was that, psychologically, criminals often pick their hideaways next door to a police station, on the theory that it is the very last place anyone would think of searching. This device is commonly used even in the home. When we want to hide a precious article from burglary, we do not use safe boxes, but an open drawer with towels or shirts, which theoretically a thief would not consider a likely security spot. Saypol had touched early on Schneider's testimony. It was a passing remark. Undoubtedly, it was to receive more concentrated treatment later.

He returned to the Jell-O box signal, and argued that the piece of cardboard carried by Gold had been last seen in Julius Rosenberg's hands. Gold had received it from Yakovlev. How else could Yakovlev have gotten it, but from Rosenberg?

It was Gold who testified, "I come from Julius," and was given Julius Rosenberg's telephone number by Greenglass, thus, further establishing the identity of "Julius." Of course, he bore down on Gold's imperviousness to doubt.

SAYPOL . . . as far as he is concerned, the die has already been cast. The charges against him have already been disposed of. He has been sentenced to thirty years, the maximum term of imprisonment. He can gain nothing from testifying as he did in this courtroom except the initial relief, the moral satisfaction in his soul of having told the truth and tried to make amends. Harry Gold, who furnished the absolute corroboration of the testimony of the Greenglasses, forged the necessary link in the chain that points indisputably to the guilt of the Rosenbergs.

Not one question was asked of him by any defendant on cross-examination.

Saypol attacked Bloch's main thesis that there was no documentary evidence against the Rosenbergs.

SAYPOL The atom bomb secrets stolen by Greenglass at the instigation of the Rosenbergs were delivered by Harry Gold right into the hands of an official representative of the Soviet Union. The veracity of David and Ruth Greenglass and of Harry Gold is established by documentary evidence and cannot be contradicted.

You have in evidence before you the registration card from the Hotel Hilton in Albuquerque, which shows that he was registered there on June 3, 1945. You have before you the transcript of the record of the Albuquerque bank, showing that on the morning of June 4, 1945, Ruth Greenglass opened a bank account in Albuquerque and made an initial deposit of $400 in cash—just as she and David testified they did here on the witness stand right before you.

When David Greenglass came home on his furlough in September, he gave Julius "a cross-section sketch of the atom bomb itself and a twelve-page description of this vital weapon." Here Saypol indulged in a melodramatic image.

SAYPOL This description of the atom bomb, destined for delivery to the Soviet Union, was typed up by the defendant Ethel Rosenberg that afternoon at her apartment at 10 Monroe Street. Just so had she on countless other occasions sat at that typewriter and struck the keys, blow by blow, against her own country in the interests of the Soviets.

He argued that Rosenberg was so high "in the Soviet espionage hierarchy" that he knew Gold had made contact with Dr. Fuchs as well as with Greenglass. Therefore, when he heard of Fuchs's arrest and confession, he knew that Gold would be involved, and then Greenglass. He and Ethel might be next.

SAYPOL That is when Rosenberg hurried to Greenglass to convey to him the necessity, the urgency of getting out of the country.

Bloch had made much of Greenglass' failure to recognize Gold's picture in the newspaper shown to him by Rosenberg. The prosecutor feared this point might raise a credibility doubt. He reminded the jury that Greenglass had only seen Gold on one occasion before.

SAYPOL Anyone might hesitate before positively identifying such a picture of one whom one hasn't seen but briefly five years before. But while Greenglass had his doubts, Rosenberg had none. If Greenglass was falsifying, couldn't he have said he recognized the picture right away? Who could contradict that?

When Gold was arrested, Rosenberg wanted to get the Greenglasses out of the country.

SAYPOL The truth was beginning to catch up with the Rosenbergs and their crowd. The passport photos of the Greenglass family were taken at Rosenberg's insistence. Rosenberg asked for five sets, but Greenglass had six sets taken. The five sets are now undoubtedly in the hands of Rosenberg's Soviet partners, but the sixth set is here, in this courtroom, before you as Government's Exhibits 9-A and 9-B.

Saypol asked the jury to infer that the reason six sets of passport photographs were taken by Greenglass on Rosenberg's instructions,

(313)

rather than one set of three, was that in fleeing from country to country, forged passports were necessary. To avoid the danger of mutilation, five extra sets were prepared.

He detailed the evidence that Rosenberg gave Greenglass $1,000 and then $4,000 to flee, and how the money landed in the hands of Greenglass' attorney.

SAYPOL Where did Rosenberg get this $4,000? Certainly it is evident that Greenglass never had that much, and it appears that Rosenberg never could have had that much.

This money like other sums given in cash to Greenglass came from the Soviet Union.

SAYPOL . . . an investment which paid handsome dividends to the Soviet Union at a cost to this country, the extent of which must be measured in lives more than in money.

The prosecutor turned to Ethel's visit to Ruth Greenglass "laden with gifts," to ask for assurance that David wouldn't talk "so that the truth of Rosenberg's treachery and disloyalty would not be discovered."

One of the devices of summation is to repeat testimony already analyzed, as a launching platform for new arguments. It is the technique of summaries within the summation. Like a tune which becomes more enjoyable as it becomes more familiar, facts repeated often enough acquire a glow of recognition. Here is an illustration:

SAYPOL Added to the testimony of the two Greenglasses, Max Elitcher, the testimony of Harry Gold, the registration card, the bank account, the Jell-O box, you have the testimony of Ruth Greenglass' young sister, Dorothy, who told you how Julius Rosenberg chased her into the bathroom, behind closed doors, so that he could talk to Ruth Greenglass alone. You have the testimony of Dr. Bernhardt about Rosenberg's inquiry concerning vaccination for a veteran who was going to Mexico. The testimony of these witnesses proves beyond any doubt the verity of what the Greenglasses have sworn to in this courtroom.

Saypol referred scornfully to Rosenberg's "glib denials," which had to yield to the admission of two incidents where third parties were present. For that reason, Rosenberg had to admit talking to Ruth alone, when Dorothy was banished. Was his mission merely to give her advice that David should not steal?

SAYPOL We know what Julius Rosenberg told Ruth Greenglass on that occasion and what he and his wife told Ruth and David on every occasion when they were together. The Rosenbergs told them to go and commit espionage in the interests of communism in the

Soviet Union, just as Rosenberg and Sobell told that to Elitcher and countless others, and that is what happened.

Saypol contended that Rosenberg "had to admit" asking Dr. Bernhardt for vaccination information "because he knew that no one would take his word against that of the doctor, a disinterested witness. Rosenberg's explanation that Greenglass demanded $2,000 or a certificate of smallpox vaccination, "is an explanation that requires vaccination."

He pointed out that Rosenberg admitted walking with Greenglass in May 1950 "because he heard Greenglass testify that they ran into the Einsohns, two friends of the Greenglasses. That meant two more living people to give him the lie, if he should deny this incident."

Summations roll like hills and valleys. The lawyer recites detail which gives him momentum to rush up to a peak. There he holds forth triumphantly, descends to lesser matters, and gathers himself for another dash to the top. Persuasion results from how skillfully the "little arguments" create speed for the ascent. It is an art in timing, not unlike that in music in which a soft lyrical passage prepares for the thundering effect of a fortissimo section, or in acting in which low-keyed, almost monotone delivery makes an explosion of feeling a stunning experience; or in painting in which brilliance is most effective against a dark background.

One of the peaks, as it turned out, in the Rosenberg trial was the console table. Saypol reached it and held forth:

SAYPOL You heard the testimony about what was done to that console table, so that it was used for microfilming. How strange, on the one hand, the testimony from the Greenglasses that that was a present from the Soviet, the testimony from the Rosenbergs that they paid $21 for it in 1944 or 1945, when furniture was scarce, at Macy's; and then a disinterested woman (Mrs. Evelyn Cox), even in the face of adroit cross-examination, resolute in her determination, told the truth. She saw the table. Mrs. Rosenberg told her it was a wedding present from a friend of Julius, whom they hadn't seen for many years. And this remarkably strange behavior taking the best piece of furniture in the house and storing it in the closet—why did they have to hide it?

The prosecutor declaimed from the top of another hill. Greenglass testified that Rosenberg ordered him to leave the country, just as Joel Barr had succeeded in doing; that he took six sets of passport photos, and that Rosenberg told him they would run away, too, and meet him in Mexico. Yet Ethel testified she never took such photos. To admit that she did "would be to admit the preparation for flight as Soviet espionage agents, for an ultimate destination behind the Iron Curtain."

SAYPOL Yesterday you heard Mr. Schneider identify both of them as those who had come to him at his place of business on a Saturday in the middle of June 1950, with their children. He told us nothing of snapshots, taken for amusement of precocious children. He told us of an order for three dozen passport photos for Julius and Ethel Rosenberg and their family, who told him that they were going to France.

Down to the valley again. Of course, there were no negatives. The pictures were three for a dollar. These were not real sittings. An· old box was used for a camera. There was no quality involved, no reorders.

He described the credibility conflict between Schneider and the Rosenbergs, as one between a disinterested, truthful witness, and those with a positive motive for deception and lying.

Once more, he returned to an accusation which is the bane of all prosecutors—their reliance on criminals to establish the facts. The defendants' counsel "had bitterly attacked many of the Government witnesses."

SAYPOL   But it is these very witnesses whom they now attack that they themselves chose as their partners in crime. While Rosenberg attacks the Greenglasses today, seven years ago it was the Rosenbergs who took this same David Greenglass and set him to betraying his country. It was Sobell at Rosenberg's instigation who recruited Elitcher. The only ones with knowledge about the activities of these defendants are those who participated in the same activities. These witnesses were not your choice, nor were they mine, these witnesses, Elitcher and the Greenglasses. They were selected by these defendants as their associates and partners in crime.

Once more, the prosecutor resorted to a summation within a summation, but this time he trumpeted a grand conclusion.

SAYPOL   . . . we have not only the testimony of Ruth and David Greenglass about Rosenberg's espionage activities. We have Elitcher's, a man who never saw Ruth and David Greenglass or Harry Gold. Elitcher has placed the brand of Soviet spy on Rosenberg. You have the documentary evidence of Gold's registration card, the bank account, the wrapping paper, the testimony of Dr. Bernhardt, Dorothy Abel, Evelyn Cox, of Schneider, who took the passport pictures. That is why the evidence as to the Rosenbergs' guilt is incontrovertible.

Their guilt is established by the proof not beyond a reasonable doubt, but beyond any conceivable doubt.

The court, acting as timekeeper, was calling out the time left, so that Saypol could guide himself to finish within the allotted time agreed to by both sides for summation.

He turned his guns on Sobell. The same month·that Greenglass was ordered to flee the country to Mexico and the Rosenbergs got their passport photos in preparation for flight, Sobell and his family did get out of the country and landed in Mexico City.

Sobell went to the airport in Vera Cruz, and then to Tampico, in exactly the same way that Greenglass had been instructed to do, before his awareness that FBI eyes were upon him and that flight was impossible.

Sobell roamed in Mexico, trying to go farther, under "a string of aliases, using people in New York and in New Mexico as mail drops." He also gave fictitious addresses.

SAYPOL   If he was not running away from anything why did he have to go under a false name and give a false address in Philadelphia?

Kuntz had denounced Elitcher as a rat and the lowest of miserable creatures. But who had picked Elitcher as his best friend? Sobell, not the government. Elitcher knew the truth, because it was Sobell who had tried to pull him into espionage activities.

SAYPOL   The cost of the truth and his testimony to Elitcher was the ruination of his reputation. He lost his job. He has admitted he had been a Communist and that he had been recruited into this Soviet espionage ring by Sobell and by Rosenberg.

Saypol reached the top of another hill, but he was defensive and not as candid in explanation as he might have been. He dealt with the sensitive question as to why Ruth Greenglass had not been arrested or indicted, despite her confession, and why Elitcher had not been indicted for perjury, though he conceded lying under oath when he denied in a government questionnaire that he was a Communist.

Saypol explained that the decision of the grand jury not to indict Ruth was "its prerogative and is foreign to the single issue in this case." He called the defendants' attack as "diversionary" as the one they had made on him.

SAYPOL   These defendants seek to escape the consequences of their own acts by hiding behind straw men like that. Greenglass is a confessed spy and Elitcher has admitted that some years ago he did not disclose his Communist Party membership in an application; but these men under the greatest stress have stood up here and disclosed the truth about their past activities. They have not compounded their sins by trying to lie to you here in this courtroom. The question here is not the fate, present or future, of other people. The question here is the guilt of these three defendants named by the grand jury here on trial before you in this courtroom. That is the single issue and the evidence on that issue is overwhelming.

Apparently, Saypol feared conceding and justifying the necessity to reward criminals in order to obtain evidence which only they could supply. By permitting one criminal to escape, many were convicted who otherwise would go free. The cause of justice was thus served, even though one of the guilty slipped out of the net. This explanation for Ruth's immunity, in order to induce David to talk, was later dealt with more forthrightly. Indeed, it was openly argued that Greenglass himself should receive only minor punishment because of his co-operation with the government. However, the prosecutor did not have sufficient confidence in this philosophy to put it bluntly to the jury. Perhaps it would tarnish his witnesses. So he skirted the problem by stating that the issue was the guilt or innocence of the Rosenbergs and Sobell, and not why the grand jury had not included others in this indictment. This was a double evasion, because realistically it was not the grand jury, but the prosecutor who presented the case to it, who had the greatest influence in determining who should or who should not be indicted.

In his conclusion, Saypol agreed fully with defense counsel on one point, the need to dissipate the prejudicial atmosphere which existed concerning communism. The defendants and their counsel must have been pleased with so fair a statement, when silence or demagogic double talk might have taken advantage of the inflamed atmosphere.

Said Saypol:

Ladies and gentlemen, you have heard statements of defense counsel here concerning the injection of communism in this case. I repeat again, these defendants are not on trial for being Communists. I don't want you to convict them merely because of their Communist activity.

Communism, as the testimony has demonstrated, has a very definite place in this case because it is the Communist ideology which teaches worship and devotion to the Soviet Union over our own government. It has provided the motive and inspiration for these people to do the terrible things which have been proven against them. It is this adherence and devotion which makes clear their intent and motivation in carrying out this conspiracy to commit espionage.

We ask you to sustain the charge of the grand jury in a verdict of guilty against each of these three defendants, on one basis and one basis alone; the evidence produced in this courtroom as to their guilt of the crime of conspiracy to commit espionage; that proof as to each defendant has been overwhelming. The guilt of each one has been established beyond any peradventure of doubt.

His time ran out, but not his emotion.

No defendants ever stood before the bar of American justice less deserving of sympathy than these three.

I am a firm believer in the American jury system. I have confidence in the perception of a jury of twelve intelligent American citizens.

I am confident that you will render the only verdict possible on the evidence presented before you in this courtroom—that of guilty as charged by the grand jury as to each of these three defendants.

CHAPTER 28

It is traditional for the court clerk to make an announcement before the judge charges the jury.

CLERK   All persons wishing to leave the courtroom should do so now, as no one will be permitted to leave until the Court has finished his charge.

This marks the solemnity of the procedure. The jury must not be diverted by the slightest movement from its concentration on the judge's instructions to it.

Even the timing of the charge is significant. It follows the summations, in which the lawyers have played on the emotions of the jury. The atmosphere is heated with contentiousness. The jury has been buffeted by the heralding of virtue and the condemnation of evil. Rampant partisanship and eloquence have assaulted their judgment. Often, jurors will be moved to tears by the plight of the defendants seen through the prisms of advocacy.

So the charge to the jury is the calm after the storm. The cold, dispassionate tone of the applicable principles of law produce a thinking process. The sanctity of reason displaces the appeal to emotion. It is a leveling process, restoring the trial to impartiality.

The judge's charge puts the scales of justice in as perfect a balance as human ingenuity can devise. It proclaims the rules of fairness in reaching a decision, which have been developed over centuries of Anglo-Saxon legal experience. It is the philosopher's touchstone. When it is expressed with lucidity, so that complex rules of law are not merely read to the jury, but are explained to achieve full comprehension, it is man's best effort to achieve equable justice.

There is a highly refined principle operating behind the final instructions to the jury. It may surprise some. It is that the rules of law as laid down by the judge for the jury must be accepted by them even if they disagree. The reason is that if the judge should err in his statement of the law, an Appellate Court may reverse the judgment. But if the jurors have not followed his instructions in the first place, the Appellate Court cannot know whether the judge's erroneous charge affected the decision. Furthermore, the judge is learned in the law, and a juror's disagreement with a rule he has set forth may well be an individual eccentric view, contrary to that which hundreds of legal philosophers and courts have reached after careful study.

When it comes to deciding facts, we consider the jurors supreme. They bring to bear their common sense and experience on credibility, which as I have written elsewhere, is based on the rule of probability. The judge, who may have spent most of his life in a cloistered tower, has no advantage over the layman in this regard. So here we exclude him from interfering with the jury's province, just as we exclude the jury from interfering with the judge's province in stating the law. The judge's charge serves one more purpose. It can wipe out minor errors or indiscretions which occurred during the trial. Emphatic instructions to disregard any impression he may have given of his own predilection, by his rulings on objections, comments to counsel, or even by jest or gesture, can set the record straight. In this sense, the judge's charge to the jury is like a powerful stream washing away the impurities, which may have crept into it during a long and arduous contest.

Judge Irving Kaufman's charge was an admirable illustration of the high purpose which can be achieved by the final step in the trial process. The lawyers on both sides commended him for his fairness in reviewing the case and the law. The Appellate Court later found in his charge explicit answers to such grievances as were raised.

He began with a general appeal for their purest judgment.

> You cannot have justice unless you are ready to approach your task of determining the issues with your minds completely barren of prejudice or sympathy. . . .
>
> The rich and the poor, the persons of every race, creed and condition stand alike before the bar of justice. . . .

He explained that they were not "supposed to be lawyers" and, therefore, must accept the rules of law as he gave them. On the other hand, they were "the sole triers of the facts."

> It is not what counsel may say a witness testified to or what counsel may say a document contained or showed, nor even what the Court might say. It is what you, the jurors, decide. And I might say at this point that counsel for both sides are to be given equal consideration—both occupy the same position before the Court.

If they didn't recall some testimony, they had a right to call for it, and the stenographers would read it to them. He urged them to exchange views with their fellow jurors and not hesitate to change their views "because of pride of opinion."

> It would be silly for you to sit in a corner and sulk because someone else does not agree with you. Talk it out. That is what deliberation means. . . .
> Justice in your hands is like a child in the hands of its parents. Just as a child will be warped in a home of bickering and wrangling—so will justice be thwarted in a jury room of heat, bickering and wrangling.

Then he turned to the law. He asked the court clerk to read the indictment out loud to the jury. He cautioned them again that an indictment "was not evidence of guilt nor does it detract in any degree from the presumption of innocence." The law's protection of the accused was stated vigorously.

> This presumption of innocence remains with them throughout the trial of the case and applies to the consideration of each of the essential ingredients going to make up the crime charged unless and until you, the jury, are satisfied beyond a reasonable doubt, from the evidence adduced by the prosecution, on whom is the burden of proof, of the guilt of the defendants as charged.

"You may well ask," he said, "what is meant by the expression beyond a reasonable doubt?" He proceeded to give the classic definition as provided by our highest courts—not without considerable struggle over the years. It is a doubt based on reason which a reasonable man might entertain because of something in the evidence or lacking in the evidence.

He also stated the negative. "It is not a fanciful doubt; it is not an imagined doubt; it is not a doubt which a juror may conjure up in order to avoid performing an unpleasant duty." Nor is it beyond "all possible doubt."

However, he combined this definition with a clear assertion that "the burden is on the Government to establish guilt beyond a reasonable doubt."

What weight was to be given to circumstantial evidence? The jury had the right to draw such reasonable inferences from it as in their judgment it deserved. Of course, this instruction was so general that it failed to narrow the alternatives, but how else can the law deal with such a precept? It is unfair to bar circumstantial evidence, and unfair to require its acceptance. The ultimate judgment, like that of direct evidence, must be based on its persuasive character deriving from probability and common experience.

(323)

The prosecution sought to draw one set of inferences from the evidence. The defense, another.

COURT It is for you to decide and for you alone, which inferences you will draw. If all the circumstances taken together are consistent with any reasonable hypothesis which includes the innocence of the defendants, or any of them, the prosecution has not proved their guilt beyond a reasonable doubt, and you must acquit them.

Espionage meant spying. It is difficult to detect and prove. Therefore, the law had made conspiracy to commit a crime a distinct offense, entirely apart from the crime itself.

What is a conspiracy? It is a combination of two or more persons to accomplish an unlawful purpose by unlawful means.

Justice Holmes wrote that "A conspiracy is a partnership in criminal purposes."

However, there can be a conspiracy without formal meetings or agreements. If there is a tacit understanding among the conspirators to achieve an unlawful purpose, and they work together to further that scheme, everyone is bound by the act of the other. It is no excuse that the activity of one of them was remote or minor.

So it followed that there could be the crime of conspiracy even if its purpose was not accomplished. However, if the conspiracy was successful, that evidence was the best proof of the existence of the conspiracy in the first place. The government claimed that the conspirators actually succeeded in stealing the secret of the atom bomb. If proved, this helped to establish the existence of a conspiracy.

The judge then explained the rule of law that every conspirator was bound by the act or declaration of his fellow conspirator, "because each is deemed to assent or to command what is done by any other in furtherance of the common objective."

Therefore, the jury's first task was to decide whether the prosecution had proved a conspiracy beyond a reasonable doubt.

If it so found, then its second task was to decide as to each defendant separately, whether he or she was a member of that conspiracy. This decision had to be based on the acts and statements of each defendant. Here the acts or statements of others did not count.

However, if the jury found that a defendant was a member of the conspiracy, then from that moment on he was bound by the acts or statements of others to achieve the common objective.

Bundled up in these instructions was the evolutionary development of concepts, which legal philosophers had refined over centuries. When I hear laymen, without awareness of the careful study given the matter, condemn from the top of their heads the crime of conspiracy as a mere gimmick to convict innocent people, or just a political device, I realize that some legal education would be as valuable to the democratic process as secular education.

The judge had only begun to explain the legal yardsticks which the jury had to apply.

In the Rosenberg case, the indictment set forth twelve overt acts to achieve the conspiracy. However, an overt act need not in itself be a criminal act. "That is the law," he proclaimed. Many things can be done to effectuate a criminal conspiracy which are not illegal in themselves; for example, traveling to a certain site, writing letters, or introducing people.

> Furthermore, the Government has to prove beyond a reasonable doubt only one of the aforementioned overt acts in furtherance of the conspiracy, in addition to proving the existence of the conspiracy and the membership of each defendant in the conspiracy beyond a reasonable doubt.

The judge then turned to definitions of certain terms in the espionage statute. It spoke of "conspiring to transmit information relating to the national defense to the advantage of a foreign nation." This referred not only to a hostile nation, but to a friendly power or even to an ally. The Supreme Court once put it tersely:

> No distinction is made between friend and enemy. Unhappily the status of a foreign government may change.

Therefore, the judge wiped out Rosenberg's contention that because Russia was our ally at the time, it was not wrong to pass on secret information to her.

The law was handed to the jury in clear terms.

> I charge you that whether the Union of Soviet Socialist Republics was an ally or friendly nation during the period of the alleged conspiracy is immaterial, and you are not to consider that at all in your deliberations.

Another element of the crime, as the statute described it, was that the defendant must have believed that the information given to the foreign power was "of advantage to it." So before the jury could convict, they had to believe "beyond a reasonable doubt" that the defendants acted in bad faith, intending the secret information to be of advantage to a foreign nation.

One of the difficult tasks of a judge in charging the jury is to review the evidence offered by both sides. He must do so with complete impartiality, his purpose being solely to crystallize the issues.

Almost all judges keep carefully written notes of the testimony and exhibits as they are offered. They can refer back to these in their charge. The law is so sensitive to the possibilities of mischief in such recapitulation that it requires emphatic instruction to the jury that the judge has no opinion of guilt or innocence, and even if he had, and the jurors could sense it from anything he said, they must disregard it. It is he who tells them so. He instructs them to decide what the true facts are, without interference from him. All this protects the defendants in an ordinary case, where there is little public interest. There is an additional safeguard when the case is as celebrated as that of the Rosenbergs, and an international spotlight focuses on every detail of the trial. A judge who would violate his oath of impartiality in such a setting would be foolhardy as well as unfair.

The law is so zealous to preserve the exquisite balance between the judge's and the jury's province that it provides more safeguards. For example, at the end of the charge to the jury, the lawyer may put upon the record his objection to the judge's review of the evidence, because of its omissions or undue emphasis, or even tonal or gesturing emphasis. The Appellate Courts can then pass upon any violation of the principle of impartial statement. In this way, a judge who tries "subtly" to prejudice a jury is held in line. Such instances are extremely rare, not merely because of the "watchdog" procedure, but because of the conscientious desire of judges, trained all their lives in the law, to live up to the principle that justice comes as close to divine purpose as it is possible for humans to achieve.

Judge Kaufman's charge was an admirable illustration of these principles. He turned to the evidence with this statement:

> I believe it is my duty as a Judge to help you crystallize in your minds the respective contentions and evidence in the case and I shall therefore review briefly these contentions of the prosecution and of the defendants.

He ran through the government's contentions briefly, stopping only to give another emphatic warning against prejudice because of membership, if any, in the Communist Party.

> I wish to caution you most strenuously that proof of Communist Party membership or activity does not prove the offense charged in this indictment, but may be considered by you solely on the question of intent, which is one element of the crime charged here. It will be up to you to determine whether you believe that testimony and, if so, the weight that you will give it on the question of intention.

When he reached the government's contention that Greenglass had prepared to flee the country, and that Sobell had actually done so, he explained the rule of law which applied to flight, and the inferences to be drawn from it.

> As to any evidence of flight adduced by the Government in this case, I charge you: Evidence of flight does not create any presump-

tion of guilt, although it is a legitimate ground for an inference of a guilty mind, if the jurors conclude that such inference is justified. Flight is a circumstance which the jury may consider as having a tendency to prove the guilt of a defendant, as an indication of a consciousness of guilt. It should not be considered alone and by itself. It must be weighed with all of the surrounding circumstances.

The jury was not "to draw any inference" from Sobell's flight against Ethel and Julius. It could only consider to what extent, if any, it was pertinent to proving that Sobell was a member of the conspiracy.

The judge approached the subject of Sobell's possible guilt with meticulous care. Sobell and his lawyer must have glowed with hope as the instruction was given to the jury:

If you do not believe the testimony of Max Elitcher as it pertains to Sobell, then you must acquit the defendant, Sobell.

Having concluded the review of the government's case, the judge turned with similar even-handed neutrality to the contentions of the defense.

Now, on the other hand, the defendants' version of this case is as different as night is from day. The two versions are not reconcilable. You must determine which one you will believe.

He listed the defendants' denial of each of the government's contentions. In view of the irreconcilable conflict, the judge not only stressed that "you are sole and exclusive judges of the facts," but took pains to prevent his own standing and influence from affecting their decision on the facts.

No matter how careful a judge may be to avoid it, there is always the possibility that the jury or some particular juror may get an impression that the judge has some opinion with reference to the guilt or innocence of the defendants, or that he thinks that some particular phase of the case is more important than another, or that some particular witness is more credible than another. . . . If you have formed any such impression you must put it out of your mind and utterly disregard it. . . . Despite anything said by me or by counsel, your recollection of the testimony must prevail whenever your recollection differs from what I have said or what counsel for either side have said in argument or otherwise.

He even warned the jury not to draw any inference from the fact that in summarizing briefly the contentions on both sides, he may have inadvertently given the impression that his statement of some facts and not of others was "an indication as to my opinion of the comparative importance or weight of that particular evidence."

Such sincere, clear and repeated statements by the court satisfied all counsel, as we shall see, that whatever bias might have been inferred by the jury, from the court's comments, during a long and heated trial, had been fully purged by these instructions. It is impossible in a court contest to avoid every semblance of emotion either by counsel or by the judge. The test is whether it has tainted the case so substantially that the damage is irretrievable. That is one of the reasons for the judge's charge. It is to wipe away any adulterating influences. I have observed that in the many severe critiques of the trial, the author never refers to the judge's charge, and its corrective or ameliorating effect. Since the upper courts reviewed the charge, to ignore its impact reflects on the critic's evaluation.

The law does not expect a perfect trial any more than a perfect man, be he judge or lawyer. If any flaw in the ideal were enough to reverse the verdict, no verdict would ever stand. Those who do not perceive this and harp on an error or claimed prejudice, here or there, invalidate the whole process and enthrone technicality, at the very same time that they condemn it. The pragmatic view—the necessary view—is that unless the error is so substantial that it corrupts the core of the contest, the verdict should be upheld, with appropriate warning of the defect, so that in the future, it will not be repeated. Perfect justice—impossible. Approximate substantial justice—acceptable. Determined effort to achieve more perfect justice—always. Isn't that the rule for all other activities of man?

Having sharply etched the conflict in testimony and the jury's sole responsibility for determining who was telling the truth, the judge set forth the law on credibility.

> Each juror must form his or her judgment solely upon the evidence presented in the court, uninfluenced by anything read in the newspapers or heard on the radio or in private conversation. The juror "sizes up the witness"—so to speak. To reconcile all the testimony is impossible, and it is for you, members of the jury, upon careful consideration of all the proven facts and incidental circumstances, to determine what the truth is.

How was the jury to gauge a witness' honesty? In the same way that we judge peoples' veracity in ordinary social contacts.

> You should consider—and naturally would, I think—a witness' demeanor, his background, his or her candor, or lack of candor, possible bias or prejudice, means of information, and accuracy of recollection. You should consider whether the witness' testimony is supported or whether it is contradicted by other credible testimony or circumstances.

He cautioned them to take into consideration the witness' interest in the outcome of the case. "The greater a person's interest, the stronger

(328)

the temptation to falsify testimony." However, it did not follow that an interested witness may not also be truthful. It was simply a factor in the scales to consider with all other weights.

The law on accomplice testimony was favorable to the Rosenbergs.

As to the testimony of David Greenglass, Ruth Greenglass and Harry Gold, you must consider it carefully and act upon it with caution, for they are accused of being accomplices. An accomplice in this case is anybody that the prosecution charges agreed or confederated with any or all of the defendants in the commission of the crime charged as alleged in the indictment.

Suppose the jury believed that a witness had lied. Must it disregard everything he has said? No, it has an option. If he has lied on a material matter deliberately, it may, if it chooses, throw out all of his testimony, or it may accept that part which it still believes truthful. If, however, the lie is as to an immaterial matter, or is not intentional, then the jury has no right to disregard all of his testimony. This is the classic rule and the judge so charged the jury.

The right of a defendant not to take the stand was stated in unequivocal language.

The fact that the defendant Morton Sobell, who has a right so to do, has not seen fit to testify in this case cannot be considered by you as any evidence against him or against any of the other defendants, or as a basis for any presumption or inference unfavorable to him or to them. You must not permit such fact to weigh in the slightest degree against any defendant, nor should it enter into your discussion or deliberation. The prosecution must prove defendants guilty by the required degree of proof as explained in these instructions. They are not required under our law to establish their innocence.

The judge then dealt with the Fifth Amendment plea. Once more, as he had done many times during the trial, he instructed the jurors that they must draw no inference against Ethel or Julius for refusing to answer on the ground that to do so might tend to incriminate them. The jury could consider their plea only to the limited extent of judging her credibility when she answered the same questions at the trial without protest.

The judge concluded that punishment was solely his responsibility and should not affect the jury's duty in deciding whether the defendants were guilty or innocent.

In lengthy trials, it is the practice to select fourteen or sixteen, instead of twelve jurors, so that in the event of illness or accident, a mistrial will not result from the failure to have a minimum of twelve. In the Rosenberg case, there were four alternates. They heard the case until the very end of the judge's charge. When the jury was about to retire for deliberation, the alternates had to be excused. It is just as improper to have more than twelve jurors as to have less. He dismissed them with thanks and cautioned them not to discuss the case with anybody.

Then the marshals, who were to escort the jurors to and from a restaurant and a hotel, were sworn in, taking an oath not to interfere or talk with the jurors, carry any messages to them and to shield them from any information or influence.

Very well, the jury will retire.

It was 4:53 P.M. The jury was led to a spacious room behind the jury box. It was bare, except for a large, oblong wood conference table and twelve armchairs. On one side was a door leading to a bathroom. Pads, pencils and ash trays were spread out on the table. They began their deliberations immediately.

An hour and a half later, they sent a written message to the judge. He called the lawyers into the courtroom.

I have a communication from the jury, gentlemen. The jury would like a copy of the indictment and the jury would like a list of the witnesses. This is signed by the foreman.

The requested data was gathered, counsel examined it and agreed that it could be sent to the jury room. Once more, the door was locked. No one knew what was happening behind it. That mystery was particularly wearing on the defendants and their lawyers seated in a conference room in the basement prison, almost directly underneath the jury room.

CHAPTER 29

U. S. MARSHAL I can have dinner brought here, whenever you wish.

ETHEL ROSENBERG No, thank you. I couldn't eat. (She looks at Julius) How about you, dear?

ROSENBERG I think we could have coffee—and maybe a piece of cake.

ATTORNEYS That will do for us too.

SOBELL (Nods)

E. H. BLOCH I thought the judge's charge was pretty fair on the whole.

ETHEL ROSENBERG (Nervously) What time is it?

A. BLOCH Five minutes after 8. You know it is an old rule that the longer the jury stays out, the better it is for the defendants.

ROSENBERG Why is that?

A. BLOCH Because it means there is a lot of discussion, perhaps even quarreling among the jurors. That's what takes time. Remember, the Government must get a unanimous decision to convict. We need only one to prevent a conviction.

PHILLIPS But there is no significance yet to the three hours or so that have passed. In a case of this length, with so many exhibits, and all those witnesses, it would take a long time for any jury to even sift through the evidence, before they can begin getting down to brass tacks.

The coffee arrived. As they began to sip it without appetite, Julius finding it hard to swallow, a court attendant entered hastily. He tried to be calm, but there was excitement in his voice.

The Judge wants everybody in the courtroom. The jury has returned.

(331)

The marshal put manacles on the Rosenbergs and Sobell, and led them to the elevator, which rode up to the courtroom level. The elevator was encased in solid steel mesh, and the corridor into the courtroom was guarded by an additional uniformed attendant. They entered into the much better lighted courtroom, blinking in the glare. The courtroom was crowded. They were seated at counsel table, Julius and Ethel holding hands despite the manacles. They were pale and frightened, and breathing hard. The jury box was empty.

There were three knocks on the judge's door and he mounted the bench amidst the shuffling noise of a rising audience.

It was 8:10 P.M.

COURT   I have a communication from the jury reading as follows: "One of the members of the jury would like to hear Mrs. Ruth Greenglass' testimony starting with the first approach that Rosenberg made to her regarding securing of information for Russia." Now what I would suggest, if that is agreeable, I want to know where they want to end. So what I think I shall do is send back a communication to the jury, for them to specify just where they would like to end. Then we can have that part marked. Is that agreeable?

SAYPOL   Yes.

E. H. BLOCH   That is fair.

COURT   (To Clerk) Would you write on here please, Mr. Schaefer, "Judge would like to know at what point you would like the reporter to stop with his reading of this testimony?"

The clerk left with the note. The defendants were relieved that no verdict had been reached. But it had already dawned on them that rereading the hostile testimony of Ruth Greenglass, of how Julius and Ethel urged her to persuade Dave to obtain information, boded no good.

A few minutes later, the clerk brought back a note.

COURT   (Reading) "Up to the line that David came home for his first furlough in January 1945" is the reply from the jury. So let us get the testimony at that part.

A. BLOCH   I think that covers quite a bit. It goes to conversation before she went out West; conversation she had with her husband out West and also cross-examination on that point.

LANE   And the conversation she had when she came back from the West, and conversation as she testified to.

SAYPOL   I don't think they have asked for any cross.

COURT   I am not going to read the cross to them unless they request it.

A. BLOCH   Well, I think when they ask for testimony, it means all the

(332)

testimony on the subject. Will you ask them whether they want the cross?

COURT   I won't put it in their mouths, but I will ask them whether there is anything else they want. The jury is intelligent. If that is what they want, they will ask for it.

The jury was called in. They had the earnest, distracted look of people engaged in debate. The judge asked the stenographer to read the typed minutes of Ruth Greenglass' testimony.

COURT   Have we read what the jury wanted?

JURORS   Yes.

COURT   Very well, the jury may retire.

But before they could rise, E. H. Bloch addressed the court:

If the Court please, I make the request that the stenographer also read the cross-examination of Ruth Greenglass on this specific point—

COURT   Your request is denied. That has not been requested by the jury. The jury will retire.

We will give the jury exactly what they request.

E. H. BLOCH   I respectfully except.

So the jurors had heard the request that they ought to hear the cross-examination of Ruth Greenglass reread too. They never asked for it.

A United States marshal led Ethel and Julius, followed by their lawyers, out of the opposite door through which the jurors had passed, and took them down in the caged elevator to the conference room below. It was 8:30 P.M. The coffee had turned cold. The cakes were untouched. No one looked at them.

KUNTZ   I certainly don't like their asking for that bitch's testimony.

E. H. BLOCH   Did you notice though that the request was made by only one of the jurors, not the whole jury?

ROSENBERG   Is that so?

E. H. BLOCH   I am sure of it. I noticed the wording in the jury's letter. But how could the judge keep the cross-examination from them? I am positive their request was not intended to be limited to direct testimony, but to all her testimony on that subject.

ETHEL ROSENBERG   (Hopefully) Well, the Judge said he would ask them if they wanted anything else? Maybe one of the jurors will ask for the cross.

Waiting for a jury verdict is a unique experience in painful suspense. The lawyers and their clients carry on conversations intended to comfort whoever needs it most at the moment. Surprisingly, it is sometimes the lawyer, particularly if he is emotionally involved with his clients' fate as E. H. Bloch and Kuntz were. While talk is exchanged on one level, the participants are functioning on another. They know that the unexpressed thoughts are different from what is being said. Fears and misgivings cloud their minds, while their tongues speak of hope. Also, their ears are cocked for approaching footsteps, which might signal that a verdict has been reached. So the conversation is an interference with the sounds they dread, but for which they listen hypnotically.

Sometimes, there is an attempt to divert by small talk but the effort is so strained, it only calls attention to the heavy atmosphere which brooks no irrelevancy. Sometimes there is even a resort to levity, but smiles quiver with heartbreak and only add to the poignancy of the unbearable waiting.

The Rosenbergs, Sobell and their lawyers struggled with both banter and with silence. Nothing gave relief.

Suddenly, their antennae picked up the distant whirr of a starting elevator. All eyes darted to the door. Yes, there weré steps. Fast ones too, connoting urgency.

A marshal entered, his face registering excitement. It was 9:45 P.M.

"The Judge wants the defendants and counsel in the courtroom at once."

They hastened to the prison elevator, their hearts beating wildly. When they entered the courtroom, Judge Kaufman was already on the bench, but the jury box was empty.

COURT The jury wants all the exhibits except that which has been impounded, so will you gentlemen please get all the exhibits together in evidence?

A. BLOCH Satisfactory to us.

COURT Except those that have been impounded, and check them off together and give them to the bailiff so that they can be sent in. All right.

Once more, they took the bleak ride down. There was relief that a verdict had not yet been reached. They clung to the rule that the longer the deliberation, the more remote a conviction. They were willing to suffer the agony of uncertainty, rather than the certainty of agony.

An hour and twelve minutes later, at 10:55 P.M., their oversensitive ears again heard the click of a starting elevator. The court wanted "everybody in the courtroom." They filed out in moist anxiety.

Again, the jury was not in the box.

COURT I have a communication from the jury which reads as follows: "Judge Kaufman:
"One of the jurors has some doubt in his mind as to whether he

can recommend leniency for one of the defendants. He is interested in knowing your mind on the matter."

I might say that I am not prepared as yet to give the answer. I want to give some thought to it.

Do you gentlemen have any thoughts on the matter?

A. BLOCH   I can't very well suggest anything. It is all up to you, Judge.

COURT   Yes.

A. BLOCH   Because ultimately you will be the one who will pass on it.

COURT   My present inclination is to just read back to them that portion of my charge which dealt with punishment. I have sent my clerk to look up cases on the subject.

The judge summoned the jury. There was a decided change in their demeanor. Their faces were flushed and they looked tired and subdued.

COURT   I shall reread to you, members of the jury, that portion of my charge which dealt with the matter of punishment. Then I will give you some short explanation.

I said to you in my charge, you are instructed that the question of possible punishment of the defendants in the event of conviction is no concern of the jury and should not in any sense enter into or influence your deliberations. The duty of imposing sentence rests exclusively upon the Court. You cannot allow a consideration of a punishment which may be inflicted upon the defendants to influence your verdict in any way. The desire to avoid the performance of an unpleasant task cannot influence your verdict.

Now I want to say that if you want to make a recommendation, you can if you desire, but I believe it should be stated to the jury that the recommendation that you are going to make or intend to make should not in any way affect your decision. The decision is to be based on the evidence, and it is my prerogative to follow or disregard any recommendation that you may make on the matter of punishment. Is that clear?

All right; very well, you will retire.

An hour and ten minutes later, at 12:10 A.M., the call came again to ascend. Numb with fear and ominous expectation, Ethel, Julius and Sobell ascended. This time, the jury was in the box. The defendants gazed at them. Were they executioners or angels of freedom? In a moment, they knew once more that it was a false alarm.

COURT   Madam and gentlemen of the jury: I want to suit your convenience as much as I can. However, I also must take into mind the problems which the Marshal has. Now, if you feel that you believe a verdict can be reached in a reasonable period of time, why then, I think it would probably be a good idea to continue your deliberations. Otherwise I will have to advise the Marshal that I will consider locking you up for the evening, and it will take him, I imagine, about an hour to make arrangements for accommodations, and so forth. I would suggest with that in mind, you go back into your jury room and formally send me a communication on the wish of the jury, and also, if there is anything else that I can be of any help on.

All right, you may retire.

Within ten minutes, the judge received an answer. He read it.

"Judge Kaufman:
"Will you kindly make arrangements as you suggested from the bench due to still existent dissident vote amongst us."

I think that what I am going to do is to ask the jury whether they have arrived upon a verdict as to any defendant, under Rule 31, and if they have, then I will ask them to go back and give us the verdict on that.

A. BLOCH Tonight?

COURT Yes.

A. BLOCH That is cruelty to us.

COURT Why prolong the agony? If they have it, they have it.

KUNTZ Judge Kaufman, I have a sort of a feeling that if you do that, that juror—now, I don't know who it is and I don't know for whom it is—might feel that this is a suggestion—

COURT What I will do, if you agree, I will simply say, send in a note without sending for them again, and ask them if they have agreed upon a verdict as to any defendants. If so, to return the verdict as to that defendant or defendants, and then we will continue the deliberations as to others.

He dictated the following question to the jury:

"Judge Kaufman would like to know if you have agreed upon a verdict as to any of the defendants? If so, you may return your verdict as to the defendant or defendants as to whom you have agreed. . . ."

E. H. BLOCH Your Honor, I think that the hour is quite late. We came in very early this morning. It is not that we are tired but I think the jury is pretty tired and I think in all fairness to the defendant, as to whom the jury has been unable to agree, they ought to get a night's sleep and resume their deliberations.

COURT Well, I shall do that.

The order was given to accommodate the jurors for the night. There was a wave of relief among the defendants. The jury had been out almost eight hours and there was no agreement. As so often at the high

(336)

point of hope came the warning of despair. It arrived in a note from the jury.

"Judge Kaufman:
"We have reached our verdict on two of the defendants and we prefer to reserve rendering our verdict on all three defendants until we have complete unanimity."

What was the portent? Could it be acquittal of two and doubt about the third? If so, what two? Could it mean a finding of "guilty," then would it not be likely to be the Rosenbergs, while there was debate about Sobell? That night must have been more than usually tormenting for the defendants and their counsel, as they reviewed the possible permutations of the teasing puzzle, presented by the jury's note. To the ordinary suspense was added the half knowledge of a decision reached and not revealed. If the court and jury had planned to punish the defendants with certainty made uncertain, they could not have done better.

Court recessed until 10:00 A.M., the following morning, March 29, 1951.

CHAPTER 30

It was not until 11:00 A.M. that everyone was summoned to the courtroom.

COURT Bring the jury in.

The jury entered the courtroom at 11:01 A.M.

CLERK Will the jurors please answer as their names are called?
(Juror's names called by the clerk.)

CLERK Mr. Foreman, have you agreed upon a verdict?

FOREMAN Yes, your Honor, we have.

CLERK How say you?

VERDICT

FOREMAN We the jury find Julius Rosenberg guilty as charged.
We the jury find Ethel Rosenberg guilty as charged.
We the jury find Morton Sobell guilty as charged.

CLERK Members of the jury, listen to your verdict as it stands recorded.
You say you find the defendant Julius Rosenberg guilty, Ethel
Rosenberg guilty, and Morton Sobell guilty and so say you all?

JURORS Yes.

Though trembling, Bloch continued to perform his duty. Perhaps, perhaps, a juror who had resisted the verdict might change his mind.

E. H. BLOCH If the Court please, I ask that the jury be polled as to each defendant.

COURT Very well.

CLERK Members of the jury, listen to your verdict as it stands recorded as to Julius Rosenberg. You say you find Julius Rosenberg guilty—

FOREMAN Yes.

COURT Ask each one as to each defendant.

Do you find Julius Rosenberg, Ethel Rosenberg and Morton Sobell guilty, Mr. Lebonitte?

FOREMAN Yes, your Honor.

COURT All right.

The clerk polled the jury and each of the jurors confirmed the announced verdict.

CLERK The jury has been polled.

E. H. BLOCH If the Court please, I would like to ask leave to make any motions with respect to the jury verdict—

COURT On the day of sentence.

It is customary for the judge to express his appreciation to the jury and counsel for their conscientious service. Sometimes, he reveals his own opinion of their verdict. The judge proceeded to do so.

> My own opinion is that your verdict is a correct verdict, and what I was particularly pleased about was the time which you took to deliberate in this case. I must say that as an individual I cannot be happy because it is a sad day for America. The thought that citizens of our country would lend themselves to the destruction of their own country by the most destructive weapon known to man is so shocking that I can't find words to describe this loathsome offense.

In view of the importance of the case, the prosecutor also sought permission to speak:

> The conviction of defendants in a criminal case is no occasion for exultation. It has been said that the Government never loses a case —because if there is a conviction the guilty are punished, and if there is an acquittal, the presumption of innocence must permanently prevail. The conviction of these defendants, however, is an occasion for sober reflection. That you the jury so considered it is evidence from the fact that you deliberated for six and a half hours last night, and the nature of your requests as to the evidence and the identity of the witnesses amongst other things demonstrates that you complied throughout with the instructions of the learned Court; and that your conclusion is a mature, a reflected one. . . .
>
> The jury's verdict is a ringing answer of our democratic society to those who would destroy it. First, because a full, fair, open and complete trial—in sound American tradition—was given to a group of people who represented perhaps the sharpest secret eyes of our enemies. They were given every opportunity to present every defense and I would fight at all times for their right to defend themselves freely and vigorously.
>
> Secondly, your verdict is a warning that our democratic society,

while maintaining its freedom, can nevertheless fight back against treasonable activities.

It was natural for the judge and the victorious prosecutor to make these declarations. But there followed statements by defense counsel of a most extraordinary nature. Kuntz, who had rained verbal blows on Saypol in his summation, arose to speak.

KUNTZ If your Honor please, I wonder if I may have the privilege of a few words in my own behalf.

COURT Yes.

KUNTZ I do want to thank the jury as your Honor did for the patience and care with which they sat in this case.

I wanted to say to them through you that it was my duty as an officer of this court to defend the rights of my client zealously and strongly; and that I wanted to assure the jury and the Court, as one officer of the court to another officer of the court here, that what I might have said during the trial or summation was said as an officer of the court, and was not said against any person as an individual.

I want to assure this jury that to the best of my ability I did strive hard on behalf of my client.

COURT I am sure you did.

KUNTZ And I want to say to Mr. Saypol, as one officer of the court to another, I am willing to shake his hand after a job that we both had to do.

COURT Well, I am certain that that is so.

What did Sobell think of this exchange of courtesies? Carried away by the "sportsmanship" of the occasion, Bloch made the most startling of all speeches.

I want to extend my appreciation to the Court for its courtesies, and again I repeat I want to extend my appreciation for the courtesies extended to me by Mr. Saypol and the members of his staff, as well as the members of the FBI, and I would like to say to the jury that a lawyer does not always win a case; all that a lawyer expects is a jury to decide a case on the evidence with mature deliberation.

I feel satisfied by reason of the length of time that you took for your deliberations, as well as the questions asked during the course of your deliberations that you examined very carefully the evidence and came to a certain conclusion.

COURT Thank you.

The judge dismissed the jury with a final "God bless you all."

CHAPTER 31

April 5, 1951, was the day of sentence. If the defendants thought they would know their fate quickly, they were in for another agonizing experience. Before sentence, the lawyers made motions "to arrest judgment," for dismissal of the indictment or for a new trial, citing legal grounds, including constitutional violations. In this way, every basis for appeal was reserved. Bloch made such motions on behalf of the Rosenbergs. They were immediately denied. This took only a few minutes.

But when Phillips arose to make his formal motion on behalf of Sobell, the wrangle which developed took several hours. It seemed that nothing in this trial accorded with usual experience.

Phillips began with a melodramatic announcement.

> I shall be constrained, if your Honor please, to reveal some shocking circumstances which I shall do very, very reluctantly. I shall do so only from the conviction that the most important thing in my life at the present moment, more important than the two billion people living on this planet, are the rights of my client, Sobell. . . .
>
> In the thing that I am about to reveal, if your Honor please, there is much that is not beautiful, much that is not creditable to the law enforcement agencies of the United States of America, and I loving my country more than anything else feel that in revealing those circumstances I might injure my country in the eyes of the world, but I am powerless to stop and not to say what I must say.

He sounded as if he was about to drop a scandal bomb as powerful as the atom bomb. He continued to be mysterious. He picked up Exhibit 25, a card produced by the witness Huggins, who had been flown in from Texas, which bore the notation "Deported from Mexico." Those

(343)

words were "a downright falsehood," he screamed, and the FBI must have known that.

COURT   Well, you had your opportunity at the trial to show it, didn't you?

PHILLIPS   Just a moment. I expected to be met by that point and I shall meet that. I shall come to it eventually. First, let me state my facts on which I base my points.

COURT   Very well.

PHILLIPS   Then if I have omitted anything before, if I haven't done my duty heretofore, if I was too stupid perhaps to see the point at the time—

COURT   You can be accused of many things, but not that, Mr. Phillips.

PHILLIPS   The three words "Deported from Mexico" are as untrue as if I said "The sun ceases to shine."

He waved an affidavit of Morton Sobell and told the court that his shocking revelations were in sworn form.

COURT   I see. He had an opportunity at the trial to take the stand, did he not? You can't have your cake and eat it, you know. You had an opportunity to put him on the stand. He decided he didn't want to take the stand and deny these allegations.

Phillips persisted, and the court permitted him to read Sobell's affidavit. I reconstruct the events described in it.

———>✕<———

Sobell and his wife were in their apartment in Mexico City. They were lingering over their coffee. One of their children, a year old, was in bed. There was a knock on the door. Sobell's older daughter opened the door. Three men dressed in civilian clothes "burst into the room with drawn guns raised for shooting." They were Mexicans but they spoke English.

SOBELL   What do you want?

MEXICAN   You are Johnnie Jones and you have robbed a bank of $14,000 in Acapulco. You are coming with us.

SOBELL   I am not Johnnie Jones. My name is Sobell. I am an American. You are making a terrible mistake. Look, I will show you my papers, my visa.

MEXICAN   (Exhibiting a piece of metal) We are police and you are under arrest.

They seized him. He struggled while Mrs. Sobell screamed. The baby cried.

SOBELL   I insist on calling the American Embassy. You will see you are wrong.

A fourth Mexican joined them, also in civilian clothes. They picked Sobell up bodily and carried him kicking from the fourth floor down to the street. Sobell was yelling for the police. A taxi pulled up. The Mexicans tried to force him into the taxi. He was resisting successfully, when two more men joined the abductors. They beat Sobell over the head several times until he dropped unconscious, and hurled him onto the floor of the taxi. Three Mexicans sat on the seat, the other two joined the driver on the front seat.

While the car was driving, Sobell recovered consciousness. Blood was running down his face. It soaked his shirt. He looked up at the three Mexicans seated above him.

The car stopped in front of a building. They lifted him out of the taxi onto his feet.

MEXICAN We are going into that building. If you "make a scene" we will "plug" you.

They held him as he staggered into the building. They rode up an elevator, entered an office, sat him down in a chair and waited until a slim, dark man entered. He looked at Sobell.

SOBELL What is this all about?"

The slim Mexican slapped him in the face violently.

MEXICAN We ask the questions here.

A photographer entered and snapped pictures of him from all sides. He was put into another room, and one of the men stood guard over him. He was there from 8:30 P.M. to 4:00 A.M., dozing in a state of collapse. At twelve o'clock midnight, the guards offered him something to eat, but he was too ill, and declined.

At 4 A.M., the men entered, half carried him down the elevator, into the street and into a large four-door Packard.

On each side of him sat an armed guard.

Then the same, tall thin man approached and said to the two guards in English:

"If he makes any trouble, shoot him."

The driver of the car, whom the guards called Julio, said:

"We are going to the Chief of the Mexican Police for further action."

The car set off on a long ride. Occasionally, Julio stopped and telephoned.

At one-thirty in the morning, the car arrived at Nuevo Laredo. Julio again left and returned in ten minutes.

JULIO I have spoken to the Chief of Police. We are taking you across the border and will let you go.

They stopped at the Mexican Customs on the Mexican side of the bridge across the Rio Grande. This is the boundary between the United States and Mexico. Just as they approached the bridge to cross into the United States, a car came toward them. They stopped. A man left the approaching car, opened the door and showed his badge. He was a United States agent. He entered.

The car then drove to the United States Customs; Sobell was given a card and asked to sign it.

Then they arrested him and searched him. They put handcuffs on him. They slapped him into jail. He remained there for five days.

He was offered an opportunity to waive extradition. He did so at Laredo, and was taken a prisoner back to New York.

——→←——

When Phillips had finished describing this "kidnapping" of Sobell, he was again confronted with a question which he tried to dodge, but the judge was no longer patient.

COURT Why didn't you submit that to the jury?
PHILLIPS I beg your pardon?
COURT Why didn't you submit that to the jury?
PHILLIPS Now, just a moment. I will answer that, of course.
COURT Answer it right now.
PHILLIPS I am coming to that.
COURT Would you answer it right now?
PHILLIPS Am I right in saying—
COURT Answer it now, Mr. Phillips.
PHILLIPS You want me to answer first?
COURT Yes.
PHILLIPS Well, in order to answer that, we would have to place Sobell on the witness stand. I took the position that we ought to put him on the witness stand. My colleague took a contrary position. We discussed that pro and con until almost the last day of the trial, when he came in and told you in the courtroom there that we had decided to do otherwise. I yielded to the superior experience in criminal trials of my colleague, Mr. Kuntz. I still believe he was right.
    Without that flight, there is absolutely no case whatsoever.
COURT Well, I don't agree with you.

Thus, he revealed the internal disagreement between counsel. Kuntz, the more experienced criminal lawyer, thought the evidence against Sobell was so thin that he ought not take the risk of testifying and subjecting himself to cross-examination. Phillips believed that even if the government's case against Sobell was not as powerful as against the Rosenbergs, nevertheless, his flight from the country and use of disguised names, combined with Elitcher's and Danziger's testimony, created enough aura of guilt to require his denials from the stand. The differences between the lawyers were, of course, made known to Sobell and his family, and they tipped the scales toward silence. This decision

(346)

was all the more difficult, because it prevented him from presenting his story of forcible seizure and the forged entry of deportation. Also, the jury would not hear his melodramatic version of a brutal beating which accompanied his being dumped into the United States.

Of course, there was one other choice. It sometimes is possible "to have your cake and eat it." He might have taken the depositions of various Mexican officials to develop his version of being brought to the border bloody and semiconscious. Sobell's wife could have taken the stand to tell of the thugs she said carried her husband kicking out of their apartment in Mexico City. She would have been less vulnerable to cross-examination on the conspiracy charges since no one claimed she was involved. Accompanying her husband in flight might have been explained, if true, as loyalty to him, rather than guilty conscience.

At the very least, a venturesome cross-examination of the government witnesses, who testified to the "deportation" entry, might have revealed to the jury Sobell's claim of duress. In this way, Sobell could have stayed off the stand and had others present his grievance. But having staked his all on silence and lost, how could he now cry out, when the jury was no longer there?

The judge, therefore, rejected his plea, but in the course of the exchange, Phillips made a vital admission.

COURT Mr. Phillips, the jury has spoken. You and your co-counsel have been eloquent in his defense. You have heard the evidence. He has been tried in the American way. The accuser was on the stand subject to cross-examination, the most exhaustive kind of cross-examination, and the jury has spoken. I believe, I firmly believe that I was as impartial as any human being could possibly be in this trial.

PHILLIPS Right, no doubt about that.

Phillips continued to fight valiantly. He was the kind of lawyer who holds his feet in a storm—an admirable and unusual quality. He insisted that the "United States of America having secured the body of Sobell by a criminal illegal act must send him back to the place where they took him to deal with him accordingly some time in the future."

He assured the court that he was not trying to "create a scandal, and your Honor will now understand my reluctance during the trial" to bring the matter up. This earned him a painful rebuke.

COURT That I will never understand.

He persisted; he had an additional reason. He knew that Sobell and his wife had traveled to Mexico in their own names. The judge pointed out that he hadn't even proved that. He had not put an airline official on the stand as he might have done. Nevertheless, the judge had permitted him to argue this to the jury.

Finally, Phillips was subdued, and Saypol, who had been aching to

(347)

have his turn, replied. He revealed that when he went to Mexico City, he learned that Sobell and his wife "had cashed in the return portions of their tickets to come back to this country." He insisted that Sobell's arrest was based "on a lawful warrant." Why, he asked, had not Sobell's wife testified to the story of his forceful abduction? She had been there and was present throughout the trial.

COURT I think I have enough.

The motion to dismiss Sobell's case was denied.

All formal motions had been acted upon. The breathless moment of sentence had arrived.

CHAPTER 32

CLERK For sentence Julius Rosenberg and Ethel Rosenberg.

Ethel and Julius stood up, their faces a smudge of pallor, except for her tiny rosebud lips compressed as if she were about to whistle. They moved forward to the front rail to face the judge. They continued to clutch hands.

The judge suggested that chairs be placed there for them to sit, while counsel made long statements concerning what their fate should be. Once more, Ethel and Julius had been brought up to the moment of decision and then were pushed back into the darkness of delay.

Usually, the prosecutor makes a recommendation of punishment on behalf of the government. So Saypol spoke first.

SAYPOL Chief Judge Learned Hand of our Court of Appeals in his opinion in United States v. Dennis in the course of discussing the clear and present danger doctrine reviewed present world conditions in these words, with this warning: "and we shall be silly dupes if we forget that again and again in the past thirty years, just such preparations in other countries have aided to supplant existing governments, when the time was right."

He argued that a society which did not defend itself was not worthy of survival, and that the espionage statute was a weapon in defense of freedom.

Although he said he did not wish to translate these matters "into a direct issue of life and death," he, nevertheless, foreshadowed the latter when he tied the war in Korea to Russian instigation, and her audacity, to the possession of the atom bomb. On this premise, he attributed the deaths of American soldiers in Korea to Rosenberg's treachery.

SAYPOL How could the life of a single individual engaged in such
treasonable activities be weighed against the life of a single American soldier fighting in a distant land. . . . In terms of human life,
these defendants have affected the lives, and perhaps the freedom,
of whole generations of mankind.

There followed a series of rhetorical questions the answers to which
could only be "Death, death, to the Rosenbergs."

In the light of these considerations, is there room for compassion or
mercy? Is there not an absolute duty to exercise the only weapons
of defense available to our free judicial system which is here
charged with acting in defense of our society? Leniency would be
merely an invitation to increased activity by those dedicated to the
concept that compassion is decadent and mercy an indication of
weakness.

Having thus clearly recommended the severest penalty, he submitted
"the matter for the consideration of the court."

E. H. Bloch then was given the opportunity to plead for mercy.
He made a gracious opening, but some of his words were to come back
later as echoes of admission. "We can all say," he began, "that we
attempted to have this case tried as we expect criminal cases to be
tried in this country; we tried to conduct ourselves as lawyers, and I
know that the Court conducted itself as an American judge."

A plea for mercy reaches the heart best if it is accompanied by
contrition. Humility and regret evoke compassion. The anger of the
community is somewhat appeased by the simple words "I am sorry.
Please forgive me." But such words are not in a revolutionist's vocabulary. Defiance of authority is a stance he will not abandon even
when he faces retribution. He asks for no mercy, though he is at its
mercy. The Rosenbergs took this position. It could have been their
innocence rather than their ideology which made them unyielding.
But Bloch announced their position to "the entire world," thus heighten-
ing the impression that the process of political martyrdom had begun.
He was very skillful and graceful in stating the handicap imposed upon
him by his clients and yet fulfilling their wishes.

Because this case has become a celebrated case, and long before
we walked into this courtroom it had been the subject of report
and comment throughout the press of this country as well as the
press of the entire world, I hope your Honor will understand that
at this time as an officer of the Court I am bound by the jury's
verdict, and I am therefore circumscribed in what I say to the
Court, but indeed I would be remiss in my duty if I were not to
tell the Court and the entire world that my clients, Julius Rosenberg and Ethel Rosenberg, have always maintained their innocence;

they still maintain their innocence. And they have informed me no matter what, they will always maintain their innocence.

That makes my task here at this moment much more difficult. If these defendants came in crying *mea culpa* and showed that routine display of penitence that so many criminal defendants usually demonstrate to the Court on sentence, I could see things properly which would act as mitigation and which would move the Court, at least, in considering that state of mind in the imposition of sentence. I cannot say that. I am enjoined from saying that.

He, nevertheless, felt that the court should consider two "salient features" before prescribing punishment.

The first involved political considerations. He had wanted to keep these out of the case, but the prosecutor had made them the essence of his argument for severe punishment. He reminded the court of the warm atmosphere of 1944 and 1945, when Russia was our ally, and was highly praised by Winston Churchill and Franklin Roosevelt. Whereas, in 1951, the atmosphere was chilled with hostility toward Russia.

The Rosenbergs' intentions ought to be gauged in the beneficent light of the earlier period. Otherwise, we might be applying ex post facto emotion, which is as wrong as ex post facto law. He tried to express this thought in a series of questions:

I would like the Court to ask itself this question. Assuming that the United States Government had found out in 1945 what they found out years later and which impelled them to bring these charges; one, would these defendants find themselves in a criminal court? And two, would there be the hullabaloo and hysteria which has accompanied the progress of this criminal procedure?

COURT You overlooked one very salient feature, and that is that their activities didn't cease in 1945, but that there was evidence in the case of continued activity in espionage right on down, even during a period when it was then apparent to everybody that we were now dealing with a hostile nation.

Bloch persisted that it was "unduly harsh" if an act inspired by motives that were "prevalent amongst great sections of the American population in 1944, were transformed into something as heinous as Mr. Saypol has just stated."

Bloch's second point was that the atom bomb "was not the horrible thing that is represented to the Court." He said this was "a very startling statement," but just as he would consult the judge on law, so he would consult scientists on the bomb, and he wanted to prove

(351)

his assertion by reading from an article in the *Yale Law Journal* which gave the opinion of foremost scientists.

COURT Well, I don't think that is a sound argument, because if you are going to say to me that "with the dropping of one bomb you can't conquer a nation," or "with the dropping of one bomb you can't kill ten million, but you may kill a hundred thousand, therefore, it isn't so grave," I must say that that is not a good argument.

E. H. BLOCH I am not going to say that.

The judge permitted him to read from the article. It asserted that a number of countries, including Russia, would only be "a few years behind us" in developing the bomb. "The likelihood of marked differences in the evolution of scientific thought corresponding to geographical differences, is small." It concluded that any secrets known "by these scientists, many of whom returned to their own countries, have been disclosed to fellow workers in nuclear physics in other parts of the world."

COURT None of them had returned in 1944 and 1945.

"That is true," said Bloch, "but it was inevitable that the United States would lose its monopoly of the bomb." The court retorted that that did not excuse an American citizen's act in accelerating the process. Bloch agreed but contended that there was "a myth about the monopoly of the bomb" and that it was a huge exaggeration for Saypol to say that "our boys are dying in Korea because of the Rosenbergs." When the judge observed that the possession of the bomb did "play a very important part in power politics," the Rosenbergs were given advance notice that the grimmest view would be taken of the consequences of their acts.

An entirely different approach to mitigate punishment was possible, and Bloch presented it forcefully. Whatever we thought of the Rosenbergs, what about international relationships?

E. H. BLOCH I hope that any sentence of this Court will not exacerbate the tensions that exist in the world today. I believe that we can be more hopeful at this moment in the arena of international relations than ever before. We find strenuous efforts on the part of the greatest statesmen throughout the world to bring the Soviet Union and the United States into some orbit of understanding; and today, as in the last few weeks, our best brains are sitting with the best brains of the Soviet Union, in order to prepare an agenda to discuss outstanding differences.

Now, certainly that is not my business in this case to talk about too much, except as it impinges upon how your sentence may

11. Klaus Fuchs, a key figure in the Rosenberg case.

12. Morton Sobell being led into Federal Court House during Rosenberg trial.

13. Morton Sobell with wife after release from prison, 1969.

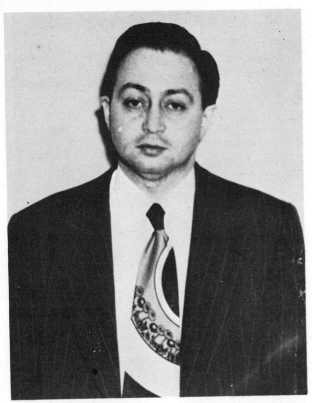

14. Harry Gold after conviction, 1950.

15. Harry Gold leaving Federal Penitentiary, Lewisburg, Pa., 1966.

16. Emanuel Bloch with Rosenberg children, Michael, ten, and Robert, six, after visiting their parents on "Death Row."

17. Rally for Julius and Ethel Rosenberg in New York's Union Square, June 1953.

18. Demonstration in Paris for the Rosenbergs.

19. Demonstrators march around Grosvenor Square, London.

20. Demonstrators for and against the Rosenbergs in front of the White House.

21. Michael, holding hand of Grandmother Mrs. Sophie Rosenberg, and Robert join demonstration in front of the White House, asking presidential clemency for their parents.

affect relations, precisely because this case is a celebrated case, and any sentence that your Honor imposes will be radioed throughout the world within three minutes and may be construed in a political way, when I know your Honor is merely trying to discharge his duty as a Court and impose a legal sentence.

The judge replied that his sole duty was "to the American people," which, of course, did not exclude Bloch's argument.

Bloch proceeded to cite analogies of proper punishment, for which he gave credit to Harry Gold's counsel, Mr. Hamilton, when he pleaded for his client. Tokyo Rose and Axis Sally had been convicted of treason and aiding Nazi Germany during the war. They received sentences of ten to fifteen years.

E. H. BLOCH ... and so I must say that I was extremely shocked, extremely shocked, despite everything that I have read in the newspapers, to hear Mr. Saypol ask for the severe penalty that he requested the Court to impose upon these defendants.

Usually, a plea for light sentence stresses the human aspects of the case. The private life and background of the Rosenbergs lent themselves to such purpose. Bloch avoided the emotional approach. He did not even mention their children. Instead, as must have been his instructions, he stressed their resoluteness and belief in their innocence.

E. H. BLOCH ... my clients have stood up with that kind of courage that can only come from persons that are convinced of their innocence. The worst that can be said about them is that, ideologically, during the years when we were allied with the Soviet Union, they were extremely sympathetic to the Soviet Union. ...

I am going to ask you to say to yourself, in your own conscience, your Honor, whether or not these people are the type of people that ordinarily come before you in a criminal case. I am through, your Honor.

In one respect, the defendants did not follow the pattern of fanatical ideologists. They did not speak in their own behalf. Extraordinary statements have been made by "political" defendants such as Sacco and Vanzetti, Tom Mooney and others. The Rosenbergs were more literate than any of these, and much later demonstrated great skill in their exhortations written in prose and poetry. I shall later quote from the extraordinary love letters they wrote to each other while in jail. But on this occasion, perhaps because they would not stoop to begging for mercy, and feared provoking the judge, by denouncing the verdict, they stood mute.

COURT Is there anything defendants wish to say?
ROSENBERG No, sir.

COURT Do you care to say anything?

ETHEL ROSENBERG No, sir.

At long last, the time had come to hear their fate. But even now, they were to stand a long time while the judge explained the reasons for the sentence he was about to impose.

They were no more than fifteen feet from the judge. They looked him in the eye, apprehensively, while holding hands tightly to derive courage from each other's warmth.

CHAPTER 33

The judge began by stating that "the seriousness of the case" and lack of precedent made his responsibility so great, that he felt he must accept it alone without calling on the prosecutor for his recommendation.

The Espionage Statute under which the Rosenbergs were convicted was passed in 1917 when "the Russian international spy ring did not present the threat to all of us which it does now."

He tore from the defendants any heroic cloak which they or their supporters might imagine was around their shoulders.

COURT Espionage, as viewed here today, does not reflect the courage of a Nathan Hale, risking his life in the service of his own country. It is rather a sordid, dirty work—however idealistic are the rationalizations of the persons who engaged in it—with but one paramount theme, the betrayal of one's own country.

He would not permit them the solace of even mistaken idealism.

COURT The nature of Russian terrorism is now self-evident. Idealism as a rationale dissolves.

He referred to the "life and death struggle" between the Russian and American systems, in which "as this case shows," Russia used our own citizens to betray us. The bomb could "wipe out millions of Americans." The Rosenbergs blanched at the next sentence.

COURT The punishment to be meted out in this case must therefore serve the maximum interest for the preservation of our society against these traitors in our midst.

The judge pointed out the irony of the fact that the country which they had betrayed gave them a fair and impartial trial which

(355)

consumed three weeks. As Rosenberg had admitted on the stand, the American system of justice was superior to that of Russia. Would a Russian national, who had been accused of the same crime, been given a trial of more than one day as a mere formality for a conviction agreed upon before the hearing? Yet, the Rosenbergs, he proclaimed, had chosen to devote themselves to Russian ideology, rather than to the "cause of liberty and freedom."

If the Rosenbergs had any lingering hope of a compassionate sentence, it was lost in the next pronouncement:

COURT I consider your crime worse than murder. Plain deliberate contemplated murder is dwarfed in magnitude by comparison with the crime you have committed. In committing the act of murder, the criminal kills only his victim. The immediate family is brought to grief and when justice is meted out the chapter is closed. But in your case, I believe your conduct in putting into the hands of the Russians the A-bomb years before our best scientists predicted Russia would perfect the bomb has already caused, in my opinion, the Communist aggression in Korea, with the resultant casualties exceeding 50,000 and who knows but that millions more of innocent people may pay the price of your treason. Indeed, by your betrayal you undoubtedly have altered the course of history to the disadvantage of our country.

He pointed out that "the evidence" of their treachery was "all around us every day—for the civilian defense activities throughout the nation are aimed at preparing us for an atom bomb attack."

There was still a possibility that the judge would deal differently with Ethel than with Julius. She was a devoted wife and mother of two children who needed her. Then came crashing down on her head the following pronouncement:

COURT The evidence indicated quite clearly that Julius Rosenberg was the prime mover in this conspiracy. However, let no mistake be made about the role which his wife, Ethel Rosenberg, played in this conspiracy. Instead of deterring him from pursuing his ignoble cause, she encouraged and assisted the cause. She was a mature woman—almost three years older than her husband and almost seven years older than her younger brother. She was a full-fledged partner in this crime.

It was twelve noon. Directly behind the Court House on Duane Street is St. Andrew's Roman Catholic Church. At twelve o'clock, its bells began to roll and peal sonorous deep clangs, and higher pitched, more melodious chimes. The evenly spaced variations became louder and more rhythmic as the bells obtained swinging momentum and filled the courtroom with echoing sounds. Time and again, they have stopped proceedings as their immense waves drowned out the voices of witnesses and lawyers. Clerks seized huge poles and closed the windows, but the ringing sounds, like radio waves, entered easily, as if their religious origin would brook no interference from mundane activity.

When Judge Kaufman reached his final words, St. Andrew's bells began their accompanying din. His voice, flat, soft, and hoarse from emotion, struggled against their melodious thunder. The spectators strained to hear the judge as he denounced Ethel and Julius for placing their devotion to their cause above their own safety and consciously "sacrificing their own children, should their misdeeds be detected." His next words hurt them more than any others in the entire trial.

COURT Love for their cause dominated their lives—it was even greater than their love for their children.

As the judge's voice grew fainter from his own emotion, the bells became more dominating. Judge Kaufman tried to describe his own struggle between compassion and duty. His conscience had been troubled. He had gone to a synagogue to pray for guidance.

COURT What I am about to say is not easy for me. I have deliberated for hours, days and nights. I have carefully weighed the evidence. Every nerve, every fiber of my body has been taxed. I am convinced beyond any doubt of your guilt. I have searched the records —I have searched my conscience—to find some reason for mercy —for it is only human to be merciful and it is natural to try to spare lives. I am convinced, however, that I would violate the solemn and sacred trust that the people of this land have placed in my hands were I to show leniency to the defendants Rosenberg.

It is not in my power, Julius and Ethel Rosenberg, to forgive you. Only the Lord can find mercy for what you have done.

The Rosenbergs straightened up to prepare for the blow.

COURT The sentence of the Court upon Julius and Ethel Rosenberg is, for the crime for which you have been convicted you are hereby sentenced to the punishment of death, and it is ordered upon some day within the week beginning with Monday, May 21st, you shall be executed according to law.

Julius fell backward a step as if the judge's words had physically struck him in the chest. Ethel hung on to his hand.

There were cries of surprise and horror from the back of the room, which joined with St. Andrew's bells tolling doom. Reporters rushed out, startling the spectators with their haste. As the doors swung open repeatedly, the shouts outside spurted into the room, adding to the confusion.

(357)

The marshals mercifully stepped in quickly, took Ethel and Julius firmly under the arms, half lifting and leading them out of the back door to the elevator. When Julius reached the chair below, he collapsed into it. His restraint and control broke, and he burst into loud sobs, holding his head with his hands and swaying forward almost off his seat to the cement floor. Ethel seized him around the waist and tried to comfort him through her own tears. Bloch put his hands on their shoulders, his head sunken on his chest and his eyes closed. They formed a tableau of desolateness.

———>←———

Up above, court attendants had finally quieted the spectators, with repeated calls for orders.

CLERK For sentence, Morton Sobell.

Saypol said the court was familiar with the evidence and he had no statement to make.

Phillips made an appeal for a merciful sentence. He pointed out that Sobell did not transmit any information to a foreign power. At most, it could be argued that he was agreeable to others doing so. Not a single overt act was charged against him in the indictment.

Phillips argued that the statute did not prescribe minimum punishment—only maximum punishment. So he told the court that "You have the privilege to impose almost no sentence."

Sobell was invited to speak for himself if he wished to do so. He remained silent. The court proceeded to sentence him, offering a brief explanation first. He had "not the slightest sympathy" for him because he had undoubtedly been involved in espionage. But he had no part in the atom bomb theft, and "I cannot be moved by hysteria or motivated by a desire to do the popular thing." Since Sobell was involved to a lesser degree, he must take that into consideration.

COURT I, therefore, sentence you to the maximum prison term provided by statute, to wit, thirty years.

While it may be gratuitous on my part, I at this point note my recommendation against parole.

Mrs. Sobell's shriek was heard above the new outburst in the rear.

The court quickly announced an adjournment to the next day, April 6, 1951, for the sentencing of the confessed spy David Greenglass, who had been the government's most important witness.

———>←———

Saypol was placed in the unusual position of pleading for mercy for Greenglass, a defendant. He took great pains to explain the consideration due to those who co-operate with the government.

(358)

Crimes are not usually "committed by clerics, or barristers, or medics. It takes a thief to catch a thief." So it is the prosecutor who must decide what reward he will give to a culprit who exposes criminality. He cited a Supreme Court decision justifying non-prosecution of a criminal who confessed and made possible the conviction of his accomplices.

Saypol revealed for the first time how Ruth Greenglass had earned immunity. When David Greenglass was arrested, his attorney, Rogge, appeared and protested his innocence.

SAYPOL Through Ruth Greenglass, his wife, came the subsequent recantation of those protestations, their co-operation and the disclosure of the facts by both of them. They were told before that their conduct in these disclosures in no way implied any commitment to them regarding the prosecution of either.

It was now evident said Saypol that his decision not to indict Ruth was morally justified.

The question of David Greenglass' punishment involved similar considerations of reward for his assistance. The prosecutor held no brief for him. Greenglass would carry forever a moral and legal burden. The death penalty given to the Rosenbergs could easily have been his too. But there was in him now "an equitable right to mercy." The court ought, therefore, be inclined to recognize "the presence of penitence, contriteness, remorse and belated truth." He recommended that Greenglass receive a fifteen-year prison sentence.

O. John Rogge lost not a second in expressing his shock at the severity of this suggestion. He did not consider it showed mercy at all.

ROGGE If the Government wants help it must give help. If it wants people in the position of David Greenglass to come forward and co-operate, it must give him a pat on the back. It must give example to which investigative agencies can point, and say "Now, if you will be helpful, the Government will be helpful."

Even now, the whole story had not yet been told. If the government approached others to learn more, what incentive would there be for them to talk, if such sentences as thirty years to Gold, and fifteen years to Greenglass were all that they could look forward to?

The court wanted to know where Rogge would draw the line, when the penalty called for death or maximum of thirty years? He replied that anything in excess of five years would defeat the good purpose which a considerate sentence could have.

He then gave a sympathetic picture of the Greenglasses' background. They had married when he was twenty and she eighteen, and his mother had to accompany them because David was under age. They had two children, Stephen, four and a half, and Barbara, ten months.

He claimed that Julius Rosenberg tried to indoctrinate David into communism. He brought books and chemical sets to David's home when he was "a well-intentioned, impressionable lad of thirteen. He flattered him; David was going to be a scientist."

Ethel Rosenberg had made a similar effort to indoctrinate Ruth Greenglass. Ruth was only eighteen and looked up to Julius and Ethel, but she and David resisted the effort to make them Communists.

Yes, Dave and Ruth Greenglass wanted to see a better world, but not to see a Communist one.

When David went into the Army, he did not seek Los Alamos. The government sent him there. Although he made a misstep, he did not persist in it. He got out and "never liked it."

Rogge revealed incriminating facts against the Rosenbergs, some of which had not been disclosed, even at the trial.

ROGGE Julius wanted him to keep on at Los Alamos. He refused. David was given an offer to—and I think it was at a rather high salary—to go for six months on an atom bomb test out of the country. Julius wanted him to do it. He refused. Julius made him an offer to go to school for four years at $100 a week and maintenance, something which very much appealed to David at that time more than anything else. David refused him. Julius offered him an apartment rent free. David and Ruth refused. Julius in this last year gave David $5,000 to flee the country. David refused to do so.

However, when Rogge mentioned Greenglass' "fuzzy thinking" as typical of many important persons during the 1944 period, he ran into resistance from the judge.

COURT I want to make sure that I understand you. You are condoning, are you, that any individual in America had a right to set himself above his Government and determine what type of information should be furnished to Russia?

ROGGE I am not condoning that in the slightest, your Honor.

COURT I wanted to make certain of that.

Rogge persisted that there was an atmosphere at that time which should be considered in judging Greenglass' vulnerability. General Mac-Arthur had sent a warm telegram of congratulations to the Red Army. Judge Learned Hand was a member of the National Council of American-Soviet Friendship. President Roosevelt made many speeches praising the Russians. "Borough President Lyons, up in the Bronx, believe it or not, declared a 'Red Army Day.'"

COURT Well, let's get one thing clear. Russia didn't come to our aid in this war. We came to Russia's aid.

ROGGE That is quite true, Judge, but the point I am making is
that: Many people far wiser than David Greenglass spoke in
terms of aid and admiration for the Russians, and I say that—
COURT I am getting a bit confused by this argument, Mr. Rogge.
I want to make certain that you are not condoning any thinking
on the part of anybody, even at that time, who would determine
for himself or herself how much aid should be given Russia.

New light was shed on the government's success in rounding up the
conspirators. Greenglass' description of how Communists escaped from
the country had made possible the apprehension of Sobell.

Rogge revealed that he represented six people involved in the case:
David and Ruth Greenglass, Max Elitcher, his wife, Helene Elitcher,
Louis Abel and his wife, Dorothy Abel. His secretary, Helen Pagano,
had also testified for the government. It became clear that he had
guided them all to co-operate with the government, and he sought
to transfer the gratitude the prosecution owed him to consideration
for Greenglass. The judge apparently was aware of Rogge's assistance
and paid him a handsome tribute.

COURT I must say, Mr. Rogge, that I think that you have done
service to the profession and to the country in assisting these clients
who came to your office to think clearly on the subject, because
it is my opinion that a lawyer plays a vital part in clarifying in
a witness' or defendant's mind the proper thinking on the subject.
I am firmly of the opinion that it is the duty of a lawyer to
ascertain the truth and then to give the best type of advice in
his client's interest, and I believe you did it.

The "proper thinking" which Rogge had instilled in Greenglass
was, of course, a calculated strategy to save him from much worse.
Now Rogge was almost pleading to make good on his implied
promise to his client, that if he confessed, he would probably be rewarded with a very light sentence.

While it was not said, the fact was that Greenglass had been called
upon to do more than bare his soul as a spy. He had to suffer the
anguish of destroying his sister, a pain which would imprison him
for life. Was he not, like Faust, entitled to the temporary reward
for which he had sold his soul?

Punishment could be a deterrent, argued the lawyer, but it would not
deter political fanatics. They would persist in their rebellious ways. It
could deter non-malicious "fuzzy thinkers," like Greenglass, who would
seek lighter sentences by confessing. Why discourage them by severe
penalty?

Another purpose of a sentence was punitive. Greenglass had come
forward from the beginning and told the government all. "He should
be praised, not punished."

Finally, there was the objective of rehabilitation. Greenglass had quit the conspiracy long before he consulted counsel. He didn't need reform.

Whenever Rogge turned to arguments which might have been suitable for the Rosenbergs, too, he lost ground with the court. So when he launched on a demonstration that the information given by Greenglass was not as valuable as the government contended, he incurred the open opposition of the judge whom he was trying to persuade. But not before he urged that American publications were so informative that "the Russians didn't have to go through all the trouble that they do, if they just would read."

COURT Well, I don't think there is much point to that argument, Mr. Rogge, because your client testified—I believe he told the truth in every respect—testified to the vital character of the information which he gave to Julius Rosenberg; and, if you will recall, Dr. Koski, attested to the tremendous importance of this information.

Rogge abandoned the argument instantly, and turned to his last "topic." It involved a remote and circuitous argument that our troubles were due to a hasty disarmament and "bringing the boys home" too soon, thus leaving Russia in command. We ought not put the entire blame on the Greenglasses (and while he didn't say so, inferentially, the Rosenbergs) for our own sins.

He concluded with personal touches, which for the purpose of a lighter sentence, are more effective than sophisticated argument.

Greenglass had given blood during the Second World War. "I see he has an emblem on his coat today that he gave blood recently. This is the kind of man you have, a well-intentioned person, without malice."

He described his hard beginnings, being reared in a cold-water flat on the lower East Side. He had made a mistake, and atoned for it.

Rogge thought a sentence of one year and a day would be sufficient in view of Greenglass' "courageous cooperation." He wound up recommending three years.

Saypol insisted on the privilege of reply. He criticized Rogge's "arrogating to himself the function of the District Attorney" and advising the court what kind of sentence would be most helpful in future prosecution. He felt "that Rogge was stepping out of his role" in diminishing Greenglass' part in the "sordid" events. Those in the prosecutor's office charged with continuous investigation were "entirely in disagreement with" Rogge's thesis for so light a sentence.

COURT (To the defendant) Have you anything that you want to say?
GREENGLASS Nothing.

(362)

The judge stated that he did not intend to mete out a light sentence nor a heavy sentence, but "a just sentence within the framework of the facts in this particular case."

He was about to show some consideration to Greenglass, but not because he condoned his acts. "They were loathsome; they were contemptible." However, he wished to recognize Greenglass' help in bringing to justice "the arch criminals in this nefarious scheme, Julius Rosenberg and Ethel Rosenberg."

Greenglass had not added to his sins "by committing the additional crime of perjury." He had been of a great assistance to the government.

COURT   I realize the courage that was required for you to give your
testimony, and I must say that you were the recipient of the best
kind of legal advice in doing so.

He concluded that justice required balancing the gravity of Greenglass' offense against the aid he had given to the government. He would follow the prosecutor's recommendation.

I sentence you to fifteen years in prison.

An unhappy Greenglass was led away. Now it was Ruth Greenglass' turn to weep.

CHAPTER 34

The government has no federal execution chamber in the New York district. It was decided to execute the Rosenbergs in Sing Sing, New York State's prison, equipped for dealing death.

In the meantime, pending appeals, the defendants were to be kept in a detention prison in New York. Only if the appeals were unsuccessful would they be shipped to the death house in Sing Sing. This, too, presented a problem. There were no facilities in the Women's House of Detention for a woman who, like others sentenced to death, had to be kept in isolated quarters. So the government had to send Ethel to the death house in Sing Sing early. Julius remained in the temporary New York prison. While all this was being decided, the defendants were maintained in the small jail underneath the courtroom.

Understandably, Greenglass was kept apart from the other defendants. The Rosenbergs, Sobell and their attorneys were permitted to gather in the conference room next to the cells.

They huddled together theoretically for discussion, but more to banish the most terrible loneliness of all, that which is filled not with boredom, but with terror.

United States Marshal William Carrol had authorized a lunch conference. Ethel and Julius sat close to each other, their shoulders and legs touching to provide as much contact as possible. They were red-eyed and in despair. The Sobells sat next to them, she more dejected than he. Their lawyers were on the other side of the table. They nibbled on sandwiches, finding it difficult to swallow.

As in all such desultory meetings, the lawyers tried to lift the spirits of their clients with expressions of confidence in the ultimate outcome.

Bloch, looking as if he needed encouragement himself, nevertheless said: "Remember this is only the first round. We have an excellent chance—an excellent chance on appeal."

Julius had his mind on other things. "Please, somebody call my mother and, if she doesn't know, try to break the news to her gently."

Phillips continued "Operation Hope": "I have practiced law for more than fifty years. I have never seen a clearer reversible record. Keep your courage up. These verdicts will never stand."

"We have a fine Circuit Court of Appeals," continued Bloch. "They are not only brilliant judges, who will pierce the many legal errors made during this trial, but Jerome Frank sits on it. He is a liberal judge, sensitive to the rights of the individual. He will never stand for the prejudicial atmosphere which railroaded all of you."

The mood brightened under these verbal ministrations. Even though they suspected that the words were sedative pills, not cures, they welcomed them. Their lawyers should be confident. It increased their effectiveness. The mere utterance of hope cushioned their forebodings. It was a welcome offset to the nightmares which persisted during their waking hours.

"Do you think they will permit us to see the children?" asked Ethel. "They are old enough to understand. Tell Tessie to have someone talk to them who can explain our innocence, and that we'll be back."

"We have already taken care of it," Bloch assured her. "Don't worry. Children are resilient. You know how they take even death— I mean they will accept the news with hope. I will arrange for visits with you."

Rosenberg voiced the concern which the lawyers felt too, but suppressed. "I know you are right about the legal situation—the chances on appeal. That would be true if this was any other kind of case, even a murder trial. But communism has been dragged into our case. It has poisoned the air. There is hysteria in the country. The government is really trying to stifle dissent and we are the guinea pigs. I am afraid we cannot get a fair hearing anywhere."

"Don't say that," Bloch insisted. "Our courts have reversed cases time and again involving sensitive political issues. I think the very inflamed atmosphere in which the case was tried, will be an excellent ground for appeal.

"The thing is a joke. The judge tells the jury communism is not the issue, but he lets in all the prejudicial stuff about Communist activity through the back door—motive, motive!"

Ethel spoke up bitterly. "I resented most the judge's comments about how we let down the children. What does he know about our love for the children? What kind of animals does he think we are?"

There was a reason for her special hurt. A completely outrageous accusation doesn't pain much. It can be ridiculed. Few believe it. More

(366)

important, the victim doesn't, so he does not suffer from the recognition of the truth. But an accusation that is even half true rankles and festers. Julius, and particularly Ethel, never got over the judge's condemnation of them for "sacrificing their children." Even his death sentence did not make them hate him as much as his slur on them as parents. The reason was that they knew subconsciously, at least, that there was some validity to the accusation. They had failed their children even before their arrest. Although brimming with love, they had not communicated it sufficiently to Michael and Bobby to prevent their neurotic behavior. Hadn't their intense activity for a better Communist world deprived their children of a better home? A happy home, goes a proverb, is an early heaven. The Rosenbergs may have begun to suspect that in searching for a heaven for society, they had denied their children a heaven at home. Furthermore, their activities (even on the assumption that they were innocent of espionage) had involved them in a tragedy, not only to themselves, but to their children. Little wonder that Ethel kept harping on the judge's comment about the children. It had pierced the outer shell we all have to protect us against a complete lie. Half lies seep through such armor.

Bloch was sensitive to all this. He had not limited himself to legal service. He had undertaken paternal care of the children, and, therefore, understood and felt her anguish. Now that she cried out, it released his own pent-up emotions, resulting from the shock of the verdict and, to him, the unspeakably extreme sentence. He exploded in self-recrimination.

"If only I had been able to shake up the Greenglasses on cross. They are responsible for everything. But I failed. I did nothing to them. Or if I had forbidden you to take the Fifth Amendment. After all, the jury knew you were Communists, what good did it do? If I had to do it over again—"

Ethel Rosenberg leaned over and patted Bloch on the hand comfortingly. "Don't blame yourself. You did everything you could. It is not your fault. With the way things are in this country today, we would have been convicted if there was no testimony."

Bloch looked up gratefully at her and squeezed her hand in appreciation.

The United States marshal directed that Sobell be taken back to the Tombs and that his wife should leave. He then placed Julius and Ethel Rosenberg in two separate but adjoining cells near the conference room for the night. One of the marshals told Julius that they were waiting for instructions from Washington whether to transfer them immediately to Sing Sing.

Julius feared that Ethel might hear this. He called out to her in the next cell:

"Ethel, don't be scared if some clown tells you we may be taken to the death house tonight. Everything will be all right. They won't do it."

To give him assurance, Ethel began to sing. The marshal and other prisoners were startled. She sang "Un Bel Dì Vedromo," ("One Fine Day He Shall Return") from Puccini's *Madame Butterfly*, a message of hope. Her coloratura small voice fluttered with tearfulness.

When she finished, Julius called out, "Ethel, the other one."

She sang "Ah Dolce Notte! Quante Stelle!" from the same opera. Then she said softly, "Are you all right, dear?"

"Fine. Sing some more."

She sang the popular ballad of the day, "Goodnight, Irene."

As if he had to respond, Julius sang "The Battle Hymn of the Republic." His voice was bad and he had trouble reaching notes, but the guards and other prisoners were moved by the communication in song.

The next morning they were both taken to the House of Detention in a large prison van (Julius to the prison on West Street, and Ethel to the Women's House of Detention on Greenwich Avenue). They were separated by a steel mesh screen, which divided men from women prisoners. When the doors were locked, there was pitch blackness. A prisoner struck a match for her cigarette. In the flickering light, she saw Ethel and Julius flattened against the mesh screen, frozen in an endless kiss. She quickly put out the match without lighting the cigarette. The van drove on in darkness.

The Rosenbergs would not be executed in the week of May 21, 1951, as the judge had directed. The law grants automatic stays to permit time for appeals. The Blochs, father and son, and their associate, Miss Agrin, slaved on an appellate brief, night after night. There are illimitable possibilities in the presentation of facts and law to make a brief persuasive. The Blochs "squeezed every drop of blood" out of the record, as the saying goes among lawyers. The selective process of emphasis and organization is not mere totaling of points, but a creative effort. The result is larger than the sum of its parts. The form and placement of the arguments can create momentum toward the desired conclusion which sweeps away contrary considerations.

The Blochs made deep research of the law, raising no less than twenty-five points of alleged errors. Furthermore, the writing was as felicitous as it was eloquent. Like singers who have favorite registers and feel uncomfortable in others, lawyers, too, have greater strengths in some areas. The Blochs and Miss Agrin were more particularly effective in brief writing. Their printed arguments were of the highest order in learning and persuasive presentation.

When the lawyers had agreed with the prosecutor on the accuracy of the printed record, which is called "settling the record," corrected the proofs of the brief, and sent it to the printer, they had time to visit Ethel, who was then ensconced in death row in Sing Sing.

CHAPTER 35

Ethel was advised that her attorney had arrived. The opportunity to leave her cage was a thrill. To converse with her lawyer and gratify her burning curiosity gave meaning to the day. Her matron escorted her to the lawyer's conference room. She embraced and kissed Bloch heartily, saying, "How glad I am to see you, Manny."

A client facing death sees in her lawyer not merely an adviser, but a friend and champion. He is her only and last hope. No other professional relationship, not even psychiatry, creates such dependence. The lawyer, understanding this, must be unusually careful, lest by a flicker of his eyelid, he should reveal a doubt, which, due to her hypersensitivity, may bring about a hysterical reaction. Bloch's personal warmth and devotion lifted Ethel out of periods of despondency which came frequently during the coming struggles.

He observed that she looked haggard and unkempt. Her face, without lipstick, looked like a white slate. She was carelessly dressed, even in simple gray prison garb, which took no effort for neatness. After a few moments of chatting about Julius, who was still in the House of Detention in New York, and the children, he told her he had come to report.

"Ethel, I have good news. Our appeal has been filed, and this automatically stays the execution date of May 21st, indefinitely. Not only am I confident that we will reverse the verdict, but even if worst comes to worst, there is the Supreme Court for final review, and many other legal moves. So please take the May date out of your mind. It will be years before a final decision, and you will walk out free. I am sure."

"How did Julius take it?" she asked.

"Of course, he was relieved, even though I think he was confident anyhow. He sends you his love. He said he wishes they would transfer him here too, because then I will be able to arrange for you to see each other at conferences with me."

"That would be wonderful."

"Here, I brought you some reading matter. I know you will be interested in these books."

He gave her Beard's *The Rise of American Civilization* and Vernon Parrington's *Main Currents in American Thought.*

"I also brought you some sheet music. This is Brahms' 'Lieder' and songs by Schubert and Schumann."

Ethel accepted them eagerly. Her wan face showed the first sign of excitement.

"And oh, yes, believe it or not, I had to go to five stores to get this." He handed her a plastic pitch pipe.

"You see, they don't permit any metal to be taken in. Now where do you think one can find a plastic pitch pipe?"

She blew it. "You're a darling." She kissed him.

"Now, tell me, Ethel, how are your spirits? How are you getting on?"

"Well, I am the only woman in a death cell. I have the distinction of occupying the same cell from which Martha Beck was executed. Oh, don't worry. I don't consider it an evil omen. There have been so few of us. I read that the only other woman ever condemned to die by a federal court was Mary Surratt. She was hanged for her part in the Lincoln assassination. Good company, huh, Manny?"

"I would suggest you read less morbid material."

"When did you see the children last?"

"Not for a week. They are getting on as well as can be expected. I can bring them now. When do you want to see them?"

"Not yet. It is eight months now, but I will wait until Julius gets here. I do not want them to visit each of us separately. We will plan to see them together. You can help us arrange it, can't you, so that the shock will be as little as possible?"

"Of course. When Julius gets here, we can have a joint meeting once a month. Then we'll bring the children in while all of us are present."

"Wonderful. Julius and I will have to prepare a campaign of how to treat them, when they know where we are and what may happen to us." Bloch saw her slipping away to despair, and he chopped away her mood.

"The real purpose of my visit is to cheer you up a bit. Look at you— no lipstick, hair all over the place. Come on, you have had so much courage up to now. Don't let up."

"Wait till Julius gets here. I'll doll up to kill."

"I'll come back soon, and I will bring you the best present of all, a passport to freedom, our appeal brief to the Circuit Court of Appeals. We have all worked like dogs to make it irresistibly persuasive. We present twenty-five separate legal points for reversal, and each of them has merit."

"I am dying to read it."

"Watch your language, lady."

They burst into laughter.

CHAPTER 36

There is a "cluster" phenomenon in nature which defies explanation. At infrequent periods in history several geniuses appear at the same time. Usually they know each other. Their fame will last through the centuries. Then a century or two later, another cluster of transcendent, talented men will dominate the scene, and like comets disappear, their like not to blaze across the horizon for hundreds of years. Shakespeare and Bacon are an unforgettable cluster. Leonardo da Vinci and Verrocchio worked together. During their lifetime, Michelangelo and Raphael vied with each other in exhibitions. Da Vinci and Michelangelo compared their work in Florence in 1504.

Two centuries later—Mozart, Beethoven, Hayden and Schubert.

A century later—Brahms, Liszt and Schumann.

In the philosophical field—Voltaire, Rousseau and Diderot.

This "cluster" phenomenon has occurred among scientists, violinists and judges. Holmes, Brandeis and Hughes sat on the Supreme Court at the same time. The Court of Appeals of New York at one time was presided over by Chief Judge Benjamin Cardozo, who was flanked by Pound, Lehman and Crane—all giants in the law. Indeed, this particular court had such prestige that its opinions were honored by judges throughout the nation, and many a tribute was paid to it by the Supreme Court.

The Rosenberg appeal came before a court which had a "cluster" of brilliant judges. The great Learned Hand was the Chief Judge. With him sat Jerome Frank, Augustus N. Hand, Thomas W. Swan and Harrie B. Chase.

Lawyers are always eager to know who the trial judge or appellate judges are who will preside over their case. If justice was an abstract ideal, untouched by the judge's mind processes and predilections, it would not matter who was sitting. But it does, because interpretive discretion is necessary, and it is shaped by indefinable forces. Whatever their origin or mysterious their application, they do not long remain unrecognized. We speak of some judges as "plaintiffs' judges" and others as "defendants' judges." Their decisions have marked them. Some judges are more compassionate than others. Although they instruct juries not to permit sympathy to affect their judgment, their own conclusions usually favor those who have suffered. Who can say whether the heart has interfered with the purity of the intellectual process?

If the Rosenbergs had had the choice of selecting one judge in the entire nation to review their appeal and write an opinion, it would have been Judge Jerome Frank. As was evident from his extensive writings he, more than even Learned Hand or Cardozo, was philosophically conditioned toward every argument for reversal which they made. In the first place, he was a passionate exponent of civil rights. Long before those words achieved popular identity, he had espoused them in books and dissertations which drew from Aristotle's philosophy of respect for the individual. He was the only judge who considered and answered every communication from a prison inmate. He despised mob prejudice such as engendered by the McCarthy crusade. He wrote eruditely about legislative encroachment on the individual's exclusive domain. More important, he had written *Courts on Trial*, a most penetrating analysis of judicial tyranny. So he would be most sensitive to the insidious impact of the word "Communist" on the impartiality of the judicial process. He had, time and again, unerringly pierced the formalism of a trial to detect ugly bias, sometimes flowing right from the judge's bench. It could not escape his eye because it was disguised as innocent inquiry to develop the facts. So he was attuned to Rosenberg's charges that the jury had been unfairly influenced by the judge's comments and questioning.

Furthermore, he was the enunciator of a theory which criticized our fact-finding processes. His book *Law and the Modern Mind* had received international attention in scholarly circles. He virtually psychoanalyzed the process by which we selected the truth from conflicting testimony, and pointed out its perils and defects. He delved into the uncertainty of memory and the emotional impact which distorted fact. He did more. He weighed the myriad elements which affected a jury or judge in determining the truth, and made us conscious of the subjective elements affecting the decider of the facts. Since these stimuli were changeable, the risks were even greater than we had supposed.

Despite his profundity, he was a gay and kindly man. He reveled in humor. His coruscating and restless mind developed different approaches to his theory of fact skepticism. He justified his repetition with an illustration:

Mr. Smith of Denver was introduced to Mr. Jones at a dinner party in Chicago. "Oh," said Jones, "do you know my friend Mr. Schnicklefritz, who lives in Denver?" "No," answered Smith. Later in the evening, when Smith referred to Denver, Jones again asked whether Smith was acquainted with Schnicklefritz, and again received a negative reply. As the dinner party broke up, Smith remarked that he was leaving that night for Denver, and Jones once more inquired whether Smith knew Schnicklefritz. "Really," came the answer, "his name sounds quite familiar."

To him the law was like the wanderer Ulysses, "a part of all he has met," and "an arch through which gleams that untraveled world whose margin fades forever when we move."

Most important from the Rosenberg point of view was his abhorrence of capital punishment, first, because he didn't believe it deterred crime; and second, because of his "fact skepticism," he feared convicting and executing the wrong person.

The appeal was argued on January 10, 1952. The court sat silently during a lengthy argument giving no indication of its reactions to the many contentions. A month and a half later, on February 25, 1952, the court clerk called Bloch and government counsel to announce that the court's opinion had been filed. The lawyers rushed to the courthouse to obtain a copy. Breathlessly they turned to the last page. Was the conviction reversed? Was the death penalty commuted?

—→←—

Frank, Circuit Judge:

> Since two of the defendants must be put to death if the judgments stand, it goes without saying that we have scrutinized the record with extraordinary care to see whether it contains any of the errors asserted on this appeal.

This assurance of thoroughness was demonstrated in the twenty-four-page printed opinion which followed. It was a meticulous review of the facts; a scholarly testing of the law; and a detailed analysis of every grievance presented in the defendants' briefs and arguments. It was clear that the three judges had studied and absorbed every line of the testimony. They set forth their analysis and conclusion on each point.

This was in accordance with a tradition that judges should reveal themselves in their opinions. Due to the backlog of appeals, courts sometimes save time by writing "Affirmed. No Opinion." How are the litigants to know why the judge rejected their assignment of errors? If the appellate judges have erred, a higher court may review their opinions and reverse. But if the lower court has not exposed its reasoning, the

(375)

higher court must sail into a fog of silence with no compass points to guide it except the original record and the result. Judge Frank's opinion was a model of explicitness.

The Rosenbergs' lawyer had, with great ingenuity, raised legal questions about the validity of the Espionage Act and the sufficiency of the indictment. Did the government have to prove only that the information given to a foreign nation was of advantage to it, or also that the result was "to injure the United States"? The prosecutor had presented evidence to prove the former, but there was no direct testimony of injury to the United States. Judge Frank held that was not necessary. He cited the Gorin case in the United States Supreme Court on this point. That case had also held that it made no difference whether the information was given to a friendly or hostile nation. "Unhappily, the status of a foreign government may change." Therefore, he upheld Judge Kaufman's charge to the jury that it may not consider the fact that at the time the secrets were pilfered, Russia was our ally.

Bloch's brief also claimed that the indictment was defective because it did not say that the stolen information had not previously been made public. If it had, there would be no secret. Judge Frank not only analyzed Supreme Court decisions which upheld the language of the indictment, but pointed out that one of the overt acts referred to the receipt of sketches by Julius from Los Alamos, "a good indication that the material involved was secret."

A criminal statute must not be vague. If it is, it is unconstitutional. The reason is that a citizen should not be entrapped by ambiguity. The statute must be clear enough, so that it gives fair warning to an average man of what he may or may not do. He should not be required to guess at his peril. Since intention to commit a crime is essential to guilt, how can one have such intention, if he is not sure that what he does is a crime?

Rosenbergs' counsel raised the issue of vagueness. What, they argued, is the meaning of "National Defense"? Judge Frank carefully explored the contention. The Supreme Court in the Gorin case had passed on this very point, and held that National Defense referred to military and naval establishments and national preparedness. That language "was sufficiently definite to apprise the public of prohibited activities and is consonant with due process."

The Rosenbergs had also raised the point that giving information to a foreign government was communication, and to prohibit it, violated free speech and the First Amendment guarantee. Judge Frank rejected this contention with brief incisiveness. Having disposed of the basic legal challenges to the statute itself, the court turned to arguments involving the evidence.

The main attack was on the reliability of testimony by self-confessed spies, "and particularly the credibility of the Greenglasses, one of whom the Government has not prosecuted and the other of whom received a relatively mild sentence."

Judge Frank agreed that if the Greenglass testimony was disregarded, "the conviction could not stand."

> But where trial is by jury, this court is not allowed to consider the credibility of witnesses or the reliability of testimony. Particularly in the federal judicial system, that is the jury's province.

That "province" included, of course, the "sizing up" of the witnesses, an invaluable determinant, not available to appellate judges. Furthermore, Judge Frank pointed out the "warning" given to the jury by Judge Kaufman that the testimony of the Greenglasses and Gold must be scrutinized carefully and "with caution" because they were accomplices.

> So instructed, the jury found defendants guilty. Faced with such a verdict, this court is obligated to assume that the jury believed the evidence unfavorable to the defendants. On that assumption, the evidence to sustain the verdict is more than ample.

The opinions then turned to the grievance "that the trial judge behaved himself so improperly as to deprive the Rosenbergs of a fair trial."

As would be expected of Judge Frank, whose antennae were sensitive to such a charge, he examined the matter with microscopic thoroughness.

Bloch, he said, had first broached this suggestion on a motion for mistrial after all the evidence had been heard. Even then, he had called the judge's action "inadvertent" and added that the judge had "been extremely courteous to us and afforded us lawyers every privilege that a lawyer should expect in a criminal case."

> Soon after the denial of this motion, counsel for the Rosenbergs, summing up for the jury, stated that "we feel that the trial has been conducted . . . with that dignity and that decorum that befits an American trial." Still later, the same counsel said that "the court conducted itself as an American judge." These remarks, by a highly competent and experienced lawyer, are not compatible with the complaints now made.

Up to this point in the opinion, it might have appeared that Bloch's comments waived an otherwise just grievance. Judge Frank was not one to deny justice to a defendant because his lawyer had made a generous gesture to a judge who had the power of imprisoned life or death over his clients. He searched the record and found that Judge Kaufman had "stayed well inside the discretion allowed him" and the complaints against his conduct were undeserved. In this way, he really absolved Bloch of responsibility. How had Judge Frank come to this conclusion?

(377)

He applied his judicial scalpel to each accusation against the trial judge. Had he taken too active a part in the trial process by his questioning of witnesses? The charge was that he had thereby:

(1) emphasized key points of the government's case; (2) protected and rehabilitated government witnesses; (3) commented on evidence as immaterial or dismissed contradictions brought out by defense attorney as not very important or convincing; (4) examined the defendants with hostility. We have carefully examined each of the hundred or so incidents cited by defendants.

Judge Frank was not content with analyzing "the hundred or so incidents." He set forth detailed illustrations in each category. For example, under the heading of "alleged emphasizing of key points of the Government case," he cited the instance when Dorothy Abel was being cross-examined, and she quoted Julius as criticizing our government because it was "capitalistic . . . that is about all I can remember." The judge asked whether that was the reason that the Rosenbergs assigned for preferring the Russian form of government, and she replied, "Yes."

As an illustration of "alleged protecting and rehabilitating of Government witnesses," Judge Frank cited the instance when Elitcher was under cross-examination and admitted that he had not remembered being at Julius' home, Christmas 1946. Bloch asked, "You forgot about that?" Judge Kaufman commented:

He wasn't asked about it if I remember and it might have been nothing to the Government's case. There is a certain inference in your question that he deliberately withheld it.

Another instance was Ruth Greenglass' answer on cross-examination that she didn't know the printed language on the Jell-O box side, and that she didn't consider that "pertinent." The court intervened to ask "What was important to you?" thus drawing the answer that it was matching the pieces for identification.

As an illustration of "alleged improper comments on evidence," Judge Frank cited the instance when Ruth Greenglass was asked by Bloch to repeat certain testimony, and he claimed that it was a "verbatim repetition of her direct testimony." When the prosecutor objected, the court said:

COURT Your objection is sustained. I don't know exactly what the point is. If the witness has left out something, Mr. Bloch would say the witness didn't repeat the story accurately, and the witness repeats it accurately and apparently that isn't good.

As an illustration of "alleged hostile examination of defendants," Judge Frank quoted the court's questioning of Julius:

"What were your own views about the subject matter of the United States having any weapon that Russia didn't have at that time? That is, in 1944 and 1945."

"A I don't recall having any views at all about it."

"Q Your mind was a blank on the subject. . . . There were never any discussions about it at all."

"A Not about that, not about the weapon."

Another instance was when Julius told Ethel that David Greenglass was attempting to "blackmail" him. The trial judge intervened with these questions:

"Court:

"Q Blackmail you. When did he try to blackmail you?"

"A Well, he threatened me to get money. I considered it blackmailing me."

"Q What did he say he would do if you didn't give it to him? You said he said you would be sorry."

"A Yes. I consider it blackmail when somebody says that."

"Q Did he say what he would do to you?"

"A No, he didn't."

"Q Did he say he would go to the authorities and tell them you were in a conspiracy with him to steal the atomic bomb secret?"

"A No."

"Q Do you think that was what he had in mind?"

"A How could I know what he had in mind."

"Q What do you mean by blackmail then?"

"A Maybe he threatened to punch me in the nose or something like that."

Having given illustrations in each category, Judge Frank addressed himself to the proper function of a trial judge in a federal court.

He ruled that "in general we can find no purpose in the judge's questioning except that of clarification." A judge has the "unchallenged power" to bring out the facts of the case. If there is a contradiction in a witness' testimony and the judge gives him an opportunity to resolve it, it is not wrong even if it "took away defendants' temporary advantage with the jury."

He cited the classic language in the Simon case (in which the United States Supreme Court had denied certiorari):

It cannot be too often repeated or too strongly emphasized that the function of a federal trial judge is not that of an umpire or of a moderator at a town meeting. He sits to see that justice is done in the cases heard before him; and it is his duty to see that a case on trial is presented in such a way as to be understood by the jury, as well as by himself. He should not hesitate to ask questions for the

(379)

purpose of developing the facts; and it is no ground of complaint that the facts so developed may hurt or help one side or the other. . . . The judge is the only disinterested lawyer connected with the proceeding.

Judge Frank explained that a federal judge "may comment outright on any portion of the evidence, telling the jury how it struck him, whom he believed, or disbelieved, provided only that he advises the jury that they are in no way bound by his expressions of such views." He backed up this rule of law by citing many Supreme Court cases.

In the Rosenberg trial, Judge Kaufman had not gone at all as far as he had the right to go, and besides he had given the most emphatic charge to the jury, which Judge Frank quoted, to the effect that if a juror had obtained any impression of the judge's opinion of guilt or innocence, he must "put it out" of his mind and "utterly disregard it." The trial judge had borne down as heavily as words would permit on the fact that the jurors "were the exclusive judges of the facts in this case; you, and you alone, will pass on the credibility of witnesses."

Should the judge be merely an impartial referee, as he is required to be in most state courts, or an active participant in the trial, as he is permitted to be in the federal courts? The question poses another illustration of a philosophical dilemma.

Historically, the Anglo-Saxon tradition was that the judge should question witnesses closely, criticize or aid counsel, and even indicate his belief or disbelief of testimony, all to achieve a just result. The federal courts adopted this rule. The advantage is that an experienced judge, who has no ax to grind for either party, prevents the trial from becoming a game, in which the more skillful lawyer may have an advantage. It provides at least a partial answer to those who complain that the affluent who retain the ablest counsel may prevail in an unjust case. The judge keeps the scales of justice even by his intervention. Such a judge may help a floundering lawyer, or even guide him in making necessary motions to protect his client. Time and again, I have heard such a judge say, "Objection sustained," when the neophyte lawyer failed to object as he should have.

The danger of such a rule is that judges, like other men, need little help to become tyrannical. Given the power to conduct, rather than preside over the trial, they may interfere with the lawyers who have the advantage of thorough preparation, and thus prevent the fairest presentation of a complicated case. The judge who takes the case out of the hands of the lawyers, and tries it for them, may often unbalance the judicial procedure, not because his intentions are not of the best, but because he doesn't know the facts and applicable law which the attorneys painstakingly studied for months. The "take charge" judge may wish to speed up things and get to the root of the matter, but in doing so he may deprive one side or the other of an opportunity to develop the facts. Such judges are frequently reversed, and the timesaving becomes time wasting.

The power of the judge to participate in the development of the facts is salutary, provided it is combined with humility. The know-it-all judge steps in where not only angels, but advocates fear to tread, and thus unwittingly creates reversible error. One of the reasons is that in the course of cross-examining witnesses, he may be caught up in the fires of battle. He may be rebuffed by a skillful witness and, in his frustration, become emotionally involved. These are the human hazards which abstract theoreticians often underestimate.

The judicial system tries to provide against such imperfections. It has its own checks and balances. The law requires the judge to tell the jury that it may disregard his views. It is their evaluation of the witnesses which counts, not his. In this way, the jurors may listen to his appraisal of witnesses but are instructed by him that they may ignore his views.

The state courts follow the opposite rule. A judge must be neutral in manner and conduct. If he comments on credibility or is partisan in his questions, the verdict will be reversed. The reasoning is that a jury usually looks at the judge with respect and even awe. His high position gives him unusual influence over them. No matter what precautions are taken to preserve the jurors' predominant role as fact finders, they will not readily shed the judge's opinions. Therefore, it is contended that the purity of the judicial process is best preserved if we limit the judge to legal rulings, and keep him out of the fact-finding process.

Obviously, the question of which is the better rule is a difficult one. As all this applied to the Rosenberg case, the Appellate Court held that it was clear that Judge Kaufman had not availed himself of all the permissible prerogatives to question witnesses and comment on their testimony. His intrusions were very limited, and Judge Frank held that they were elucidating rather than prejudicial. Even if one thought otherwise, Judge Kaufman's instructions to the jury were emphatic models of neutrality, and wiped out the momentary incidents of possible prejudice in a long trial, where a comment or question here or there recedes into the background and becomes a blur in the total context of the dispute. In this sense, Bloch's compliments to the judge that he tried the case as an American trial should be conducted was a sincere over-all appraisal, rather than courteous expression.

Judge Frank turned to the most serious point the Rosenbergs raised, and one to which he would be most likely to incline. He analyzed the issue of communism as it affected the trial. He referred to the evidence that the Rosenbergs "expressed a preference for the Russian social and economic system over ours" and that they were Communists. Did this evidence inflame the jury against them? Was it competent "to show that they would commit espionage for Russia?"

We think the evidence possessed relevance. An American's devotion to another country's welfare cannot of course constitute proof that he has spied for that other country. But the jurors may reasonably infer that he is more likely to spy for it than other Americans not similarly devoted. Hence this attitude bears on a possible motive for his spying, or on a possible intent to do so when there is other evidence in the case that he did such spying. We have held such testimony admissible in a similar case involving espionage for Nazi Germany.

The next question, said Judge Frank, was more difficult. Was evidence of Rosenberg's membership in the Communist Party relevant or just prejudicial? It was relevant if the government could prove that such membership was a tie to Russia and, therefore, created a motive or intent to aid Russia. He quoted Judge Kaufman's instructions to the jury, early in the trial:

> "I want you to understand right at the outset that the fact that they were members of the Communist Party does not establish the elements necessary to prove them guilty."

Elizabeth Bentley had offered testimony that the American Communist Party took its orders from Russia. If the jury believed her, she supplied "the missing link" which made Communist membership "probative of intent to aid Russia."

"Of course," wrote Judge Frank, "such evidence can be highly inflammatory in a jury trial." Therefore, how much of such kind of evidence should come into a trial is a matter "for carefully exercised judicial discretion." He held that Judge Kaufman had not abused that discretion. Each time Party membership was alluded to, and again in his final charge, the judge warned the jury not to determine guilt or innocence on whether the defendant was a Communist. If the crime itself was proved, Communist membership simply supplied a motive.

There followed a remarkable passage in which Judge Jerome Frank set forth his theory of "fact skepticism" which had shaken up the legal fraternity:

> It may be that such warnings are no more than an empty ritual without any practical effect on the jurors. If so, this danger is one of the risks run in a trial by jury; and the defendants made no effort to procure a trial by a judge alone, under Criminal Rule 23(a).

The assumption that unlike a jury, a judge would have been impervious to possible prejudice from Rosenbergs' communism is, of course, highly questionable. Judge Kaufman's strictures, when he sentenced them, showed his deep concern with the Communist menace.

Judge Frank's observation about the risk of jury prejudice may have been a just critique of human frailty no matter how many safeguards we construct to insure godly impartiality. But, at least in a jury, there is the chance of canceling out prejudice through multiple judgments. There is a small army of twelve to attack one another's conscience. The risk where a trial judge alone makes the decision is no less than when a jury does. For who can be sure that the blows and triumphs of his life have not conditioned him to a prejudicial view, even though he strives for fairness and is unaware of the forces which have battered against his high purpose and fashioned his judgment? I had occasion to exchange philosophical views with Judge Frank on this subject, but except for the immense stimulation I received from his learning and agile mind, I was not convinced, and remained a champion for the jury system, and he held fast to his own convictions. We did agree that the objective of perfect justice was not attainable, and that we were both looking for the best methodology to overcome the defects inherent in any activity managed by man.

The appellate opinion then delved into the defendants' argument that certain testimony which Elitcher gave was hearsay and, therefore, improperly received. It related to Sobell's quoting Rosenberg that there was nothing to worry about because although he talked once to Elizabeth Bentley on the phone, she didn't know who he was. Bloch had not objected to this testimony and "the record shows that defendants' counsel was singularly astute and conscientious," and may have chosen deliberately not to do so. In a footnote, the opinion pointed out that if the failure to object is due to incompetence, the Appellate Court will consider the matter as if proper objection had been made.

The record in this case showed that the hearsay evidence was corroborated by other testimony. Greenglass had quoted Rosenberg as saying that Elizabeth Bentley "probably knew him." Therefore, it was no error to permit Bentley to testify that she received phone calls from a man who called himself "Julius" and that as a go-between for Golos and "Julius," she learned that Rosenberg lived in Knickerbocker Village.

Also Greenglass had sworn that Rosenberg told him an emissary would contact him in Los Alamos, bearing greetings from "Julius." Gold had used the password "I come from Julius." It was, therefore, no error for the judge to leave it to the jury to accept or reject the inference that it was Rosenberg who spoke to Bentley.

Another specification of error claimed by the Rosenbergs was Judge Kaufman's statement to the jury that there were tensions among nations and that "our national well-being requires that we guard against spying on the secrets of our defense."

In this way, the appellants argued, the jurors were asked to yield to their emotional bias, and that "it would be a reflection" on their patriotism, "if they returned a verdict other than guilty." Judge Frank answered:

> We do not agree. For the judge also said that he did "not mean that the mere allegation or use of the word 'espionage' should justify convicting innocent persons"; and he cautioned the jurors that it was their duty "to approach [the] task of determining the issues with . . . minds completely barren of prejudice or sympathy," to "weigh the evidence in this case calmly and dispassionately."

It could hardly be contended that the jury was given "a green light to convict on emotions rather than evidence."

The appellate opinion disposed with equal care contentions about Judge Kaufman's inadequate instructions to the jury concerning the Greenglasses; the charge that the evidence of Rosenberg's spiriting away a proximity fuse should not have been received; and that the sketches of the bomb drawn by Greenglass should not have been admitted. After analysis, Judge Frank held that none of those grievances were meritorious.

The defendants stressed the "error" which Judge Kaufman had made when he complied with the jury's request to read a portion of Ruth Greenglass' testimony, but refused to read the cross-examination of the same subject matter unless the jury specifically asked for it. When the direct testimony had been read, the judge asked the jury whether that was what they wanted. They said, "Yes." In the presence of the jury, Bloch requested that the cross-examination also be read, and the judge again ruled that he would do so if the jury requested it. They remained silent.

Furthermore, Judge Frank pointed out that the cross-examination in this instance did not attempt to contradict the direct. On the contrary, its purpose was to show such close repetition as to indicate that it was a rehearsed falsehood. Bloch had made this argument to the jury in summation only a short time before. If the jury had been impressed with it and wanted to review the parroted version, it would have asked for it, particularly when it heard Bloch's request.

> Accordingly, we hold that the refusal to have the cross read was within the trial judge's discretion.

The final point reviewed involved the last witness, Schneider the photographer. His name was not on the witness list. But he was not known or subpoenaed until the morning before he testified. The witness rule does not apply to rebuttal witnesses. They may be called to refute unanticipated testimony, and therefore notice cannot be given weeks in advance.

The next question was whether Schneider was really a rebuttal witness. Did he answer a new charge or did he merely corroborate what the

government had already claimed, that the Rosenbergs had taken passport photos in preparation for flight? The Appellate Court was not
unanimous on this subject. By a vote of two out of three, Judge Frank
being in a minority, it held that Schneider was a rebuttal witness. But
the court was unanimous that the testimony should have been received
in any event. The only possible remedy was for the defense lawyers to
claim surprise and ask for a brief adjournment. They did not do so. Had
they made such a request and been denied, "it might have been error."

The judge considered the argument that the photographer Schneider,
according to later revelation, had been brought to the courtroom by the
FBI the morning before he testified and that his statement on the stand
that he had not seen the Rosenbergs since the time he photographed
them was therefore false.

On the motion for a new trial before District Judge Ryan, he ruled
that this misstatement, if it was a misstatement, was immaterial. The
Court of Appeals held that it was, in fact, hardly a misstatement, since
the court understood it to mean that the photographer had not seen
them between the time when he took their picture and the time of the
trial, rather than the specific day on which he testified.

Before taking up the question of the death sentences, the opinion
addressed itself to Sobell's appellate points. One of these was so impressive that Judge Frank felt Sobell should receive a new trial. However,
the majority disagreed and upheld the verdict. He expressed his dissenting view.

It involved a philosophical question, which to the uninitiated might
sound like the ancient debate of the metaphysicians of how many angels
could stand on the head of a pin. Actually it was a profound interpreta-
tive dilemma, and a man's incarceration for thirty years or his possible
freedom hung in the balance.

Were there really two conspiracies or one? Sobell's counsel claimed
that the proof showed two. One was the conspiracy to steal the atom
bomb. This involved the Rosenbergs, Greenglasses and Gold. Con-
cededly, Sobell had no part in obtaining secrets of the bomb and
transferring them to Russia.

The other conspiracy was to send to Russia information involving
military engineering and fire control. This involved Sobell, Elitcher
and Rosenberg. If these were really separate conspiracies, it was prejudicial to include Sobell in the first one, where he had to share responsibility for the revelation of implosion to the Russians.

Judge Kaufman had ruled, and the majority of the Court of Appeals
agreed, that there was one over-all conspiracy to transmit information
relating to national defense to Russia. The value of the information was
not the crux of the matter. It might be a proximity fuse, a fire control

device, an atomic plane drawing or the atom bomb secret. The "common end" determined the conspiracy. If Sobell was part of this conspiracy, then in accordance with well-established law he was bound by the acts of his fellow conspirators, even if he did not participate in them.

Since Judge Frank was writing the opinion for the majority, he set forth its reasoning faithfully and with full appreciation of its strength. This was typical of his intellectual integrity. It was also a reflection of his personality. His fellow judges and friends were impressed with his lack of rancor when he was outvoted. His good humor and wit survived the most vigorous contests within the court. So, in his opinion, he went on to build up the structure of the majority's argument. It ran as follows: Judge Kaufman had properly ruled that the question of who had joined the conspiracy was separate from the nature of the conspiracy. The jury had to decide first whether Sobell was a member of the conspiracy. Elitcher and Danziger had testified that he was. The judge had given Sobell the benefit of every doubt, by telling the jury that if it disbelieved Elitcher, Sobell must be acquitted. They held otherwise. Therefore, he was bound by the acts of his fellow conspirators. It did not matter that he personally did not participate in the atom bomb phase of the over-all objective.

Why did Judge Frank disagree? He reasoned that Elitcher's testimony was susceptible of two interpretations; either that there was one or two separate conspiracies, or there would be one conspiracy to steal the bomb and another to transmit other classified information. That question was one of fact, and should have been submitted to the jury. It never was. The court ruled as a matter of law, that there was only one over-all plan.

The legal analysis which led Judge Frank to this conclusion is instructive on the intricacies of forensic philosophy. He fought his way through two Supreme Court decisions. In one (the Katteakos case), the defendants separately obtained fraudulent loans from a government agency. They did so through a single broker, and had similar objectives, but the court held there was no "single unified purpose of co-conspirators." In the other (the Blumenthal case), whiskey salesmen illegally sold a certain brand above ceiling price. Here the court decided that there was one conspiracy.

> The whiskey was the same. The agreements related alike to its disposition. . . .
> The salesmen knew that others unknown to them were sharing in so large a project.

Judge Frank felt that the Rosenberg case was closer to the loan case than the whiskey case.

He pointed out that the can of film delivered by Sobell to Rosenberg did not make him a member of the atomic bomb conspiracy, because there was no testimony of what was on the film. In any event, he would have left the issue of the contours of the conspiracy to the jury.

Sobell's appeal claimed that the prosecutor's "ill attempts" at courtroom humor and "questions" deprived him of a fair trial. Judge Frank said that an examination of each such incident showed that alone or cumulatively the effect on the jury was not so adverse as to overcome the cautioning instructions of the judge to decide on the evidence only. Furthermore, the court had admonished the prosecutor on the very few occasions where such a charge could be made. Also, Sobell's counsel, at the end of the trial, said that the prosecutor had conducted himself fairly; "I am willing to shake his hand after a job we both had to do." Similarly, Rosenberg's counsel had acknowledged the good behavior of the prosecutor.

With methodical completeness, the opinion then tackled Sobell's claim that the card bearing the notation "Deported from Mexico" should not have been admitted into the evidence because it was irrelevant and hearsay. The Appellate Court held that it was relevant, because otherwise the jury might have thought that Sobell's return for trial was voluntary. It was not hearsay, because an entry made "in the regular course of business," is admissible under a statute which changed the rule that the witness who made the original entry must be produced for any hospital, governmental, police or business record.

A more substantial query involved the kidnapping story presented in Sobell's affidavit, when he moved for a new trial after the verdict.

A complete answer was the rule of law, supported by many cases, that in a criminal case, unlike a civil case, it doesn't matter how the defendant was brought into court. If he is physically there, the court has jurisdiction over him. Judge Frank pointed out that since the anti-kidnapping law, there might be a different rule. However, it wasn't necessary to resolve that matter. If Sobell wanted to make such a challenge to the court's jurisdiction, he had to do so by a motion before trial: Sobell did not do so, even though he knew "the facts" which he put in his affidavit long before the trial. Furthermore, when the government offered evidence of legal deportation, Sobell made no move to bring to light the facts of his alleged abduction.

> He preferred to take his chances on the verdict, withholding his trump card until the trial was over. The Federal Rules of Criminal Procedure allow no such tactic.

—→←—

There was still one hope left for the Rosenbergs. Would this court reduce the death sentences? Judge Frank not only made a penetrating study of the question for the majority, but departed on a scholarly treatise of his own, which comes as close to a definitive review of the subject as will ever be written.

First he presented the full contention of the Rosenbergs. They conceded that the death penalty could be imposed for the crime of which they were convicted. However, they argued that even if they were properly found guilty, it was unconstitutional and an abuse of discretion to exact the extreme penalty in their particular case. What were those special circumstances?

> They did not act from venal or pecuniary motives; except for this conviction, their records as citizens and parents are unblemished; at the most, out of idealistic motives, they gave secret information to Soviet Russia when it was our wartime ally; for this breach, they are sentenced to die, while those who, according to the government, were their confederates, at least equally implicated in wartime espionage—Harry Gold, Klaus Fuchs, Elizabeth Bentley and the Greenglasses—get off with far lighter sentences or go free altogether. Finally, they argue, the death sentence is unprecedented in a case like this: No civil court has ever imposed this penalty in an espionage case, and it has been imposed by such a court in two treason cases only.

To this they added the claim that the information which the Rosenbergs gave to the Russians "would have become known to Russia in a matter of a few years."

The law was that an Appellate Court would not interfere with a sentence if it does not exceed the authority in the statute. This had been the "undeviating" rule for sixty years. The court could not overrule such a long-standing precedent. He cited thirteen cases which had supported this non-interference doctrine, and quoted from one of them:

> "If there is one rule in the federal criminal practice which is firmly established, it is that the Appellate Court has no control over a sentence which is within the limits allowed by a statute."

Where the sentence seemed "unduly harsh," an Appellate Court would be "more inclined to regard as harmful an error otherwise probably harmless. We have, however, found no such errors affecting the Rosenbergs."

This is another aspect of evasive tactics in the face of a harsh result. Sometimes a jury refuses to convict in the first degree, because it cannot stomach the death penalty. Here it is the austere law, supposedly immune from sympathetic considerations, which finds an otherwise non-reversible error a ground for reversal because it disapproves of the severe sentence and is powerless to reduce it.

The Supreme Court once gave a rationale for its non-interference with a severe penalty. In the Blockburger case, it said, "There may have been other facts and circumstances before the trial court properly influencing the extent of punishment."

Judge Frank traced the history of the rule that penalties will not be reviewed. At one time in 1879, there was the power to correct harsh sentences on appeal. When the statute was changed in 1891, such power was not incorporated, and the courts thereafter kept hands off.

Where the crime does not fall under the statutory provision, the Supreme Court has not hesitated to review the punishment, as for example, its reduction of a fine imposed on the United Mine Workers for contempt.

So, Judge Frank concluded for a unanimous court that the death penalties for the Rosenbergs could not be reviewed or reduced. But he was not one to leave the matter there. Why shouldn't the court have this power?

> Further discussion on this subject my colleagues think unnecessary. Consequently, the subsequent paragraphs express the views only on the writer of this opinion.

In these days when, as the Supreme Court said, "retribution is no longer the dominant objective of the criminal law," it would seem desirable that harsh sentences should be reduced by the upper courts. In the Middle Ages, justice popularly meant the gallows. Up to 1826, every felony in England was punishable by death.

Today in Canada, England and some of our states, power to reduce sentence exists, but always under a statute. By involved deduction, Judge Frank thought that if the Supreme Court wished to enlarge its review powers to include reduction of harsh sentences, it could do so. His legal citations were a brief on which it could rely, if it chose to do so.

> As matters now stand, this court properly regards itself as powerless to exercise its own judgment concerning the alleged severity of the defendants' sentences.

He noted that the court's judgment, not the "common conscience," was the test. Therefore, in the Rosenberg case, the court could consider that their espionage activities took place after Germany's defeat (and not being aid to any enemy in war, was not treason, only espionage). It also might consider that the evidence "came almost entirely from accomplices." His dissertation was virtually an appeal to the Supreme Court to do something about the matter. He was bowing to its supreme authority, and yet nudging it to change the precedent which tied his hands.

Then he considered a different argument for reducing the sentence, which Bloch, in a resourceful brief, had raised. Were the death sentences unconstitutional because they violated the Eighth Amendment which forbids "cruel and unusual punishment"? If so, then there was an independent reason and authority to change the sentence.

Judge Frank found this argument unsound. First, the law was that if a statute, which is passed by Congress and signed by the President, provides for certain punishment, the imposition of such punishment cannot be deemed a violation of the Constitution. The statute itself, might be unconstitutional, but until it is so condemned, its penalty provisions are legal.

Still, reasoned Judge Frank, it might be contended that "a particular sentence" is cruel and unusual, because "it shocks the conscience and sense of justice of the people of the United States." In other words, the test might be shifted from the judge's reaction to that of the community conscience. But Judge Frank held that such a test was "not met here."

> In the first place, how is the community conscience to be proven? It is unknowable. It resembles a slithery shadow, since one can seldom learn, at all accurately, what the community, or a majority, actually feels. Even a carefully-taken "public opinion poll" would be inconclusive in a case like this. Cases are conceivable where there would be little doubt of a general public antipathy to a death sentence. But (for reasons noted below) this is not such a case.

If the evidence was as the Rosenbergs depicted it, he reasoned, then a death sentence would shock the conscience of the community.

> They say that they were sentenced to death, not for espionage, but for political unorthodoxy and adherence to the Communist Party, and that (assuming they are guilty) they had only the best of motives in giving information to Russia which, at the time, was an ally of this country, praised as such by leading patriotic Americans. But the trial judge, in sentencing the Rosenbergs, relied on record evidence which (if believed) shows a very different picture. If this evidence be accepted, the conspiracy did not end in 1945, while Russia was still a "friend" but, as the trial judge phrased it, continued "during a period when it was apparent to everybody that we were dealing with a hostile nation." For, according to government witnesses, in 1948, Julius Rosenberg was urging Elitcher to stay with the Navy Department so that he might obtain secret data; in 1948, Rosenberg received "valuable" information from Sobell; in 1950, Rosenberg gave Greenglass money to flee to Russia. This court cannot rule that the trial judge should have disbelieved those witnesses whom he saw and heard testify.

He quoted from the Williams case in the Supreme Court, that a judge may avail himself of out-of-court information in making the awesome choice between death and life imprisonment.

Then, in one final paragraph, he rejected comparison with punishment for other defendants, like Greenglass or Gold, or with punishments handed out by other judges in other cases.

> We must, then, consider the case as one in which death sentences have been imposed on Americans who conspired to pass important secret information to Russia, not only during 1944–1945, but also during the "cold war." Assuming the applicability of the community-attitude test proposed by these defendants, it is impossible to say that the community is shocked and outraged by such sentences resting on such facts. In applying that test, it is necessary to treat as immaterial the sentences given (or not given) to the other conspirators, and also to disregard what sentences this court would have imposed on what other trial judges have done in other espionage or in treason cases. For such matters do not adequately reflect the prevailing mood of the public. In short, it cannot be held that these sentences are unconstitutional.
>
> Affirmed.

Despite this stern and unyielding conclusion, there was balm in a footnote:

> The Rosenbergs, of course, may ask the Supreme Court, considering 28 U.S.C. section 2106, to overrule the decisions precluding federal appellate modification of a sentence not exceeding the maximum fixed by a valid statute, and to direct us accordingly to consider whether or not these sentences are excessive; or the Rosenbergs, pursuant to Federal Rule of Criminal Procedure 35, may move the trial judge for a reduction of their sentences; or, if those alternatives fail, these defendants may seek relief from the President.

In his final salute to legal helplessness to change the death penalty, Judge Frank had outlined for the Rosenbergs the various steps they could take to avoid death. And at the same time, as a revered judge, only one rung beneath the Supreme Court, he was clearly suggesting that the punishment was excessive, and that there were legal avenues for redress. Whether this was due to his aversion for the death penalty or for human considerations, apart from the crime, he was holding out his hand to the Rosenbergs, empty of immediate relief, but full of promise.

I have set forth the Court of Appeals opinion in such detail, because of its immense importance in evaluating the case. Only by a close study of this first opinion (there was a second by the same court on reargument), can one understand how meticulously every conceivable point, legal and factual, raised by the Rosenbergs and Sobell, was examined; how painstakingly it was researched; how diligently and profoundly it was decided; and how fully it was expounded so that it could be the subject of review and criticism.

Above all, it was written by a brilliant judge, whose predilections were in favor of the defendants, and whose opinion was unanimously endorsed by Judge Swan and Judge Chase, two of the most learned and respected circuit court judges in the nation.

Such an affirmance had enormous weight, and it fell heavily on the Rosenbergs and their counsel.

CHAPTER 37

Ethel heard the bad news on the radio, which by special dispensation
had been placed in her Sing Sing cell. Early the next morning, she
wrote to Julius.

> My dear one, last night at 10 o'clock I heard the shocking news.
> At the present moment, with little or no detail to go by, it is difficult
> to make any comment, beyond an expression of horror at the haste with
> which the government appears to be pressing for our death. Certainly it
> proves that all our analyses regarding the political nature of our case
> have been amazingly correct.
> Sweetheart, if only I could truly comfort you. I love you so very
> dearly.

Emanuel Bloch rushed to the Detention House to report to Julius and
cushion the shock. The moment he saw him, he knew that he had
heard. Julius' eyes were puffed, and his drained face sagged, as he
greeted his lawyer without looking at him.

Bloch immediately set out to encourage him. Hiding his own con-
sternation, he pictured the procedures still available, and his confidence
in ultimate victory. This time Julius did not respond to the injection of
hope. With head bowed, he listened but his inert figure registered the
torpor of cynicism.

He had believed with all his heart that relief would come from the
Appellate Court. He was sure the death sentences would be set aside.
He had been convinced that there was foul play in the trial procedure.
The daily expressions of resentment by those around him, for the judge's
"unfairness," the "lies of the Greenglasses to save their skins," the
"prejudicial tactics of the prosecutor," had by sheer repetition become
an accepted truth. He was not sure of prevailing with the jury. The
poisonous atmosphere against communism might well have seeped into

the jury room. But he believed that a fine Appellate Court, on which Jerome Frank sat, would be outraged by the faulty proceedings.

"The essence of justice will escape the bottle, no matter how tightly corked," once wrote Learned Hand. Julius, Ethel and the Blochs had faith in the judicial process. They had awaited the upper court's opinion eagerly and with the greatest expectations of relief. Bloch had cited that court's reversal of other "demagogic" mishaps. Julius had read of its reversal in the Remington case.

He had heard of Jerome Frank's civil rights achievements, when at the invitation of President Franklin D. Roosevelt he had left Yale Law School to go to Washington and formulate a new body of civil rights legislation.

On June 13, 1951, Julius had written to Ethel:

> Our spirit is good and our hopes for a successful appeal are based on solid ground. Given an even chance, under law, we must win. Adorable wife, we're pulling hard, but the reward is great. Keep it up—
>
> Your own—Julie.

So the rejection of all points by the Court of Appeals was a devastating blow from which he never recovered. He wrote bitterly to Ethel:

> February 28, 1952
>
> My Dearest Ethel,
>   I'm still terribly shocked by the horrible affirmation of our conviction in such apparent haste.
>   I can't help but see the deceit and sophistry used by a so-called "liberal" and honorable man to continue this political frame-up.

Just as Julius had been turned away from a religious career to political revolution, so the disillusionment of the Frank opinion turned him in another direction for remedy.

He became convinced that only an aroused public could save him. "We must soberly realize," he wrote Ethel, "that our only hope rests with people. Only they can stop this legal lynching."

We shall see how he and Ethel nourished this hope, and how world protest developed beyond their fondest dreams. They later told Bloch, "We will never be executed. There will be such an upheaval throughout the world, they won't dare do it."

While Bloch continued the long legal struggle, and the Rosenbergs followed it avidly, they no longer had confidence in it. So when Bloch told him that he had immediately prepared an application for rehearing, Julius barely nodded. Bloch struggled to overcome his hopelessness, although not fully convinced himself.

To prepare Julius for another shock, Bloch "guessed" that in view of the affirmance, he might be transferred to Sing Sing. Julius knew that this meant death row near the electric chair, but Bloch cheered him with the thought that once there, he could see Ethel at lawyers' conferences.

It brought Julius out of his stupor. He looked up with tearful eyes, and said, "That will be wonderful." Being near the room of death was preferable to the detention prison, if he would also be near Ethel.

The very next day, flanked by two heavyweight detectives, he was taken in handcuffs on a long car ride to Sing Sing. He suffered the indignity of having his mustache shaved off, showered and scrubbed, as if diseased, and clothed in ill-fitting gray prison garb. Then he was led to death row, but he did not see Ethel although she was in an opposite cell. He wrote her, "Say, darling, I'm only 30 feet from you! But the steel doors are equivalent to endless distance." She, too, was tortured by useless proximity. "Why do I need this miserable pencil and paper, when you're just across the hall. Love you dearly. Ethel."

$$\longrightarrow \!\!\leftarrow\!\!\longrightarrow$$

Emanuel Bloch had obtained special privilege to confer with his clients not in the usual visitor's room, separated by a wire grating, but in a private conference room.

He told Ethel that Julius had arrived, and that they would all meet. As if she were going to a gala event, she took the greatest pains to look beautiful. Her matron supplied her with a comb and lipstick. She had lost weight, and she tightened her skirt, to reveal a slimmer waist. Her hair was neat and soft. Her eyes needed no artificial beautification. They glowed with expectation, and so did her cheeks. She was at her prettiest.

Bloch was delighted with the change in her appearance. It showed the will to live, which he was striving to maintain. For several months, she had been slipping into despondency, brooding silently and not moving for hours. He had seen her in these withdrawals more and more frequently. Each time, it had become more difficult to shake her out of her self-willed numbness. So he was thrilled to see her almost trembling with excitement as she prepared to see Julius.

She and Bloch were escorted by an armed guard and a matron to a private bare room with only a table and chairs. Julius had not yet arrived. She sat, her eyes riveted on the door.

"He'll be here soon," said Bloch. Impatiently, she rose and faced the entrance. Then there was a clanging noise, and a guard's face could be seen through the bars of the door. It opened with heavy slowness. There stood Julius. He was motionless for a moment taking in the scene. Then he saw her.

"Ethel!" he cried. They rushed at each other and embraced tightly, covering each other's faces with fierce kisses. Before anyone knew what was happening, they began pawing one another with wild abandon. They lost all control and wrestled passionately. The witnesses to the scene were stunned by the suddenness and violence of the outburst. They looked on in amazement at the writhing, groaning figures.

Finally, the guards and matron recovered. They pounced on them, pulling them apart. Julius was lifted bodily and plumped hard into a chair. Ethel was dragged away none too gently. They were still panting.

It took a few moments for them to become conscious of their surroundings. Then they were as embarrassed as their viewers.

Julius' face was so smeared with lipstick, it looked as if he were bleeding. He laced his hair back with his fingers; Ethel pulled her shirt together in a modest gesture which was ludicrous under the circumstances. She pulled her skirt down and demurely patted her disheveled hair. She could not see the red blotches on her face from her own lipstick smudged off from Julius'. When Bloch's face came into focus, she felt humiliated and began to cry.

The guards announced that there would be no conference. They would return the prisoners to their cells, and report the incident to Warden Denno.

Bloch was relieved. How could he conduct a prosaic discussion when the room was still filled with shock? Instead, he visited the warden to plead that the privilege of future private conference should not be withdrawn. He contended that this was no mere exhibition of passion. The severe sentence, the affirmance by the Court of Appeals, the proximity of the death chamber a few yards from their cells, the agony visited on their children, all had combined with their longing for each other, to seek some outlet for their unbearable pain. All this, as much as their love, had broken down the inhibitions of a lifetime. They had gone berserk not merely with passion, but with the need to share the collapse of their dreams, and the resulting shame, which they could no longer suppress. It all seemed unreal to them. Was it a nightmare? Were they dead? They had reached out for the sensation of being alive.

Bloch gave assurance that it would never happen again. The warden made certain that it would not. He ordered that henceforth they were to be handcuffed. They were to sit at opposite ends of a seven-foot conference table, with a guard and matron behind each. There were strict instructions that they must never be permitted to touch again.

CHAPTER 38

How many bites at the cherry may a loser in the courts have? Under our American system of justice, more than in any other country in the world. Although Judge Frank had written an all-encompassing opinion for a unanimous court, the Rosenbergs and Sobell still had the right to petition that same court for a rehearing. They did so. They filed briefs criticizing the court for its various dispositions, and insisting that they were entitled to relief. They requested the court to reverse itself, before they took an appeal to the Supreme Court.

The brief signed by Emanuel Bloch was a brilliant presentation of the claimed mistakes Judge Frank and his fellow judges had made. It was enforced with legal citation and felicitous wording. For example, in attacking Judge Frank's conclusion that the trial judge's comments were for the "purpose of clarification," Bloch wrote:

> Judicial bona fides is an irrelevance; honest or careless overzealousness, like deliberate design, can produce the interdicted consequences.

Judge Frank's conclusion that the judge's careful and emphatic charge to the jury wiped away any possible prejudice from his earlier comments, received this rebuke in Bloch's brief.

> While, in some instances, instructions to a jury may correct prior judicial aberrations, this is not the case. A jury, impregnated with three weeks of impressions of an attitude of constant judicial disfavor toward these defendants, coupled with its respect for the authority of the bench, must defy the accepted laws of psychological behavior to be able to free their assailed minds and to restore lost objectivity by the patent of a three-minute homily. Certainly in a capital case, legal abstractions should yield to the facts of life.

Most important, the Rosenbergs raised a new point on their request for reargument. In effect, they said, they were really tried for treason rather than espionage. This not only had "passion-arousing potentialities," but resulted in a death penalty which is customary for treason. Sobell, through his attorneys, also filed a brief in support of a rehearing.

One month later, on April 8, 1952, Judge Frank wrote another opinion on behalf of a unanimous court, rejecting the petition. He gave particular attention to the "treason" argument which had not been made previously.

It was true that if the charge had been treason, namely aiding an enemy during war (Russia was not), that the requirements of proof would be different. Every overt act would have to be testified to by at least two witnesses.

The Appellate Court analyzed the Espionage Act, which involved an offense similar to treason, but subject to separate prosecution. Judge Frank quoted at length from the Supreme Court decision in the Quirin case, which held to this effect.

So, the Rosenbergs and Sobell had lost again. Judge Frank signed an order extending their time to June 7, 1952, to apply to the Supreme Court for leave to appeal, a procedure called certiorari. He also signed an order staying the executions until the Supreme Court had acted.

Once more, death was postponed, while the prolific repetitive procedures for testing the verdict were carried on in accordance with the American tradition that slow justice is better than unexplored error.

When Ethel and Julius learned of the new setback, they were not surprised but their spirits dropped even lower. They fought collapse by writing love letters to each other.

> Dearest Julie, They'll be putting the lights out soon and then I'll be alone with you. So I pretend, anyway. Oh, how I miss you and long to be in your arms where I belong. Good night, darling.

He replied,

> Hello, Honey, Just a little warmth and love. How I miss it. But enough of that. As jailbirds, our lot is to be thoroughly mechanical, devoid of physiological needs.

When despair enveloped her, she held on with words:

> Within me somewhere I shall find that "courage, confidence and perspective" I shall need to see me through the days and nights of bottomless horror, of tortured screams I may not utter, of frenzied longing I must deny! Julie, dearest, how I wait upon the journey's end, and our triumphant return to our precious life! Darling, I love you. Ethel.

As if their personal plight was not bad enough, they had to bear the burden of re-establishing their relationship with their children. Could there be a worse setting than the death house?

They finally authorized Bloch to bring the children to visit them. They had not seen them for a year, and yet they feared facing them more than they yearned to see them.

They had planned carefully with Bloch how they would conduct themselves. The most important thing was to appear confident. Tears must be avoided. The shock would be reduced if they could blot out the abnormal surroundings with calm behavior.

On July 25, 1951, she wrote,

> My Darling Julie,
> If we can manage to give the children the impression that we are not unduly upset, we will be setting the stage for the proper reaction.
> Here is what I have been dreaming up as a sample of the conversation that may take place. I'm putting it in the form of a monologue:
> "Of course, it's not easy to know about the death penalty and not worry about it sometimes, but let's look at it this way. We know that a car could strike us and kill us, but that doesn't mean we spend every minute being fearful about cars.
> "You see, we are the very same people we ever were, except that our physical selves are housed under a different roof from yours."

Could they discipline themselves to carry off such an act? They trained themselves day and night for the confrontation, even practicing the light touch and laughter, to assure their small visitors that all would be well. In this task, too, Julius leaned on Ethel. On July 25, 1951, he wrote:

> Hello, my Pretty,
> Finished winning my chess at 9:15 p.m. and it was a long battle right down to the finish, and I have to hustle to get this note off to you.
> Time doesn't stand still. Right now I'm looking forward to seeing my own sons after more than a year. Even though it's an entire week off, the tension is mounting and I'm going to have to exercise a maximum of control to keep my anxiety down.
> I am glad you are going to break the ice with the kids because I am certain you will come through beautifully and set the stage for my visit.

She replied,

> Hello, Darling,
> I shall do all that is within my power to set the children at ease and prepare them for your coming. Do try to lay aside some of the anxiety meanwhile. Believe me, I am trying to convince myself, at the same time!
> Oh, yes, if Michael neglects to question me as to the form of the death penalty, this job will fall to you. In which case, answer briefly.

that it is painless electrocution, which we believe will never come to pass, of course.

Believe me, children are what their parents truly expect them to be. If we can face the thought of our intended execution without terror, so then will they. Certainly, neither of us will seek to dwell on these matters. But let's not be afraid, and they won't be either. All my love, darling,

Ethel

Ethel and Julius asked for permission to have their handcuffs removed for the visit by their children. It was refused. The privilege of a private conference room with counsel and family was as far as the rules would be stretched. So they decided to see them separately.

Bloch had placed Michael, nine years old, and Robert, five years old, in a Bronx shelter home. He had arranged for them to move into the new home of Julius' mother in Washington Heights. He, too, had the delicate task of informing the children that they were going "upstate" to visit their father and mother. Although they had not seen them in a long time and missed them sorely, they looked forward with mixed degrees of puzzlement and anxiety to the trip.

Michael was old enough to understand. He had heard the bubbling excitement wherever he appeared, "That is the Rosenberg boy." He was an object of sympathy, which embarrassed him even more because it resulted from contempt for his parents. He had already been the victim of an incident, which might leave its mark on him for life. A friend had invited him to his home. On learning who he was, the mother angrily threw him out of the house. She had never heard that the sins of the father must not be visited on his sons. This cruel incident had made Michael even more morose. Ethel did not know that her son was unwittingly sharing her moods of despondency.

Robby was too young for such introspection. The bizarre events were simply an adventure to him. The long automobile trip to Sing Sing was part of it.

When they arrived at the gate, a guard asked for admission identification from Bloch.

Robby spoke up. "Aren't you going to frisk Michael and me?"

"Not necessary, kids."

Robby screamed at him. "You must frisk us. Frisk us!"

The guard sheepishly touched their pockets. Robby walked in happily, Michael trailing. They were taken to Ethel first. She steeled herself for the first view of the children. Her resolution was broken by Robby's first words.

"You look much smaller, Mama."

"No, it is you who are growing bigger," she replied in a shaky voice.

Michael was standing off on the side, frightened and solemn. Robby continued to chatter on.

"When are you coming home?"

"I don't know yet, but we'll all be together soon."

Michael felt he ought to say something. "When are we going to see Papa?"

Bloch answered. "Right after lunch."

"Yes, from now on, we will see each other regularly," said Ethel. "Once every month, isn't it, Manny?"

"That's right."

Robby exclaimed, "Oh, good. I like the ride."

Ethel now dared to touch him. She drew him to her. "Yes, it is good, isn't it?" she said, kissing him. Michael approached and leaned over. She lifted her head and kissed him too. She began to tremble.

Bloch stepped in quickly. "Well, now, we'll visit your father."

Robby pulled out of her arms unceremoniously.

"Can we see the electric chair?" he asked.

His innocence and directness could not diminish the horror that gripped everyone in the room, the guard and matron included. After a few seconds of silence, unnoticed by the child, Bloch said, "We are going to see your father. Don't you want to see him?"

"Sure," he replied, running out lightheartedly. Michael tarried, kissed his mother lightly, and left sadly.

Bloch smiled meaningfully at her, as if to say she had survived the test, and followed the guards out. But she felt otherwise. She later told Bloch that the children were disturbed. To Julius she wrote:

I experience such a stab of longing for my boys that I could howl like a she-animal who has had its young forcibly torn from her! How dared they, how dared they, the low, vile creatures, lay unclean hands upon our sacred family? And tell me, oh, my sister Americans, how long shall any of your own husbands and children be safe if by your silence you permit this deed to go unchallenged!

In another letter, she referred to the children's visit as opening "a wide floodgate; I am one vast vessel of pain. It feels as though every inch of me beats with hurt."

Julius was waiting in the conference room, a guard behind him. The children entered. Robby immediately exclaimed, "You have no mustache. What happened to your mustache? You look different."

The unexpected, trivial approach made it easier for Julius.

"Come here. You look different too—grown up, like a big man."

Michael stood shyly near the door. Two days earlier he had sent a card to his father. It had a picture of a sailboat on a lake. Underneath he had written, "The merry wind is blowing, My lovely words are flowing. Michael." But none were flowing as he looked at his father in prison garb.

Julius had bought candy from the prison canteen. He held some out.

Michael approached hesitantly, took a piece, withdrew and sucked it without relish. Robby filled his mouth and gobbled eagerly.

Knowing that Michael had inherited his mother's love of song, and how he used to join eagerly in folk melodies, Julius invited him to sing. He chose an old Yiddish folk song and began to sing softly:

"Uf dem Pripitchickel
Brent a fier-il
In die shtieb is kalt
Zugt shoin nuch a mool
In takke nuch a mool
Kumitz ahliv—ooh
Zugt shoin nuch a mool
In takke nuch a mool
Kumitz ahliv—ooh.

"In a little home at Pripitchik
A fireplace is burning
But the room is cold,
The rabbi is teaching the children, 'Say A-B-C,
Repeat after me, A-B-C.'"

Robby loved the song and jumped on his father's lap. Michael stood aloof. Julius held out his hand, as if the music was a string by which he would pull his son to him. Michael began to sing hesitantly and moved toward his father. As he touched him, his voice grew stronger. He came close. His father put his arm gently around his shoulder. Michael leaned his head on his father. Both closed their eyes. The prison surroundings disappeared. They were transported to the past when they were home. They had escaped on a carpet of music.

CHAPTER 39

Supreme Court jurisdiction is severely limited. The extensive appellate procedure in the lower courts is usually deemed final. Otherwise, the highest court would be so deluged with appeals from the ten circuit and fifty state courts that it would be unable to function. Only where there are constitutional questions, or conflicts between federal courts or several other special circumstances may an appeal be taken to the Supreme Court as a matter of right. Otherwise, the Court's permission must be obtained. This procedure is called a petition for certiorari. If four of the nine judges believe that the question is one which the Court ought to review, certiorari is granted and the case set down for oral argument. Otherwise, certiorari is denied. The Court of Appeals judgment remains final.

Like other Appellate Courts, the Supreme Court will not review disputes of fact. It, too, recognizes that the jury had the benefit of appraising the live witnesses, which it has not. It will not substitute its judgment of credibility for that of the jury from such an inferior vantage point. Only if there is a novel question of law may it entertain jurisdiction. So the Rosenbergs' and Sobell's chances depended on whether the Court detected legal error in Judge Frank's opinion. Realistically, this did not provide much hope. However, Julius had studied Bloch's petition and he wrote Ethel,

Hello, Darling,

I am so completely enamored of our petition that I have high hopes we will be granted certiorari, if it gets the attention it should receive. It is a stupendous legal document, displaying a beautiful integration of concise and poignant language and devastating legal argument.

On reflection, he grew more cautious.

September 7, 1952

Ethel, My Sunshine,

Slowly but surely we are coming to the date of our next major hurdle, the writ of certiorari. I'm optimistic, but no one can predict the idiosyncrasies of the courts.

I need you more than anything else. Your devoted husband,

Julie

He advised her that Station WFAS would report the Supreme Court decision on Monday at 12:45. He listened and in his own words, "took the hammer blow with self-control."

His mother visited him that day but he didn't "let on, because I wanted her to be home and have people near her when she hears the bad tidings."

The Supreme Court denial of certiorari was unanimous, and it stated that no legal question had been raised which had not previously been decided by it.

Following the highest court's denial of certiorari, Judge Kaufman set a new execution date: January 12, 1953.

To the morbid, it must have seemed as if each legal proceeding cheated the executioner of his due, and each rejection by the court was a triumph for him.

Bloch petitioned the Supreme Court for a rehearing. One month later, this, too, was denied eight to one, only Justice Black dissenting.

Bloch could not be discouraged. He seemed to gather strength for a new attack each time he was defeated. He moved in the District Court before Judge Sylvester Ryan to set aside the verdict on the ground that both David Greenglass and photographer Schneider had perjured themselves. Judge Ryan, who later became Chief Judge, was a highly respected jurist. His denial of the motion was another severe blow, particularly when he would not stay the execution because "no substantial question of law has been raised."

In desperation, the family stepped in. Julius' mother, Sophie Rosenberg, and his two sisters, Mrs. Lena Cohen and Mrs. David Goldberg, obtained Judge Irving Kaufman's permission to visit him in his chambers. They begged him to reduce the sentence.

"Look at me. Look at my eyes," the mother said. "I want to see your face. My two children are innocent. They are pure like the snow. If you give it to them, then you must give it to me, too, for I do not wish to live."

The judge explained his anguished duty and the long thorough proceedings by which he was bound. They left, sobbing hysterically.

The same day, Bloch moved before Judge Kaufman to reduce the sentence on the same grounds that Judge Frank had rejected, but which he indicated were not in his province. Judge Kaufman weighed the matter for three days before denying the motion. However, he granted another stay of execution, which was only ten days off, in order to permit the Rosenbergs more time to petition President Truman for clemency.

In the meantime, Bloch appealed to the Court of Appeals from Judge Ryan's decision. It unanimously upheld Judge Ryan's refusal to reduce the verdict on the theory of perjured testimony. It also refused a further stay of execution.

On January 10, 1953, President Truman received a petition for clemency. It was written in Ethel's name with the help of Bloch. It was a lengthy document presenting not only considerations for mercy, but a review of the legal arguments which had failed in the courts, but which might have residual force in avoiding the extreme penalty. Although "beyond a reasonable doubt" is necessary to convict, "any doubt" is pertinent in granting clemency. Ethel's petition became a twenty-four-page pamphlet which was distributed by the International Association of Democratic Lawyers of Brussels, Belgium, in the burgeoning public appeals. It concluded with a plea, which did not depend on innocence for effectiveness.

> To let us live will serve all and the common good. If we are innocent, as we proclaim, we shall have the opportunity to vindicate ourselves. If we have erred, as others say, then it is in the interests of the United States not to depart from its heritage of open-heartedness and its ideals of equality before the law by stooping to a vengeful and savage deed . . .

With only ten days left of his term of office, President Truman ignored the sign on his desk which read "The buck stops here," and passed it to the incoming President, Dwight D. Eisenhower.

This was unfortunate for the Rosenbergs. As a General of the Armies, he had expressed his firm belief in execution as a deterrent, and authorized the first shooting of a private for desertion—Private Slovik. Also, Judge Kaufman's assertion that fifty thousand American casualties in Korea might be ascribed to Russia's possession of the atom bomb was likely to evoke a receptive echo from the new President.

On February 11, 1953, less than a month after he took office, President Eisenhower denied the petition for clemency. He issued a statement stating that he had given the record of the case

> earnest consideration, but the nature of the crime involves deliberate betrayal of the entire nation and the cause of freedom for which free men are fighting and dying at this very hour. We are a nation under law and our affairs are governed by the just exercise of these laws. The courts have provided every opportunity for the submission of evidence bearing on this case. In time honored

tradition of American justice, a freely selected jury of their fellow citizens considered the evidence and rendered its judgment. All rights of appeal were exercised and the conviction was upheld after four judicial reviews, including that of the highest court in the land. I am determined that it is my duty in the interest of the people of the United States, not to set aside the verdict of their representatives.

It appeared that there was nothing left to do, but Bloch had just begun to fight. Doggedly, he went back to the Court of Appeals to ask for a stay of execution on the ground of judicial prejudice. He was rewarded for his persistence. Suddenly, the landslide of defeats stopped. Judge Jerome Frank was still on the bench, but Chief Judge Thomas Swan had retired. The famed Learned Hand presided. Also, Judge Augustus Hand sat in place of Judge Harrie B. Chase.

During the argument, Judge Frank, who in his original opinions had virtually outlined possible relief from the death penalty, which only the Supreme Court could grant, again asserted that "I believe the Supreme Court should hear it."

Judge Learned Hand was even more emphatic.

> People don't dispose of lives, just because an attorney didn't make a point . . . You can't undo a death sentence. There are some Justices on the Supreme Court on whom the conduct of the Prosecuting Attorney might make an impression.

When the prosecutor pointed out that the proceedings had lasted years, and that it was time they came to an end, Judge Learned Hand retorted with characteristic tartness:

> Your duty, Mr. Prosecutor, is to seek justice, not to act as a time-keeper.

Judge Hand's acerbity was not to be interpreted as a criticism of Judge Kaufman. He later recommended that President Kennedy promote him to the Court of Appeals to sit with him. President Kennedy did so and the Senate confirmed the appointment.

The Court of Appeals granted a stay of execution, so that another petition could be filed with the Supreme Court.

This was the first victory Bloch had won in the case. He filed a new and carefully devised petition with the Supreme Court. Before it could rule, a startling development occurred and a wave of excitement and hope swept through the defense ranks.

CHAPTER 40

On April 13, 1953, the *National Guardian,* a pro-Communist paper, announced that the missing console table had been found. The Rosenberg Committee claimed that it disproved Greenglass' story that it was a Russian gift and had a hollowed-out microfilming section for Rosenberg's use in espionage activities. This "discovery" attracted the attention of Professor Malcolm P. Sharp of the University of Chicago Law School. At the invitation of Bloch, he joined defense counsel immediately, and helped to prepare a motion for a new trial on the ground of newly discovered evidence. The motion papers were rushed out and served on the prosecutor on Saturday, June 6, 1953, at two in the morning. The argument was heard by Judge Irving Kaufman on Monday, June 8, 1953, in the afternoon.

Bloch advised the judge that the table was an ordinary Macy table, which its markings would show, and that Greenglass had lied.

The judge asked, "Where did you find it, and when?"

Bloch told him it was in the home of Julius' mother, and had been discovered in March more than "two months ago."

Judge Kaufman wanted to know when Bloch had first seen it. He replied that because of his supervision of the children, who were living with their grandmother, he had been to Sophie Rosenberg's house a number of times. "But frankly, Judge, I never noticed it before."

He had an affidavit from Julius' sister that when the furniture in the Rosenberg apartment had been sold for $100, she had kept the console table and a few other items because they were too good to dispose of as junk. Later, she had given the table to her mother.

COURT Didn't anyone in the family tell you they had this table?

E. H. BLOCH No, sir. They didn't realize its importance.

SAYPOL May I be heard, your Honor. When we were served with these affidavits, we investigated this matter. We are submitting affidavits of Macy employees, which show that the markings on this table were not the kind which Macy placed inside its tables in 1944. They marked their tables with colored crayon. This table has white chalk marks. Also, in 1944, they had code markings for the price, which this table has not got.

Your Honor will recall that the witness Evelyn Cox testified that Ethel Rosenberg told her the console table was a gift from Julius' friend. Ethel never told her it was bought at Macy's. So Evelyn Cox corroborated the Greenglass testimony. Now, at this late date, the defendants find a table. Even if it was bought in Macy's, it would mean nothing. Hundreds of such tables were sold by Macy's.

COURT Mr. Bloch, when you were confronted with Greenglass' testimony about the console table, you had weeks in which to contradict it. Did you ask the Rosenberg family where the console table had been disposed of?

E. H. BLOCH Frankly, I didn't consider the Greenglass testimony on this point very significant. I knew the furniture had been sold as junk and I didn't attempt to trace it.

COURT But you could have asked the sister or mother whether they knew where it went.

You tell me you were actually in the mother's home and didn't ask about it or notice it standing there, even after the testimony was given, isn't that right?

E. H. BLOCH Yes, your Honor. But I can bring the table in, and also the witnesses whose affidavits I have submitted. I would like you to hear them and look at the table.

COURT I don't see how that will do any good. There are many Macy tables. That is not the point. Furthermore, if you didn't consider the original testimony to be of much significance, I don't see how raising an issue of credibility on this point can overcome all the other evidence in the case.

I deny the motion.

E. H. BLOCH Will your Honor stay the execution until we take an appeal? You have set June 18th as the new execution date and this only gives us ten days.

COURT If the Court of Appeals or the Supreme Court finds any merit in the application, they can stay the execution. It has been stayed four times already. That is up to them. I will expedite the order so that you can appeal immediately.

Once more, Bloch, his associate, Miss Agrin, now joined by Professor Sharp, rushed to the Court of Appeals. Their chief problem was the stringent rules which govern the right to a new trial on the ground

(408)

of newly discovered evidence. These are not technical, as might appear at first blush. They were formulated to prevent the tactic of withholding or ignoring certain proof, and then if the verdict was adverse, coming forward with it to obtain a new trial.

So to qualify for a new trial, the "new" evidence must be shown not to have been available, even if diligent search had been made. It must also be substantial enough to have materially affected the outcome. The burden is heavy upon the movant to meet these tests, or there would never be an end to a trial. It is rare that after a trial a lawyer doesn't discover a new witness or document which has turned up and which might have thrown more light on the facts. This does not justify a new trial. Diligence before trial, not after, is required, and cases are few indeed which are reopened because of "newly discovered evidence."

As this rule operated on the console table, the Rosenbergs had the burden of explaining why they had not sought to trace the whereabouts of the table, even if they thought it had been disposed of to a second-hand furniture dealer. If he had been interviewed and recalled that it was not in his purchase, would they not have been led to Julius' sister, who supervised the sale? Apart from such inquiry of the dealer was it not natural to inquire of Julius' family whether they knew where the table was?

In view of the defense efforts to trace the sale at Macy's, it was almost inconceivable that they had not also attempted to check with the family. Why had not the sister and mother been put on the stand, as Macy executives had been, to reveal an effort—even if ineffectual? Instead, Bloch explained he did not consider the Greenglass testimony on this point important.

This could be interpreted to mean that it was not substantial in its effect on the verdict, any more than the watches supposedly given by the Russians to Julius and Ethel. In other words, it was cumulative on a peripheral issue and, therefore, did not meet the substantiality test required of new evidence.

On the other hand, Bloch and Professor Sharp could contend that Greenglass' credibility was the decisive factor in the case. The Court of Appeals had so found. If he had concocted the story of the hollowed-out console table and been caught in a lie, might not his entire testimony have crumbled? What could be more substantial than this? But then Evelyn Cox's testimony that Ethel had told her the table was a "gift from a friend," and that it had been kept mysteriously in a closet, would shore up Greenglass. There would be a conflict of testimony as on other subjects. Perhaps, Greenglass could have survived, despite the new evidence?

Furthermore, the assertion that the found table was the one in the Rosenberg home, and not one of the many Macy tables sold to others, was challenged by the government.

Finally, none of this put to rest the failure of the defense to have presented the evidence, which they said was right in their own relative's home, during the trial, so that the jury could have weighed its effect. The explanation for the "oversight" had to be very strong, if the extraordinary relief of a new trial was to be granted.

This demonstrates the involvements and uphill struggle the Rosenbergs had on this point.

However, in one respect, the incident was very favorable to them. New trial or not, any doubt, no matter how vaporous, was persuasive on the subject of clemency, if not on guilt. Execution is final and irreversible. If the remotest possibility of error exists, how can the death penalty be justified even by its adherents? It seemed that the Rosenbergs had at the very least strengthened their appeal for clemency.

The Court of Appeals ruled that it would hear the appeal and the application for a stay at the same time. On June 11, 1953, one week before execution, the Court unanimously affirmed Judge Kaufman's decision denying a new trial on the ground of newly discovered evidence. Bloch and Professor Sharp added this to Judge Hand's ruling in a final rush to the Supreme Court to stay the fast-approaching day when the electric chair would terminate any further legal struggles.

CHAPTER 41

Ethel and Julius had spent three years in jail, two of which were in the death house. They were permitted to see each other behind a visitor's screen every Wednesday. "Time marched on without us," she wrote, until "wondrous Wednesday" arrived. Monday and Tuesday were particularly difficult as they counted the hours when they could whisper endearments while the mesh hid most of their faces. The contact of voice and sentiment sustained them for days.

> November 1, 1951
>
> Hello, Julie Dearest,
>   Since Wednesday and all the good, sweet words that passed between us, I have been walking on air. My dear one, rest easy; I am ever-fortified in your love.

Man's adaptability, and in this instance, woman's too, is revealed dramatically in a jail cell. Julius made a collection of insects which had invaded his "privacy." He wrote excitedly of having captured a dragonfly and a locust to add to "a small brown butterfly and a nice white moth." He went "hunting" for cockroaches and "massacred" them. Like good health, which is seldom appreciated until it fails, the little joys provided by nature became great events when they are inaccessible. Julius learned this lesson in jail and described it to Ethel.

> About three months ago one of the fellows here planted an orange pip in the dirt in a crack in the concrete. As all of us are interested in living things in this bleak place, we watered it, nursed it along and it took firm root in the soil and began to flourish. By now it has grown to eight inches, bloomed, flowered, and has small oranges on the branches. Can you imagine the contrast? Bars, concrete, walls—and an orange tree growing in a crack. Thriving freshness, beauty and life—in this tomb.

We, too, will continue to grow in this negative atmosphere. I think of the time when we'll enjoy our home again and our children's sweetness.

All my heart I send you,

Julie

Julius became a voracious cigarette smoker and prided himself on his "uncanny knack" of flipping the butt from any place in the cell "right into the bowl."

He played chess by pushing his arm through the bars to a board placed between two cells. He never saw his adversary, only an opposing arm. But he complained that his opponent had become unavailable because he had received appellate briefs from his lawyer and was immersed in them. Julius, too, studied the record of his trial, and the many briefs and petitions prepared by his lawyers. So did Ethel. When they met with Bloch in the conference room, they had lists of suggestions.

This was not unusual. Even illiterate prisoners become "jail house lawyers," a term well recognized in all prisons. There is no more satisfying effort than to work for one's own freedom. It gives the illusion that the bars are being bent and an exit can be glimpsed. A lawyer must be sensitive to his client's yearning, and not cast aside his most worthless suggestions. A prisoner's participation in the legal effort is psychological medicine of which he should not be deprived.

Due to bad lighting, Julius could not read much, but he enjoyed particularly Thomas Wolfe's *You Can't Go Home Again* (was he attracted perversely by the title?) and Forbes's *History of Technology and Invention*. He was not permitted to write much. Pens and pencils were given for short periods and withdrawn at 9 P.M. as dangerous instruments.

He looked forward avidly to the fifteen-minute exercise periods, which gave him the opportunity to be in the yard. He had never before appreciated how wonderful it was to see the sky and breathe outdoor air. The movement of running or playing handball made him feel free. The breeze against his face was life, when contrasted with the stagnation in his cell.

Any visitor was doubly welcome because he was permitted to "walk out" to the visiting room. It was an escape from his cage.

Yet he took care to make that cage his home. He scrubbed and cleaned it. He gloried in a better mattress. When he received snapshots of his sons, he improvised a cardboard frame and mounted them. They would smile at him whenever he chose to look up. He tried to care for his children vicariously. He wrote instructions to Bloch and it made him feel that he was stretching out his hands through the prison gate to act as a father should.

Michael appears to squint badly in the last set of photos. Since you already made a note of an audiometer test for Robby, add one that Mike should have his eyes examined.

Ethel even suggested to Bloch the books to get for the children: *Be My Friend, Tony and the Wonderful Door* and *The Races of Mankind.*

You see, I am determined to go on living and planning as though naught awaited me save a husband's fond kiss, a son's noisy welcome.

Ethel

Ethel was also living in *gehenna* (Julius' Hebrew word for hell). She wrote that she never fell asleep until she had exhausted herself sobbing. She suffered from severe migraine headaches, and her cell mate applied cold compresses at all hours of the night. They were never helpful, but she needed the kindness. She hugged her pillow so tightly, she had cramps.

She, too, had to contend with prison animals.

I awoke at 4:30 A.M. to hear a mouse squeaking almost in my ear, it was so close. A few hard bangs on the spring and he scampered out into the corridor, where he proceeded to protest loudly, but to no avail. No one else seemed anxious to invite him in. The damage was already done, because try as I would I could not get back to sleep.

Do you know how dear you are to me? Oh, please, honey, be strong for me—I need you so to be strong for me. Lovingly,

Ethel

The prison chaplain, Rabbi Irving Koslowe, conducted services, not necessarily on the Sabbath, but on any day of the week. In prison there are no days, only time, and every day, indeed every hour, was suitable for prayer. Rabbi Koslowe set up a table in front of the cells, and his congregation remained behind bars. Those who chose not to participate lay down on their cots and ignored him. Those who wished to join in the service took front pews by moving a chair to the bars. Ethel, being the only woman in the death house, was permitted to leave her cell and sit in the corridor out of sight of the prisoners. However, when the service concluded with collective singing of the hymn "El Kalohenu," her voice rang out with unique feminine beauty against the croaking male voices. Julius was particularly thrilled by it and considered it not merely an ode to God, but a personal message, to which he responded by drowning out the spiritless voices of his fellow prisoners. Then they wrote to each other of the vocal contact they had achieved, he lavishing praise upon her for her "magnificent singing," a tribute she could not return, but instead expressed her excitement at being "touched by your voice."

It was her own mother, Tessie Greenglass, who gave Ethel the greatest anguish. As death drew near, her estranged mother asked to visit her. Ethel eagerly agreed. A reconciliation and love would ease

(413)

her torment somewhat. She brightened when her mother arrived. She described what happened in a letter to Bloch.

> Dear Manny,
>   This is to let you know that my mother was here on Monday . . .
> I am still in a state of stupefaction over its bold-faced immorality
> . . . Our conversation follows . . . Said she: "So what would have
> been so terrible if you had backed up Davey's story?" I guess my mouth
> kind of fell open. "What," I replied, "and take the blame for a crime
> I never committed, and allow my name and my husband's, and chil-
> dren's to be slandered to protect him? . . . Wait a minute, maybe I'm
> not getting you straight. Just what are you driving at?" She answered,
> "Yes, you get me straight; I mean even if it was a lie, you should have
> said it was true anyway! You think that way you would have been sent
> here? No, if you had agreed that what Davey said was so, even if it
> wasn't, you wouldn't have got this!"

Although she proclaimed boldly, "I am made of the stuff of the early pioneers, and in my veins beats the blood of the Maccabees!" her periods of depression grew more frequent and longer.

> September 15, 1952
> Sweetest Julie,
>   More and more I tend to withdraw into myself, emerging fully only
> when you are with me. Day by day our separation grows more intolera-
> ble; day by day the assault upon mind and spirit grows the more
> viciously insistent.
>   Sweetheart, I love you with a strength that defies my pain. Still,
> hold me close, my heart is so heavy with wanting you—Always your
> own wife,
>
> Ethel

———>←———

Most agonizing of all were the visits of the children. The joy of seeing them turned into stabbing pain which lasted long after they left. On January 3, 1953, the children were permitted to stay two hours. Julius held Robby at the barred window and they looked at the seagulls and a tugboat pulling a string of barges on the Hudson. Robby drew crude pictures of what he had seen. He circled his father's neck with his little arms and kissed his cheeks.

Later, when they had to leave, Michael clutched Julius and stam-mered, "You must come home. Every day there is a lump in my stomach, even when I go to bed."

When the door clanged shut, wrote Julius,

> I broke down and cried like a baby because of the children's deep hurt.
> With my back to the bars, I stood facing the concrete walls that boxed
> me in on all sides, and I let the pain that tore at my insides flood out
> in tears.

(414)

Under the circumstances, each visit was a mixture of joy and tragedy. On one occasion, the children arrived playful and happy. They hid under the table and when Julius arrived, Robby's giggles gave them away. They rushed at him and embraced him.

Julius showed them his collection of insects. He also brought them two Hershey bars and a couple of bananas. Michael remonstrated, "Daddy, please don't stuff us," but Robby devoured all of them. His father carried him around on his shoulders. All seemed well.

Then Michael began to put questions to him. He had read about the death sentence. Was there an electric chair in this prison? How certain was his father that he and Mother would not die? Julius told him about the appeals and assured him of victory. "Suppose you lose the appeals?" asked the child.

As they were about to leave, Michael said, "Daddy, maybe I'll study to be a lawyer and help you in your case." Julius replied, "We won't wait that long as we want to be with you while you're growing up." Each visit left a similar trail of torment. Recollection of physical pain does not reproduce the pain itself. But emotional pain is experienced all over again and sometimes is even enlarged, when it is recalled.

It undermined their health. Julius had to have teeth pulled. Warden Denno did not lift his spirits when he ordered a temporary plate installed. Ethel's curved spine vied with her head in giving pain. To all this was added a continuous stream of defeats in the courts. They might have collapsed from the harsh blows which beat upon them from all directions—their children, her mother and the judges—were it not for one saving grace.

They were scoring triumph after triumph in another arena. Those victories freed their spirits if not their bodies. Their misery turned to the elation of martyrdom.

CHAPTER 42

Job, tested by God, cried out, "I am declared guilty. Why then should I toil in vain? . . . O, that there were an umpire between us . . ."

The Rosenbergs chose public opinion as an intercessor. It is difficult to move a mass. To arouse the public in a large country has taxed foremost experts, even with millions of dollars at their disposal. To achieve international reaction requires nothing short of a miracle. Yet the Rosenbergs, starting without a penny, accomplished this feat.

Curiously, it was the legal defeats which provided the motive power for an organized protest. Each time the courts rejected a plea and moved them nearer to execution, new momentum was created for the "Don't Kill the Rosenbergs" committees.

It is interesting to trace this phenomenon. Like almost everything else in this case, it is unique.

Aside from the wide coverage of the trial itself, there was a silent lull for months after the verdict. Even the Communist press played it low, not having decided yet whether to disclaim the Rosenbergs or assert that they were martyrs.

In August 1951, the *National Guardian* decided on the latter course. It published a series of articles denouncing the "verdict of passion." This had been the line of the *Daily Worker* immediately after sentence. Its news heading read "ROSENBERGS MADE SCAPEGOATS FOR KOREAN WAR."

The *National Guardian* claimed there was a plot "to silence through mortal fear, all who may dare to hold views at variance with those of the administration . . ." This was "America's Dreyfus Case," an anti-Semitic plan "to persecute Jews."

Just as the Russians had invented everything first, including baseball, it also knew all along how to build atomic weapons, but humanistic considerations had deterred it from doing so.

Naturally, such fulminations received no attention, except from devoted Communists who required no persuasion. But the Rosenbergs were thrilled by this series. The large black type didn't reveal the pitifully small circulation and even more insignificant acceptance. They gladly suffered the illusion that the revelations would awaken Americans to the charge that Nazi tactics were being employed, that fascism had succeeded in our country; that "It could happen here."

Although the Blochs were eager to kindle their clients' hopes, they felt duty bound to limit their enthusiasm by pointing out the ineffectiveness of the source. To no avail; Ethel, particularly, believed this was the beginning of a world-wide movement to save them. Who could have dreamed that she was right?

She sent a letter of gratitude to the *National Guardian*. This was a scoop. It was featured in a special box, and said:

> It is because we are relentless, uncompromising, implacable in implementing our beliefs with action, that we sit today in the gray walls of Sing Sing awaiting we know not what further pain and sorrow and emptiness.

Alexander Bloch did not like this Communist lingo. He thought she was destroying sympathy for herself. What would people think of her statement that she had implemented her "beliefs with action"? What action? He exercised his "fatherly" prerogatives to tell her so. Her eyes blazed with anger. She yelled at him and told him that the *National Guardian* had received a flood of letters. She continued to "reward" it with more contributions. The concluding article suggested the formation of a Committee to Secure Justice in the Rosenberg Case. There was the seed, unnoticed and unheralded.

A committee was formed by William A. Reuben, author of the series, Joseph Brainin and David Altman. They asked two Communist-front organizations, the Civil Rights Congress, which is not to be confused with the American Civil Liberties Union, and the International Workers Order, to assist. These new allies succeeded in forming chapters in fifty cities. Suddenly, there was a national organization.

In the meantime, the New York committee developed a letterhead with sponsors' names on it. This involves a technique which can be insidious. The unwary are persuaded by a high-sounding title, which usually includes the word "Peace" or "Justice," to lend their names to a letterhead. When a respected name is obtained, it is used as leverage to persuade others that they are in good company. Sometimes the name is exploited without express permission, by the device of stating in the invitation that if there is no reply, assent will be assumed. If, later, there is protest, the name is withdrawn and an apology given for the mistake.

The point is that few sponsors have the time and means to investigate who is really behind the impressive title of the letterhead. So, distinguished sponsors are listed on letterheads, who might be horrified if they knew what they were really sponsoring and who was behind the movement. Furthermore, these committees raise funds, and often there is no real accounting of their use.

A customary device is to attract sponsors by representing an issue which may only be tangential to the real purpose of the committee.

In the Rosenberg case, this was capital punishment. Millions of people were opposed to the death penalty. The Supreme Court, reacting partially to this public aversion, held nineteen years later that it violated the Eighth Amendment which prohibits cruel and unusual punishment. This decision saved six hundred prisoners from execution, but it came too late for the Rosenbergs. Ironically, they had raised that very point on appeal. But no grievance can be belatedly raised on this account.

The law is not an inanimate solid structure. It is a living breathing mechanism, which changes and grows with the evolution of ideas and the shifting of standards. Therefore, we cannot bemoan the effects of change on those who would prefer a permanent status quo. Slavery was once legal, but who would criticize "the injustice" to widows who lost their only property because of emancipation? Income tax was once illegal, but would anyone restore that rule? No great moral is therefore to be drawn from the misfortune to the many who died on the gallows, in currented chairs and pellet-filled chambers, because the law was changed. If it were otherwise, we could never correct a wrong interpretation by the highest court (yes, it has conceded having erred), or alter the law to accord with changing social conditions and new judicial concepts. President Kennedy once commented on the vagaries of the draft as "a built-in inequity" which, as in many other areas, is part of life.

The Rosenberg Committee's appeal to commute the death sentences was particularly powerful. They were not hardened criminals, rapist killers or presidential assassins, for whom capital punishment would be emotionally acceptable even to its opponents. They would be the first husband and wife to be electrocuted, and the plea not to make their two innocent children orphans was a call for mercy not easily resisted.

The committee gathered in thirty-seven sponsors, some of whom were non-Communists, like the author Waldo Frank and the editor Robert M. Lovett. Still it achieved no success at first. When Emanuel Bloch argued his first appeal before the Court of Appeals, only a few newspapermen attended. However, the rejection of the appeal created momentum for organized protest. The founders of the committee, joined by Mrs. Morton Sobell, went on speaking tours, describing the horrors of the death house, and appealing for funds "to fight Fascism." Mrs. Sobell became an effective speaker. They created a revival-meeting atmosphere, and collections were timed expertly.

Thus, possessed of funds, full-page advertisements appeared, featuring noble quotations from Ethel. The first large public meeting was held on March 12, 1952, at Pythian Temple in New York City. There followed a mass meeting in Chicago, and one in Far Rockaway under the auspices of the International Workers Order. Dr. S. Andhil Fineberg of the American Jewish Committee attended as a critical observer. In his book, *The Rosenberg Case,* he described the curious goings on at this meeting. A question-and-answer period had been announced, and so he sought to ask Mrs. Sobell a question. He was repeatedly put off. After a collection had been taken, he was finally permitted to put his query. She fell in a faint. The audience was indignant at the questioner and she was escorted out. He had sought to dig into a statement she made in her speech: "Julie and Ethel could save their own skins by talking, but they will never betray their friends." Just what did this mean?

The propaganda program took hold and the Rosenberg cause blossomed. It was not a gradual growth. There was a geometric progression of interest.

A theater rally sponsored by Paul Robeson, Ruby Dee and Rockwell Kent in New York drew two thousand people. Large sums of money were collected. Thousands of "fact sheets" were distributed in which Ethel and Julius wrote emotional appeals. From reading them one would have thought Ethel and Julius were prosecuted for making a speech, rather than for espionage.

> We are an ordinary man and wife, and it was inevitable that ordinary people would be grievously persecuted by the history of these past few years.
>
> Like others we spoke for peace, because we did not want our two little sons to live in the shadow of war and death. Like others we spoke for the liberties of our fellow citizens, because we believe, and want our children to believe, in the fine democratic traditions of our country.
>
> That is why we are in the death house today, as warning to all ordinary men and women, like you yourselves, that there are forces today which hope to silence by death those who speak for peace and democracy.
>
> But you see, we are not silent today, even though we are behind bars. And we say to you that no matter what happens to us, you must not be silent.

At Christmas time, a picket line marched around the White House chanting pleas to save the Rosenbergs. Eight hundred New Yorkers chartered an eight-car New York Central train to go to Sing Sing and bring Christmas greetings to the Rosenbergs. They were not allowed to approach the prison, but they sang songs of solidarity.

The International Communist Party perceived the value of the protest. As if on command, Rosenberg committees appeared in London, Paris, Rome, Vienna and Copenhagen. They bombarded United States consulates and embassies with protest literature.

At about this time in 1952, the Communist government in Czechoslovakia tried Rudolph Slansky and seven other "bourgeois Zionist Jews" and hung them. There was an international reaction to this deed. The Communists used the Rosenberg case to retort. Jacques Duclos, the French Communist leader, declared that "the conviction of United States atom spies Julius and Ethel Rosenberg was an example of anti-Semitism, but the execution of eight Jews in Czechoslovakia last week was not." This argument made millions of Europeans, aroused by the Slansky case, aware of the Rosenberg case with which it was coupled. New impetus was given to the Rosenberg committees.

The capital punishment issue had great public appeal, but there had been no dent made on the merits of the case. Although the committee's literature asserted vehemently that the Rosenbergs were innocent victims of a Fascist plot, there was no acceptance of the claim among the general public. What the committee needed to turn the appeal for mercy into a crusade for justice was a statement by a responsible non-Communist source that there was doubt about guilt.

This came from Dr. Harold C. Urey, the distinguished Nobel Prize nuclear chemist, discoverer of heavy water, and developer of the gaseous diffusion process of Uranium 235. In a letter to the New York *Times* in January 1953, he supplied the forensic chemical to give the protest movement an implosion effect. He attacked the rule that accomplice testimony should be sufficient to convict, when the co-conspirators could profit by their confession. He pointed to the disparity of the sentences given to the confessed spies and to the Rosenbergs. Dr. Urey concluded:

> We are engaged in a cold war with the tyrannical government of the U.S.S.R. We wish to win the loyalty and approval of the good people of the world. Would it not be embarrassing if, after the execution of the Rosenbergs, it could be shown that the United States had executed two innocent people and let a guilty one (Ruth Greenglass) go completely free? And, remember, somewhere there is a representative of the U.S.S.R. who knows what the facts are.

(421)

Immediately thereafter, Albert Einstein urged clemency, stating that his reasons were the same as those set forth "by my distinguished colleague, Harold C. Urey."

Could there be better auspices to sow a doubt that something had gone awry? The committee's literature widened its attack. No longer was its aim to commute the death penalty. Its slogan became "Free the Rosenbergs."

Ethel and Julius understandably saw no reservations in these developments. They considered them a verdict by the highest court of all, the public, reversing their conviction. Triumphantly, she wrote to Bloch, of course, for distribution:

> While the entire world storms, thunders, exhorts, and pleads, we are witnessing the astounding spectacle of the most powerful nation on earth, bound helpless, powerless to reverse itself because it is always so much easier to commit new errors than to right old ones!

The florid approach of martyrdom was in her words.

> All, all past, and decision close at hand; for us, sitting here and fighting for breath in an ever-narrowing circle of tightening time, it looms large and unknown, color-blurred and shapeless upon the gigantic canvas of a furious age.

Julius, too, drank deeply from the cup of confidence handed him by the committee. He wrote to Ethel:

> My Sweet,
> The attendance at rallies, the contributions and the petitions coming into the Committee office are bearing out our faith in the American people.

A little later:

> Sweetheart Darling,
> The world has come to recognize the true nature of our case and the people, the most effective force on earth, are behind us and are demonstrating a thorough awareness that they know how to fight for peace and freedom.

The committee pressed for an all-out public appeal before the final appeals went to the Supreme Court. It wanted to muster Michael and Robby into the ranks. The Blochs, of course, were opposed to that. Manny had adopted the role of child psychologist in protecting the children as much as possible from the trauma of their parents' plight.

However, the Rosenbergs were carried away by what they thought was the winning battle and felt every contribution should be made. Perhaps they even reasoned that if the public relations battle was won, the children would be saved too. Without doubting their love for their children, their decision nevertheless was to assign them actively to the committee's activities. So the children were cast into the limelight at public meetings, as sympathetic exhibits for the denunciation of the death sentence. There they sat while speakers pointed at them and harangued audiences that they must not become orphans. Repeatedly, they heard the gruesome references to death in the electric chair, and the short time remaining before their father and mother would die in it. They were even exploited as pickets, carrying signs which read "Don't kill my mommy and daddy!" Undoubtedly, they brought tears and contributions from the audiences, but Alexander Bloch, particularly, was disgusted with the ruthlessness of the campaign. Emanuel also disapproved, but he could not distinguish emotionally between Ethel and Julius' struggle and their children's "duty" to co-operate.

The rallies multiplied. Attendance increased. Two thousand people cheered speakers at Carnegie Hall. A record-breaking ten thousand persons appeared at Randall's Island Stadium. Committees proliferated in forty more cities. Hired organizers rang doorbells to collect signatures and contributions.

The committee sold Rosenbergs' "Death House Letters" and a book of poetry, some written by Ethel. The record of the trial was printed in pocketbook size and sold for ten dollars. Ten thousand were bought.

All in all, one million dollars was collected.

The public furor seemed to have reached its climax as the final legal battle in the Supreme Court was about to begin. Crowds hovered ominously around the Court, chanting songs and demanding "justice." The State Department was deluged with appeals on behalf of the Rosenbergs, which came from American embassies throughout the world. President Eisenhower received fifty thousand letters begging for clemency.

It was in this setting that Bloch went to the Supreme Court to make his final plea. He couldn't anticipate the fact that despite all judicial precedent, it would not be final, nor that world-wide public support would explode beyond the expectations of the most rabid committee leaders.

CHAPTER 43

Five days remained to save the Rosenbergs from electrocution. What was desperately needed was a stay from the Supreme Court, so that a petition for certiorari could be granted to argue the appeals from Judge Kaufman's denial of a new trial, and Judge Ryan's decision rejecting the claims of perjury and prejudice. The only other legal weapon left, if the stay was not granted, was a writ of habeus corpus which on any ground would test whether the Rosenbergs were being legally detained. After that, there was only a second appeal for clemency to President Eisenhower. A new attorney, who had fought for Sacco and Vanzetti, offered to help in the emergency. He was John H. Finerty, seventy-four years old. He had a ruddy Irish complexion. His cheekbones were high and his chin long, giving his face a vaselike contour.

The legal staff had grown sufficiently so that the intense labors could be divided among Professor Sharp, Bloch, Finerty and Agrin. They rushed out sets of papers, and on Friday, June 12, they were referred by Chief Justice Fred M. Vinson to Supreme Court Justice Jackson, who came from the New York district and was authorized to hear applications for stays. He examined the papers, heard argument and felt that the matter should be passed upon by the entire Court. This was a victory. Had he denied the stay, they would be scurrying around for other individual justices with diminishing chances because of previous rejection. In view of Justice Jackson's recommendation, the full Court sat in conference on Saturday, June 13, 1953, and adjourned at five o'clock without announcing its decision.

Monday morning, June 15, 1953, was the last day of the term. It was also three days before execution. If the Court denied the stay, it would disband for the summer holiday and not meet again until October. There would be neither time nor a court to which any plea could be made. The lawyers and reporters, representing many nations throughout the world, sat nervously in the courtroom waiting for the last decisions of the term to be announced.

In Lafayette Park, thousands of pickets were marching four abreast, their signs proclaiming that the Rosenbergs must not be "murdered." Some carried red flags and sang Communist hymns to the displeasure of committee organizers, who sought to make the protest universal.

Hundreds of sympathizers, who could not get into the crowded courtroom, marched silently in front of the Supreme Court building, made of white marble as if it had been cut out of the sky.

Michael and Robby were kept in the hotel room on this occasion, the older boy biting his nails continually.

Finally, the clerk announced that the Court would read its decision on the petitions of several defendants in the case of the United States of America against Ethel Rosenberg, Julius Rosenberg, Morton Sobell, and Anatoli Yakovlev.

> The application for a stay is denied. Oral argument is denied.

The decision was by a vote of five to four, Justices Douglas, Frankfurter, Black and Jackson dissenting. The Court immediately announced adjournment until the October term. Before the judges could rise to file out through the red plush curtain behind them, Finerty sprinted to the podium, from which lawyers make their argument, and yelled, "Excuse me, your Honors, but we have a petition for a writ of habeas corpus which must be acted upon before your Honors leave. We have delivered the motion papers to the clerk. Otherwise, executions will take place without an opportunity to review a meritorious application."

Chief Justice Vinson, standing to depart, looked at his fellow judges, and said, "We will consider it at once and advise you." He canceled the adjournment by instructing the clerk to announce a recess.

Several hours later, the clerk rapped his gavel and announced, "The Honorable Justices of the Supreme Court of the United States." All jumped to their feet with a mixed feeling of respect and anxiety. The judges filed in, the Chief Justice first, and the others in the order of seniority which also determined their seats to the right and left of him.

The Chief Justice announced:

> In the petition for a writ of habeas corpus on behalf of the defendants Ethel and Julius Rosenberg, unanimously denied.

At a nod of his head, the clerk announced adjournment until the October term. The judges rose and disappeared through the slit in the curtain.

Reporters rushed out of the courtroom, and on their race to the telephones, replied to eager questions, "Stay denied." The words spread as if on wings to the hundred of spectators and protesters in the corridors and in the streets. Wails of disbelief and anger rose from the crowds. Men and women wept. Some made ugly threats. There were only two days left before execution.

As Bloch, Finerty and Sharp fought their way through the crowd, down the esthetically designed multiple steps, microphones were pushed into their faces. Shaken by the calamitous finality of the decision, they were asked to offer plans when they had none. They improvised, Finerty saying breathlessly as he pushed through the blocking phalanx, "We will apply for a stay of execution to individual judges." "But the decision was unanimous," replied a correspondent. "Do you really think there is any hope of preventing the executions Thursday night?"

Bloch replied, "Yes, this can't happen. We will submit a new petition for clemency to the President."

"Have you heard," said the reporter from the Washington *Post*, "that the President was visited by a group of ministers today, and that he said, he did not intend to interfere in the Rosenberg case?"

Bloch's knees buckled. He turned a shade paler. "No, I haven't heard," he stammered. "Please, gentlemen, let me through. We have petitions to prepare."

Completely disheartened, the lawyers returned to the Statler Hotel where one bedroom served as an office, three typewriters being spread on a bed. They avoided plopping into armchairs, lest coming to rest might complete the collapse. They had to fight time. To stop was to default. They drove themselves to work. Futile though it appeared to be, there was comfort in action.

Finerty assigned the tasks. He and Miss Agrin would dictate a second petition for clemency to President Eisenhower. There were new points to be made. Judge Learned Hand could be quoted. Even if President Eisenhower considered the Rosenbergs unworthy of mercy, was it not in the interest of the United States to prevent international ill will, which their execution would cause?

Bloch was given the awesome task of finding Judge Douglas and obtaining a last second stay. He reached him in chambers and made a tearful plea. The judge explained to him what he already knew, that he could not overrule the Court, which had passed on the same arguments. Bloch left in despair, knowing not where to turn.

Then the most remarkable incident of the Rosenberg case occurred. If mathematicians had attempted to calculate the possibility of its happening, they would have had to employ infinity as a measure of the odds.

CHAPTER 44

In Greek tragedies, the dramatic technique of *deus ex machina* was employed to solve impossible problems. At the last moment, a god appeared from nowhere and unwound the tangles of the plot. So, in *Orestes* when the actors were about to kill each other, Apollo appeared and made peace among them.

Molière copied this technique. In *Amphitryon,* just when the complexities were too great for human solution, Jupiter descended, "announced by thunderclaps, armed with a thunderbolt, in a cloud on an eagle" and resolved everything. Molière's stage directions provided for pullies and ropes to lower the actors who would play god *ex machina*.

In the Rosenberg case, two characters were dropped from above, right into Judge Douglas' chambers to give last-minute succor which could only have been interpreted as divine intercession.

Who were they? Two lawyers, who had never met the Rosenbergs, and had no authority to speak for them. They had been rejected by Bloch and Professor Sharp. They had been retained by an ex-Communist, Irwin Edelman, a soap-box orator and left-wing pamphleteer from Los Angeles. He sent them on a mission to save the Rosenbergs.

The first was Fyke Farmer, a Nashville, Tennessee, lawyer, who was a campaigner for World Government. He was fifty-one years old, tight lipped and angry looking. His brown hair was parted in the middle and plastered down shiningly. He wore round, wire-framed spectacles.

The second attorney was Daniel Marshall, fifty, a crusading liberal. He had wavy gray hair. He was tall, loose jointed and well spoken, and had a pleasant, open face.

At six o'clock in the evening, while Justice Douglas was disposing of last-minute chores and packing his books and briefs to leave for his summer vacation, Farmer and Marshall descended upon him. They sought a stay in the Rosenberg case.

Of course, the judge told them it was an impossible request.

"We have a new legal point which conclusively demonstrates that the Rosenbergs were illegally sentenced," they announced.

Justice Douglas barely looked up. The pause was an invitation to state the point.

They did. The Rosenbergs were convicted under the Espionage Act of 1917. In 1946, Congress had passed the Atomic Energy Act, which also made it a crime to reveal atomic secrets. However, the death penalty was permitted only if the jury recommended it.

The jury in the Rosenberg case made no such recommendation. Therefore, Judge Kaufman had no authority in 1951 to impose the death penalty. The sentence was illegal!

Justice Douglas looked up. "This contention was never made before?"

"Never!" they assured him.

He sat silently for a while. Then, as if shaking off a bad impulse, he said, "It is an interesting point, but I am not sure it has merit. Look, gentlemen, my car is packed downstairs. I am driving to the Coast in the morning. I have no time to study the matter. Why don't you make your application to Judge Black or one of the other judges?"

"We have learned that Judge Black has gone to the hospital to have some minor surgery. He left word with his secretary that he will entertain no petitions, and he even included the Rosenberg case by name. No other judge can be reached. Most have already left the city. Your Honor, two lives are at stake. Should they be snuffed out because this point was not made previously?"

Judge Douglas leaned back reflectively. Marshall took advantage of the silence. "There is also new evidence in the case. A console table has been found which is objective evidence that the Greenglasses lied when they described it as an espionage tool for microfilming."

Douglas replied, "I know, but Judge Kaufman and the Court of Appeals denied the motion for a new trial on that ground."

"Yes," replied Farmer, "but Judge Learned Hand thought the Supreme Court ought to review the matter."

Fyke Farmer returned to surer and newer ground. "The main point, your Honor, is that even if the Rosenbergs were guilty, they could only be sentenced for the lesser punishment of two overlapping statutes. The death penalty was illegal, because no jury recommended it. This is purely a legal point, not a factual dispute like the console table. It should be reviewed by the Supreme Court. It never has been."

The judge sat deep in thought for a minute. Then he stirred. "How soon could you submit a brief on the legal question?"

The lawyers were so eager to answer, they could not speak. Finally, the words came. "Within an hour or so. We have our research notes with us." Farmer fumbled in his brief case and brought out a sheath of loose papers. "Here, we can leave this with you in the meantime."

"And how soon can I have the trial record and a memorandum about the new evidence?"

"We'll call Mr. Bloch and Professor Sharp and get it promptly."

"Do that," said the judge. "Come back as soon as you are ready."

"Thank you, thank you," said the gods *ex machina*. They dashed out to a telephone and called Bloch. He answered. There were "the two crackpots" again. How could he get rid of these nuisances? He was desperately trying to draft an appeal to the President. Every moment was precious, and here again were these interlopers with their wild idea. He was about to hang up when he heard Fyke Farmer say that he and Marshall were outside Judge Douglas' chambers and that the judge had agreed to consider an application for a stay on the new point they had raised. Bloch could only shout, "What!"

Farmer rushed on to tell him that the judge would also read the record of the trial, and wanted a memorandum on the newly discovered evidence point. "Can you bring the papers at once? He is waiting."

Bloch and Professor Sharp seized the heavy volumes of the trial minutes, the briefs for a new trial, and ran for a cab to take them to the Supreme Court. They were fearful of a hoax, but the urgency in Farmer's voice was convincing. Breathless with their burden and excitement, they rushed into the courthouse. Farmer and Marshall met them, and they were ushered into Judge Douglas' chambers. In a moment, they knew it was all true. The judge took the briefs and asked them to place the record on the table. He buzzed for his secretary.

"I am not leaving in the morning. Telephone ahead that I am delayed. Call my law secretary to work with me tonight. Tell Clerk Wiley to stay too. How about yourself? Can you stay?"

"Yes, sir," she said with a rueful smile.

Then he addressed the lawyers, "All right, gentlemen. I will be staying here probably through the night. My secretary will advise you of my decision, when I am ready."

There was an emotional babble of thank you's. "It is wonderful of you, your Honor, to consider this matter at this hour," said Bloch.

"Oh, don't thank me," said Judge Douglas. "Justice has many lanes and we must traverse all of them."

CHAPTER 45

Bloch embraced Marshall and Farmer and their idea enthusiastically. The enlarged team of counsel returned to the hotel in high spirits. Their entrance, as if on air, made unnecessary any report of what had happened. All tiredness disappeared. There was new hope that the executions scheduled to take place in forty-eight hours would be stayed.

Nevertheless, a petition for clemency had to be completed. There had been too many reverses in the courts, when better possibilities than the present gambit existed. If Justice Douglas were to find that the new legal theory was unsound, the stay would be denied, and an appeal to the President was all that was left.

Petitions for clemency must be signed by the condemned. Bloch had, therefore, made arrangements to fly to Ossining and also to take the children with him. This might well be the last time they could see their father and mother. Bloch dreaded the meeting. He, too, could hardly face his clients, who had become dear friends, knowing that it might be a last farewell.

The defense forces were spread strategically. Farmer and Marshall sat in the lawyers' room in the Supreme Court to await Judge Douglas' decision.

Bloch and the children headed for Sing Sing. Michael and Robby, spruced up in Eton jackets and pants, carried marigolds and roses to give to Ethel. When they arrived at the jail, the flowers were taken from them. They were against the rules.

The imminence of death had overcome Ethel and Julius' reluctance to meet with the children while handcuffed. They wanted the family to be together for the last meeting. Julius sat at one end of the seven-foot conference table, a stiff sentinel guard behind him, and Ethel at the other end with a matron at her shoulders. Ethel and Julius were looking at each other intently, like a painter who peers at his subject to fix the image indelibly in his mind.

The children burst upon the scene shattering the picture. Robby rushed to his mother, shouting, "They took our flowers away." She kissed him. "It was lovely, darling, of you to bring them."

"You look just like your picture. They carry your picture and Papa's all over," he said excitedly.

Bloch approached and kissed her, Robby running to his father. Michael, tense and pale, embraced her silently.

Bloch seated himself in the middle of the table and called for the boys to be quiet. He announced that he had good news and he wanted everyone to listen. Robby was fascinated by his father's handcuffs and played with them silently.

"Last night, Judge Douglas took under advisement out application for a stay of execution. Two lawyers submitted a new point to him and he thought well enough of it—"

Julius interrupted excitedly, "Do you think he will grant a stay?" The reference to the new lawyers went by them.

Ethel pre-empted the answer. "He will. He will. Tomorrow is our fourteenth wedding anniversary. It is an omen. It will be a gift for us."

"Well," said Bloch, "we have a right to be hopeful. Judge Douglas is a compassionate man. You know he had his car packed to ride to the Coast, and he postponed his time of leaving. He is working all night reading our papers, including our briefs on the newly discovered evidence point."

"When will we know?" asked Julius. He was sweating.

"Maybe today, or tomorrow. That is why I must rush back."

Ethel broke in. She threw her head back defiantly. "They won't dare go through with it," she said. "The people are aroused. They are protesting all over the world. You got my letter, Manny, about the visit from the prison director, Bennett. He offered us relief if we would talk. It is the government which is afraid—not us." Her voice had risen to a scream.

"Ethel is right," said Julius. "A stay will be granted. What will happen then?"

"That's just it," said Bloch. "If we get a stay, it goes over the summer to October. That's the next term of the Supreme Court."

He referred to the time element triumphantly. There was a gush of relief in the room. When one is fighting desperately for hours, a few months seem like years.

But now, Bloch had to obtain their signatures on the petition for clemency. How was he to broach the subject without piercing the euphoria which he had created?

"Still, we must be prepared for every emergency," he said. "So I have brought a petition for clemency even though we are confident we won't have to use it."

He reached into his brief case and brought out a thick set of papers backed with a blue cover. He moved his chair next to Ethel, and turned the pages for her like an assistant for a concert pianist. When she had completed reading it, she said,

"This is very good. But, Manny, I have written a letter to Eisenhower and I would like you to use it—that is, if you have to."

She asked the matron to give it to him.

"Certainly, I'll insert it in the petition," he said, not stopping to read it, to continue the impression that it was all academic.

The guard spoke up to say that the letter could not be taken out unless it was submitted to the warden for approval. Bloch asked him to take him to the warden as soon as he was ready to leave.

He was eager to end the session. Seconds were ticking away and despite the brave talk, they seemed to be moving nearer to that door of death at the end of the hall.

Ethel felt Michael shivering next to her. He had not followed the talk. His mind was filled with vivid images created by "orators" who had aroused audiences by morbid descriptions of his father and mother writhing against the straps of the electric chair. The family that was housing him reported that time and again, they were awakened by his shrill nightmare screams.

When, despite the manacles, the petition was signed, Bloch tried to harness the rampant emotions he felt everyone but Robby was experiencing. As lightly as he could, though the quiver in his voice betrayed him, he said, "Well, I must rush off to catch the plane back, and get the good news. Come, boys, say good-bye."

He embraced Ethel. She clutched him and he felt this was her final expression of gratitude. He turned away without looking at her, to shake hands with Julius, who drew him toward him and put his head against his chest. Robby kissed both and ran to the door, but when Michael put his arms around Ethel, he began to shake with suppressed sobs. The matron, in tears herself, gently separated them, and led him to his father. He covered his father's face with kisses, mumbling incoherently. The matron pulled him away and with her arm around him tried to lead him out. Suddenly, he broke out of her grasp, and began to scream hysterically.

"I'll never see you again! They're going to kill you! I won't let them! I'll kill them first. They are murderers! I won't let them kill my mother and father!"

He ran to Ethel and threw his arms around her. His face was contorted. The guard seized him, lifted him up bodily and carried him out kicking wildly. Ethel tried to run to him, but the matron held her down. Robby dashed at the guard, pounding his fists at him. Bloch, weakened by his exertions, could not absorb another blow. He tottered, holding the door to steady himself, as the wails in the room finally ushered him out.

Julius sat frozen and choked. He lifted his chained arms high above his head, tears flooding down his cheeks, and then there came from him an animalistic, unending bellow—"No-o-o-o!"

CHAPTER 46

Ethel's reference to James V. Bennett, federal prison director, involved visits by him to her and Julius separately the preceding week. He had been sent by the Department of Justice to offer a recommendation to commute the death sentences, if they would co-operate with the government and reveal what they knew about the spy ring.

The versions of these remarkable meetings differ. Ethel and Julius wrote Bloch lengthy descriptions of the confrontations, obviously for propaganda use. They were self-serving inflammatory descriptions characterized by Julius as "the ugly brutality of police state tyranny." Ethel considered them a sordid attempt to pressure them into confessing or forfeiting their lives. Although it was never suggested that only one of them would accept the proffer, she assumed that was the intent and wrote a searing letter, pitting her love and loyalty against her life:

> So now my life is to be bargained off against my husband's! I need only grasp the line unchivalrously held out to me and leave him to drown without a backward glance! How diabolical! A cold fury possesses me and I could retch with horror and revulsion, for these saviours are actually proposing to erect a sepulchre in which I shall live without living, and die without dying. By day there will be no hope, and by night, there will be no peace. Over and over again I shall see the beloved face and fancy I hear the beloved voice. Over and over again, I shall sob out the last heartbroken, wracking good-byes and reel under the impact of irrevocable murder! . . .
>
> I should far rather embrace my husband in death than live on ingloriously upon such bounty.

This was all to be translated into public resistance. "The people must be told all about what took place for there is great danger in our land if this Fascist stuff is not stopped now," wrote Julius. "We must live to defeat the plans of the Justice Department to kill us because they could not use us."

On the other hand, the FBI claimed it had information which, though not in evidentiary form for court, proved that the Rosenbergs could give invaluable help to the government in exposing the spy ring which was still operating in the country. The Department of Justice proposed that such co-operative information would warrant a reward, just as the Greenglasses and Gold had escaped death sentences by "coming clean." Apparently, Judge Kaufman had been informed of this fact, because when the Rosenbergs applied to him to reduce the sentence, a year and a half after they were convicted, he wrote:

> The Rosenbergs have not seen fit to follow the course of David Greenglass and Harry Gold. Their lips have remained sealed and they prefer the glory which will be theirs by the martyrdom which will be bestowed upon them by those who enlisted them in this diabolical conspiracy (and who, indeed, desire them to remain silent).

This expressed the theory that the Communists had organized the international protest not to save the Rosenbergs, but to shackle them with martyrdom, so that they would die in silence; that they would find it more desirable to achieve immortality as revolutionary victims than to confess. Indeed, many non-Communists, who recommended clemency, used this very argument to commute the death sentences. They contended that the Communists wanted the Rosenbergs to die in order to silence them, and that a prison sentence would hold the sword of revelation over Communist heads.

On this theory, the more Ethel wrote poetry about her heroic resolve, and Julius about Fascist infamy, the more contrition became impossible.

The opposite view was simple. They were innocent and had nothing to confess. Julius wrote to Bloch, of course not for his eyes alone:

> Dear Manny,
> Before God and man I must blazon forth these truths: We are completely innocent. Nothing can change this . . .
> Don't be too hasty, gentlemen, in pulling the switch. Remember, it is a two-way affair. The world is watching our government's action in this case and the conscience of men of good will is outraged by the brutal sentence and the miscarriage of justice in the Rosenberg case.

Even the fate of the children, an almost irresistible appeal for mercy, was rejected by Judge Kaufman in his later decision not to reduce the sentence.

He wrote:

> The families of these defendants are victims of their infamy, but I am mindful that countless other Americans may also be victims of that infamy.

(438)

The defendants were not moved by any consideration for their families and their children in committing their crimes, but have urged such consideration upon the Court. In considering mercy I am reminded of this passage from George Eliot's *Romola:* "There is a mercy which is weakness, and even treason against the common good."

Ethel felt his equal in a poetic contest. She wrote to Bloch:

Enamored of quotations as the good judge seems, however, I would hazard the guess that a study of the following excerpts from Shaw's *Saint Joan* would not have inclined him to use them against the Rosenbergs! As you will recall, John de Stogumber, the English chaplain, who had been one of the most bloodthirsty advocates of Joan's proposed burning, comes rushing in from this spectacle, overcome with remorse and sobbing like one demented:

"You don't know; you haven't seen; it is so easy to talk when you don't know. You madden yourself with words; you damn yourself because it feels grand to throw oil on the flaming hell of your own temper. But when it is brought home to you; when you see the thing you have done; when it's blinding your eyes, stifling your nostrils, tearing your heart then—then—O God, take away this sight from me! O Christ! deliver me from this fire that is consuming me! She cried to thee in the midst of it: Jesus! Jesus! Jesus! She is in Thy bosom; and I am in hell for evermore!"

And there shall you be, Judge Kaufman, for a crime "worse than murder!"

Ethel

The Rosenbergs' main thesis that they were the victims of a civil rights crisis in the nation was refuted by many liberals, including the American Civil Liberties Union. That organization, which had vigorously opposed the Smith Act aimed at Communists, nevertheless declared through its national board of directors that there was no civil liberties issue in the Rosenberg case. Further, that the death sentence was not so disproportionate to the severity of the crime to amount to a violation of due process. It found the death penalty was not motivated by political or religious considerations and that Judge Kaufman had the right to evaluate the effects of the crime on the international balance of power. The sentence under these circumstances, was a matter of discretion, not civil rights. Indeed, William L. White, a distinguished member of the Board of the American Civil Liberties Union had written a letter to the New York *Times* months earlier, urging that "if at this late hour, the Rosenbergs could be made to see their true situation and in atonement make what the F.B.I. would recognize as a full and complete confession, then we would have a different situation."

The Rosenbergs were steadfast. They told Bennett, "Our dignity is not for sale." Their stubbornness, like some of their letters, was for outside consumption. Actually, they were both at a point of collapse and disintegration. Julius' mother revealed later that he was like a little child when he talked to her alone. With tears running down his cheeks, he said, "Mama, I don't feel good. Oh, Mama, where is my wife? Where are my children? I'm sick. If only I were home, you and Ethel would take care of me."

The government's offer to confess and be saved remained open. Would they be able to resist it if the end came?

CHAPTER 47

While Bloch and the children were at Sing Sing, Finerty, Sharp and Agrin sat in the huge, plush lawyer's conference room in the Supreme Court, waiting for word from Judge Douglas. Hour after hour passed. They ate in shifts to be sure they would not miss the fateful decision. At five o'clock, Bloch arrived. Before he greeted them, he scanned their faces and knew they were still waiting. They, on the other hand, were shocked by his appearance. He looked exhausted and sick. His eyes were sunken in. His lips were bluish, and his face had almost a greenish cast. His shoulders were so bent, it seemed he would not be able to lift his head. They dared not ask him what had happened.

"Ethel has written her own appeal to Eisenhower," he said. "It is just beautiful. Here, read it." It had none of the revolutionary fervor of her other writings. In a remarkable change of pace, she dropped her denunciation of Eisenhower as a dictator, who headed a corrupt capitalistic country. Instead, she approached him with awe, respect and flattery, beseeching him to extend mercy to a mother of two children.

Finerty read it to the group.

> 354 Hunter Street
> Ossining, N.Y.
> June 16, 1953

President Dwight D. Eisenhower,
White House, Washington, D.C.

Dear Mr. President,

At various intervals during the two long and bitter years I have spent in the Death House at Sing Sing, I have had the impulse to address myself to the President of the United States. Always, in the end, a certain innate shyness, an embarrassment almost, comparable to that which the ordinary person feels in the presence of the great and the famous, prevailed upon me not to do so.

Since then, however, the moving plea of Mrs. William Oatis on behalf of her husband has lent me inspiration. She had not been ashamed to bare her heart to the head of a foreign state; would it really be such a presumption for a citizen to ask for redress of grievance and to expect as much consideration as Mrs. Oatis received at the hands of strangers?

Of Czechoslovakia I know very little, of her President less than that, But my own land is a part of me. I would be homesick for her anywhere else in the world. And Dwight D. Eisenhower was "Liberator" to millions before he was ever "President." It does not seem reasonable to me, then, that a letter concerning itself with condemned wife as well as condemned husband should not merit this particular President's sober attention.

True, to date, you have not seen fit to spare our lives. Be that as it may, it is my humble belief that the burdens of your office and the exigencies of the times have allowed of no genuine opportunity, as yet, for your more personal consideration.

It is chiefly the death sentence I would entreat you to ponder. I would entreat you to ask yourself whether that sentence does not serve the end of "force and violence" rather than an enlightened justice. Even granting the assumption that the convictions had been properly procured (and there now exists incontrovertible evidence to the contrary), the steadfast denial of guilt, extending over a protracted period of solitary confinement and enforced separation from our loved ones, makes of the death penalty an act of vengeance.

As Commander-in-Chief of the European theatre, you had ample opportunity to witness the wanton and hideous tortures that such a policy of vengeance had wreaked upon vast multitudes of guiltless victims. Today, while these ghastly mass butchers, these obscene racists, are graciously receiving the benefits of mercy and in many instances being reinstated in public office, the great democratic United States is proposing the savage destruction of a small unoffending Jewish family, whose guilt is seriously doubted throughout the length and breadth of the civilized world! As you have recently so wisely declared, no nation can chance "going it alone." That, Mr. President, is truly the voice of the sanity and of the leadership so sorely needed in these perilous times. Surely you must recognize then, that the ensuing damage to the good name of our country, in its struggle to lead the world toward a more equitable and righteous way of life, should not be underestimated.

Surely, too, what single action could more effectively demonstrate this nation's fealty to religious and democratic ideals, than the granting of clemency to my husband and myself.

Such an act would also be a fitting reply to a small boy's desperate appeal. His bright young mind and homesick heart prompted him (even as his mother was prompted) to see in Mr. Oatis' release, a hope for the release of his own dear parents. I approach you then as he did, solely on the basis of mercy, and earnestly beseech you to let this quality sway you rather than any narrow judicial concern, which is after all the province of the courts. It is rather the province of the affectionate

(442)

grandfather, the sensitive artist, the devoutly religious man, that I would enter.

I ask this man, himself no stranger to the humanities, what man there is that history has acclaimed great, whose greatness has not been measured in terms of his goodness? Truly, the stories of Christ, of Moses, of Gandhi hold more sheer wonderment and spiritual treasure than all the conquests of Napoleon!

I ask this man, whose name is one with glory, what glory there is that is greater, than the offering to God of a simple act of compassion!

Take counsel with your good wife; of statesmen there are enough and to spare. Take counsel with the mother of your only son; her heart which understands my grief so well and my longing to see my sons grown to manhood like her own, with loving husband at my side even as you are at hers—her heart must plead my cause with grace and with felicity!

And the world must humbly honor greatness!

Respectfully yours,

(Signed) (Mrs.) Ethel Rosenberg, 110-510

Women's Wing—C.C.

"That letter ought to move a man like Ike," said Finerty, "but let's hope we don't have to use it." He gazed anxiously at the door. Eleven hours had passed. It was seven-thirty. At that very moment, Clerk Wiley appeared. All but Bloch jumped up, pushed by anxiety.

"I just came to tell you that Judge Douglas is taking a dinner hour," he said.

They left for dinner, waving to the hundreds who were standing vigil in front of the building. They ate hastily and without relish, but a cocktail or two lifted their spirits. Only Bloch remained glum, not confiding the hysterical horror he had lived through and which still kept his stomach in tremors.

It was a mild June Washington night. The air was fragrant with flowers. As they were returning to the Court, Finerty suddenly exclaimed, "I have just seen the new moon over my left shoulder. I am sure we are going to get a stay."

This broke Bloch's silence. Even superstition seemed a sturdy reed after what he had been through. "If you want another omen, tomorrow is the Rosenbergs' fourteenth wedding anniversary," he said.

"Really, on execution day?" said Professor Sharp.

"No," replied Finerty, "the day when they will be saved by a stay."

To keep the raised spirits from flagging and yielding to his tendency to sing after several bourbon sours, he began to chant,

> "We will get a stay,
> We will get a stay,
> Hi, ho, and merry-o,
> We will get a stay."

(443)

Sharp and Agrin joined in, marching to the rhythm. Bloch managed a smile, even though he was out of step.

They were near the Supreme Court, and seeing the "protesters," became self-conscious and stopped singing. But their unintended audience picked up the song, always a unifying factor for a group, and improvised the middle line of the lyrics,

"Murder No, Murder No,
We will get a stay."

The lawyers entered the courthouse serenaded by the musical expression of hope.

Buildings made for day use seem resentful of nocturnal visitors. They express it in dampness and hostile echoes. The grandeur of the white marble becomes sepulchral. For no good reason, everyone began to whisper. Bloch, completely done in, stretched out on a sofa and fell asleep in an awkward posture which revealed its suddenness. His soft snores were welcome sounds in the eerie setting.

For hours, they waited and chafed. They opened a huge window on a courtyard to give some stir to the clinging, heavy air. A few photographers who had gotten in, climbed the center table, marring its polished reflection, to take a favorite picture of the clock over the door, and lawyers lounging restlessly underneath. As the hands of the clock formed different angles, some of the lawyers took to plodding back and forth through the thick carpet. The ten-feet-high portraits of former Supreme Court judges peered down on them. The lawyers imagined their expressions changed, smiles conveying hope or the stern visages saying, "How do you expect one judge to nullify the will of the Court, after it has adjourned? It has never happened in our history."

At five minutes after midnight, Clerk Harold Wiley appeared. They could not read the decision in his face. All expression was blotted out by tiredness.

"I just want to tell you there will be no decision tonight. You can come back tomorrow at ten."

Finerty asked, "Is there any indication—" He hesitated to finish, knowing he had no right to ask.

Wiley was understanding of their anxiety. "I can only tell you that the judge is studying the voluminous papers very carefully."

He saw Bloch still in deep sleep. He pointed to him and said, "Go home and do likewise. I wish I could say the same for myself. Good night."

The next morning, they began their vigil at nine-thirty. Marshall and Farmer were with them.

At eleven o'clock, exactly eleven hours before execution time, Wiley entered the room with labored steps, like a man who is carrying too heavy a burden on his back. He was mercifully swift in his announcement.

"Stay granted!"

Before he could finish the rest of his report, a whoop of joy exploded. Fyke Farmer jumped several feet into the air shaking his fists like a cheerleader. Professor Sharp stood quietly, tears in his eyes. Marshall hugged everybody in sight, screaming, "I told you, I told you." Miss Agrin tried to catch Bloch to congratulate him. This was impossible. He was running around in circles like a wound-up toy which has lost direction, and screaming ecstatically.

Clerk Wiley gave up trying to tell them that an opinion would be filed within an hour. He watched the unorthodox scene, then decided to depart. Even though they were delirious with happiness, they noticed him leaving, and Bloch rushed to express their gratitude. "Please tell the judge, he has done a great service to America, in doing justice to the Rosenbergs. Please tell the judge, on behalf of the children as well as the defendants, we are thankful—thankful beyond words." He stammered and finished the sentence with a burst of tears.

CHAPTER 48

A member of the Washington Rosenberg Committee, Don Rothenberg, heard the bedlam. He ran out of the building, leaping down the steps, barely touching them and yelling, "Stay granted." The crowd cheered, at first in mob style and then in organized fashion. It sounded like verbal cannon salutes.

While reporters once again were dashing from the scene to convey the announcement as quickly as possible to their newspapers, television cameras appeared from nowhere, as if summoned up by the magic of the decision.

This time counsel did not have to feign confidence after defeat. They were too happy to talk and just waved to the cheering crowds. Their grins were the most eloquent statement of their triumph.

When they reached their hotel office, the rooms were not as before, a somber retreat. Dozens of reporters and adherents had invaded their quarters and there was a constant buzz of victory.

Bloch rushed to a phone and called Warden Denno. In response to calls for silence, Bloch gained a host of listeners to his critical call—one he had not really believed he would ever make.

"Warden Denno? This is Mr. Bloch. You have heard the news? Good. Thank you."

He turned to the others in the room and said, "It has already been flashed on the radio."

He continued with the warden. "I want to be sure you receive the news officially. Oh, you have received telephone notice from the Court. Good. Have you already informed the Rosenbergs? How did they take it? Of course. Of course. Will you please tell them that all their lawyers send them congratulations. Thank you. Right, tell them it is an anniversary gift.

"Yes. That's right. There will be an indefinite extension of time. The case will have to be argued in October at the next term of the Supreme Court at the very earliest. That's right.

"Well, thank you, Warden. And thank you for your prompt action on the clemency letter. No, that's right. We won't have to use it now.

"Tell the Rosenbergs that I'll be up soon and bring the children.

"Good-bye. Thanks again."

A member of the Save Rosenbergs Committee announced that he had ordered champagne. Waiters would take orders for cocktails for those who preferred more direct results.

A clerk arrived with a copy of Judge Douglas' opinion. It caused a new wave of exhilaration. It was a more complete victory than anyone had imagined. He not only granted a stay. He sent the case back to the District Court to determine whether the Atomic Energy Act of 1946 applied to the Rosenberg case, so that the death penalty could only be imposed if a jury recommended it. He suggested that whatever the decision, the Court of Appeals ought to pass upon it, and only then would the matter come before the Supreme Court "in the usual order." In other words, he was starting the judicial process all over again on the new point. This meant that the execution was stayed not only to October 5, but perhaps for a year or more after that. Ethel and Julius would not have dared to pray for so much time under the circumstances. His conclusion was forcefully stated:

> I do not decide that the death penalty could have been imposed on the Rosenbergs only if the provisions of the Atomic Energy Act of 1946 were satisfied. I merely decide that the question is a substantial one which should be decided after full argument and deliberation.
>
> It is important that the country be protected against the nefarious plans of spies who would destroy us.
>
> It is also important that before we allow human lives to be snuffed out we be sure—emphatically sure—that we act within the law. If we are not sure, there will be lingering doubts to plague the conscience after the event.
>
> I have serious doubts whether this death sentence may be imposed for this offense except and unless a jury recommends it. The Rosenbergs should have an opportunity to litigate that issue.

Bloch called back Sing Sing to advise Ethel and Julius, through Warden Denno, of the full impact of the relief Judge Douglas had given them. The warden later reported that they were "startled as well as elated" by the manna from heaven.

Judge Douglas also wrote that he had studied the grievances, first, that the trial was not fairly conducted, and second, that a new trial should have been granted on the ground of newly discovered evidence. He denied both motions because the Supreme Court had already passed on them and there was nothing new, which warranted the granting of a stay.

The drinks arrived to vivify the celebration. Bloch offered several toasts.

"First, I drink to Ethel and Julius Rosenberg. Long may they live!"

There were cheers and appreciation for the special meaning of an old toast.

"Now I want to drink to Fyke Farmer and Dan Marshall. My clients have nothing to confess, but I have. When Fyke and Dan first approached me, I resented their intrusion. Frankly, I thought nothing of their new point. That will give you a hint of what a brilliant lawyer I am. But they persisted, and they won a stay. So I love them. I would love the devil if he saved the lives of our clients. As Churchill once said about the Russians when they became our Allies, he would support the devil if he fought Hitler. So I drink to those wonderful devils, my friends, Fyke and Dan."

They were applauded heartily, as befitted heroes of the day. Marshall responded with a toast, while popping corks punctuated his words.

"There is nothing that knits men together more closely than fighting together in a common cause. I don't know whether the Rosenbergs are guilty or not, but I do know that the death penalty was not legally imposed, and now that we have battled together, I consider all of you my friends. I reciprocate the toast to my fellow devils."

Again, laughter and enthusiasm. During his toast, the telephone began to ring. It was a nuisance in the midst of the revelry. Somebody said, "Can't you shut that damn thing off." There was only one way to quiet it. A secretary lifted the receiver and took the message, whispering, "Wait a minute. I'll get him."

When Marshall was finished, everyone called on Fyke Farmer to speak. The secretary intervened, "Mr. Bloch, it is Jack from UP calling."

"Tell him I'll call back," said Bloch, eager to drink in the happy moments denied him for years.

"He says it is important."

"All right. Just a moment, Fyke."

He took the phone jauntily, and suddenly turned serious. Professor Sharp and Miss Agrin noticed it and watched him closely. In the hubbub, they could not hear what he said. He returned slowly, and obviously concerned.

"What is it?" asked Farmer.

"Oh, nothing. Go ahead, Fyke. It is a friend of mine on UP, who says he heard a report that Chief Judge Vinson was considering

(449)

a request from Attorney General Brownell to call a special session of the Court to review the stay granted by Judge Douglas."

"Oh, come now," said Farmer, "that's ridiculous. The judges are not even in Washington. They're all over the country."

"And Judge Black is undergoing surgery," added Finerty.

"Well, more than that," Professor Sharp said. "The Supreme Court always honors a stay granted by any member of the Court, until the issue is heard on the merits. They have never called a special session to vacate a stay. Don't let these rumors spoil our party."

They tried to regain their exuberance. "We want to hear from Fyke," someone shouted. Farmer lifted his glass and began, "Where I come from, we go fox hunting. No matter how wily he is, we persist and run him down. The illegal sentence has withstood all sorts of pursuit, but—"

The phone was ringing insistently again. This time everyone stopped. They looked at the instrument as if it were an enemy. Bloch lifted the receiver with foreboding.

"Yes, this is he. Who?" There was a long pause. "Tomorrow at one? Will all the judges be there? Yes, we are all here. The telegram can be sent here for all of us. We're in Room 706. Is there any order indicating the scope of the hearing? I see. I see." He listened and turned red. "Tomorrow night? That's unfair. I think that's dead wrong. I know, but there might not be time to make a clemency appeal, if it is necessary." He waited. "You *can* help it. That's wrong. Well, that's typical of the treatment we're getting." Another pause. "No, I don't think that is your duty. Well, I disagree. Yes. I'll advise them. Good-bye."

He put the phone down slowly and leaned heavily on it with both hands. His head was bowed, but the anguish from the new blow was clearly visible. Without lifting his head, he said, "This is too much. I can't believe it. I just can't believe it." He shook his head.

Everyone understood the ominous news. Out of regard for Bloch, they did not press him for details, but waited patiently until he was ready to speak. The silence after all the hilarity awakened Bloch. Still leaning on the telephone, he explained haltingly, as if the words hurt him.

"Vinson has reconvened the Court. Special session. We are to be there at twelve noon. Judge Douglas has turned back from Uniontown, Pennsylvania. Judge Black is returning from the hospital. He has not been operated on yet. The entire Court will be there.

"They will decide whether Douglas' stay should be vacated.

"Listen to this, they have rescheduled the execution for tomorrow night!"

The descent from triumph to despair left them frozen in silence. No one moved or said anything for a long moment or two. Then

Finerty, the oldest among them, slowly lifted the glass of champagne next to him and said, "I say let's drink to tomorrow."

It was a courageous toast. It was the day the Rosenbergs were scheduled to die at 11:00 P.M.

>⬤⬤⬤⬤

CHAPTER 49

The Rosenbergs went to sleep that night not knowing that the stay was in jeopardy. Relieved of the consciousness of time, they slept soundly and leisurely for the first time in months. They ate breakfast heartily. It was not until 9:00 A.M. that word came to them of a hearing that very day in the Supreme Court to review the stay. More bewildering and alarming was the news that their execution had been rescheduled for that very evening. Suddenly, their oxygen supply had been sharply curtailed. The clock's ticking once again had the ominous sound of a time bomb, about to explode in fourteen hours.

Buffeted sadistically by legal waves of hope and then of despair, they clung to the only news which was consistently good—public clamor throughout the world against their execution. They had a right to pin their lives to it, for nothing quite like it had ever occurred before, not even in the Dreyfus case. Protest was rising to an overwhelming climax.

United States embassies abroad received 10,251 petitions for clemency. Hundreds of pickets marched four abreast in front of the White House and the Treasury Building with placards calling for mercy. Fifty Washington patrolmen were sent on a special detail to keep the peace, because a small counter group had appeared with signs demanding "Death to the Dirty Spies." Michael handed a letter to the guard at the White House asking the President not to let "anything happen to my Mommy and Daddy."

The House and Senate offices were overrun with Rosenberg supporters seeking legislative pressures.

In New York, the police barricaded 17th Street west of Union Square to contain a huge rally.

At another meeting, sponsored by the national Committee to Secure

Justice in the Rosenberg Case, attended by fifteen thousand people, speakers included Sophie Rosenberg, Julius' mother, Karen Morley, film actress, and Professor Ephraim Gross of City College, who proclaimed that execution would put the United States "to shame in the eyes of the world." Day and night, floats depicting the brutality of the death sentence were towed through the streets. They announced rallies in the stadia.

In dozens of American cities, volunteers were ringing doorbells, beseeching housewives to telegraph President Eisenhower to grant clemency. The mail and telegrams pouring in from the nation inundated the White House.

A special clemency train to Washington was booked. Eight 15-minute radio broadcasts on behalf of the Rosenbergs were arranged in Washington for the three days preceding the execution.

The tumult abroad was even more intense. Conservative as well as radical protest waves smashed together to give them towering impact. Paris seethed with protest. *Humanité,* Communist-oriented newspaper, featured an appeal by Pablo Picasso for all intellectuals to write or cable President Eisenhower. *Figaro* featured a front-page appeal to defeat the Communist design. "Don't play their game. Don't give them their martyrs."

Four hundred French Communists delivered a protest to the United States Embassy. Twelve thousand French Communists, among them Simone Signoret, gathered at the Vélodrome d'Hiver and were addressed by their leader, Jacques Duclos, who charged the United States with anti-Semitism.

François Mauriac, a Nobel Prize winner, Catholic and a conservative, signed a petition demanding clemency.

The French right-wing publication *Aurore* urged the United States to pardon the Rosenbergs in return for the release of William Oatis of the Associated Press, held by the Czech Communist Government.

Le Monde, a newspaper critical of both the United States and Russia, argued that "The execution of the Rosenbergs may be a serious defeat for the whole Atlantic coalition and a victory for its enemies." In another editorial, it charged that "the President seemed to have yielded to public hysteria aroused by witch hunting."

These exhortations aroused the French to fever pitch. Bands of pickets marched through central Paris. They threatened the United States Embassy in the Avenue Gabriel. One speaker read an inciting article by Jean-Paul Sarte in *Liberation,* a Communist daily, which called the impending execution "a legal lynching." Police riot squads were called out to control the surly crowds. A seventeen-year-old boy was badly injured. Eight hundred and seventy-seven were arrested.

Maurice Cardinal Feltin, Archbishop of Paris, sent a message to President Eisenhower urging a retrial or clemency. The bishops of Orleans and Lyons joined in this plea.

Hundreds of delegations visited the United States Embassy daily. French Socialist Deputies called on C. Douglas Dillon, United States Ambassador to France, to urge clemency. June 17, 1953, was declared by French Communist leader Maurice Thorez "Save the Rosenbergs Day." Professor François Perrin, head of the French Atomic Energy Commission, and former Prime Ministers Joseph Paul-Boncour and Edgar Faure sent messages to Eisenhower recommending mercy. Notre Dame Cathedral declared a special hour of prayer. Huge banners appeared of Eisenhower with his famous grin, but each tooth was depicted as an electric chair.

In England at that time the joyous preoccupation was preparation for Queen Elizabeth's coronation. Buildings were being clothed with decorations.

The Rosenberg protest swept away the festive mood and made it riotous. Thousands marched in the streets shouting, "American assassins."

A motorcade rushed to the country home of Prime Minister Winston Churchill, pleading that he intercede with President Eisenhower to save the Rosenbergs. Churchill sent a message to the gate: "It is not within my duty or power to intervene."

In Hyde Park, more than one thousand protesters gathered and then marched out through London, disrupting traffic and carrying a special edition of the London *Daily Worker* with a one-word headline five inches high, "MURDER!"

Another marching army laid flowers at the base of the Franklin D. Roosevelt statue, with a placard which read "That Roosevelt's Ideals Shall Live, the Rosenbergs Must Not Die."

An uncharacteristic violent and insulting debate took place in the House of Commons. Steven Davis, a Labor member, attacked the impending executions and demanded the closing of the United States Embassy. In the absence of Churchill, the majority leader H. F. C. Crookshank condemned the suggestion as "mischievous and wholly without foundation." Clement Atlee tried unsuccessfully to calm the members, as he had done once before when he was under criticism for authorizing Klaus Fuchs to be England's representative at Los Alamos.

The Executive Council of the anti-Communist Transport and General Workers Union, the largest in Britain, passed a resolution for clemency.

Forty Labor members of the British Parliament sent a letter to President Eisenhower stating that the Rosenberg executions would light a fuse which would set off anti-American violence throughout Europe.

Britain's coronation preparation had been turned into "Save the Rosenbergs Week."

In Italy, too, the right as well as the left protested. The Vatican

(455)

Radio announced the sympathy of the world's Roman Catholics for clemency, distinguishing it from the "usual, organized and noisy campaign of the Communists."

Pope Pius XII sent a message to the President stating that he was acting "out of motive of charity and without being able to enter into the merits of the case."

The right-wing press urged clemency, first because "Italians are easy going generous people." Second, because they are "against capital punishment ideologically." Third, because a woman is to be executed and children would be orphaned. Fourth, because many felt that the evidence failed to prove the Rosenbergs guilty beyond a reasonable doubt.

At the other end of the political spectrum, the Italian Communist Party covered the façades and walls of the cities and countryside with chalk and crayon slogans and printed posters demanding justice for the Rosenbergs, often in vicious anti-American terms.

Two large Communist rallies were held in Rome. They were attended by thousands who sang Communist songs and cheered fist-waving speakers, who predicted that there would be a revolution in the United States if the Rosenbergs were electrocuted. In Turin, police beat back two thousand shouting protesters with clubs and fire hoses.

The United States Embassy was surrounded by a threatening mob. Clare Boothe Luce, the American Ambassador, said she was "besieged with clemency appeals."

The Communist-dominated General Confederation of Labor declared a fifteen-minute strike by public-service employees, which paralyzed Italy for that brief period.

Almost all non-Communist newspapers opposed the death penalty even though they believed that the Rosenbergs were guilty. Some argued that they had suffered sufficient anguish as a result of three stays of execution.

Demonstrations took place in Milan and Genoa, where the port was shut down for an hour by the workers.

The two Germanys found it possible to unite on the Rosenberg issue. In East Berlin, Gerhart Eisler addressed rallies in Communist-provocative terminology, likening the case to the Dreyfus affair as an outburst of anti-Semitism. He ignored the fact that the judge and prosecutor of the Rosenbergs were Jews. He read letters from Arnold Zweig to Professor Albert Einstein and from Bertolt Brecht to Ernest Hemingway urging clemency.

At rallies throughout East Germany, anti-Americanism was skillfully mixed with sentiment to move audiences to cheers and then tears. An actress read the children's letter in a choking voice.

Committees were formed in "Defense of Victims of American Reaction." A survey showed that there were more pictures displayed of the Rosenbergs than even of Stalin.

A play quickly appeared on the stage in East Berlin called *In God's Own Country*, condemning "the brutality of American justice."

In Bonn, the protests were quieter, because of the inhibition against the Communist approach in East Germany. They were limited to appeals for mercy, and featured the messages of the Pope, Protestant bishops and non-Communist statesmen and authors.

In Sweden, the predominant liberal press proclaimed the Rosenbergs guilty after a thorough trial, but argued against "playing into Moscow's hands," by executing them.

In Copenhagen, the World Congress of Women sent an appeal to President Eisenhower to stay the execution. The Communist Party in the Scandinavian countries organized meetings throughout the main cities.

In Switzerland, the United States Ambassador Robert E. Ward, rejected a petition for clemency because he "refused to be a tool in a Communist propaganda campaign."

In Melbourne, pickets kept a noisy watch at the United States Consulate. Twenty-three Christian church leaders protested the death sentence. Among the hundreds of signatures, was that of Dr. Wu Yi Fang, president of the Christian Gurling Girls College in Nanking, and T. S. Theu, chairman of the House of Bishops of the Christian Council of Asia. Tugboat crews in Melbourne threatened to boycott United States registered ships if the Rosenbergs were executed. In Sydney, Australia, Anglican, Presbyterian, Methodist, Congregational and Jewish leaders joined in a manifesto for clemency and sent it to President Eisenhower.

In Dublin, two molotov cocktails were hurled through the windows of the United States Information Agency.

In Tel Aviv, the small Communist Party led a demonstration in the streets. Rabbinical and anti-Communist leaders appealed for mercy. This expressed the ambivalent feelings of American Jews, who, through the American Jewish Committee and otherwise, refused to identify with the Rosenbergs as Jews, feeling unjustly shamed by their conviction, but expressing their disapproval of the death penalty as a matter of principle.

In Brussels, a movement was begun for a countertrial in which the Rosenbergs would be the accusers and the United States Government the defendant.

In Ottawa and Toronto, there were around-the-clock vigils of the United States Embassy. The Reverend Clendon F. G. Partridge became chairman of a committee of five hundred men and women from Montreal, Quebec; Toronto, Hamilton and Windsor, Ontario; and Vancouver, British Columbia, to save the Rosenbergs, "on purely

(457)

humanitarian grounds and not influenced in any way by the Communists."

Naturally, in Communist countries, the Iron Curtain was lifted to permit indignant epistles to be sent to the United States and throughout the world.

In Moscow, *Pravda* published a statement by Ilya Ehrenberg made at the World Peace Council at Budapest, Hungary, "This is more than a crime. It is madness."

In Kiev, there were organized protest meetings heaping abuse on the United States for "lynching" the Rosenbergs.

In Warsaw, the government offered the Rosenbergs asylum, if the United States would lift the sentence and permit them to leave. The State Department refused to answer the note, calling it "an impertinence."

Plans were announced for a new play called *Julius and Ethel*, presenting them as martyrs to capitalism and fascism.

In Vienna, Communist lawyers from Russia and the satellite countries convened an "International Conference for the Defense of Democratic Liberties," a euphemism for denouncing American justice.

A stream of protests flowed from Mexico, South America, Guatemala, and parts of Africa. Even the Rosenbergs could not have envisioned such world-wide attention and reaction.

It didn't matter that those who protested on the merits had no real knowledge of the evidence, or the trial procedures, nor that many who thought them guilty, nevertheless, sought commutation of the death penalty. It all melted into one force which spelled out to the Rosenbergs and their ardent committees a civil revolt to aid them. In their minds, distorted by desperation, it might have even appeared to be the beginning of a world revolution. Perhaps, they had become the agents through whom the Communist dream was to be realized. Religious fanatics have proclaimed the end of the world many times. Political fanatics may have thought that the Rosenbergs were the revolutionary messiahs who had come to achieve an international upheaval and bring in the millennium which their blueprints prescribed.

Ethel, in an earlier letter to Bloch, had protested an item in a column which quoted the Rosenbergs as saying that if they could have two years' delay, a Communist air armada would come to rescue them. Even though they had never said this, they might have come to believe it, as a result of the euphoric reports that heads of state, religious leaders and, above all, unions and workers in more than thirty nations were marching for them. It was enough to turn calmer heads than theirs. At the very least, they believed that the world-wide tumult would cause the Supreme Court and the President to hesitate lest they bring the full fury of hate and revolution upon their heads.

It was in this setting that Thursday, June 18, 1953, dawned. For the first time in history, the Supreme Court was convened in special session to review a stay granted by one of its judges. An unprecedented storm of domestic and international resentment beat down upon the White House.

The Rosenbergs could nurse two hopes; that Judge Douglas' stay, which stretched their time more than a year, would be honored; and that, in any event, the President would yield to world opinion, if not to their own entreaties.

CHAPTER 50

The attack on Judge Douglas was not limited to the Court hearing. That day Representative W. W. Wheeler, a Democrat from Georgia, introduced a resolution to impeach Judge Douglas for "high crimes and misdemeanors in office." The House immediately appointed a special five-man committee, headed by Chairman William McCulloch, a Republican from Ohio, to study the matter.

Aroused by the call for an extraordinary session of the Supreme Court, crowds assembled in Washington early Thursday morning. Caught by surprise, the attendants, who had prepared the courtroom for its summer slumber, had been busy removing the slip covers from the judges' different-shaped chairs (to fit their size and reclining habits) and uncover the counsel tables and seats for active use. Even some of the heavy velvet drapes, taken down for airing, had to be hastily restored.

When the Court doors were opened at 10:00 A.M., thousands tried to fill the 350 available seats. The unaccommodated filled the wide marble corridors, making it difficult to get in or out. Other thousands silently surrounded the building as if proximity would relieve their anxiety. Vociferous protesters marched opposite the White House and spilled into the city.

For the first time, reporters from many nations were in and outside the courtroom, as if an international issue affecting their country was about to be decided.

Against this background of vituperation and pleas from abroad, and feverish activity domestically, the judges filed onto the wide bench at twelve noon, after the clerk intoned the awesome announcement of their appearance.

It was immediately evident, as newspapers reported, that the judges

(461)

were in "a tense and snappish mood." There had been disagreement among them about the call for a special session. Judge Black had been particularly outspoken from his hospital bed at the attempt to review a stay, always previously honored. But he was there. So was every other judge assembled from near and far.

Chief Judge Fred Vinson announced that the Court was in session to hear an application by the Attorney General to vacate a stay granted by Judge Douglas in the case of the United States of America against Julius Rosenberg, Ethel Rosenberg, et al.

Acting Solicitor General Robert L. Stern arose to present the argument for the government. He was dressed in the traditional striped pants and cutaway black coat for Supreme Court appearance, and his argument was phrased with similar decorum. This made the contrast with defense counsel who were to speak later all the greater.

He began by referring to the numerous proceedings in the case over a period of two years. There had been appeal after appeal. Six applications had come before the Supreme Court. Execution had been stayed three times. Therefore, only a legal point of the most substantial nature might justify a stay by one judge, which frustrated the will of the entire court repeatedly expressed.

Although Stern had not made a statistical study, his point that the Rosenbergs had received more judicial attention than any case in America's history, or perhaps any in the world, was true. I have made a compilation, annexed as an appendix, which shows that there were 23 applications to the various federal courts and that 112 judges reviewed them (counting the same judges in some instances, who passed on different petitions). Of these 112 judges, only 16, counting the same way, disagreed. These disagreements never related to innocence or guilt, but rather to whether a stay should be issued or further review granted. The Solicitor General contended that "not only had all legal procedures been exhausted once, but many times."

He then turned to the new point which had been raised. He set out to prove that it was entirely without merit, and certainly didn't warrant being sent back to the District Court for determination, as Judge Douglas had unilaterally decided.

The Rosenbergs were convicted under the 1917 Espionage Act. Must the 1946 Atomic Energy Act be applied, even though the espionage occurred before 1946? To do so, he urged would violate the constitutional guarantee against ex post facto proceedings. In other words, it would apply a criminal statute passed after the act had been committed. Our laws forbid making prior conduct criminal by a subsequent statute.

Like a good lawyer, Stern did not ignore the strength of the other side. He stated it fully. It was true that the conspiracy charged that there were continuing acts after 1946. He listed them: the arrangement for Sobell's flight to Mexico, the attempts to have the Greenglasses flee, and even the Rosenbergs' plans to run away, as evidenced by their taking passport photos. But these, argued Stern, were incidental acts which did not dislodge the proper indictment, trial and conviction under the 1917 Espionage Act which applied to stealing of the atom bomb secret in 1944 and 1945, before the Atomic Energy Act was passed in 1946.

Furthermore, Rosenberg's conduct after 1946 did not relate to atomic secrets. He turned the tables by a reverse analogy. Suppose the 1946 Act provided for a severer penalty than the 1917 Act, and the government had attempted to increase the Rosenbergs' penalty. Would not their counsel argue quite properly that the provision of a latter statute could not be applied, and that only the penal provision of the 1917 Act was applicable? The rule did not change because either the government or the defendant would prefer a different punishment.

After further legal analysis, he struck a note which may have been designed for world opinion as well as for the Court.

> Your Honors, it is to the honor of our judicial system that even spies are given the fullest and fairest hearings which man can devise. No other judicial system in the world, not even England's which shares our Anglo-Saxon traditions in law, would have provided the defendants with so many appeals, so many reviews, and so much time to exhaust extraordinary legal tests.
>
> The defendants have been convicted of a most terrible crime, nothing less than the stealing of the most important weapon in history, and giving it to the Soviet Union. Haven't the Rosenbergs had their full day in court and more?
>
> The public's rights and safety are no less precious than the Rosenbergs'. We do not think those rights should be violated any longer.

He urged that the stay be vacated and that the judgment of the Court be at long last carried out. He sat down.

The Chief Judge nodded toward the many defense counsel.

—→←—

Finerty was the first to step to the lawyer's center lectern with its different-colored electric bulbs which the clerk lighted to give silent warning that only five minutes were left of the allotted time, or that the argument must be ended at the end of the sentence.

Finerty had fought for Tom Mooney forty years before. As a crusader for justice, he discarded diplomatic language as if it were a hypocritical encumbrance. He was boiling with indignation at the turn of events and his anger spurted from him like blood from an open artery. He shocked the Court immediately. He denounced the unprecedented hurried call of the Court as an insult to the integrity of Judge Douglas and the Court itself. He made a blistering attack on the Justice Department for participating in a fraudulent conviction, on Attorney General Brownell for persecuting the defendants, and sparing only the use of his name, upon the Chief Judge himself for conspiring with the Attorney General improperly to vacate the stay. Before the astonished Court could catch its breath, he took after Judge Irving Kaufman and particularly Prosecutor Irving Saypol whom he pilloried with nasty adjectives.

Judge Tom Clark leaned over the bench, stopped him, and suggested that it would be more helpful to the Court if he argued his case rather than indulged in a vituperative tirade. Finerty shouted back at him, "If you lift the stay, then God save the United States and this honorable Court." Thus, he added divine retribution to his own appraisal of their iniquity.

Finerty's defiance was a strange way to make friends and influence judges. He preceded by a generation the practice of a few "revolutionary" lawyers who deliberately disrupt court proceedings and prevent the trial from being completed.

In the past, doughty lawyers, fighting great causes, have used "open warfare" against the system. Some have denounced the prejudice of the presiding judge or the southern jury sitting in the case. At times, these orations stirred the blood with their eloquence and sincerity. But what happened to the client on whose behalf they were made? What good did it do him that the lawyer's speech was deemed grandiloquent enough to be included in anthologies, if he hanged or rotted in jail?

In the interest of his client, a lawyer must curb his sense of outrage, swallow his pride if he is humiliated or rebuked by the judge, and even bow to rudeness from his adversary. The only consideration if he strikes back is whether it will advantage his client. Playing to the gallery or to public opinion, which in this case was international, could possibly be justified if it was the best way to win. This was not the case. Finerty's bitter comments published in the American and foreign press might gratify the deep feelings of many readers, but it was not in their power to sustain Judge Douglas' stay. He had infuriated the judges before him and given an extra dimension to the unsavory position of the Rosenbergs.

Ethel Rosenberg was a better psychologist. Although she wrote imprecations for the *National Guardian,* she did not adopt any such tone when she addressed the President. She was respectful, and when she employed vivid words, they were flattering:

You, whose name is one with glory . . .

Had defense counsel been as sensitive to the persuasive art as she was, Finerty might have begun by declaring that the whole world

(464)

looked to the Supreme Court for the protection of the rights of the humblest citizen, even if he was embroiled in criminal acts. Surely, the judgment of one of the distinguished members of the Court that the finality of death ought to await a study of its legality should commend itself not only as a matter of law, but as a matter of humanity. Was not this the very reason for the many appeals permitted under our system of justice, to take every precaution against a fatal error? Ought we to defeat this purpose by last-moment impatience and intransigence, when a new point, never reviewed before, pointed to the possibility that the defendants would be executed by error? Ought not the Court be grateful for the opportunity to avoid a mistake in a capital case which could haunt the nation's and the Court's conscience forever?

Instead of such a sympathetic approach, the mood of belligerence persisted among defense counsel. Marshall, who followed Finerty, began calmly enough. He soon worked himself into the foam of a revivalist, closing his eyes, holding the lectern tightly with both hands and rocking back and forth. He demanded more time to study the legal issue. "I doubt," he yelled, "whether even a justice of the peace would call the meanest pimp before the bar on such short notice."

There was dissension in counsel's ranks. Fyke Farmer interrupted his own colleague and shouted, "I'm not maintaining we're not ready. I'm anxious to get up before the bar and argue."

Marshall settled down to arguing the doubt raised by two statutes, each of which covered the same offense, but had different penalty provisions. Judge Jackson, who had seen Bloch and later Sharp on the various applications to the Supreme Court, was intrigued by the appearance of Marshall and Farmer on the scene. He did not recognize them as *deus ex machina.*

Politely, he interrupted to ask whom Marshall represented. He replied that he spoke for one Irwin Edelman, but that his plane fare from Los Angeles was paid by "nine good Unitarians who asked me to come here and see what I could do for the Rosenbergs."

A few more questions revealed that he had never seen the Rosenbergs and had never been authorized by them to represent them. Indeed, he turned on Bloch and said that he had brought the new point to him and Professor Sharp, but that both had rejected him.

Resenting this slur on Bloch, whom the Court liked, Judge Jackson threw a barb at Marshall. Wasn't Edelman the defendant who had appeared a year ago before the Court on a vagrancy charge?

Marshall was infuriated. Pointing an admonishing finger at the judge, he shouted, "It was a free speech case. It is improper to call it vagrancy. I think it is shocking in a capital case where human lives are at stake."

Chief Judge Vinson gestured for calm. "Don't let your temperature rise," he said. But Marshall would not subside. It loosed his vitriol and he paralleled if not exceeded the offensive launched by Finerty. Probably never before had such quarrelsome scenes occurred in the Court. Usually counsel is so awed by appearing before the nine men whose picture adorns the law offices throughout the nation, that the transposition from photograph to life causes the most eloquent to lose his tongue.

After Fyke Farmer had added to the din, Bloch was permitted to make his plea for the stay, saying that counsel for both sides needed time to study and brief the difficult legal question posed by the 1946 statute. He pointed out that it had two provisions which did not exist in the 1917 statute. One was that the government had to prove that the espionage was intended to injure the United States as well as help a foreign nation. The government in the Rosenberg case had offered no proof of intention to hurt the United States. The second was that the death penalty could only be given if the jury recommended it. It had not done so in the Rosenberg case.

As Bloch grew enthusiastic about the validity of these arguments, Judge Jackson could not resist taunting him about his inconsistency. Had he not turned down these same contentions as meritless, when Farmer and Marshall first submitted them to him?

Bloch's answer was disarmingly candid. "Frankly, your Honor, I was not impressed with them originally, but I adopt them now and believe they are worthy of this Court's fullest consideration."

His embarrassment was evident. Judge Jackson regretted his rebuke. He hastened to make amends.

"I think you have done a fine professional job. You have appeared six times before this Court on behalf of your clients, and I think they are fortunate to have you for their counsel."

He later inscribed this compliment in his written opinion. Bloch responded that he hoped the judge's comment would encourage other lawyers to represent clients in unpopular causes. Thus, the atmosphere was changed for a moment from clash and dissonance to harmonious idealism. Bloch could then dare to request that months were needed to study the legal issue presented by two varying statutes. He pleaded that Judge Douglas' stay be upheld, so that the case could be returned to the District Court for disposition and appeal.

The Solicitor General replied that the point was frivolous. It was not necessary to send the case back to the District Court to begin the judicial process all over again. That would cause years of delay to no purpose. It would make a mockery of our judicial system. There were no new facts requiring determination. At most, it was a question of law, and the Supreme Court could decide it immediately.

Questions poured from the bench to counsel. They indicated the variety of reactions of the judges. After three hours of such argument and exchanges, some of which revived the acrimony, the Chief Judge announced that the Court would take the matter under advisement. A recess was declared. It was 3:00 P.M. For three more hours, the judges debated the issue behind the closed doors of their conference room. The delay indicated the conflicting contentions among them. At 6:00 P.M., the clerk announced that Court was again in session. Tremulously, defense counsel rushed to their seats. Only Judge Burton appeared to announce that a decision would be rendered at noon the next day.

The Attorney General then informed Warden Denno that the executions would be postponed for one day to Friday, June 19, 1953, at 11:00 P.M., to await the decision of the Court. The lives of the Rosenbergs were being extended dribble by dribble.

——→←——

The civilian army of Rosenberg protesters crowded the streets through the night in a sleep hunger strike. Defense lawyers discussed available remedies into the early hours, in the event the Court were to vacate the stay. Relieved by the coming of dawn which they impatiently awaited, they ate, or rather nibbled at, an early breakfast. A coffee cup slipped out of Bloch's trembling hands and fell into his lap. He had no other suit with him. It was arranged for him to go to the nearest clothing shop as soon as it opened. So it was that he appeared in Court in a new suit. They were hours early, pushing through their supporters who were strangely silent. Even Professor Sharp, a restrained smoker, was puffing continuously.

At twelve noon, the courtroom, filled for hours, rose to the announcement which ushered the judges to their seats. Everyone engaged in the psychiatric game of face reading to guess the decision. The judges looked grim. It was obvious that there was disagreement among them. But who was in the majority?

Chief Judge Vinson announced that full opinions would be filed with the clerk, but that in the meantime, he was stating the majority view:

> There is no dispute that a stay should issue only if there is a substantial question to be preserved for further proceedings in the courts. . . . Although this question was raised and presented for the first time to Mr. Justice Douglas by counsel who have never been employed by the Rosenbergs, and who heretofore have not participated in this case, the full Court has considered it on its merits.
>
> We think the question is not substantial. We think further proceedings to litigate it are unwarranted . . . we vacate the stay entered by Mr. Justice Douglas on June 17, 1953.

There was a gasp in the audience. Bloch slumped in his seat.

Judge Felix Frankfurter read a memorandum, stating that the legal question was "complicated and novel," and, therefore, he thought more

(467)

time for study ought to be allowed to both sides. He had not voted either way on the stay.

Judge Jackson then read an opinion on behalf of the majority of six judges including the Chief Judge, Judges Reed, Burton, Clark and Minton. Defense counsel squirmed as precious minutes went by while they had to listen to a lengthy rationale for a decision which doomed their clients.

Judge Jackson pointed out that all the overt acts which related to atomic energy occurred before the 1946 statute. If Congress had attempted to make that statute retroactive to 1944 and 1945, the Supreme Court would have had to declare it unconstitutional. He struck a note which even radicals would applaud:

> To open the door to retroactive criminal statutes would rightly be regarded as a most serious blow to one of the civil liberties protected by our Constitution.

Indeed, the government in 1951 could not have tried the Rosenbergs under the 1946 act for espionage committed earlier.

He quoted Judge Douglas against himself. When defendants sought a stay to raise questions about the sentence among other points, it had been denied and Judge Douglas had written "there would be no end served by hearing argument on the motion for a stay." So, after the matter of sentence was before the Court many times over a period of nine months, a new contention was now made and in an irregular manner.

He launched a severe attack on the interlopers Farmer and Marshall who had "elbowed" regular counsel out of control of their case. Edelman was not authorized to speak for the Rosenbergs and their lawyers had rejected him and his legal emissaries. As to Edelman, he cited his case before the court and said tartly:

> It does not appear that his own record is entirely clear or that he would be a helpful or chosen champion.

He praised the Blochs and decried the events which pushed them aside:

> The Rosenbergs throughout have had able and zealous counsel of their own choice. These attorneys originally thought this point had no merit and perhaps also that it would obscure the better points on which they were endeavoring to procure a hearing here. Of course, after a Justice of this Court had granted Edelman standing to raise the question and indicated that he is impressed by its substantiality, counsel adopted the argument and it became necessary for us to review it.

IIis concluding statement was balm for the Rosenbergs. Defense counsel perked up. Once more, they were lifted from despair to a last lingering hope. Said Judge Jackson:

> Vacating this stay is not to be construed as indorsing the wisdom or appropriateness to this case of a death sentence. That sentence, however, is permitted by law and, as was previously pointed out, is therefore not within this Court's power of revision.

This was virtually putting a finger in the President's eye. The Court had no power to interfere. Clemency was an executive function. By not endorsing "the wisdom or appropriateness" of the death penalty, weren't they in effect saying, "We wish we could modify the death sentence. Only you, Mr. President, can"? It was as close to a recommendation as the Court could come. The defense battery was aching to get out and submit this language to Eisenhower.

But there was more to listen to. Judge Clark read his separate opinion.

> Seven times now have the defendants been before this Court. In addition, the Chief Justice, as well as individual Justices, have considered applications by the defendants. The Court of Appeals and the District Court have likewise given careful consideration to even more numerous applications than has this Court.

He stated that since human lives were at stake, "we need not turn this decision on fine points of procedure or a party's technical standing to claim relief."

> But for me the short answer to the contention that the Atomic Energy Act of 1946 may invalidate defendants' death sentence is that the Atomic Energy Act cannot here apply.

He cited leading authorities holding that where Congress by two statutes forbids certain conduct, the government may choose to invoke either law. The later statute didn't repeal the former. Apart from this rule, the government could not have prosecuted the Rosenbergs under the 1946 statute for preceding overt acts and as to those acts which occurred later, "they related principally to defendants' efforts to avoid detection and prosecution of earlier deeds," not to atomic energy.

He concluded by lifting the sword of justice in a righteous gesture, but then he brought it down with deadly force.

> To permit our judicial processes to be used to obstruct the course of justice destroys our freedom. Over two years ago the Rosenbergs were found guilty by a jury of a grave offense in time of war. Unlike other litigants they have had the attention of this Court seven times; each time their pleas have been denied. Though the penalty is great and our responsibility heavy, our duty is clear.

(469)

Then Judge Black, followed by Judge Douglas read dissenting opinions. A losing litigant and his counsel can derive solace from a minority view, when there is an upper Court to which to appeal. Then counsel can argue that their views are not mere partisan outpourings, but that distinguished judges agree with them. But there is no appeal from the Supreme Court except to God and He doesn't accept jurisdiction for interference in the judicial system. So the highest Court, as a bitter wit once observed, is the one entitled to make the last mistake.

Of what avail were these dissenting opinions when they could not deter the executions now only ten hours away? Perhaps they could give moral force to Judge Jackson's hint to the President to prevent the extreme penalty. So counsel listened intently.

Judge Black began by criticizing the haste of the procedure. The oral arguments were "wholly unsatisfactory" because counsel for both sides didn't have time to brief the question adequately. "Certainly," he said, "time has been too short for me to give this question the study it deserves."

He expressed his doubts rather than conclusions. He was not sure the Court had the power to vacate the stay of one of its judges. He was against calling extra sessions of the Court, during vacation:

> . . . every time a federal or state official asks it, to hasten the electrocution of defendants without affording this Court adequate time or opportunity for exploration and study of serious legal questions.

He did not say that the new point was valid, but that it was substantial enough to require careful review. Why the haste in a capital case?

He argued that the Supreme Court had never reviewed the fairness of the trial itself and there might always remain a question whether the executions were "rightfully carried out."

Thus, he was calling for a review of facts, which the Court of Appeals and district judges had made on several occasions. In 1967, another federal judge, Edward Weinfeld, of outstanding reputation for scholarliness and thoroughness, ruled on an application by Sobell. After a study of the entire record, he declared:

> No act or conduct on part of the government deprived him of a fundamentally fair trial.

Judge Douglas followed with a vigorous dissent. He defended the stay he had granted and which had been struck down before his eyes. When he granted the stay after twelve hours of study, he had done so only because he believed there was a substantial question. Now he dropped the stance of uncertainty.

(470)

I have had the benefit of an additional argument and additional study and reflection. Now I know that I am right on the law.

He insisted that acts under the conspiracy took place four years after the 1946 act, and that the death sentence could therefore only be imposed if the jury recommended it. Where two statutes cover a similar crime, the lesser punishment governs.

I know in my heart that I am right on the law. Knowing that, my duty is clear.

With this ringing declaration as the Rosenberg ship was going down, the clerk announced that Court was in recess until the October term. Bloch rushed to the lectern.

Just a minute, please, your Honor. I apply for a stay to permit us time to petition the President for clemency.

There are only ten hours left before execution. We could not submit our petition to the White House until all legal remedies were exhausted.

Therefore, this is the first moment available, and the President should have an opportunity to study the petition.

The Chief Judge turned to the Acting Solicitor General.

What is the Government's position?

He resisted.

President Eisenhower has already denied a petition for clemency in this matter. There are no new facts which might be submitted to him.

Furthermore, there is still sufficient time to apply to him. I am certain a petition has been prepared and can be submitted immediately.

He turned to Bloch:

Isn't that so?

Bloch conceded:

Yes, it is ready. But there are new developments and we would seek an oral hearing before the President.

We believe the President may be impressed by the fact that three judges thought more time ought to be given to study the legal point concerning the death sentences. Surely, that is a matter which is appropriate for consideration on a petition for mercy. We must add these facts to our papers.

(471)

Judge Black intervened to help the defendants.

Mr. Solicitor General, you might consider that the majority opinion read by Mr. Justice Jackson had this paragraph:
"Vacating this stay is not to be construed as endorsing the wisdom or appropriateness to this case of a death sentence."
Don't you think the President may wish to weigh that statement in his consideration of executive clemency?

Stern replied:

Surely. We do not wish to limit the defendants' rights to submit anything to the President.
We simply think that it can be done promptly and that there ought to be no further delays in the judicial process, which has already extended beyond any previous experience.
If the President feels he wants more time for consideration, he has the power to order it or even to commute the sentence at the last moment. We don't think this Court should entertain any further stays.

The Chief Judge announced:

We will consider the matter and advise you shortly.

In fifteen minutes, they returned. The Chief Judge made his final pronouncement:

The Court denies the application for a further stay. Mr. Justice Black dissents.

Even Judge Douglas had accepted the futility of any further delays.
Clerk Wiley intoned the adjournment again, concluding with "God bless this Honorable Court and the United States of America."
Counsel remained stunned. They forced themselves to action. Bloch, with trembling hands, took the Petition for Clemency signed by Julius and Ethel out of his brief case and served a copy on the Solicitor General. He had hoped never to use it. Then he and his colleagues with heavy feet and heavier hearts started out of the building, which must have seemed to them a white tomb.
The street was blocked with pickets marching silently with signs which read "Don't Murder the Rosenbergs" and "Justice and Mercy."
There was also an opposing group of protesters whose signs read "Death to All Spies."

><del>3</del>€<del>3</del>€<del>3</del>€<del>3</del>€<

CHAPTER 51

On Friday, June 19, 1953, Ethel and Julius were informed by Warden Denno that the Supreme Court had vacated the stay. Execution was scheduled that night at 11:00 P.M.

They knew that there were frantic efforts to have the President save them. Anticipating the worst (had they not learned it always happened?), they wrote a final letter to their children.

June 19, 1953

Dearest Manny,

The following letter is to be delivered to my children.

Dearest Sweethearts, my most precious children:

Only this morning it looked like we might be together again after all. Now that this cannot be, I want so much for you to know all that I have come to know. Unfortunately I may write only a few simple words; the rest your own lives must teach you, even as mine taught me.

At first, of course, you will grieve bitterly for us, but you will not grieve alone. That is our consolation and it must eventually be yours.

Eventually, too, you must come to believe that life is worth the living. Be comforted that even now, with the end of ours slowly approaching, we know this with a conviction that defeats the executioner!

Your lives must teach you, too, that good cannot really flourish in the midst of evil; that freedom and all the things that go to make up a truly satisfying and worthwhile life must sometimes be purchased very dearly. Be comforted, then, that we were serene and understood with the deepest kind of understanding that civilization had not as yet progressed to the point where life did not have to be lost for the sake of life; and that we were comforted in the sure knowledge that others would carry on after us.

We wish we might have had the tremendous joy and gratification of living our lives out with you. Your Daddy, who is with me in these last momentous hours, sends his heart and all the love that is in it for his

(473)

dearest boys. Always remember that we were innocent and could not
wrong our conscience.

We press you close and kiss you with all our strength,

Lovingly, Daddy and Mommy,

Julie, Ethel.

P.S. to Manny—The Ten Commandments religious medal and chain
—and my wedding ring—I wish you to present to our children as a
token of our undying love.

—————→←—————

A professor of surgery once explained to his class that a cut artery
must be sewed together in two minutes, or the patient would die. "But
you can do it in two minutes, if you don't hurry." Despite the squeeze of
time, defense counsel kept their heads. They marshaled their forces and
dispatched them in all directions.

Bloch, Sharp and Finerty sent a telegram to the President, quoting
Judge Jackson's comment and asking for an immediate oral hearing.

Professor Sharp and Miss Agrin, avoiding the delay of a trip back to
the hotel and desiring to be near the departing judges, wrote out on
yellow pads five motions for a stay. With the aid of Clerk Wiley, they
were sped to individual Supreme Court judges for last-second relief.
Only Judges Burton, Black, Frankfurter and Jackson could still be found.
Each of them rejected the request.

One young member of the Rosenberg legal team, Arthur Kinoy, was
sent to New Haven to petition two members of the Court of Appeals to
issue a stay of execution to allow time for a writ of habeas corpus. He
was turned down.

Daniel Marshall took off to New York to make a final appeal to Judge
Irving Kaufman. He reached the court at 7:00 P.M. He found the city
seething. Police Commissioner George Monaghan had ordered a city-
wide police alert and all precinct captains and detective squads to remain on duty until midnight. Five thousand people gathered at Union
Square and were whipped into a frenzy by Communist speakers who
condemned Eisenhower as "bloodthirsty." Similar meetings were taking
place throughout the city. FBI agents were guarding Judge Kaufman
and his family day and night. Marshall approached Judge Edward
Dimock first, but was referred to Judge Kaufman. He had lost fifteen
minutes. He pleaded with the trial judge to delay the execution until he
finished his argument and prepared a brief, but his petition for a stay
was denied forthwith.

In the meantime, Bloch had the idea that a delay of execution might
be obtained on religious grounds. After frustrating delays, Solicitor
General Robert Stern was reached on the telephone. Bloch explained
that the Sabbath began at sundown on Friday and ended Saturday at
sundown. "It is only one day," he pleaded.

Stern undertook to submit the matter immediately to the Attorney

(474)

General "Please do so quickly," urged Bloch, "You know how little time there is. And the warden must be notified." He gave him his room number, and promised that he or other counsel would sit watch at the telephone for his answer. He thanked him "with all my heart."

Just as he hung up, a reporter dashed into the room with the news that President Eisenhower, through his Press Secretary Murray Snyder, announced that he would not grant clemency.

> When in their most solemn judgment the tribunals of the United States have adjudged them guilty and their sentence just, I will not intervene in this matter.
>
> The execution of two human beings is a grave matter. But even graver is the thought of the millions of dead whose deaths may be directly attributable to what these spies have done. I deny the petition.

Bloch and Finerty hurried to the White House with Ethel's letter, hoping that it might move the President to reconsider. They also sought a personal conference. Perhaps the Court opinions had not filtered through to him. Ignoring the cheers and boos which greeted them from the pickets, they reached the White House gate. Corporal William J. McCarthy of the White House police told them that he could not admit them unless they had an authorized appointment. There was a telephone in the guard's booth.

"Please let us telephone Sherman Adams or Jim Haggerty. We are counsel for the Rosenbergs. We must get through. It is an emergency."

"This telephone is not for private use," he replied. However, he was moved by their plight, and suggested that they would save time if they ran to a store down the block where there was a telephone booth. He also agreed to deliver Ethel's letter immediately to the President's office.

They rushed down the street followed by a screaming crowd, which made it impossible for them to hear themselves, and decided that it would be quicker if they dashed back to the hotel.

The White House switchboard kept them waiting for twenty minutes while they fretted. No one was available. At last the Assistant White House Press Secretary, Murray Snyder, answered. "Had the Court's last decision or Ethel's letter been read personally by the President?" He replied that it was not his function to ascertain this. Bloch yelled, "Damn it, people are going to die. Make it your function!" Bloch asked for an immediate appointment not only for himself but also for Julius' mother, Sophie Rosenberg, who had arrived in Washington to make a plea to the President. Snyder said he would refer the request promptly to the right channels.

Shortly thereafter came another announcement from the White House.

(475)

The President has read the letter of the defendant Ethel Rosenberg. He states that in his conviction it adds nothing to the issues covered in his statement of this afternoon.

The President also declined to see Mrs. Sophie Rosenberg.

There was a pause in the landslide of bad news. A radio flash announced that the Attorney General had ordered that the executions would not violate the Sabbath. "This will give us twenty-four more hours," Bloch said. "We must reach the President in person."

Fearful that there might be some failure of communication with Sing Sing, he asked that Warden Denno be called. The room was crowded with lawyers and reporters. He called for silence as he got on the phone.

"Warden Denno? This is Mr. Bloch. We're calling, Warden, just to confirm the fact that the executions are delayed until Saturday night—you know—on account of the Sabbath."

There was a pause followed by Bloch's scream.

"What? Moved ahead? My God, eight o'clock! It is seven-thirty now. My God—no!"

Something snapped in him and he went berserk.

"What kind of animals am I dealing with? This is barbaric. Eisenhower rejects our petition without even hearing us. He acts like a military dictator! They are all without feeling like the Nazis. I want the whole world to know what animals they are. I am ashamed to be an American!"

He became more hysterical and continued to rant almost incoherently. Several lawyers, stunned though they were, took the telephone out of his hands, put their arms around him and gently pushed him into an armchair. They brought him water. Tears were flooding down his cheeks, stopped only by convulsive grimaces.

"I am all right. Leave me alone," he said. "Get the warden back, or the marshal—what's his name, Carroll. I must get a message through to the Rosenbergs. My God, it is almost eight. Please, please hurry."

They got U. S. Marshal William A. Carroll on the phone.

"This is Manny Bloch. Please tell Julie and Ethel I did the best I could for them. Tell them I will take care of the children. Tell them I love them. Tell them . . ."

He broke down in uncontrollable sobs. The phone fell out of his hands. He slumped over his knees, and buried his head in his arms.

CHAPTER 52

There was violence but also prayers by millions of people for the Rosenberg children and their parents. The United States State Department had sent a review of the case to forty United States diplomatic missions throughout the world, outlining the charges, the evidence and the numerous appeals to clear away misunderstandings that the case involved free speech or that there was no evidence of guilt. Protests throughout the world reached an ugly climax as the execution hour drew near. Hourly bulletins were broadcast of the state of affairs which still were uncertain. Would a last-second stay come from somewhere somehow? Even if such a miracle did not occur, there was the possibility that the Rosenbergs would crack under the pressure, and confess and thereby earn a commutation of the death sentence. These uncertainties persisted until the very moment the switch was to be pulled. Never before had the law's final act hovered in suspense so long.

Fearing demonstrations outside the prison walls, such as had raged in Boston twenty-six years earlier, the night Sacco and Vanzetti were executed, the state and federal government had taken special precautions. State troopers and police barricaded all approaches to Sing Sing. They were trained and prepared to prevent any public demonstration.

As if the turbulence abroad had communicated itself to the two thousand inmates of the prison, there was unusual tension and unrest within its walls. This had nothing to do with any view of the guilt or innocence of the Rosenbergs. Execution night always brought out a tribal prison instinct of abhorrence for punishment. "There, but for the grace of a jury, go I" is the psychological compulsion for the rattling of cups, banging the iron gates, whistling and cursing, in revolt against their enslavement. Their feelings were heightened by the fact that "stool pigeons" had convicted the Rosenbergs, and even worse, one of them sent his own sister to the chair. They resented the breach of their own criminal code. Greenglass was sent to Alcatraz, where Remington had been murdered, but he would have been least safe in Sing Sing.

It was a sweltering day. Thirty-five perspiring newspapermen and women were in the downstairs waiting room of the prison. Every few seconds their eyes turned to the clock on the wall as if its message had to be continuously confirmed.

In the execution chamber, this being a federal rather than a state execution, only five witnesses were permitted. They were U. S. Marshal William Carroll, his deputy, Thomas Farley, and three representatives of the major news wire services: Bob Considine of International News Service and the Hearst newspapers, Relmin Morin of the Associated Press and Jack Woliston of United Press. They had been carefully searched for hidden cameras. They were to share their story with their confreres below.

In Washington, the Attorney General waited in his office for word either that the executions had taken place or that the Rosenbergs had accepted the government's offer to escape death, if they confessed and informed who their co-conspirators were. There was an open telephone line direct to Sing Sing in the event of last-minute repentance. The warden and U. S. Marshal Carroll had advised the Rosenbergs that the offer conveyed to them by Federal Prison Director Bennett remained until the last moment, should they change their minds.

Marshal Carroll was in the death house together with three FBI men to stop the execution if either Ethel or Julius signaled repentance.

Their gruesome preparation for execution began in the morning. All of Julius' possessions were removed from his cell. His insect collection, books, pictures of his sons, and his clothes and undergarments, all were taken, even shoelaces, belts, razor blades, a small looking glass or anything which might be utilized for suicide were removed. The illusion that he had built a little home, was shattered. The cell and he were left stripped. He was given his last garments, fresh khaki pants, a loose T-shirt and buff-colored slippers to put on naked feet.

Ethel received a cheap green dress with white polka dots and terry-cloth slippers—nothing else.

The acceleration of the death hour to eight o'clock made it the first "daytime" execution in the prison's history. It allowed no time for the famous last meal. The Rosenbergs refused any sustenance and chose to spend the remaining time talking to each other. A mesh screen was set up in front of her cell and she was permitted to leave the cell and sit on a chair facing Julius on the other side of the screen. The matrons and guards were instructed to stand back far enough so that they could converse privately.

(478)

At 7:20 P.M., the guard moved up behind Julius and put his hand on his shoulder. He knew that he had to be prepared for his death at eight. He put two fingers to his lips and pressed them toward her on the mesh screen. She did the same. They pressed so hard that the tips of their fingers bled as they touched through the mesh. This was their good-bye kiss.

A guard and prison barber were waiting for Julius in his cell. The back of his head was shaved to permit the electrode to make direct contact with his scalp. He was later to hear the rabbi intone, "Thou anointest my head with oil, my cup runneth over."

The guard scissored a slit up one leg of his pants to the knee to make room for another electrode on his calf. The barber shaved that area. Then the guard sewed the slit together loosely, so that it wouldn't flap when he took his last walk.

Julius sat numb throughout it all, as if nature had mercifully rendered him unconscious of his surroundings. He was startled when at two minutes to eight the prison chaplain, Rabbi Irving Koslowe, thirty-five years old, appeared in black robe and yarmulka (skull cap) and said, "Julius, follow me."

Two guards entered and took him by the arms. They began the march down the narrow concrete corridor toward the death chamber.

The chaplain was reading the 23rd Psalm, "The Lord is my shepherd, I shall not want . . ." Julius, pale, thin and numb with terror, shuffled behind him, partly supported by the guards. His eyes were red, but dry. There were no tears left. He was breathing rapidly.

As he entered the death chamber, the glare of the lights, made stronger by the white walls, made him stop and blink in horror. The chair in the center of the room, bolted to the concrete floor with metal braces, was made of oak wood, which acted as a non-conductor. It had wide wooden straps, and wires dangled underneath.

His eyes were dimmed by fright. He saw none of the witnesses or others in the room. His ears were probably deaf to all but the pounding of his heart. His legs gave way. The guards held him up firmly, and dragged him toward the monster. There they turned him and lowered him, like an invalid, into it. With dispatch, resulting from many re-hearsals, another guard dipped his fingers in a jar, and with a circular motion rubbed adhesive paste on the shaven part of the head. Then he knelt and rubbed conductive paste on his calf. Thereafter, he placed electrodes with attached wet sponges on both areas.

After a guard had removed Julius' eyeglasses, folded them gently and put them aside, they proceeded to strap him into the chair.

His hands were clenched in his lap. The guards forced them apart and strapped them at the wrists to the arms of the chair. His fingers seized the edge of the chair and turned white squeezing it, as if it was his support rather than the instrument of death. Another brown strap

(479)

was tied across his lap, his chest and around his head. He was breathing fast and with effort. His eyes were closed tight. His lips were sucked in. Then a wide black leather hood was dropped over his head. This was not as much a merciful act for him, as it was to protect witnesses and others from the sight of fractured lenses of the eyes, a blue burnt tongue, and fearful distortions of the muscles, as they were convulsed by shock.

The executioner was Joseph Francel, an electrician from Cairo, New York. He had performed this service for fourteen years and was paid $150 for each execution. He took his place behind a glass panel in an alcove. The warden stepped forward. It was precisely eight o'clock. He nodded. The electrician pulled a huge switch downward in a firm unhurried movement.

Two thousand volts, delivered at the maximum eight amperes, crashed Julius violently against the straps. For thirty seconds the crackling noise of the current continued, as his body snapped back and forth like a whip, the straps creaking from the strain. His neck seemed to grow several sizes. Yellow-gray smoke rose in wisps from his head.

The current was turned off. The rigid straining body collapsed limply. As the whining noise stopped, a deathly silence pervaded the room. It was broken by a second charge, reduced to five hundred volts at four amperes to prevent "cooking." It continued fifty-seven seconds.

Again, there were sizzling noises and an involuntary spastic dance of the body against the straps. When the switch was released, Julius' body collapsed like a puppet dropped unceremoniously. A third charge of less voltage was given to be certain that all bodily functions had been deranged and death insured. After fifty seconds, the switch was lifted. Julius was hanging limply over the straps.

The prison physician, Dr. George McCracken, standing with his young assistant, Dr. H. W. Kipp, directly to one side of the chair, stepped forward. He ripped the T-shirt, applied the stethoscope, nodded and said as required by law, "I pronounce this man dead!" He wiped his upper lip with the back of his hand.

There was a hideous stench in the room of burning flesh, urine and defecation. The guards stepped forward and untied the straps. They lifted Julius onto a gurney, which a third guard had brought into the room, and wheeled him out into the autopsy room.

A fourth guard entered with a mop and bucket. He wiped off the seat with a dark brown sponge. He mopped up the puddle underneath the chair and left a powerful scent of ammonia to disguise the smells of an involuntary death.

Rabbi Koslowe walked sadly out of the chamber to lead Ethel to her death. She was to be the eighth woman in Sing Sing's history to be electrocuted. When he arrived in her cell, she said, "Did it happen?"

"Yes, he is dead."

She sat still, showing no emotion.

"Ethel, for the sake of the children who need you, will you say something which can still save you? Must this tragedy be completed?"

She rose. "I have nothing to say. I am ready." Two gray-haired matrons offered their arms. She walked past them and behind the chaplain with steady step.

Rabbi Koslowe chanted from Psalm 31:

> "For I have heard the slander of many;
> fear was on every side:"

As she passed Julius' cell, she paused, looked into its emptiness, lowered her head and moved her lips silently in fleeting dedication to his memory. Then she lifted her head high and walked forward resolutely.

> "while they took counsel together against me,
> they devised to take away my life."

As she entered the white room, the skylight over the black chair had turned bluish purple from the night. The glare was replaced by a somber light.

Unlike Julius she was composed. Her controlled serenity created a heroic impression. She had a Mona Lisa smile, but with an edge of bitterness, and looked every witness in the eye. Some could not return her gaze.

She stopped in front of the chair and held out her hand to her matron, Mrs. Helen Evans, who had become her friend in the last two years. The matron took it hesitantly. Ethel drew her close and brushed her cheek with a tender kiss. The matron ran out of the room, dabbing her eyes. Then in another royal gesture, she shook the hand of the other matron.

She turned and placed herself in the chair, refusing any helping hand, and watched the guards strap her in as if it was an inconsequential act on an airplane. She shifted in the chair to help them place the leather bands across her. She tucked in her leg to help a guard adjust its strap.

However, when the electrode with the wet sponge touched her shaven scalp, she lost her beatific expression for a moment and winced. Then she cocked her head to help the placement of the monstrous crown on her head.

As the black strap was placed across her mouth, she looked straight ahead at the ashen reporters sitting on hard benches before the chair. Her eyes were open when the black leather hood was dropped over her head.

The warden signaled with a nod. Francel walked quickly into the alcove. He pulled the switch down. Her body smashed convulsively against the straps which made creaking noises under the strain. Combined with the whistling, crackling sound of the electricity, they created weird, rhythmic dissonances, as if witches were howling in the wind.

Her right index finger rose as if in silent rebuke. Her body lifted off the seat against the straps and her hands closed into fists as if she was going to charge across the room swinging.

There was a strong smell of burning flesh, as the temperature of her body reached 140 degrees. Thin smoke rose from her scalp and turned blue in the overhead light, as it flattened out in an ugly cake against the skylight overhead.

After the three long shocks, the switch was turned off.

The body hung loose. The silence and stench mixed. A guard unleashed the black strap that had been tied tightly across her breasts. Another guard unbound her arms and a leg. Dr. McCracken approached. He could not place his stethoscope into the collar of the dress. He and Dr. Kipp tore it open and listened to her heart. The doctor stepped back bewildered. Instead of uttering the ritual words, he looked at the warden and said in a hollow voice, "This woman is still alive."

The executioner came out from his alcove to consult with the warden and the doctor. He, too, could not believe that there was still a heartbeat. In a whispered conference, they decided to turn the switch on for a severe and then modified jolt.

The guards restrapped her as if for a second execution. The warden signaled again. The switch was pulled down. For fifty-seven seconds, her body bounced in convulsive movements against the straps, while sizzling skillet noises crackled in the room. The switch was lifted. She descended into the seat in slow motion. Another jolt for fifty-seven seconds made sputtering noises and sent a plume of smoke out of her head. Then silence and collapse. The doctor applied his stethoscope to the smoldering chest. He straightened and said, "I pronounce this woman dead."

Two guards untied the straps, lifted her onto a wheel table. Her right leg was flexed in a nonchalant posture as they pushed her out to the autopsy room.

It had taken two minutes and forty-five seconds to kill Julius, and four minutes and thirty seconds to destroy Ethel. She died after sundown at 8:17 on the Sabbath.

CHAPTER 53

On the evening of the execution, the kind woman with whom the children were staying sought to shield Michael from the shock. There was a baseball game between the New York Yankees and Detroit Tigers on television. She lured him into watching it. She had underestimated the overriding interest in the case. Suddenly, there was a fearful scream like those that ejected him from his nightmares. A bulletin had flashed across the screen: "President Eisenhower has turned down Ethel and Julius' final appeal. They must die tonight."

She rushed into the room and found Michael curled up in a corner of the big leather chair in a fetal position, whimpering. With difficulty, she lifted him in her arms and carried him to bed, where she held him tenderly during the sleepless night.

The Rosenberg funeral was as marred by political harangue and controversy as their lives. As many as thirty thousand people surrounded the I. J. Morris Funeral Home at 9701 Church Avenue in Brooklyn, New York, which could hold only 310 mourners. The family split in court persisted at the funeral. Julius' mother and two sisters attended, but the Greenglasses did not come, even to pay respect to Ethel in death. Michael and Robby were not there.

Joseph Brainin, chairman of the Rosenberg Committee, introduced the speakers. He described his committee as "representing a cross-section of America," a claim which James B. Kilsheimer III had branded in an affidavit filed on one of the appeals as about as true as it would be of the "national committee of the Communist Party."

Emanuel H. Bloch was the chief speaker. His anger had not diminished. What might previously have been a hysterical outburst was now a deliberate statement. It provoked an immediate rebuttal from the rabbi. Bloch said:

> America should know, as the rest of the world knows, that America today is living under the heels of a military dictatorship dressed in civilian garb. These people have no hearts. They have stones for hearts. They have hard hearts, and they have hard eyes.
> They have the souls of murderers.

He concluded:

> I place the murder of the Rosenbergs at the door of President Eisenhower, Mr. Brownell and J. Edgar Hoover. They did not pull the switch, true, but they directed the one who did pull the switch. This was not the American tradition, not American justice and not American fair play. This was Nazism that killed the Rosenbergs and if we forget that lesson we will cringe, we'll live on our knees and we will be afraid. Insanity, irrationality, barbarism and murder seem to be part of the feeling of those who rule us.

Rabbi Abraham Cronbach, elderly professor emeritus of the Hebrew Union College of Cincinnati, followed Bloch. He knew he was facing a partisan audience, because admission to the chapel was by ticket, issued by the Rosenberg Committee, and by press cards. Nevertheless, despite boos and derogatory shouts, he said:

> Let us not vituperate those who pronounced the verdict. Let us at least give them credit for this much: that they did what they thought was right.
> We must demonstrate that we are among those most loyal to America. We must not permit any ground for accusation of remission in our American citizenship. We gain when America gains, and we lose when America loses.

After the service, there was violence outside the chapel, despite the presence of more than two hundred foot patrolmen, mounted and motorcycle police and dozens of detectives.

Three chartered buses and three hundred private automobiles followed the two hearses to Wellwood Cemetery at Pine Lawn, near Farmingdale, Long Island. There Ethel, thirty-seven, and Julius, thirty-five, were interred. Acrimony accompanied them to the grave.

Even martyrdom, their last solace, did not last long. In East Berlin, their execution date, July 19, was made one of five commemorative days to be publicly observed with Stalin's birth date, Dresden's destruction, Red Army Day and World Peace Day. It was removed after one year. They are in the Communist Pantheon of the forgotten.

CHAPTER 54

Like a fever which breaks, restoring normalcy, the protest movement dissipated immediately after the execution. Thousands of placards were left by pickets in heaps on the curbs and removed as trash the next day. The Rosenberg Committee turned into a Sobell Committee, but with little notice or effectiveness.

What had been drowned out in the fury of the protest movement was the sober opinion of the American people. Editorials in leading newspapers throughout the land expressed the view that the Rosenbergs had had their full and fair day in court. They rejected the claims of a "railroaded" trial or a venal judicial system. They were impressed by the unprecedented appellate procedures and they discounted much of the criticism as Communist inspired.

Typical of these was a New York *Times* editorial of March 30, 1951:

> They have denied their guilt and have appealed their case. But to the layman it must seem that they have been convicted after a fair trial, and that their conviction rests on the testimony of their own self-confessed accomplices in a spy ring which centered around the convicted British scientist Klaus Fuchs, and was headed by a master spy disguised as a Soviet vice consul in New York. . . . They (the Rosenbergs) can only be considered, like so many others, as willing victims of the Big Lie which pictures Soviet Russia as a paradise and entices its dupes to regard any means as justified to promote its ends. If this is the explanation, it cannot in any way excuse the culprits or mitigate their crime.

The San Francisco *Chronicle*'s editorial of June 23, 1953, commented directly on Bloch's "intemperate" statement:

It was not, as he said, "the face of nazism that killed the Rosenbergs." Between the almost painfully slow processes of justice as demonstrated in the three years of the Rosenberg case, and the loaded "justice" dispensed by Adolf Hitler's courts there is a breadth of difference that is obvious to every American, certainly to any practicing attorney.

There is room for honest differences of opinion as to whether, in the absolute sense, the Rosenbergs deserved to die for their crime. There is no room for doubt that they were accorded full and fair access to the American judicial process, or that those in authority did what in conscience they felt was right.

This was not the prevailing opinion about the death sentence. Many felt that the punishment was too severe when compared with Gold's thirty-year sentence, Fuchs's fourteen-year sentence and Greenglass' fifteen-year sentence. Others were opposed to capital punishment in principle, particularly where it involved a mother of two children. The Sunday *Star* of Washington, D.C., while conceding "the monstrous nature of the crime of which these people were guilty," regretted the grimness of the penalty. Many more thought the death sentence was unwise because it amalgamated millions in protest, who otherwise would have accepted the verdict. They believed the issue of "martyrdom" could have been avoided. So, on the whole, the verdict of guilty was accepted, but the death penalty was the subject of doubt, if not absolute rejection, as either excessive or unwise.

In the introduction of this book, I said that the question "Do you think the Rosenbergs were guilty?" was a wrong question, which could only lead to a wrong answer. Without being present at the trial to evaluate the credibility of witnesses based on their demeanor, any opinion is devoid of crucial determining factors.

The right question is "Do you think there was sufficient evidence for a jury which heard and saw the witnesses, and not merely the printed testimony, to find them guilty?" To this, the answer is "Yes."

As Judge Jerome Frank wrote after a most painstaking, objective review of every word of testimony by every witness:

This court is not allowed to consider the credibility of testimony.

It is the jury which "sizes up" the witnesses, which the appellate judges do not see. Judge Frank wrote:

The jury believed the evidence unfavorable to the defendants. On that assumption, the evidence to sustain the verdict is more than ample.

So I find too.

However, the death penalty was unfortunate from every viewpoint.

(486)

The crime was serious enough to warrant it, but the disparity of punishment given to others who were equally guilty resulted in uneven justice, which is equivalent to injustice. There were other mitigating circumstances.

From a viewpoint of guilt, it did not matter whether the stolen data was valuable or valueless. However, from the viewpoint of punishment, this mattered a great deal. The judge considered the consequences of the crime horrendous, and this affected the degree of punishment. He ascribed fifty thousand deaths in Korea to the Rosenbergs' treachery. President Eisenhower denied clemency for the same reason, referring to millions who might die as a result of the defendants' perfidy.

These were assumptions, not hard fact. Klaus Fuchs, a leading physicist, had confessed that he gave secret data to Gold, the same courier who received it from Greenglass. Could it be said with reasonable certainty that it was not his spy activity, rather than the Rosenbergs', which armed the Russians?

Also, there were humanistic considerations. Even a thirty-year sentence would have deprived the Rosenberg children of a father's and mother's care, but it was worse to orphan them. It increased the horror of execution.

Capital punishment played into the hands of the Communists, who whipped up a world-wide protest, made possible only because of support from those who objected to it rather than the verdict. A prison sentence would have realistically reduced the issue to the size of Sobell's, Gold's and Fuchs's convictions.

There were other peripheral reasons to avoid the extreme penalty. The Rosenbergs were convicted chiefly on the testimony of accomplices. There is a long existing contention that allowance should be made for possible irresponsibility of such a source, so as to preclude death sentence in such a case.

Also, there was the heated atmosphere of the 1950s against communism, which led many to believe that the most careful instructions could not overcome its prejudice. All this argued for a merciful penalty, either at the hands of the judge or the President.

Bloch had been in the center of the storm so long that he could not read the weather beyond it. As an advocate he had behaved like a prince of the court. He had praised the judicial process which had found his clients guilty. He had been respectful. He probably would have remained so, but for the death penalty.

He had become so emotionally involved with Ethel, Julius and their children, that understandably the issue became one of mercy and generosity of spirit, rather than of law. Admirable as was his intense feeling, it derailed his judgment. To scream, "I am ashamed to be an

(487)

American" and to denounce the President as a dictator, and with him Attorney General Herbert Brownell and J. Edgar Hoover as "murderers" and guilty of "Nazism" was to adopt Communist semantics.

He had not evaluated the American temper correctly. Suddenly, he was dislodged from his role of doughty fighter for unpopular clients, a role highly honored by Americans and praised by the Supreme Court, to that of a propagandist, irresponsibly defiling his country and his profession.

A cry went up for his punishment. Public pressure was put upon the Bar Association to discipline him for his intemperate remarks. Proceedings were instituted by the Bar Association of the City of New York.

He was out of the city on a mission of mercy when the crushing news came to him. He was traveling from coast to coast, giving talks on the Rosenberg case, in order to raise $45,000 for the education and maintenance of Michael and Robby. He succeeded. Miss Gloria Agrin became a co-trustee, and every cent was used meticulously for the purpose for which it was raised.

Why was this arduous trip necessary? The Rosenberg Committee had collected and spent approximately one million dollars. Indeed, the Treasury Department filed a lien for $124,900 in unpaid taxes against the committee (which had failed to qualify for tax exemption). Bloch had made a promise to care for the children, and he wore himself out to redeem it.

The terrible ordeal of the trial, the scenes in the death house with the children, and the final hours of torment had undermined his nervous system. Exhausted from his trip, he was confronted with a new attack by his own profession. His standing at the bar had been his most prideful possession. His father, too, had doted on it. Now even this was in jeopardy. He faced disgrace.

He was determined to fight back. He had lost the Rosenbergs' lives, but he was not going to lose his honor. Miss Agrin offered to help. She went to the County Lawyers Library in New York City, to do legal research for his defense. He was to join her there at ten o'clock and work with her. When he did not appear by eleven, she telephoned his office. He was not there. She called his home where he was living alone, having been separated from his wife about a year. There was no answer. She called again at twelve noon, and one. Mystified by his absence, for he was a punctual man, who used to jest, "The reason some people never come on time is that there is no one there to appreciate it," she decided to go to his home.

The door was locked, but there was a key under the mat. She opened the door but was blocked by a chain inside. She heaved against the door and the rusty chain broke. She stopped short in the corridor, and suppressed a cry. Out of the bathroom extended a nude foot. She approached to find Bloch, pajama clad, a cake of soap in his extended hand, lying on his back, dead. He had suffered a heart attack.

Miss Agrin rushed to the phone and called his father, and then the police. Within minutes, the apartment was swarming not only with policemen, but a squad of FBI men who searched every inch of the premises.

Alexander Bloch stood over his fifty-one-year-old son with bowed head and tears streaming down his cheeks.

"The Rosenberg case killed him too," he said.

꘾꘾꘾꘾

CHAPTER 55

Bloch's death began another court struggle. This time it involved the children. They had been happy with the Bernard Bach family, living in Toms River, New Jersey. However, the school superintendent had advised the Bachs and ten other parents that the school would no longer admit out-of-district pupils. Michael and Robby were then put in a new foster home in New York City. There was no lack of offers to adopt the children. Almost two thousand families in Europe and the United States volunteered. Michael and Robby were attracted to one couple. The love was reciprocal. Before adoption proceedings could be consummated, the Society for the Prevention of Cruelty to Children filed a complaint, based upon an investigation by the Department of Welfare of the City of New York, that the children were being exploited by the Rosenberg Committee to raise money.

The police swooped down on the children and took them to the Welfare Department. The operation was conducted with military efficiency. Police guarded the block. One was on a roof. The children thus found themselves hunted as if they were criminals. It was another trauma they had to suffer.

Judge Jacob Panken directed that they be delivered to the Jewish Child Care Association. Miss Agrin, Professor Sharp and Alexander Bloch, fulfilling the wish of his dead son, rushed to the rescue. On behalf of the grandmother Sophie Rosenberg, they sought a writ of habeas corpus. Supreme Court Justice James B. McNally of New York State was sensitive enough to the situation to sign the writ at midnight at his home and make it returnable the next morning in court, even though it was a Saturday. The Jewish Child Care Association protested a hearing on a Sabbath. Mrs. Rosenberg filed an affidavit stating that she was Orthodox but "where the happiness of the children was concerned" she believed it was no sin. Judge McNally conferred with Michael and Robby in chambers, and after a hearing awarded the children to the grandmother, instructing her to send them back to school and teach them to be religious. "Never let anybody talk to these children in desecration of this country," he said. "You teach these children to love this country. It is their country."

As they left the courthouse facing flash bulbs by photographers, Michael turned to his grandmother and said, "Give me your hand, Bubbie, I want a hand to hold onto." Robby took her other hand and they walked out happily.

This was a stopover arrangement until the children could be adopted by their chosen new parents, whose names they took.

A psychiatrist advised that what Michael and Robby needed most was anonymity and a home with loving parents. All this they enjoyed in their new surroundings.

Over the years they grew up to be fine young men. They graduated from college. Each became successful in his chosen enterprise. Both married and have children. They are normal, decent citizens living a happy life with affectionate relationships with their new parents and friends.

Had the chaplain known, he might also have recited Psalm 102 to Julius and Ethel:

> The children of thy servants shall continue and their seed shall be established before thee.

Michael looks exactly like Julius, and Robby is the image of Ethel.

APPENDIX

Applications for relief were submitted to our federal courts on twenty-three different and separate occasions.

Totaling the number of judges who reviewed these applications, sometimes they were the same judges and sometimes not; for example, the composition of the Court of Appeals changed often, there were 112 judges. Of these (making the computation the same way), sixteen judges disagreed. These disagreements were almost always as to whether a stay should be granted or further review granted. They never were on the merits in the sense that they contended that the Rosenbergs were innocent.

DISTRICT COURT	COURT OF APPEALS	SUPREME COURT	
Trial 1	Affirmed–3	Petition for cert. denied	9 (Dissent 1–Black)
	Petition for rehearing denied–3	Petition for rehearing denied	9 (Dissent 1–Black)
Motion Sec. 2255 vacate judgment and sentence–1	Affirmed–3	Cert. denied	9 Dissent
		Petition for stay pending Petition for rehearing	9 (Dissent 1–Black)
		Petition for rehearing	9 Dissent
			8 Dissent
Two separate motions for Sec. 2255 relief–2	Court of Appeals–3		
	Court of Appeals–3		Total 45
Denied June 1 Denied June 8	Total 15		
Total 4			

(493)

DISTRICT COURT	COURT OF APPEALS	SUPREME COURT	
	Petition for mandamus directing trial judge–3 to resentence Denied	Application to Judge Jackson to stay 1 exec.	1
		He refers to full court, denied	9 (Dissent 1–Black)
		Petition for writ of habeas corpus and request for stay denied	9 (Dissent 1–Black)
		June 16– Petition to Douglas Habeas Corpus and stay denied June 17	1
		Granted stay June 17	1
		June 18– Convened special term	9 (Dissent 1–Douglas 1–Black)
		June 19– vacated stay Applications for stay pending appeal to Eisenhower	9 (Dissent 1–Douglas 1–Black 1–Frank-furter)
			Dissents–7
	Total 3		Total–39

DISTRICT COURT	COURT OF APPEALS	SUPREME COURT	
Connecticut–1 New York–2 Total 3		Application for stay to Black, Douglas and Frankfurter	3 Total 3

Entire Total 112

SUMMARY

Four applications to judges in district courts.

Six separate applications to the Court of Appeals, each application heard by three judges, not always the same.

Seven separate applications to the Supreme Court of the United States—all nine judges sitting on each occasion.

Six separate applications to individual and different judges of the Supreme Court.

Total number of judges who reviewed the various applications and appeals—112.

The number of judges who dissented—sixteen.

N52